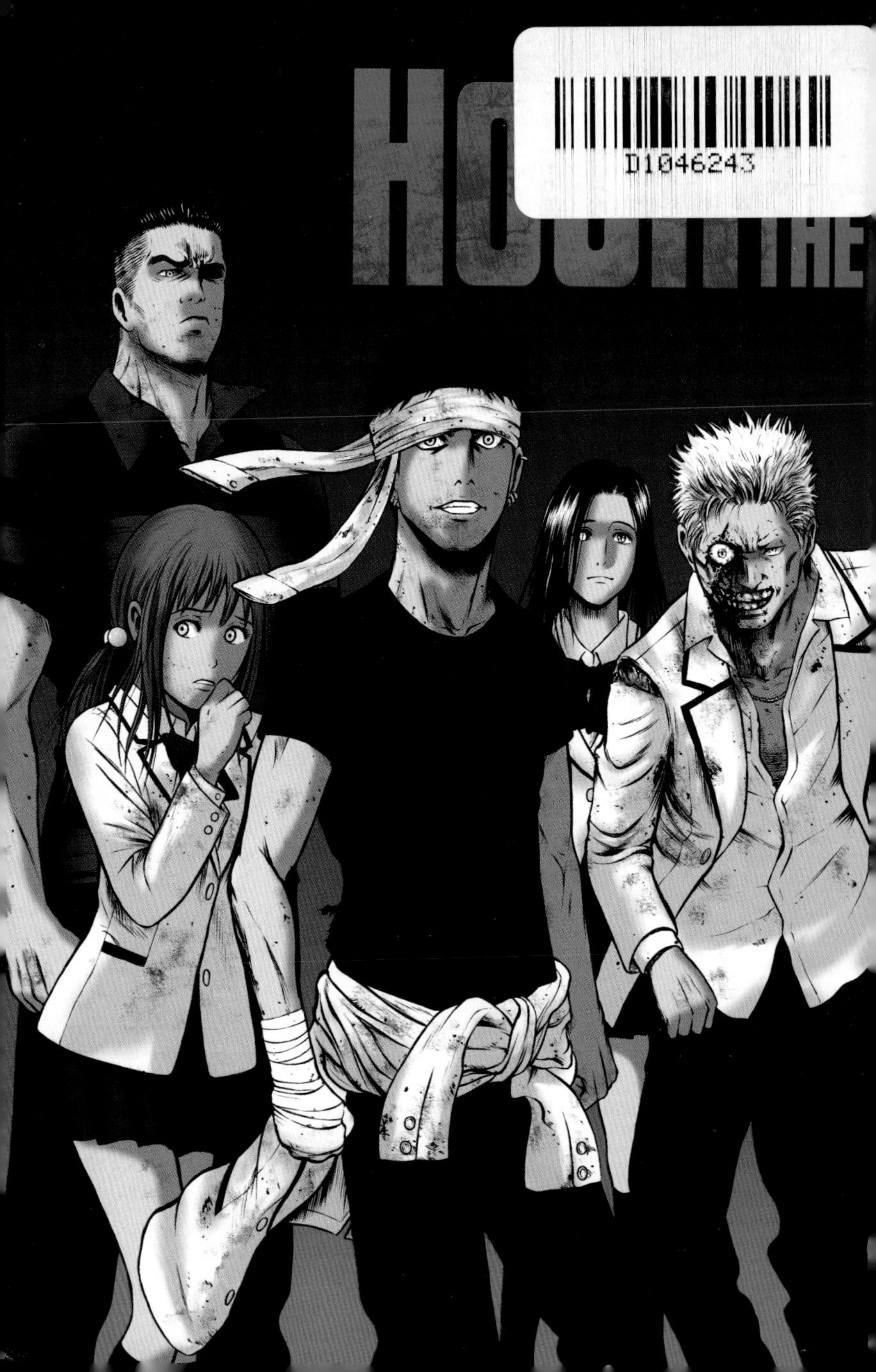

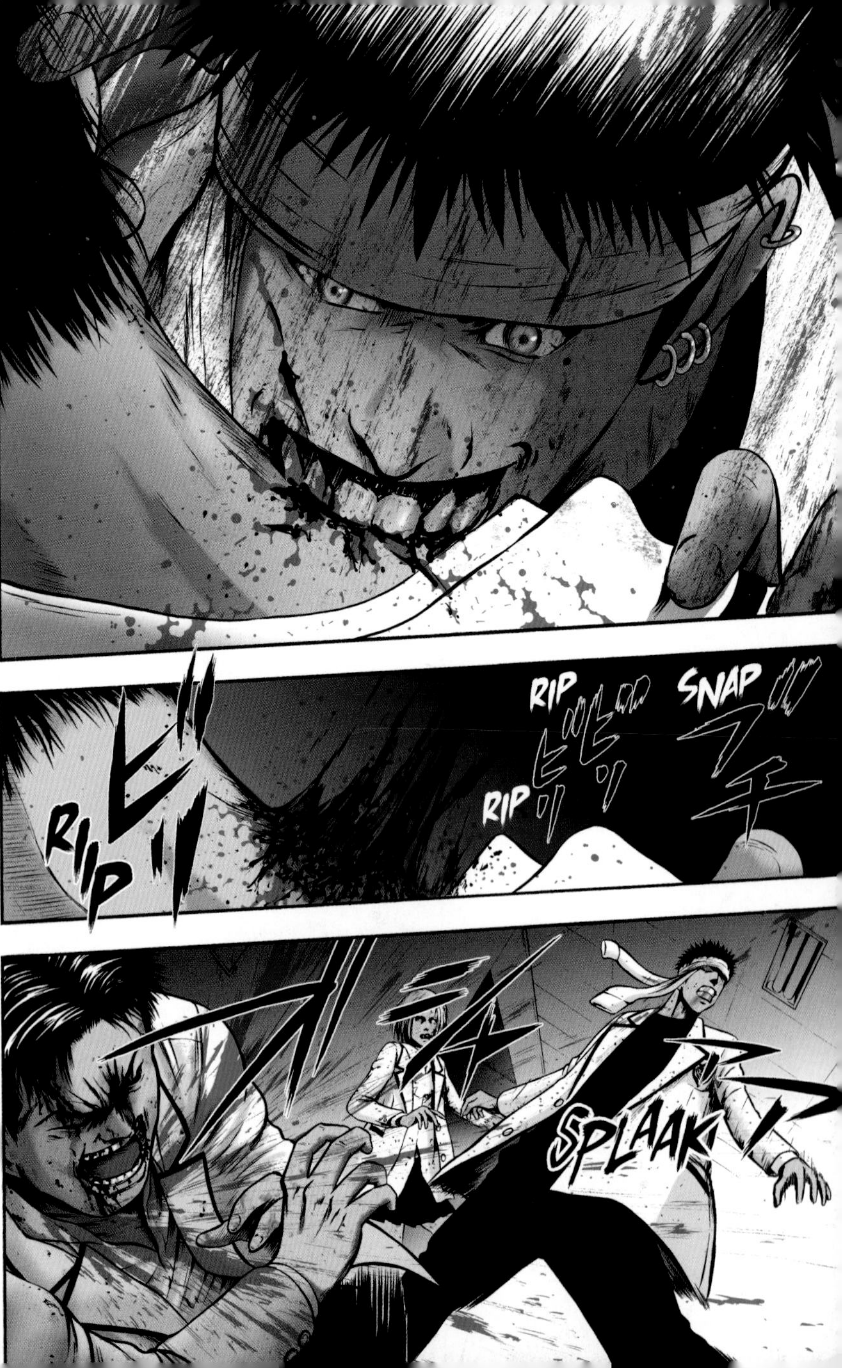
SNAP
RIP
RIP
RIP
SPLAAK!

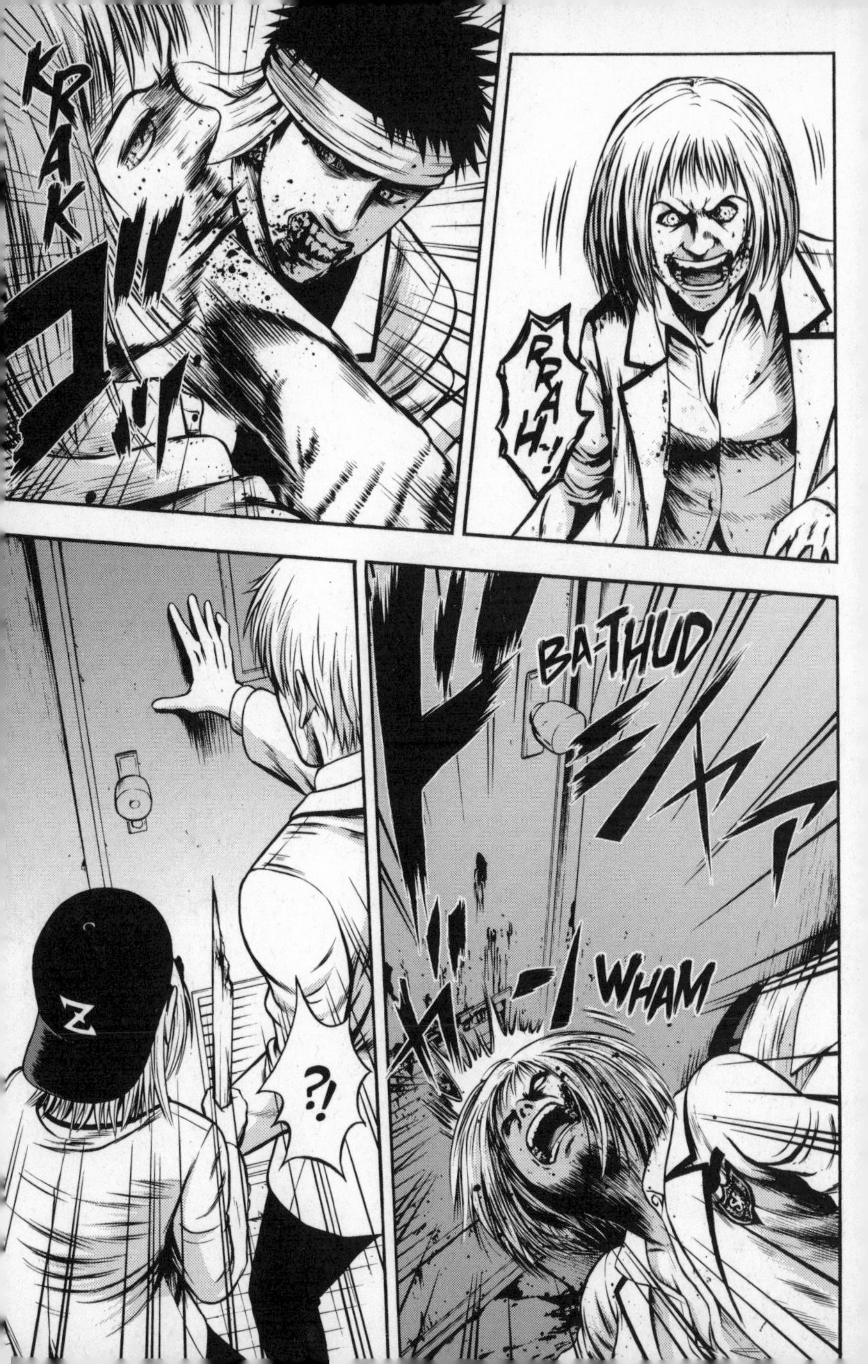
RRAH-!
KRAK
BA-THUD
WHAM
?!

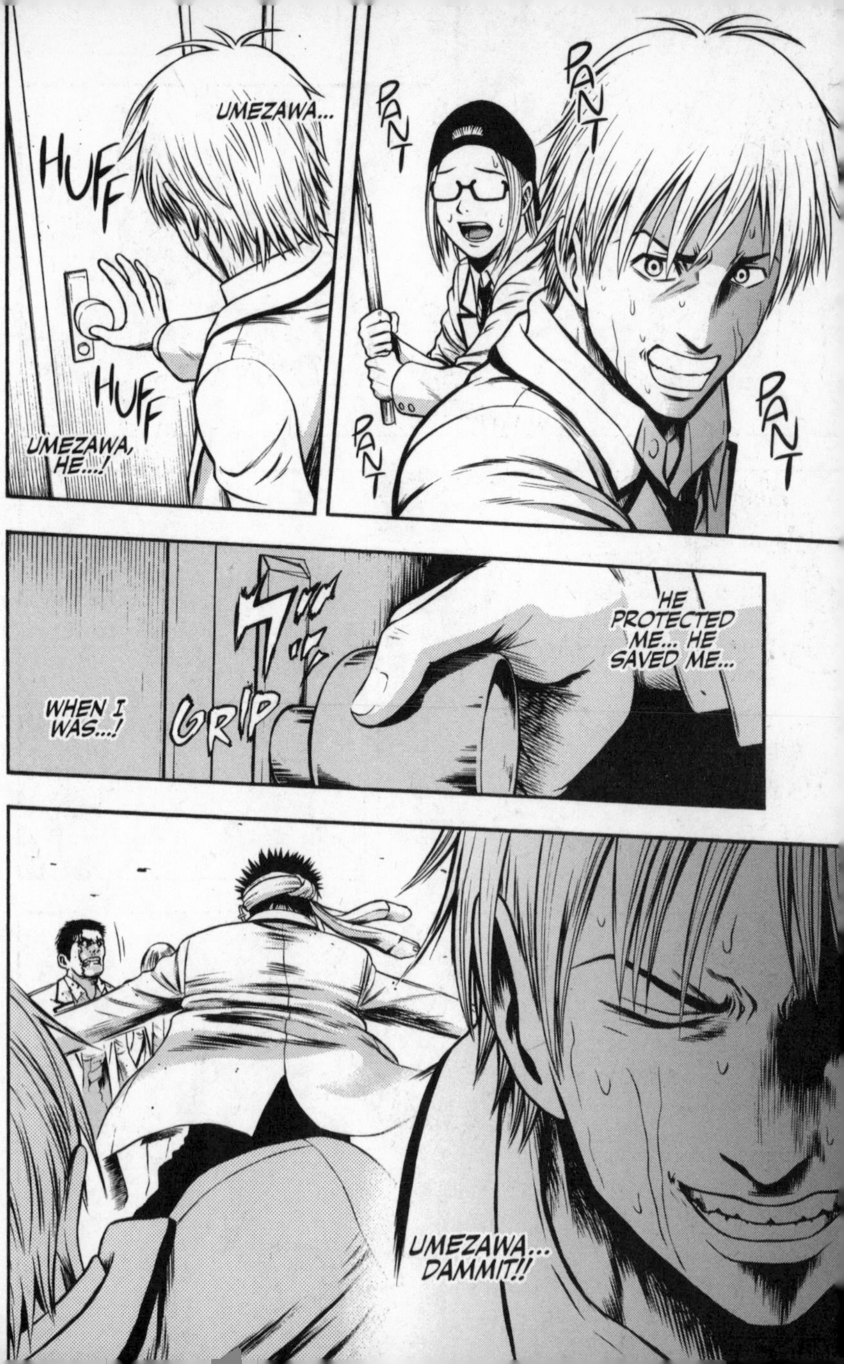
PANT
PANT
PANT
PANT
PANT
PANT
UMEZAWA...
HUFF
HUFF
HUFF
HUFF
UMEZAWA, HE...!
HE PROTECTED ME... HE SAVED ME...
GRIP
WHEN I WAS...!
UMEZAWA... DAMMIT!!

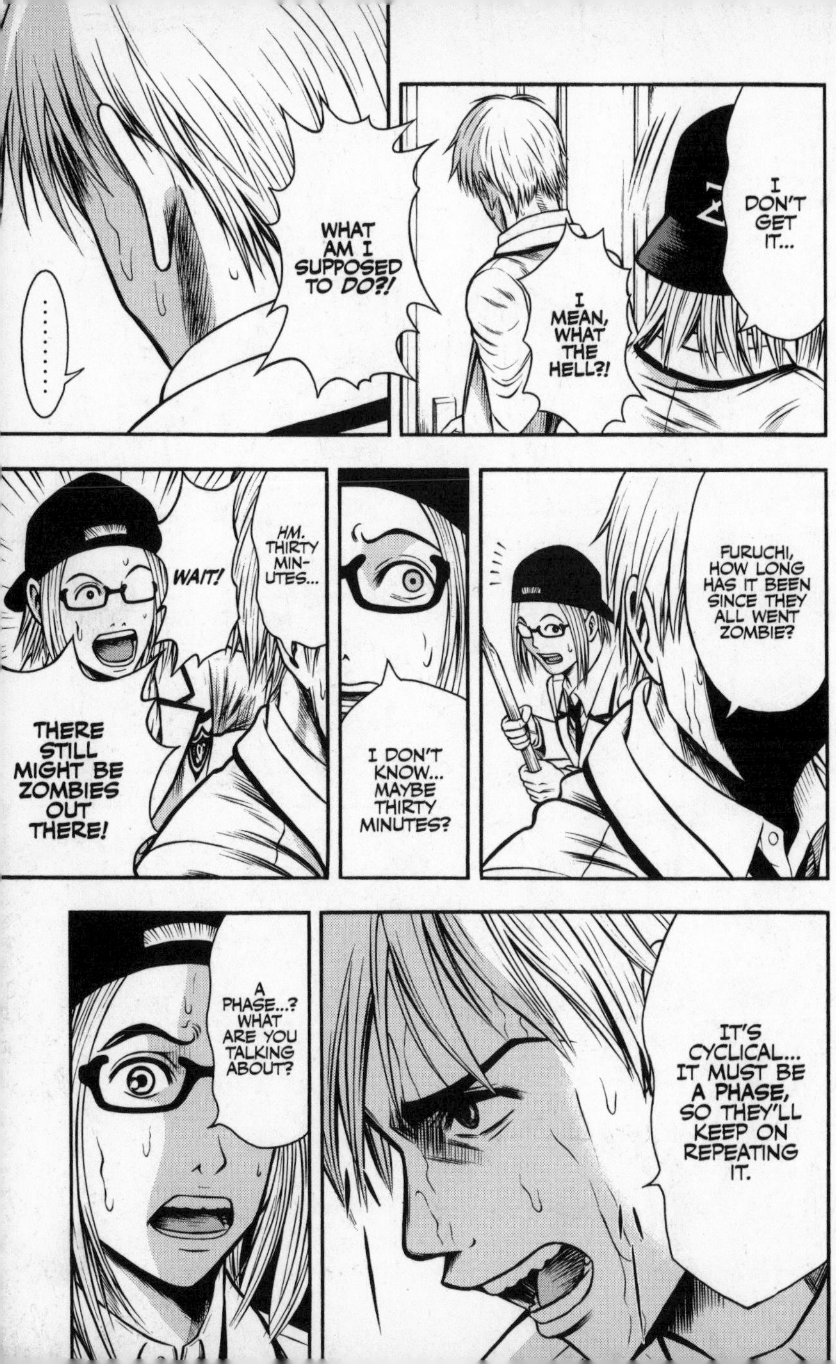
I DON'T GET IT...
I MEAN, WHAT THE HELL?!
WHAT AM I SUPPOSED TO *DO*?!
....
FURUCHI, HOW LONG HAS IT BEEN SINCE THEY ALL WENT ZOMBIE?
I DON'T KNOW... MAYBE THIRTY MINUTES?
HM. THIRTY MIN-UTES...
WAIT!
THERE STILL MIGHT BE ZOMBIES OUT THERE!
IT'S CYCLICAL... IT MUST BE A PHASE, SO THEY'LL KEEP ON REPEATING IT.
A PHASE...? WHAT ARE YOU TALKING ABOUT?

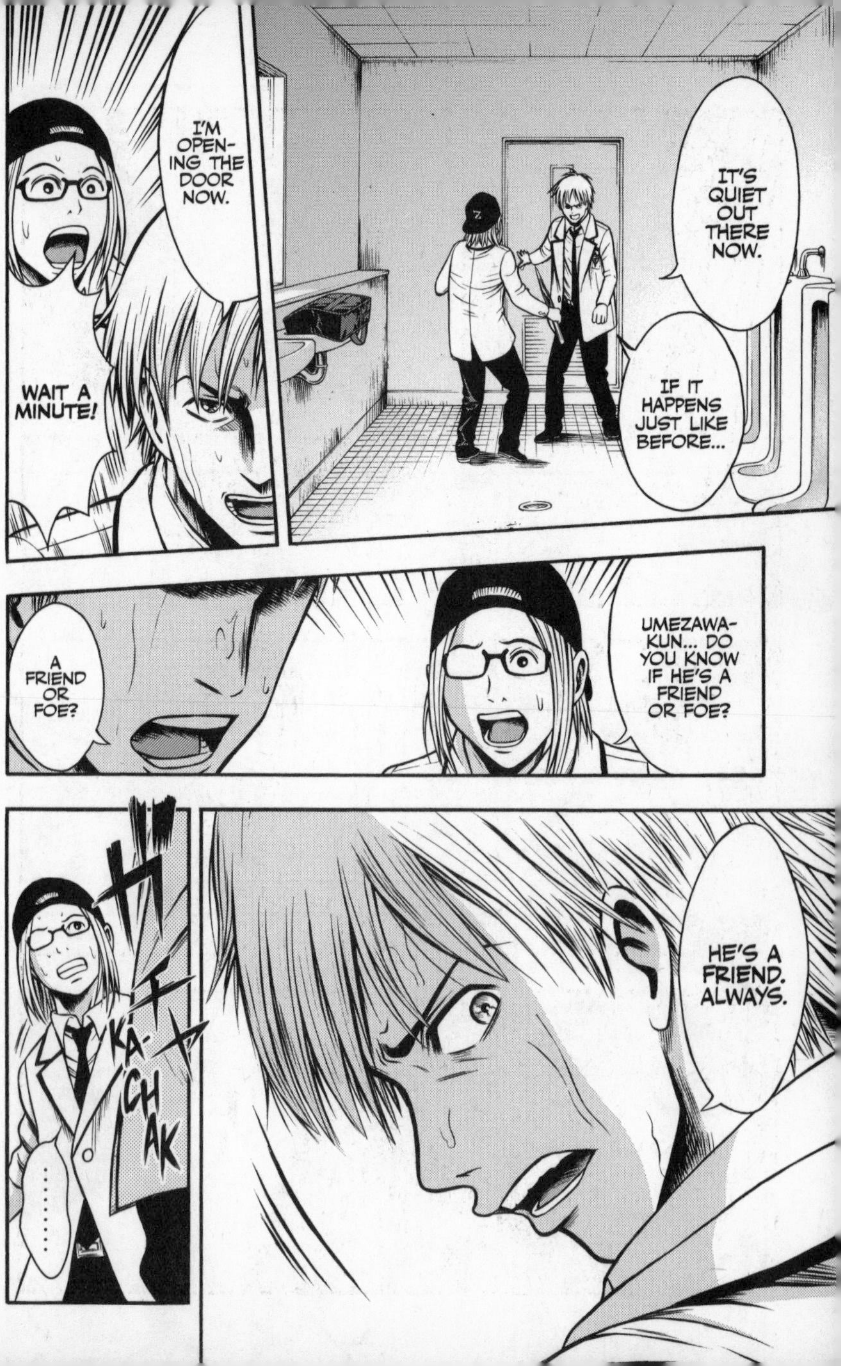
IT'S QUIET OUT THERE NOW.
IF IT HAPPENS JUST LIKE BEFORE...
I'M OPEN-ING THE DOOR NOW.
WAIT A MINUTE!
UMEZAWA-KUN... DO YOU KNOW IF HE'S A FRIEND OR FOE?
A FRIEND OR FOE?
HE'S A FRIEND. ALWAYS.
KA-CHAK
....

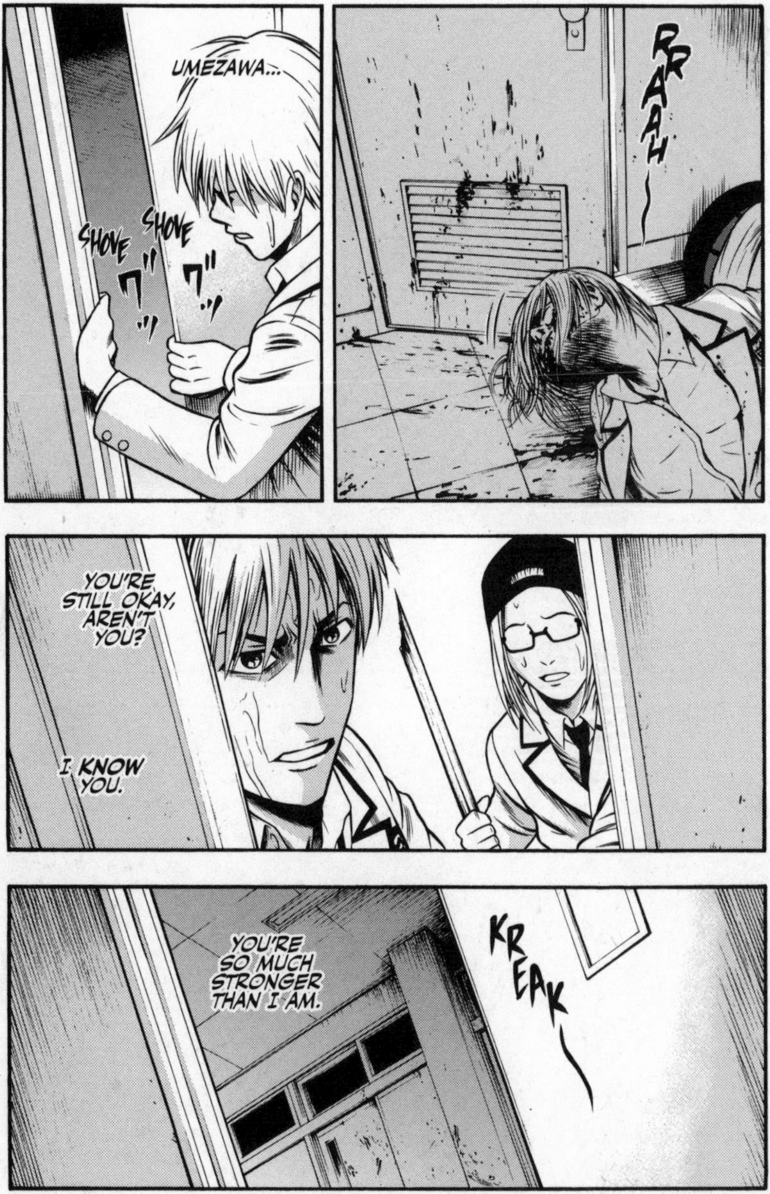
RRAAH
UMEZAWA...
SHOVE SHOVE
YOU'RE STILL OKAY, AREN'T YOU?
I KNOW YOU.
YOU'RE SO MUCH STRONGER THAN I AM.
KREAK

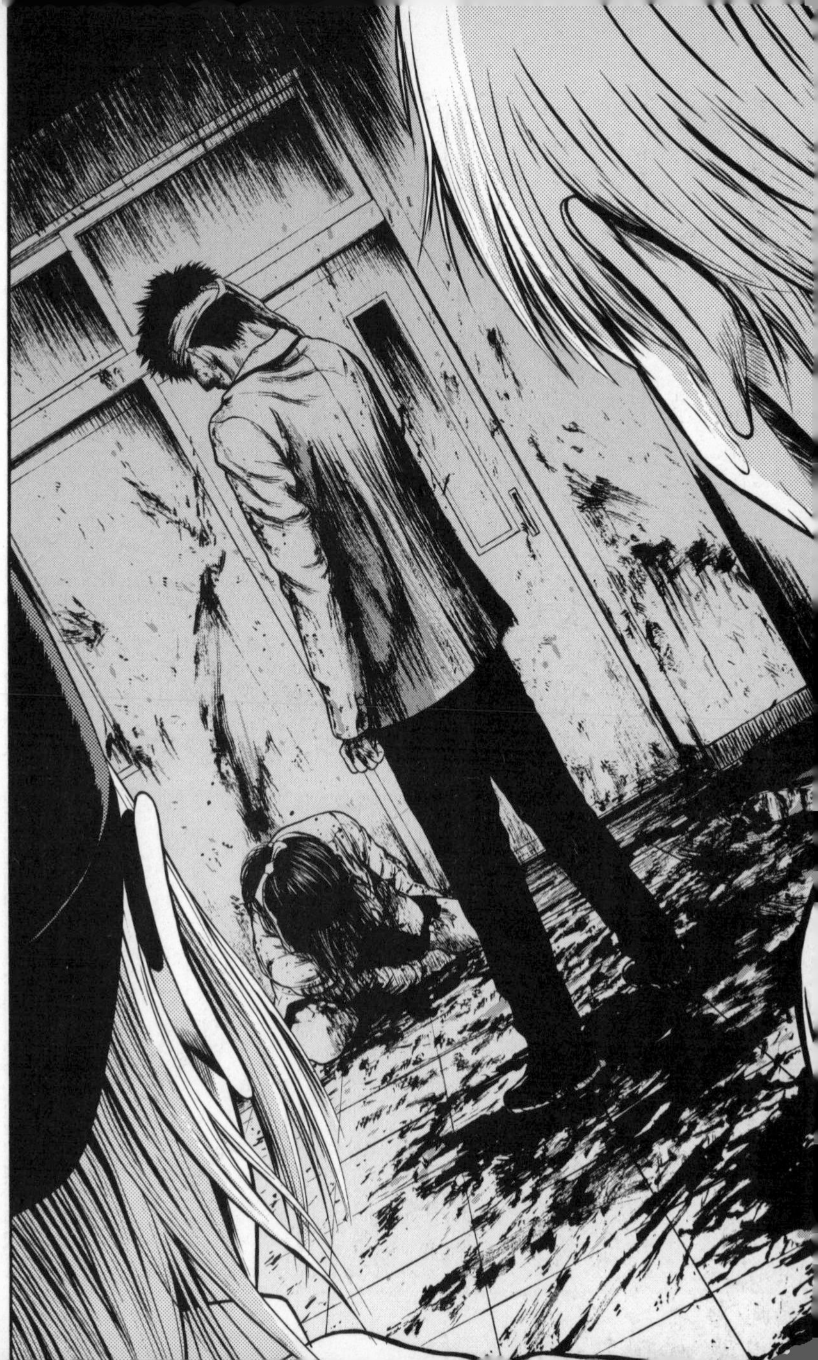

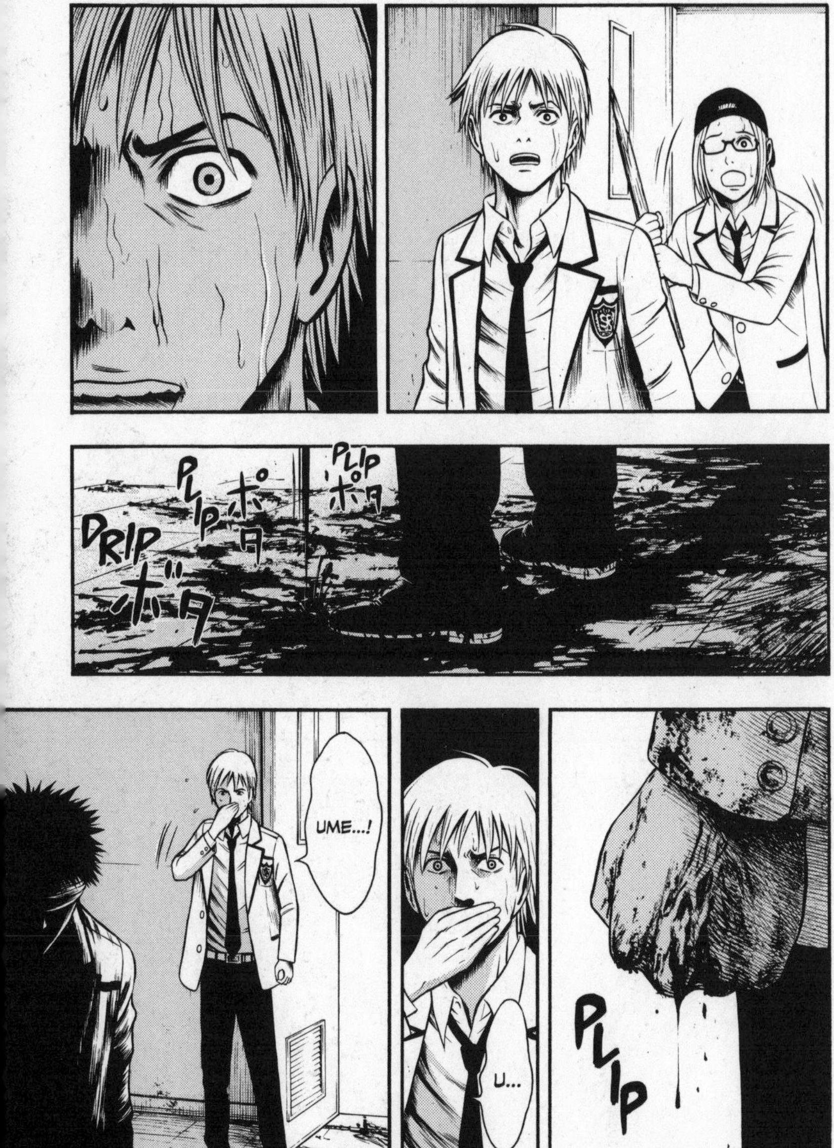
PLIP
ポタ
PLIP
ポタ
DRIP
ボタ
PLIP
U...
UME...!

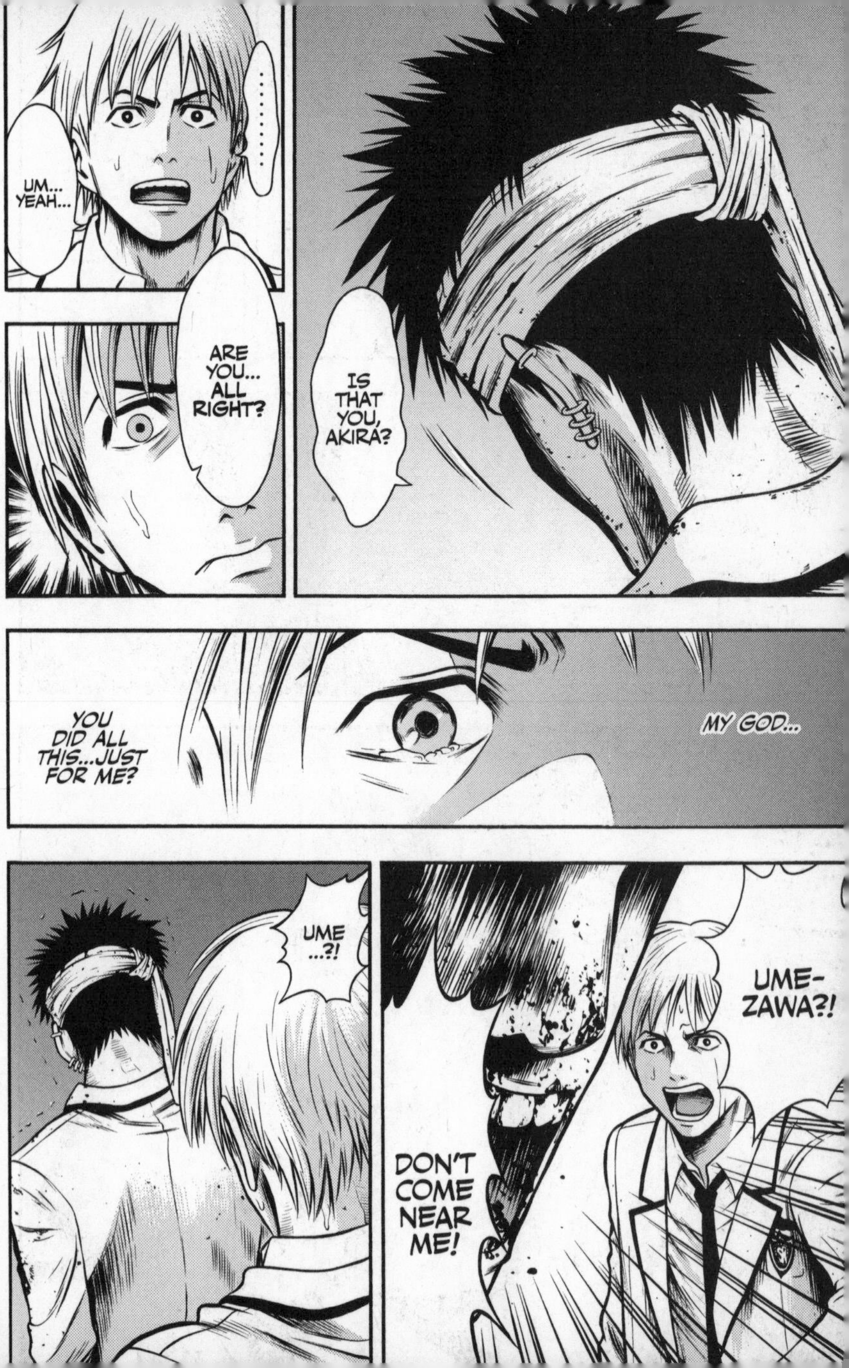
IS THAT YOU, AKIRA?
UM... YEAH...
ARE YOU... ALL RIGHT?
MY GOD...
YOU DID ALL THIS...JUST FOR ME?
UME-ZAWA?!
DON'T COME NEAR ME!
UME ...?!

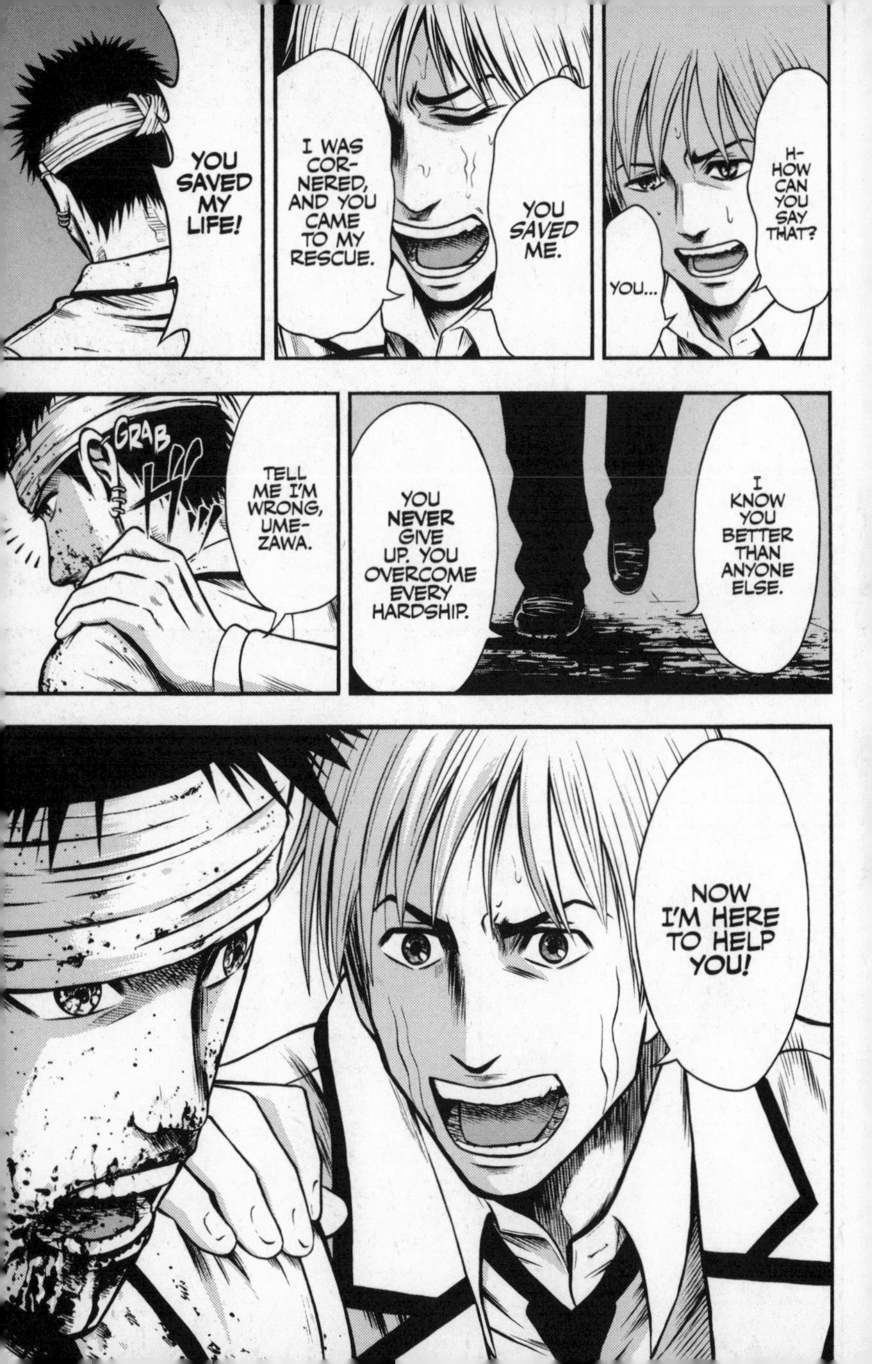
H-HOW CAN YOU SAY THAT?
YOU...
YOU SAVED ME.
I WAS CORNERED, AND YOU CAME TO MY RESCUE.
YOU SAVED MY LIFE!
I KNOW YOU BETTER THAN ANYONE ELSE.
YOU NEVER GIVE UP. YOU OVERCOME EVERY HARDSHIP.
GRAB
TELL ME I'M WRONG, UMEZAWA.
NOW I'M HERE TO HELP YOU!

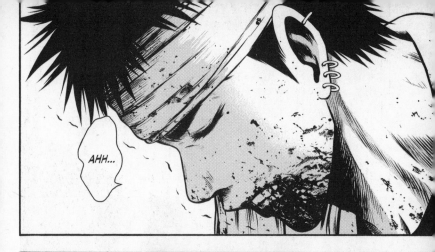

AHH...

.....

HE REALLY
IS BACK
TO HIS OLD
SELF... IT IS
A CYCLE...

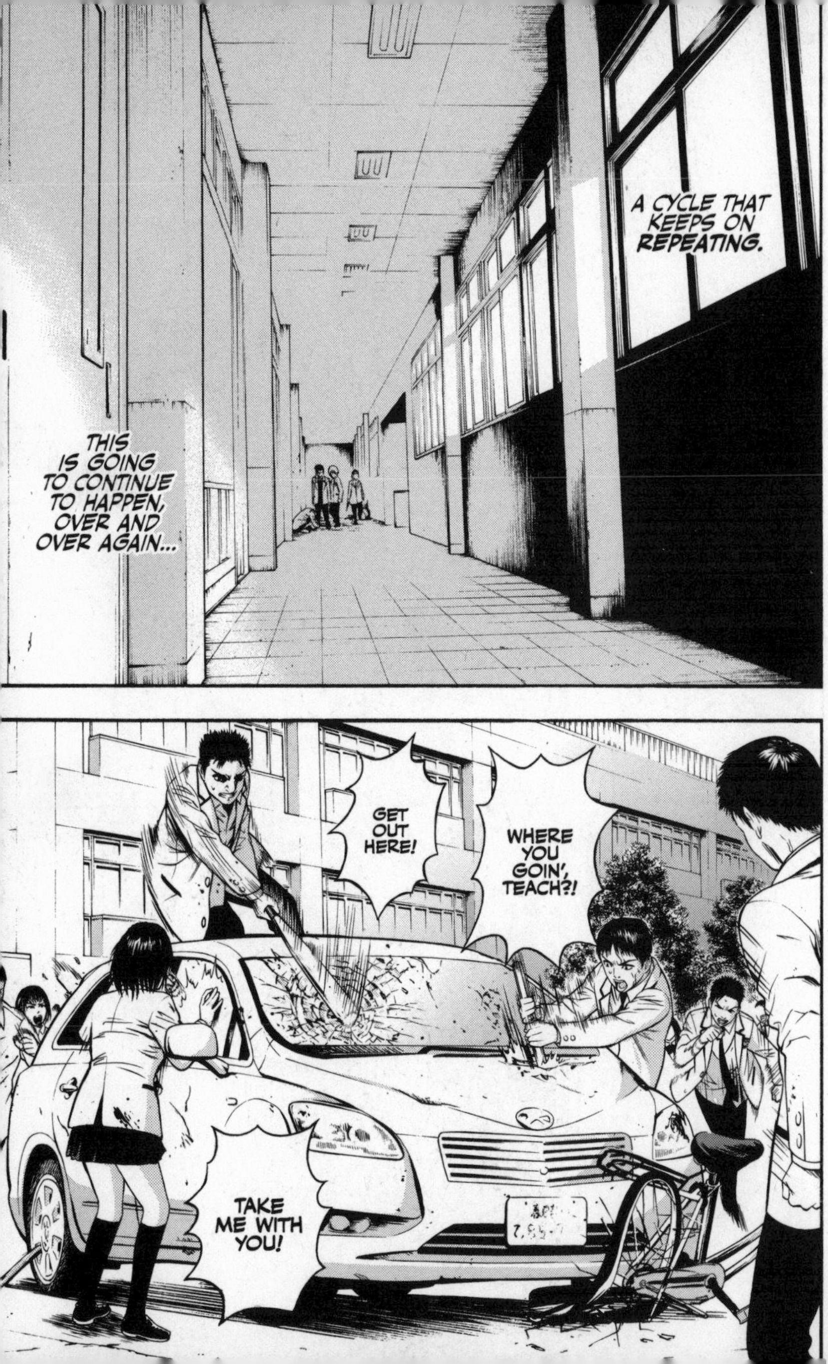
A CYCLE THAT KEEPS ON REPEATING.
THIS IS GOING TO CONTINUE TO HAPPEN, OVER AND OVER AGAIN...
WHERE YOU GOIN', TEACH?!
GET OUT HERE!
TAKE ME WITH YOU!

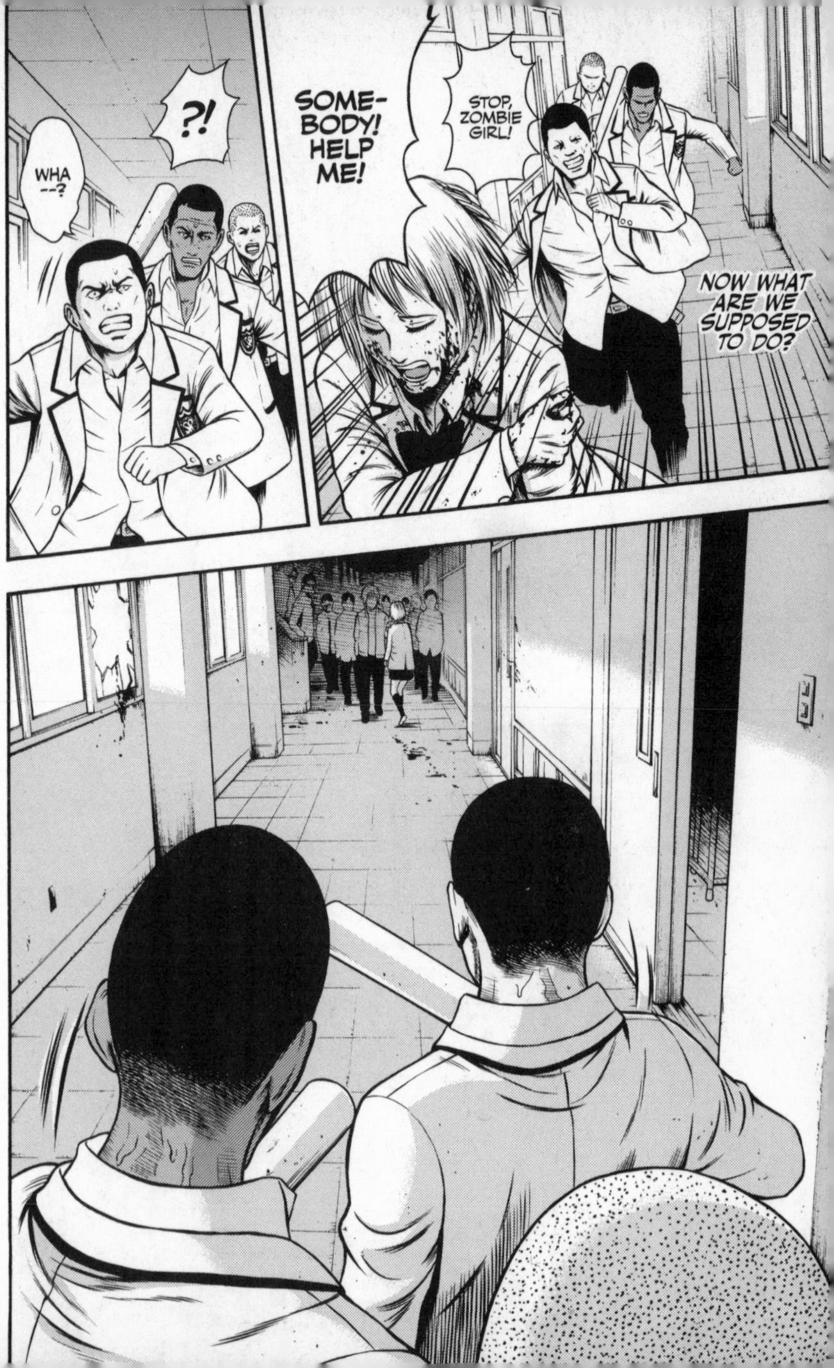
STOP, ZOMBIE GIRL!
SOME-BODY! HELP ME!
?!
WHA--?
NOW WHAT ARE WE SUPPOSED TO DO?

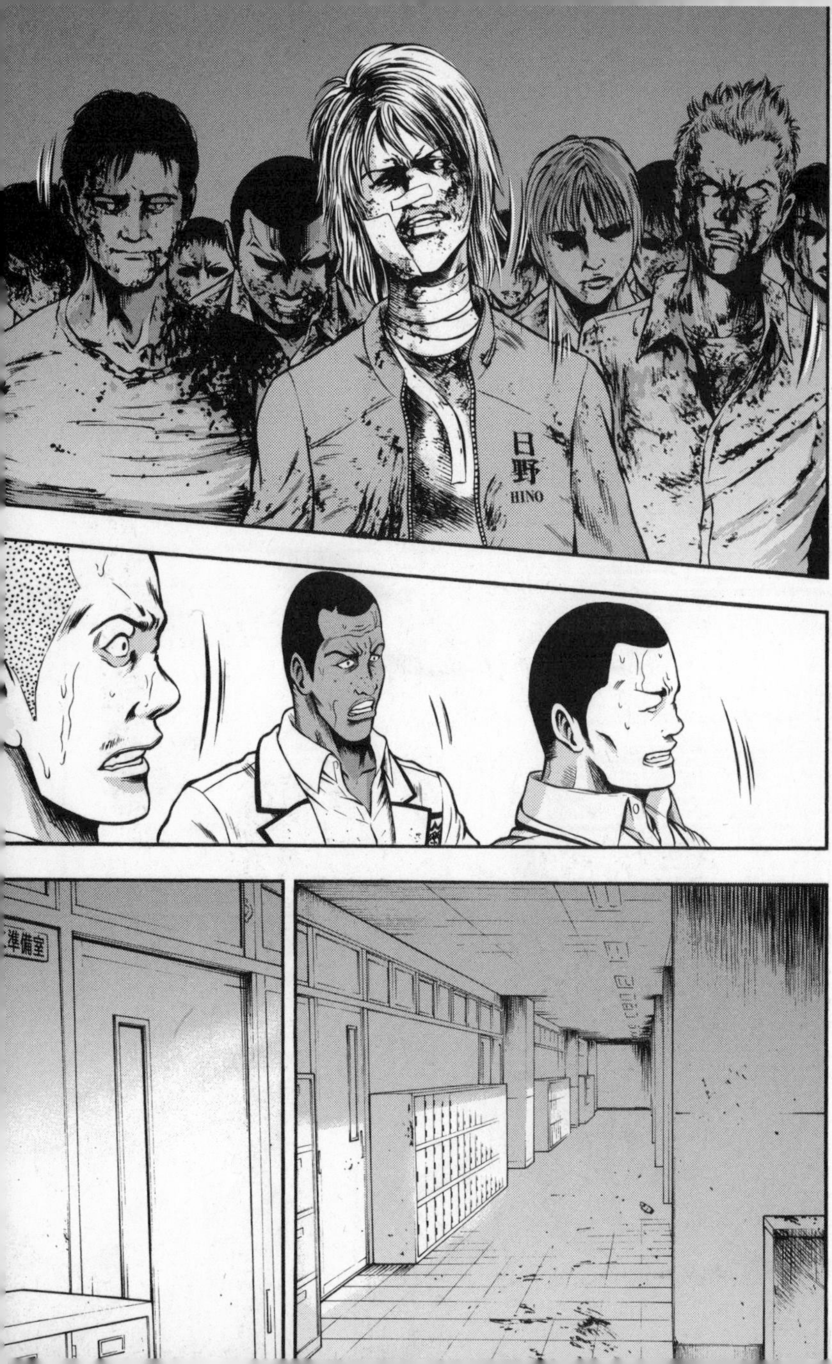
日野
HINO
準備室

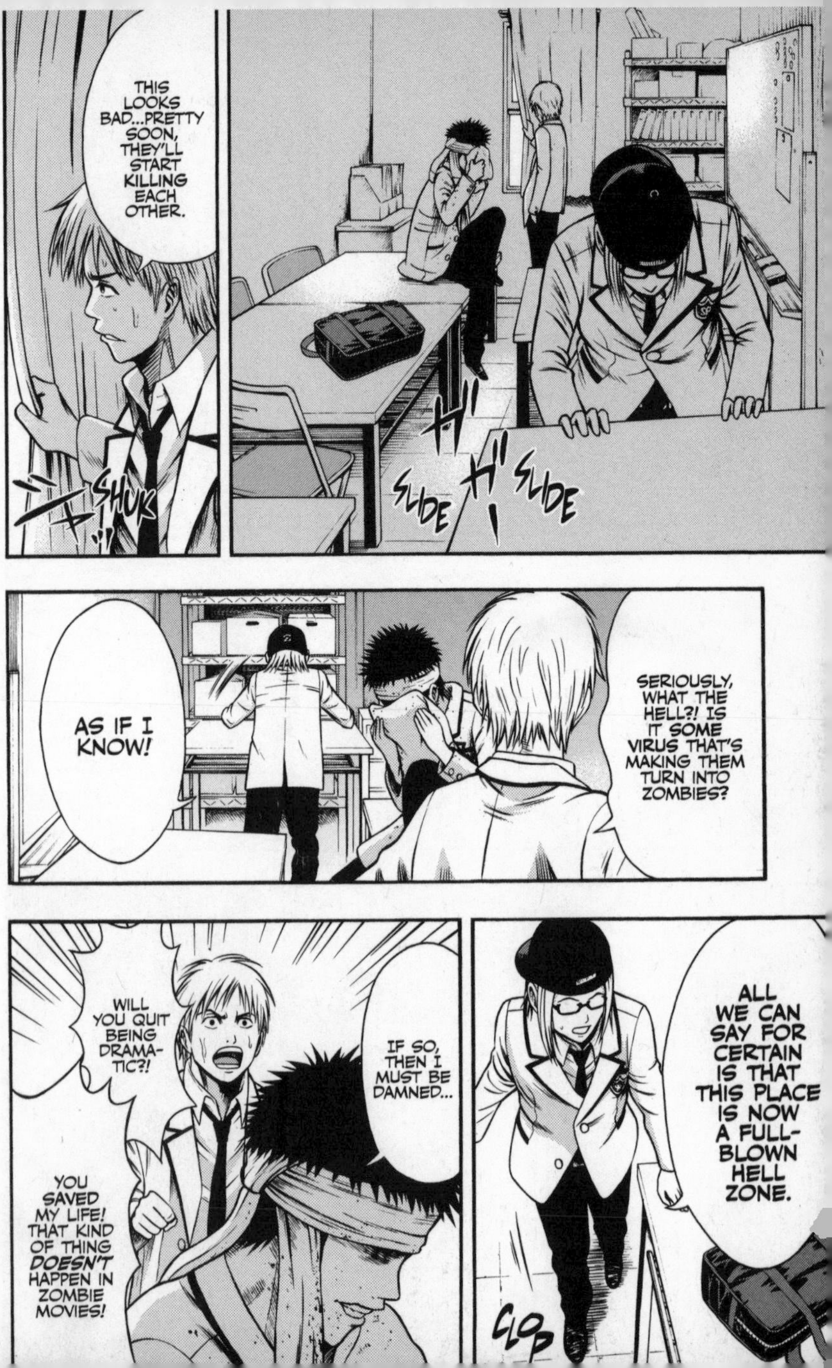
THIS LOOKS BAD...PRETTY SOON, THEY'LL START KILLING EACH OTHER.
SLIDE
SLIDE
SHUK
SERIOUSLY, WHAT THE HELL?! IS IT SOME VIRUS THAT'S MAKING THEM TURN INTO ZOMBIES?
AS IF I KNOW!
ALL WE CAN SAY FOR CERTAIN IS THAT THIS PLACE IS NOW A FULL-BLOWN HELL ZONE.
CLOP
IF SO, THEN I MUST BE DAMNED...
WILL YOU QUIT BEING DRAMA-TIC?!
YOU SAVED MY LIFE! THAT KIND OF THING DOESN'T HAPPEN IN ZOMBIE MOVIES!

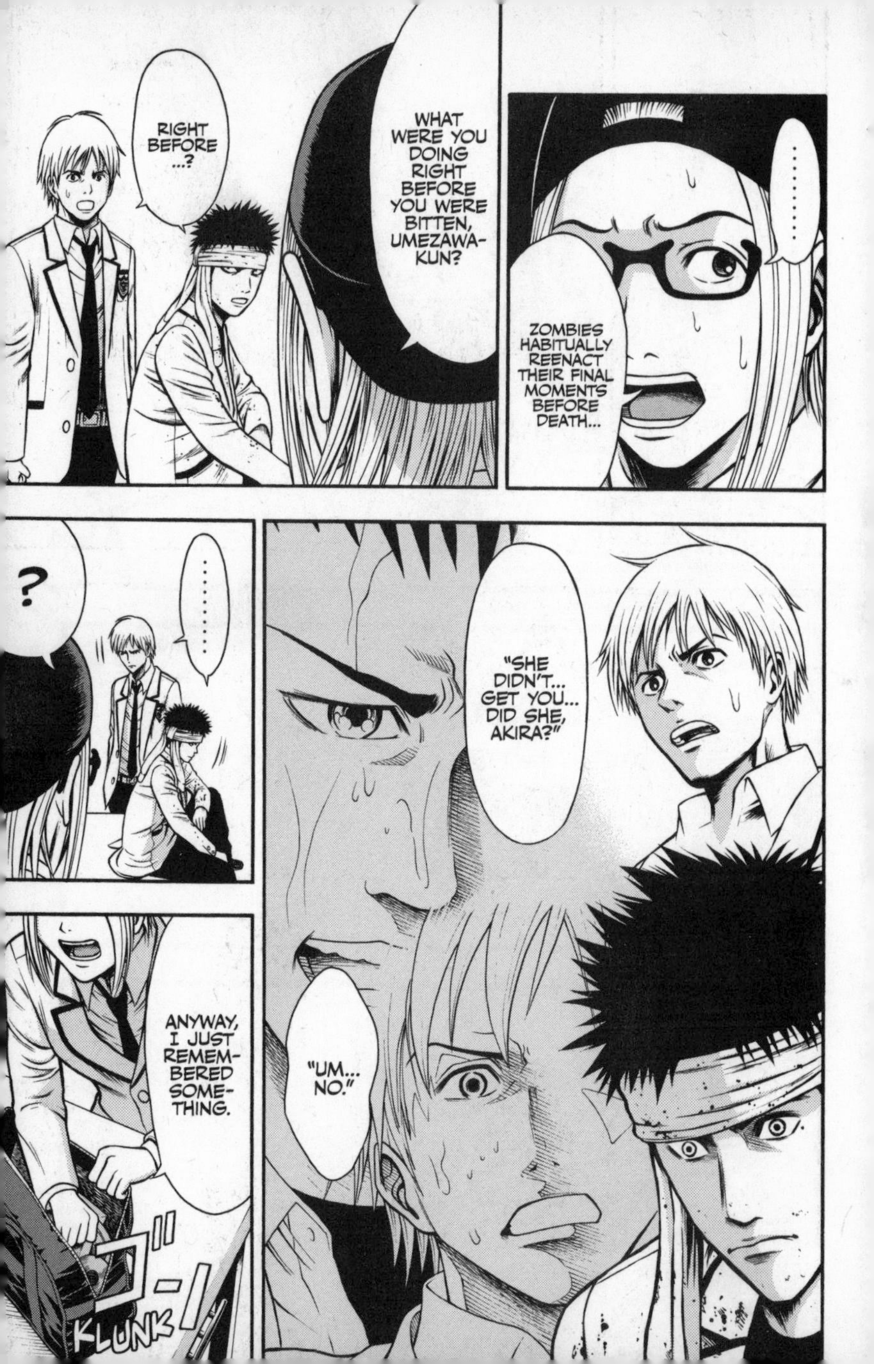
......
ZOMBIES HABITUALLY REENACT THEIR FINAL MOMENTS BEFORE DEATH...
WHAT WERE YOU DOING RIGHT BEFORE YOU WERE BITTEN, UMEZAWA-KUN?
RIGHT BEFORE ...?
"SHE DIDN'T... GET YOU... DID SHE, AKIRA?"
"UM... NO."
......
?
ANYWAY, I JUST REMEMBERED SOMETHING.
KLUNK

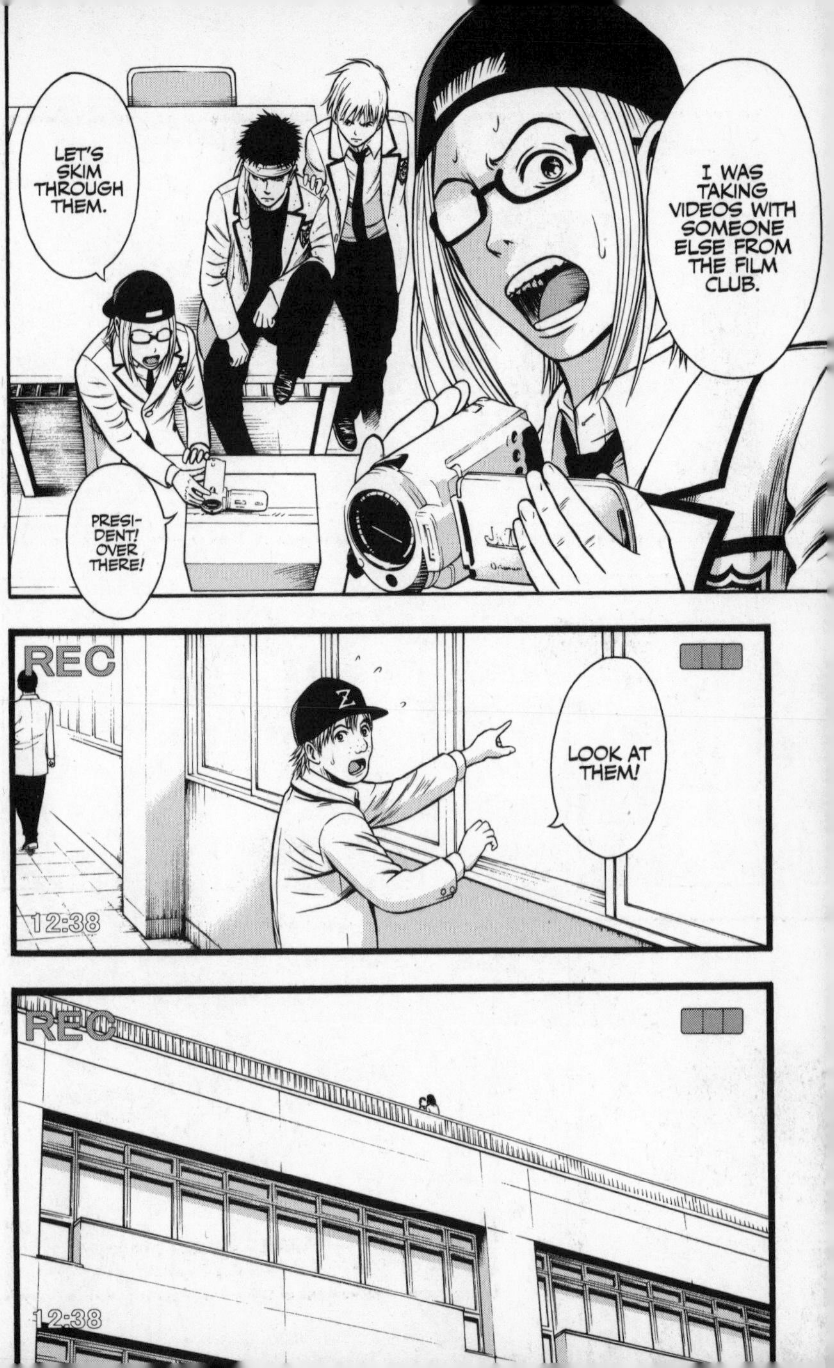
I WAS TAKING VIDEOS WITH SOMEONE ELSE FROM THE FILM CLUB.
LET'S SKIM THROUGH THEM.
PRESI-DENT! OVER THERE!
REC
LOOK AT THEM!
12:38
REC
12:38

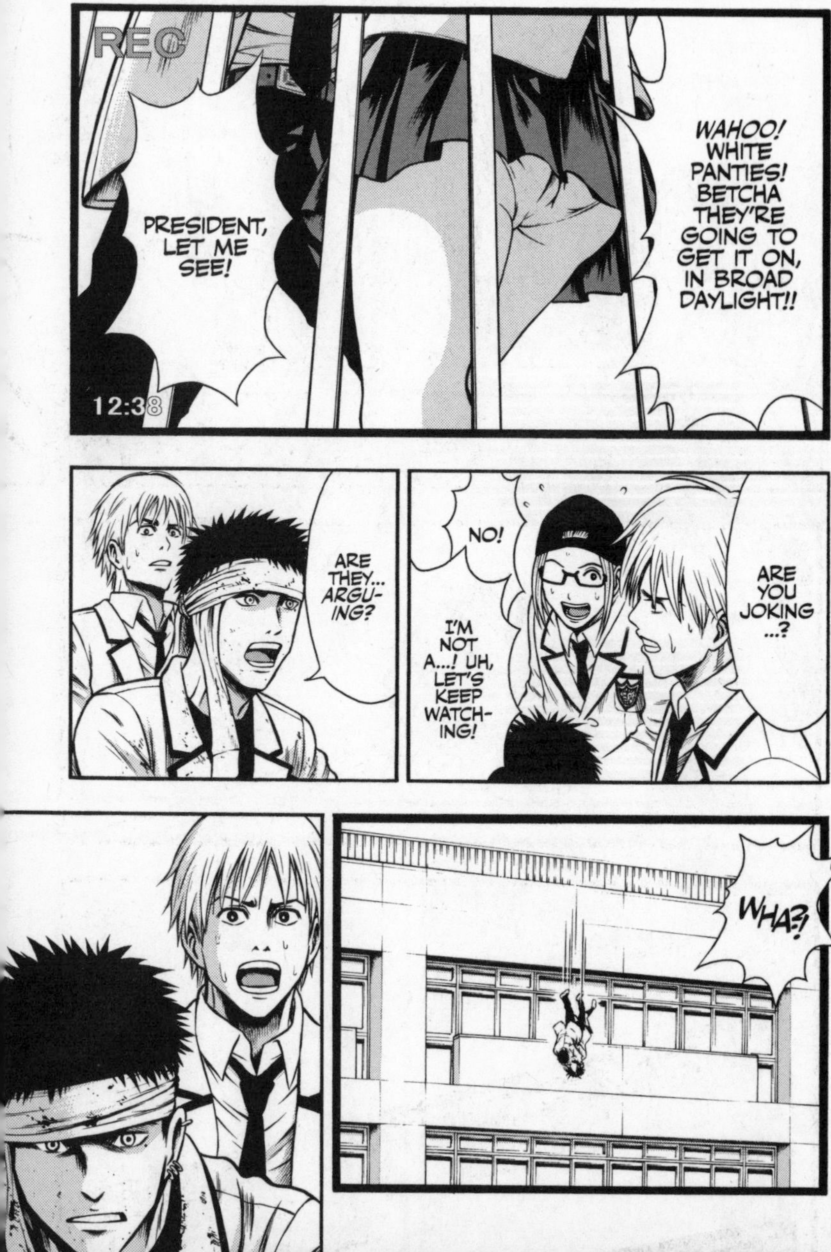
REC
WAHOO! WHITE PANTIES! BETCHA THEY'RE GOING TO GET IT ON, IN BROAD DAYLIGHT!!
PRESIDENT, LET ME SEE!
12:38
ARE YOU JOKING ...?
NO!
I'M NOT A...! UH, LET'S KEEP WATCHING!
ARE THEY... ARGU-ING?
WHA?!

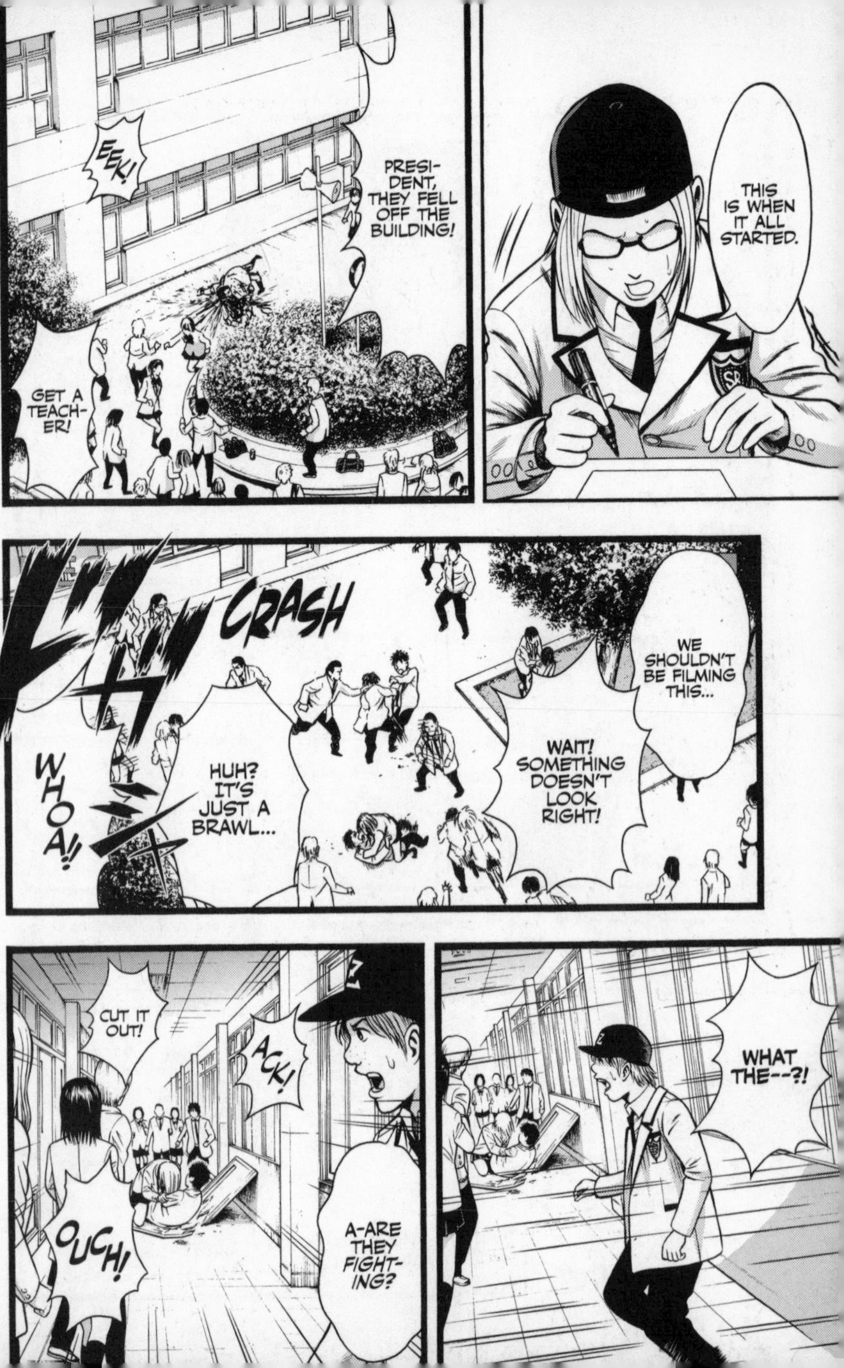
THIS IS WHEN IT ALL STARTED.
PRESIDENT, THEY FELL OFF THE BUILDING!
EEK!
GET A TEACHER!
WE SHOULDN'T BE FILMING THIS...
WAIT! SOMETHING DOESN'T LOOK RIGHT!
HUH? IT'S JUST A BRAWL...
CRASH
WHOA!!
WHAT THE--?!
CUT IT OUT!
ACK!
A-ARE THEY FIGHTING?
OUCH!

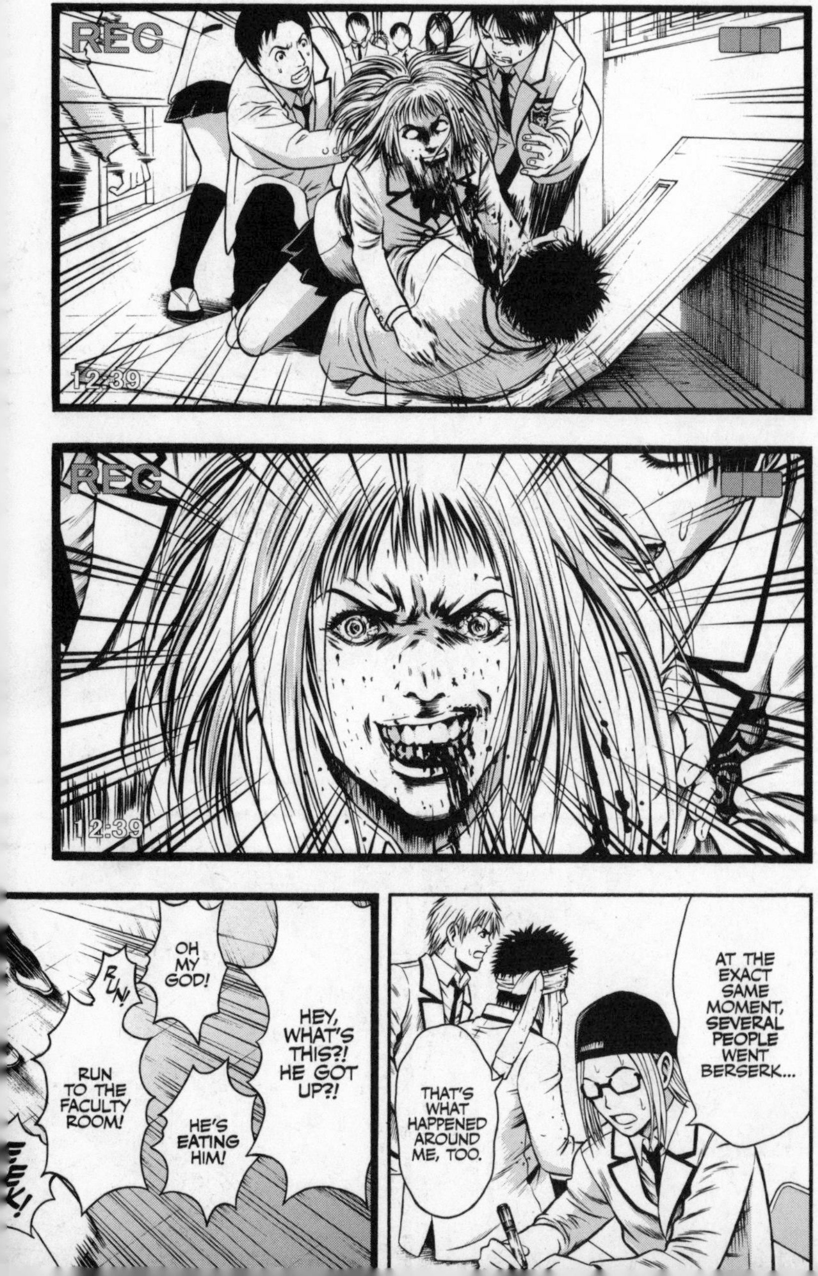
REC
12:39
REC
12:39
OH MY GOD!
RUN!
HEY, WHAT'S THIS?! HE GOT UP?!
RUN TO THE FACULTY ROOM!
HE'S EATING HIM!
AT THE EXACT SAME MOMENT, SEVERAL PEOPLE WENT BERSERK...
THAT'S WHAT HAPPENED AROUND ME, TOO.

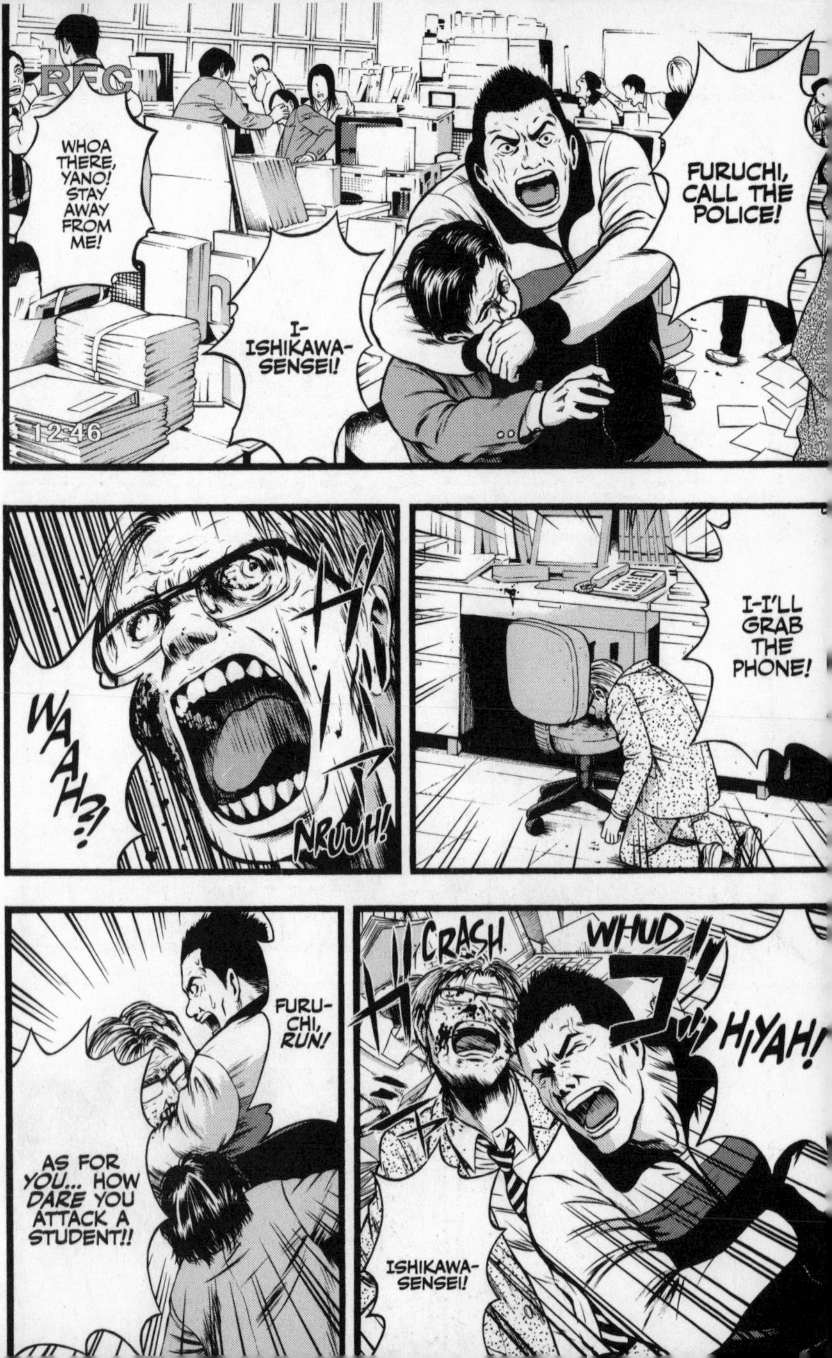
REC
12:46
FURUCHI, CALL THE POLICE!
I-ISHIKAWA-SENSEI!
WHOA THERE, YANO! STAY AWAY FROM ME!
I-I'LL GRAB THE PHONE!
NRUUH!
WAAH?!
HIYAH!
WHUD
CRASH
ISHIKAWA-SENSEI!
FURU-CHI, RUN!
AS FOR YOU... HOW DARE YOU ATTACK A STUDENT!!

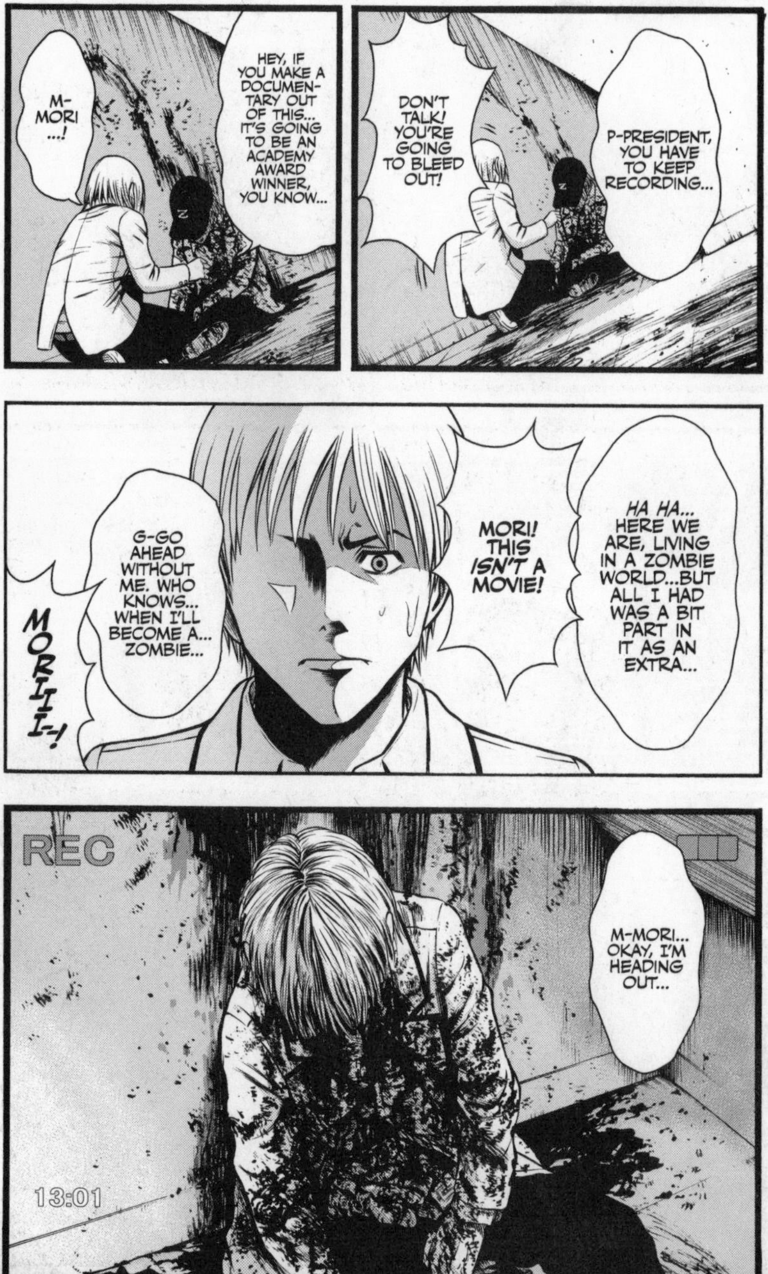
P-PRESIDENT, YOU HAVE TO KEEP RECORDING...
DON'T TALK! YOU'RE GOING TO BLEED OUT!
HEY, IF YOU MAKE A DOCUMENTARY OUT OF THIS... IT'S GOING TO BE AN ACADEMY AWARD WINNER, YOU KNOW...
M-MORI ...!
HA HA... HERE WE ARE, LIVING IN A ZOMBIE WORLD...BUT ALL I HAD WAS A BIT PART IN IT AS AN EXTRA...
MORI! THIS ISN'T A MOVIE!
G-GO AHEAD WITHOUT ME. WHO KNOWS... WHEN I'LL BECOME A... ZOMBIE...
MORIIII--!
REC
M-MORI... OKAY, I'M HEADING OUT...
13:01

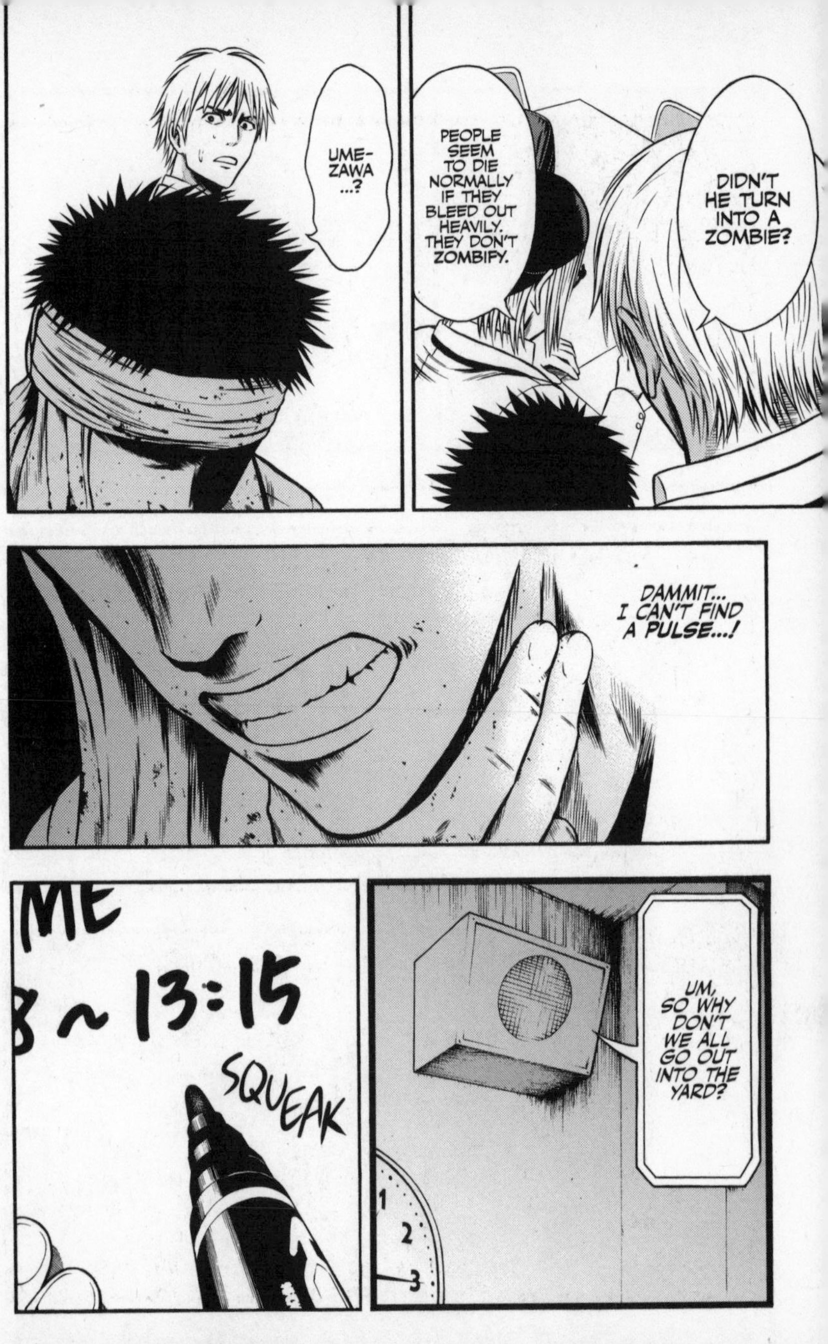
DIDN'T HE TURN INTO A ZOMBIE?
PEOPLE SEEM TO DIE NORMALLY IF THEY BLEED OUT HEAVILY. THEY DON'T ZOMBIFY.
UME-ZAWA ...?
DAMMIT... I CAN'T FIND A PULSE...!
UM, SO WHY DON'T WE ALL GO OUT INTO THE YARD?
ME
~ 13:15
SQUEAK
1
2
3

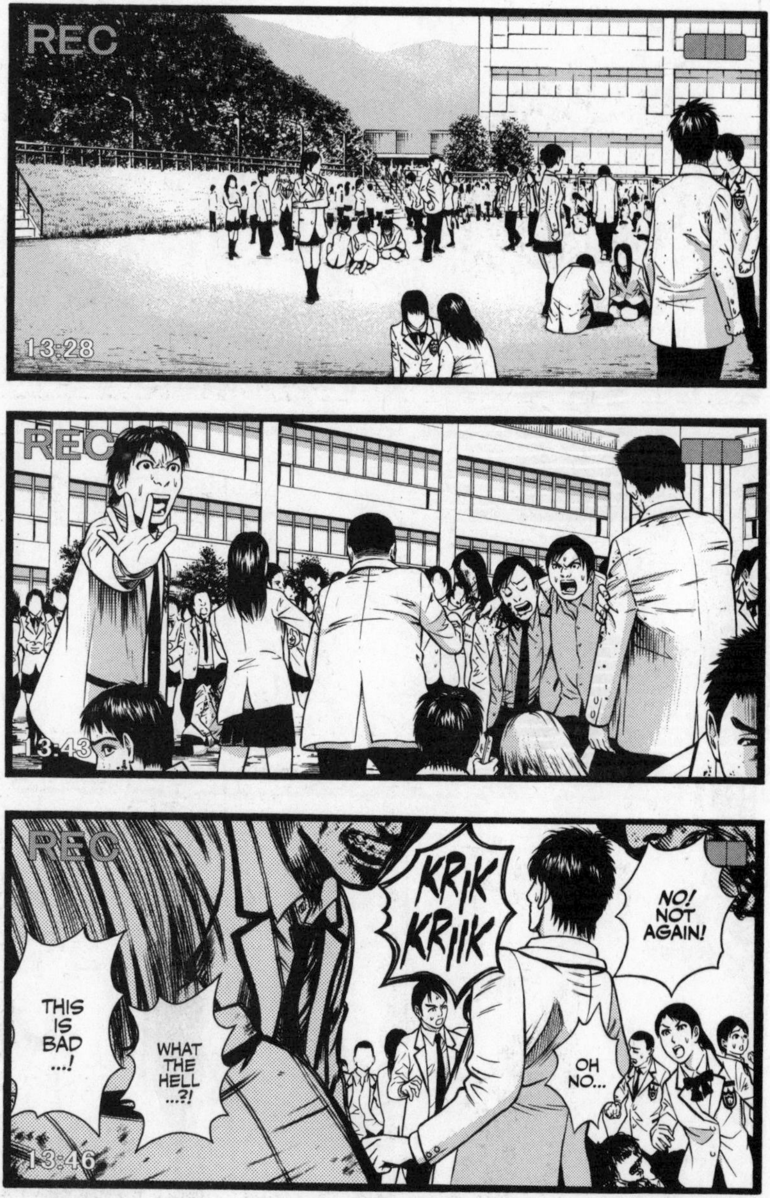
REC
13:28
REC
13:43
REC
KRIK KRIIK
NO! NOT AGAIN!
THIS IS BAD ...!
WHAT THE HELL ...?!
OH NO...
13:46

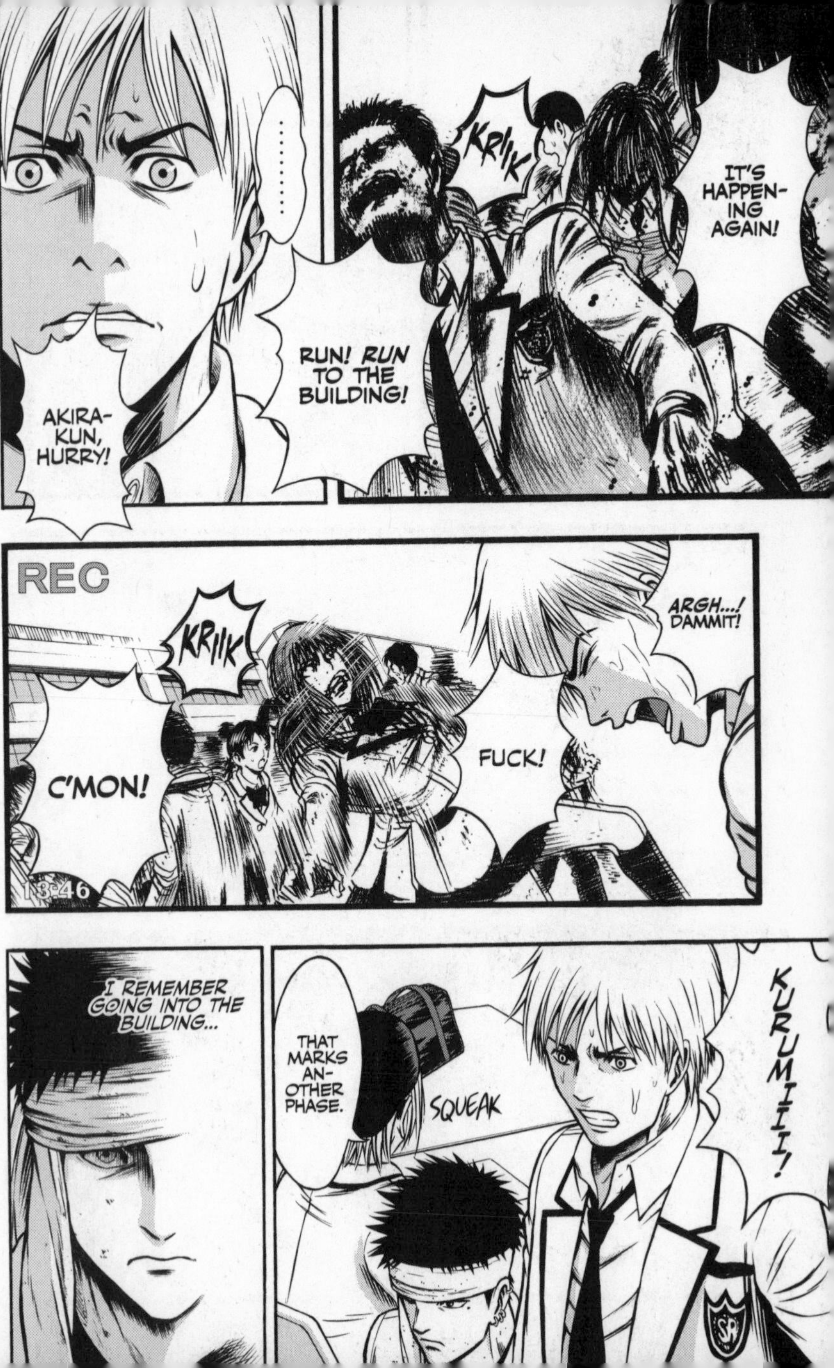
IT'S HAPPENING AGAIN!
KRIIK
......
RUN! RUN TO THE BUILDING!
AKIRA-KUN, HURRY!
REC
ARGH...! DAMMIT!
FUCK!
KRIIK
C'MON!
13:46
KURUMIII!
SQUEAK
THAT MARKS AN-OTHER PHASE.
I REMEMBER GOING INTO THE BUILDING...

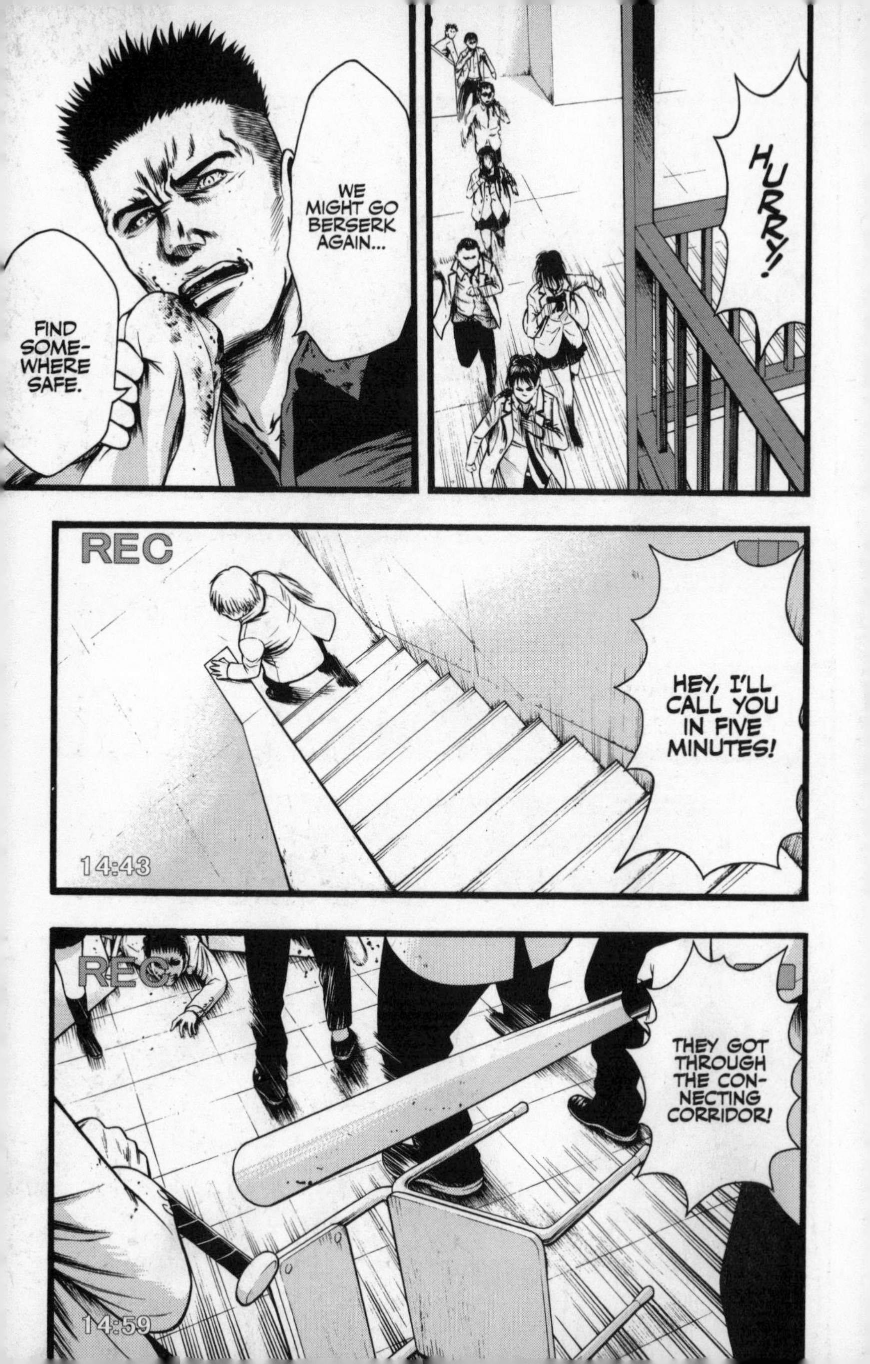
WE MIGHT GO BERSERK AGAIN...
FIND SOME-WHERE SAFE.
HURRY!!
REC
HEY, I'LL CALL YOU IN FIVE MINUTES!
14:43
REC
THEY GOT THROUGH THE CON-NECTING CORRIDOR!
14:59

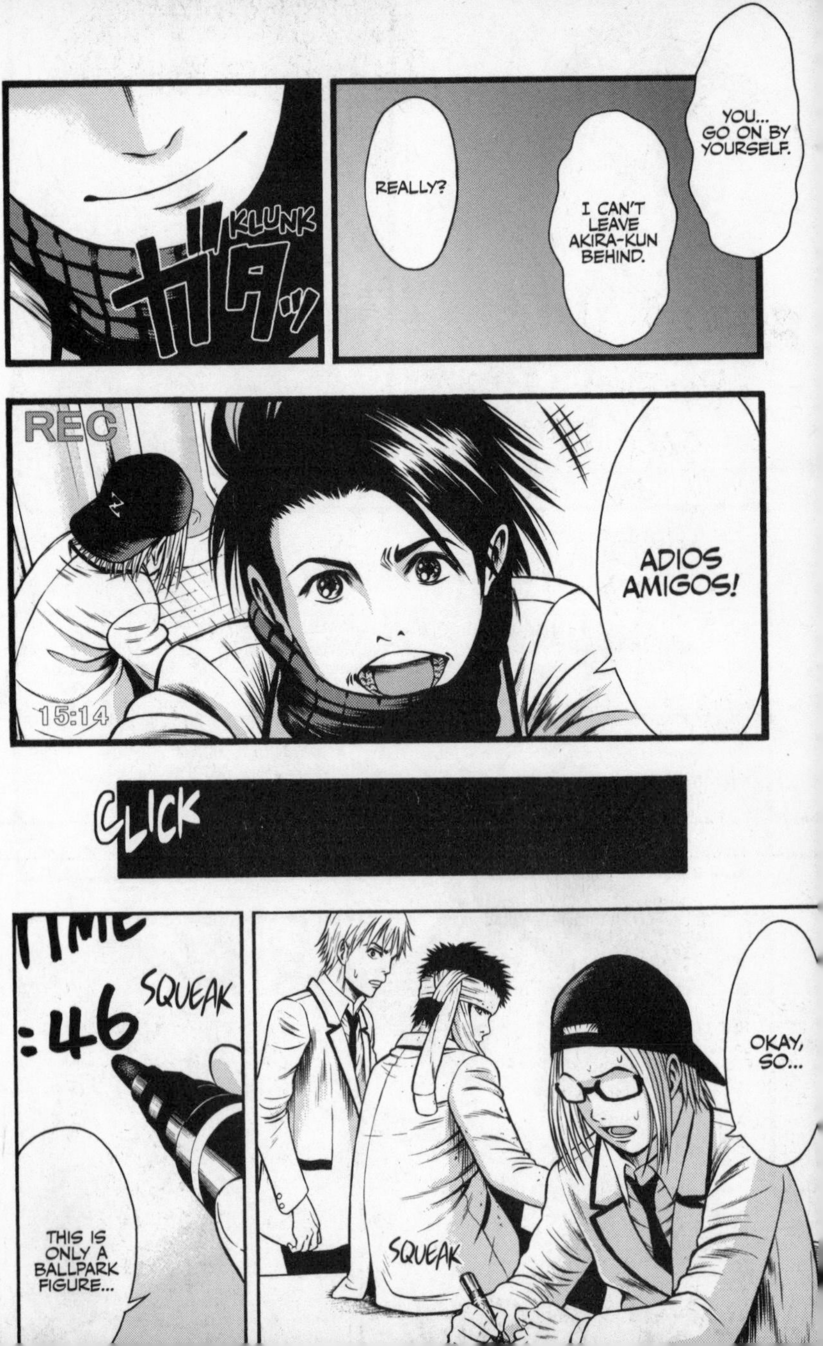
YOU... GO ON BY YOURSELF.
I CAN'T LEAVE AKIRA-KUN BEHIND.
REALLY?
KLUNK
ガタッ
REC
15:14
ADIOS AMIGOS!
CLICK
OKAY, SO...
SQUEAK
TIME
:46
SQUEAK
THIS IS ONLY A BALLPARK FIGURE...

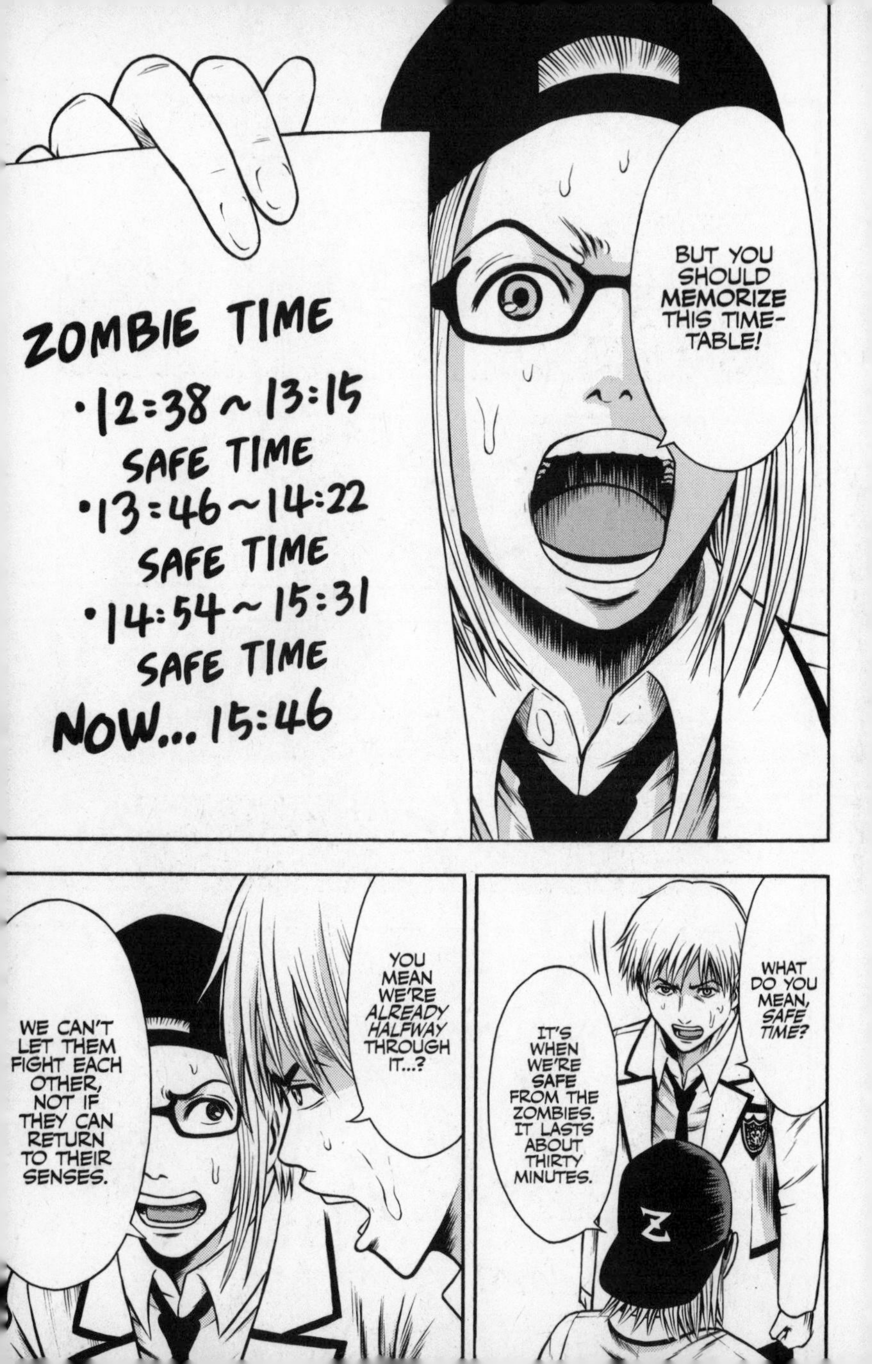
BUT YOU SHOULD MEMORIZE THIS TIME-TABLE!
ZOMBIE TIME
•12:38 ~ 13:15
SAFE TIME
•13:46 ~ 14:22
SAFE TIME
•14:54 ~ 15:31
SAFE TIME
NOW... 15:46
WHAT DO YOU MEAN, *SAFE TIME*?
IT'S WHEN WE'RE SAFE FROM THE ZOMBIES. IT LASTS ABOUT THIRTY MINUTES.
YOU MEAN WE'RE *ALREADY HALFWAY* THROUGH IT...?
WE CAN'T LET THEM FIGHT EACH OTHER, NOT IF THEY CAN RETURN TO THEIR SENSES.

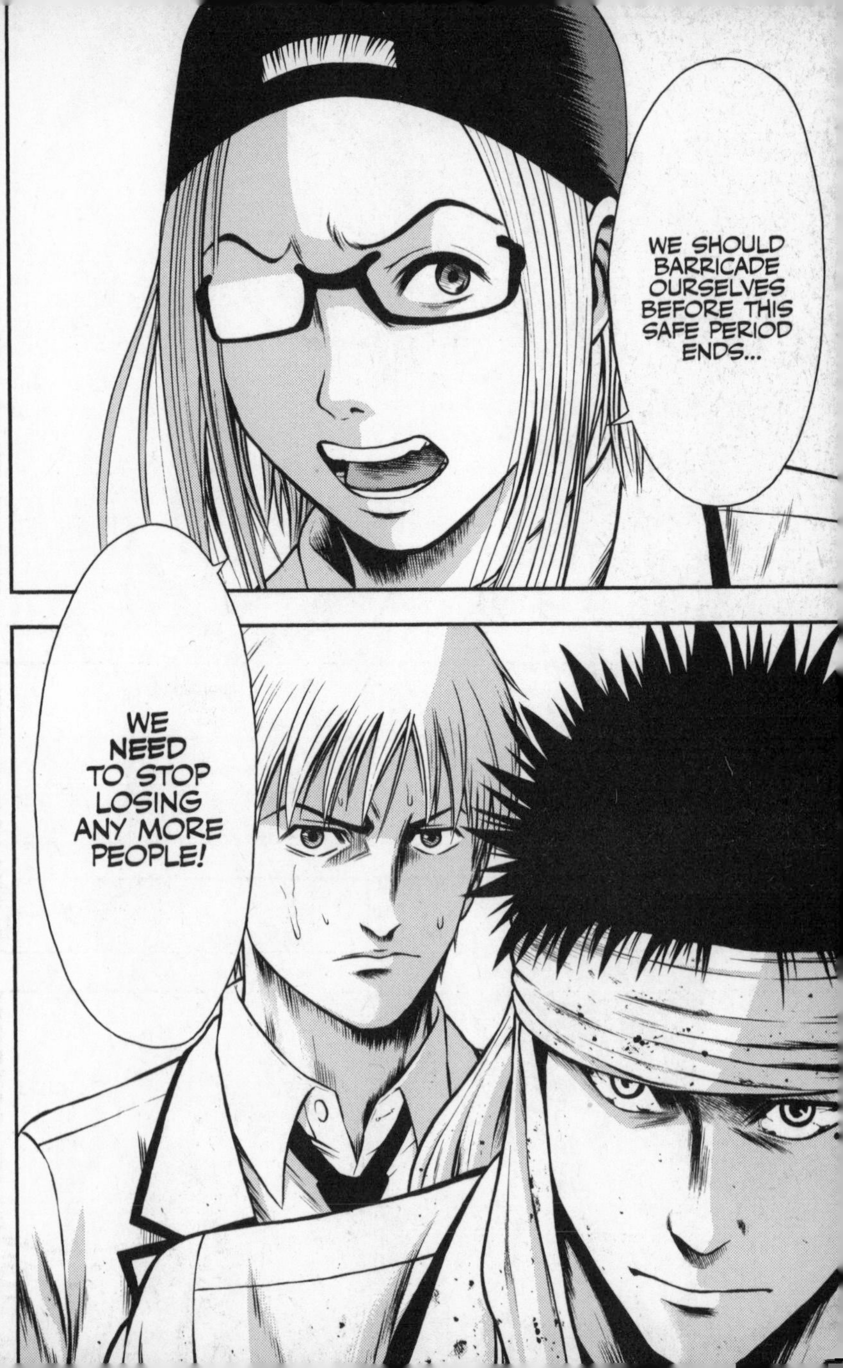
WE SHOULD BARRICADE OURSELVES BEFORE THIS SAFE PERIOD ENDS...
WE NEED TO STOP LOSING ANY MORE PEOPLE!

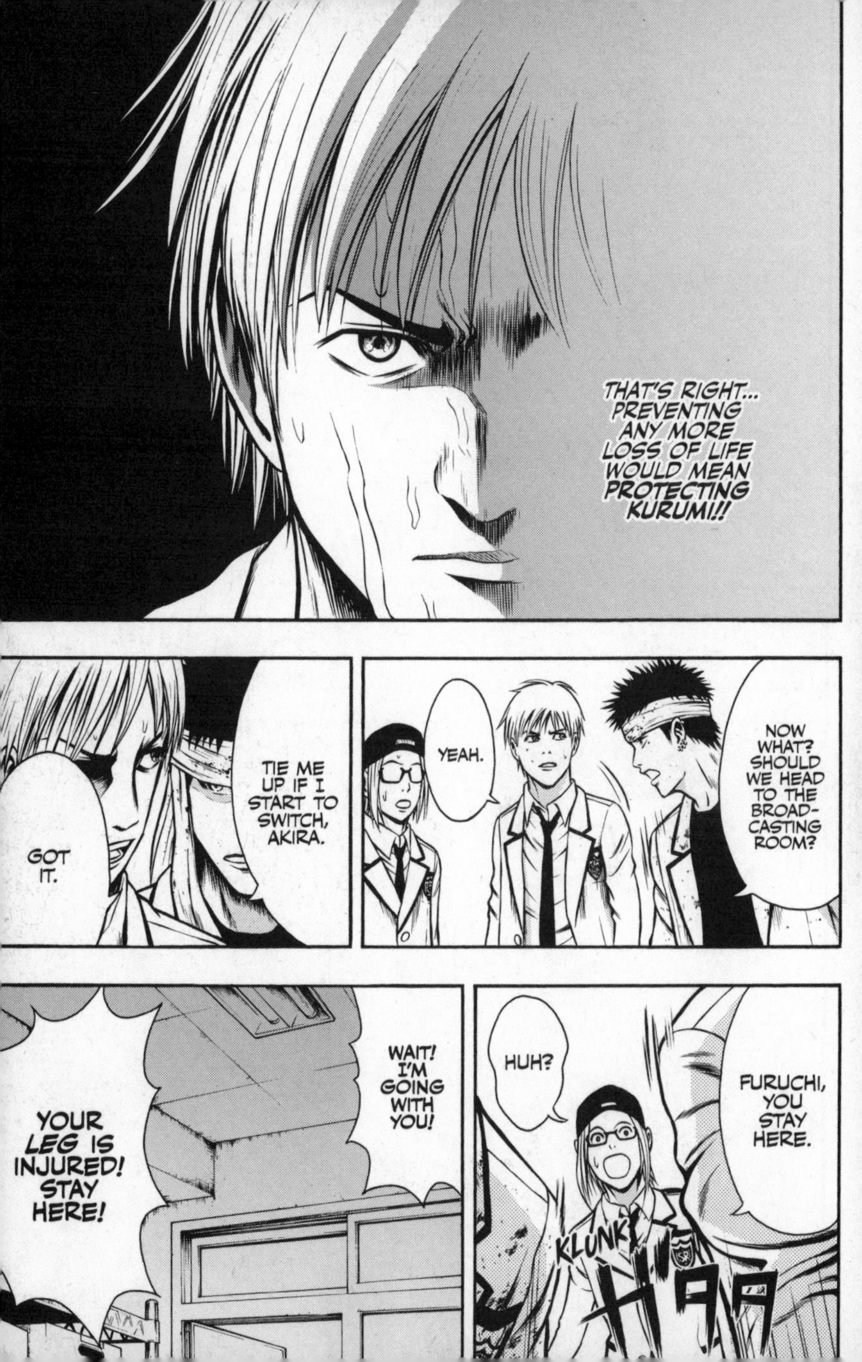
THAT'S RIGHT... PREVENTING ANY MORE LOSS OF LIFE WOULD MEAN PROTECTING KURUMI!!
NOW WHAT? SHOULD WE HEAD TO THE BROAD-CASTING ROOM?
YEAH.
TIE ME UP IF I START TO SWITCH, AKIRA.
GOT IT.
FURUCHI, YOU STAY HERE.
HUH?
KLUNK
WAIT! I'M GOING WITH YOU!
YOUR LEG IS INJURED! STAY HERE!

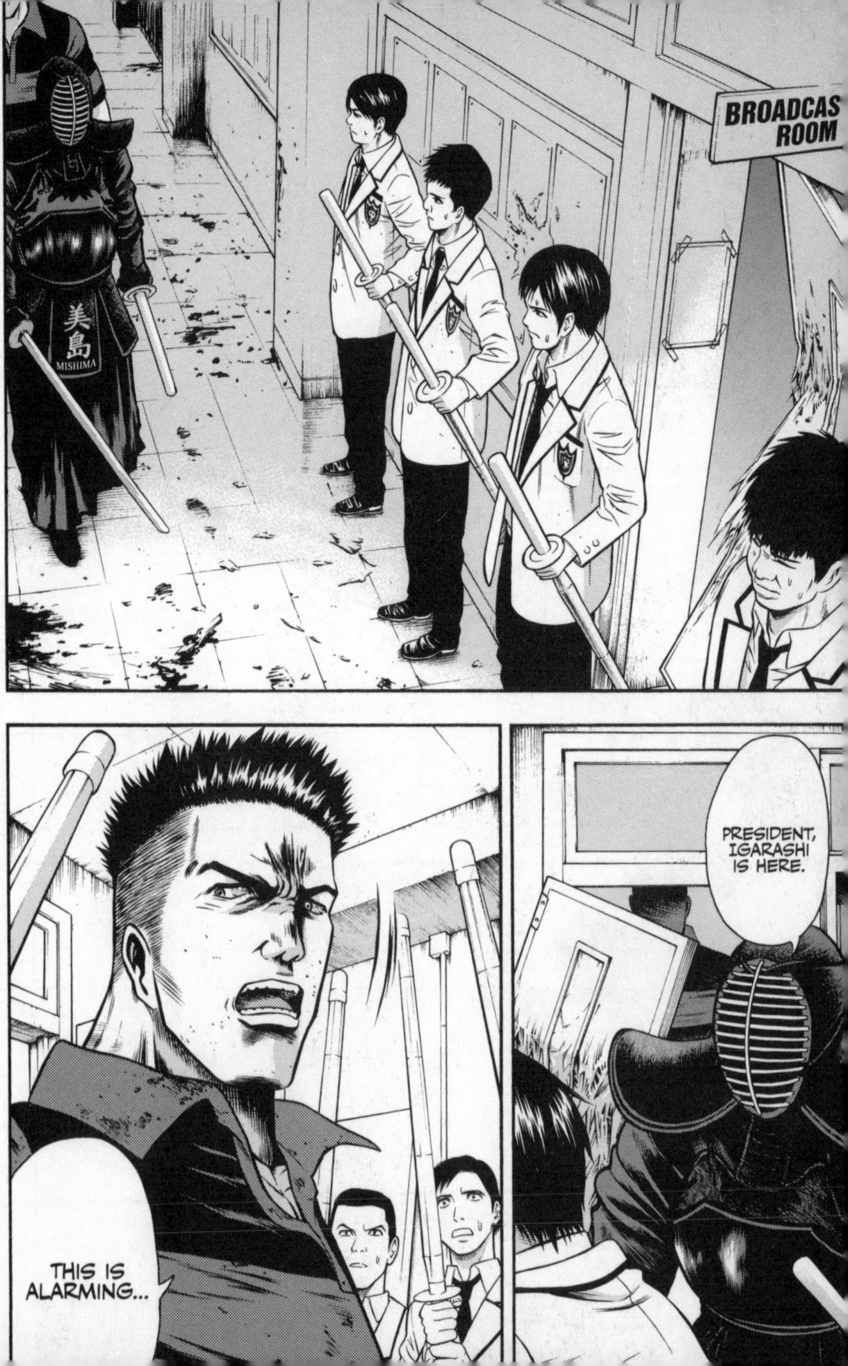
美島
MISHIMA
BROADCAS
ROOM
PRESIDENT, IGARASHI IS HERE.
THIS IS ALARMING...

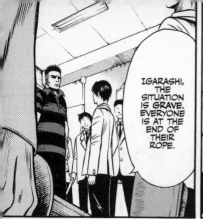

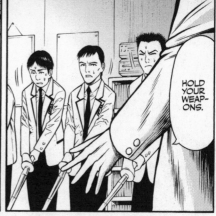

HOLD YOUR WEAP-ONS.
IGARASHI, THE SITUATION IS GRAVE. EVERYONE IS AT THE END OF THEIR ROPE.
VICE PRESIDENT HIMEKAWA TOLD ME THAT YOU GUIDED EVERYONE TO THE TENNIS COURT.
......
IT DIDN'T MAKE ANY DIFFER-ENCE, THOUGH.
WE DON'T WANT TO LOSE ANY MORE PEOPLE.
CAN YOU LEAD THEM AWAY AGAIN?

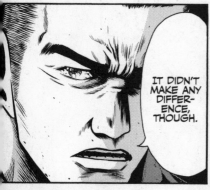

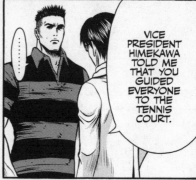

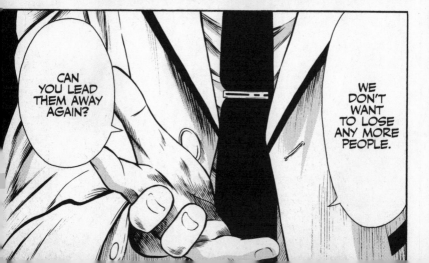

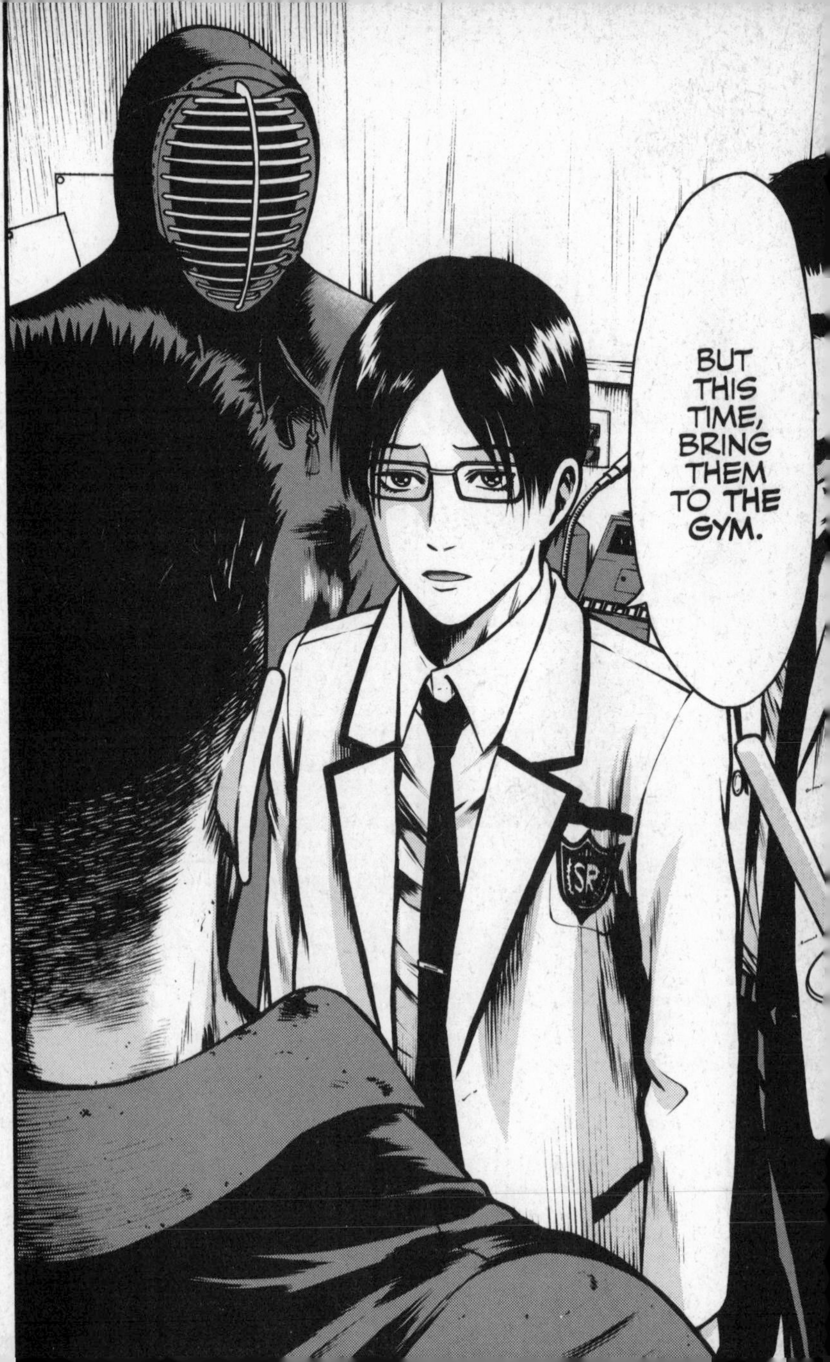
BUT THIS TIME, BRING THEM TO THE GYM.

HOUR OF THE ZOMBIE

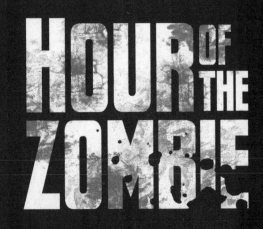

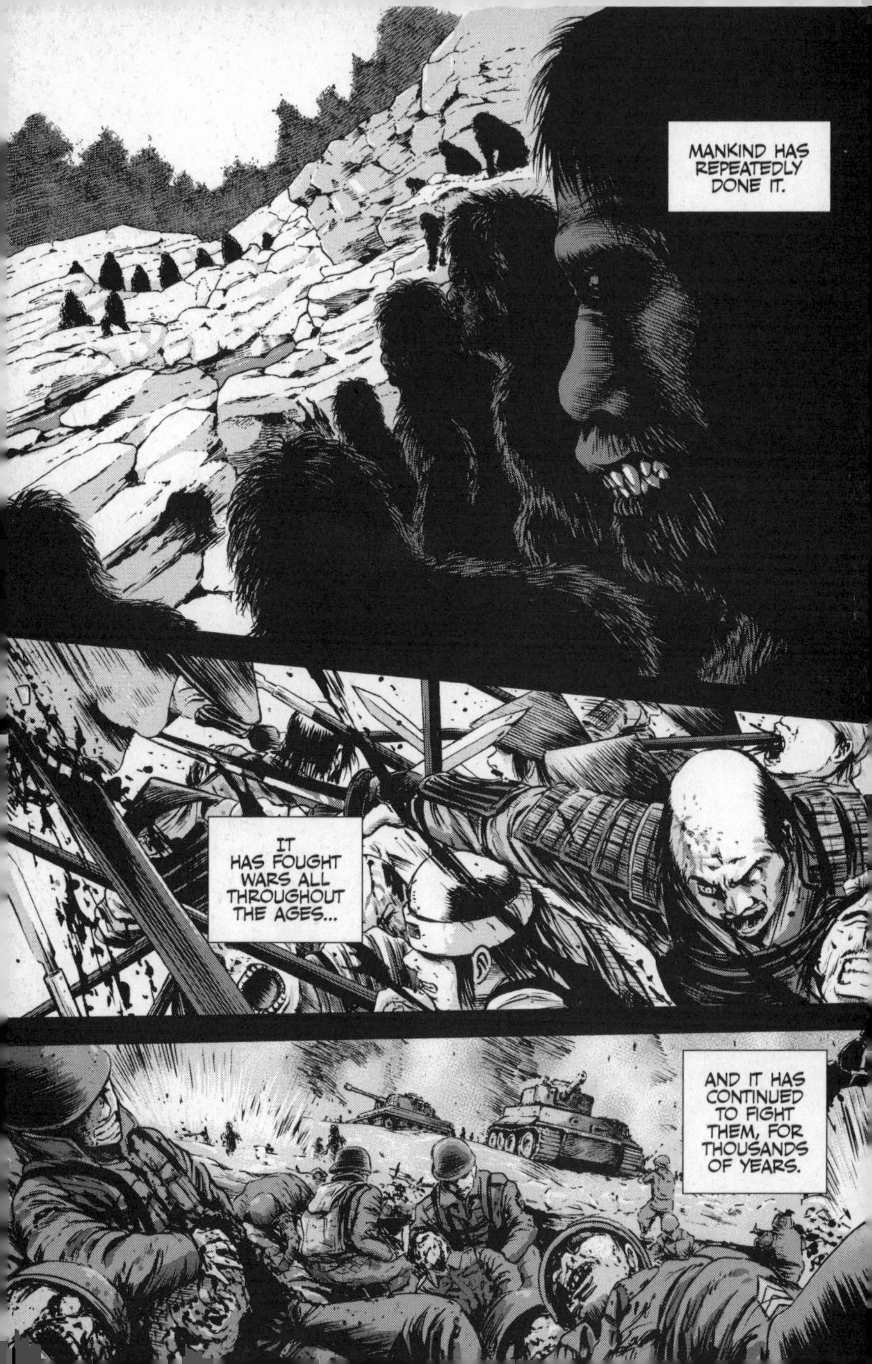
MANKIND HAS REPEATEDLY DONE IT.
IT HAS FOUGHT WARS ALL THROUGHOUT THE AGES...
AND IT HAS CONTINUED TO FIGHT THEM, FOR THOUSANDS OF YEARS.

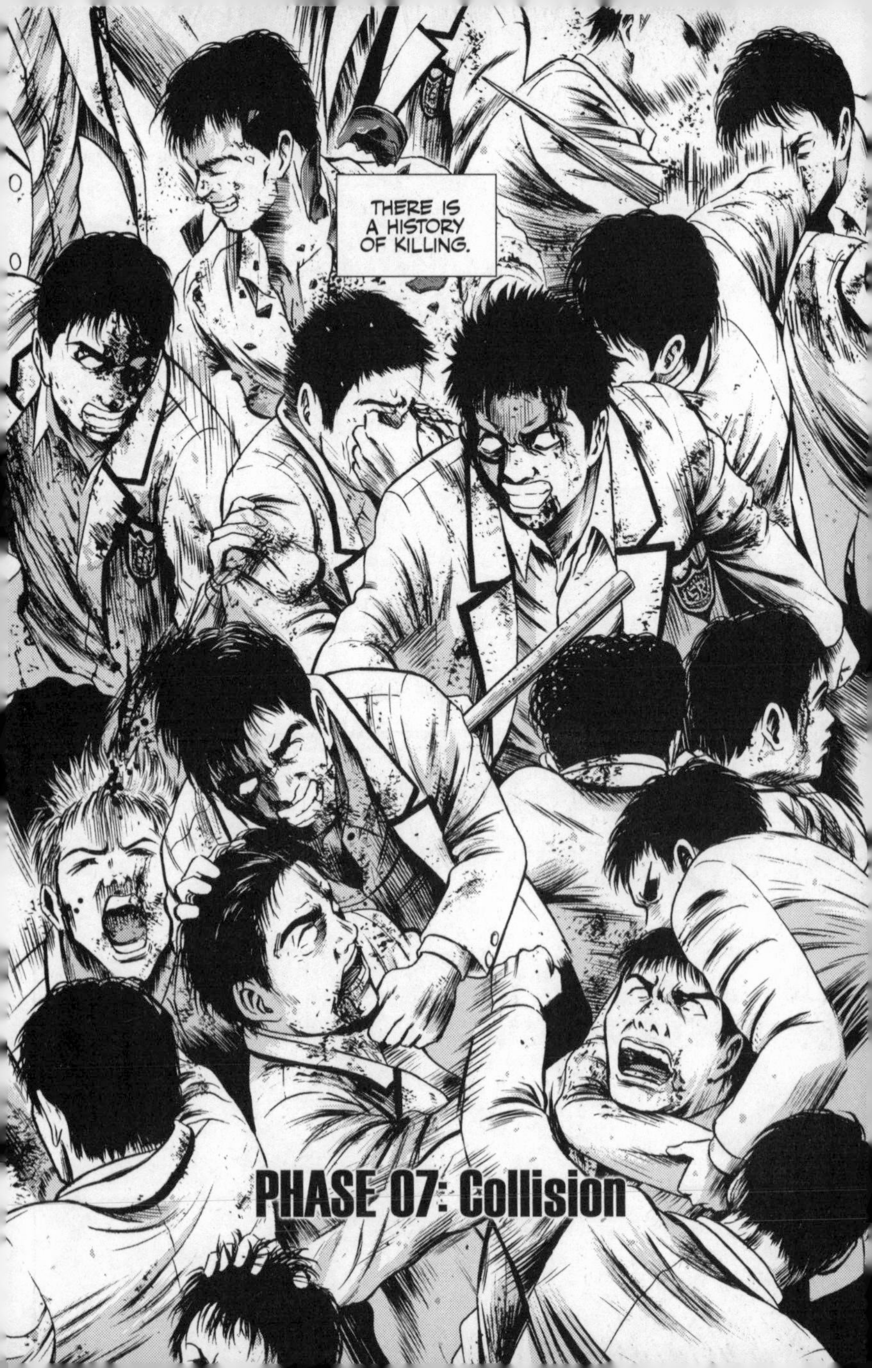
THERE IS A HISTORY OF KILLING.
PHASE 07: Collision

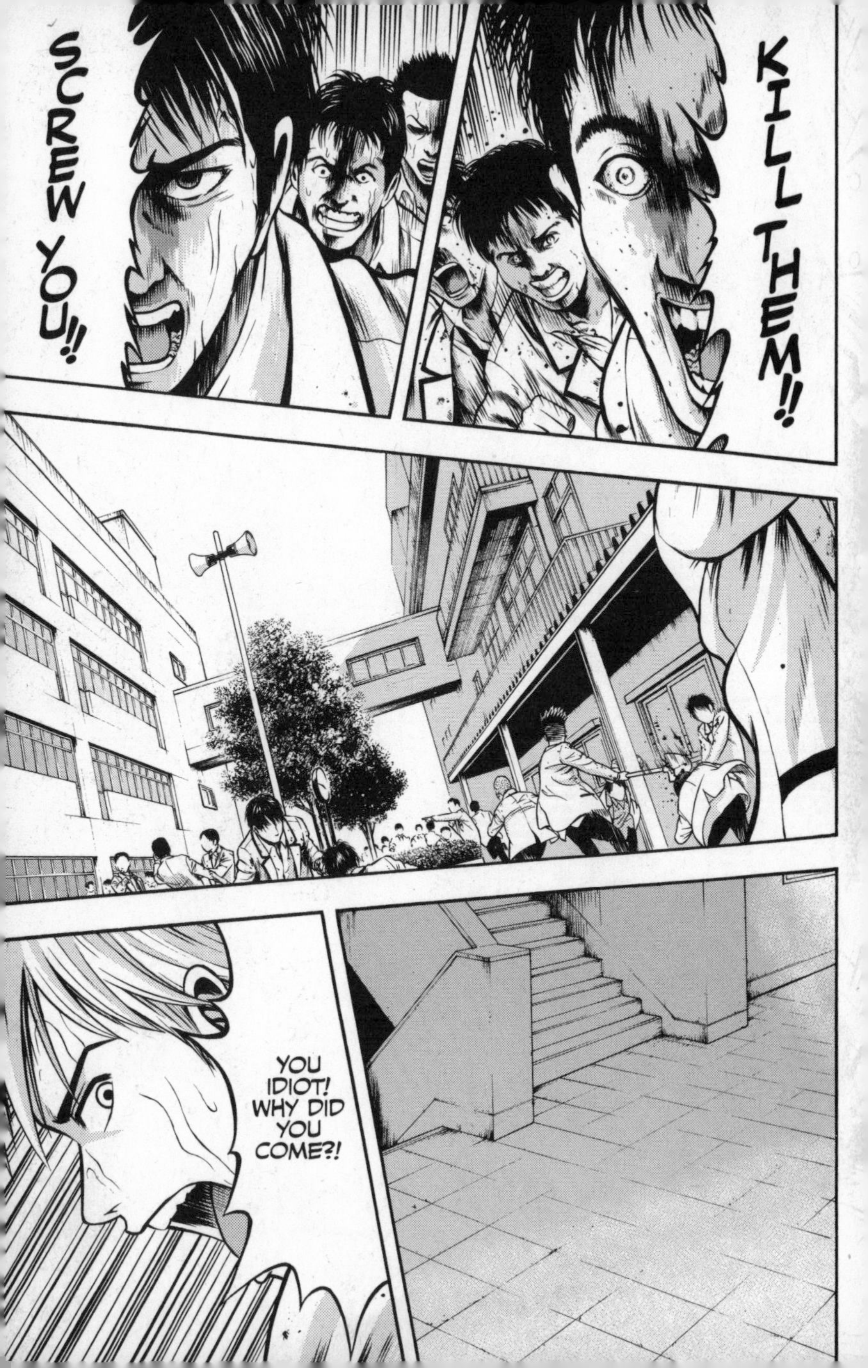
KILL THEM!!
SCREW YOU!!
YOU IDIOT! WHY DID YOU COME?!

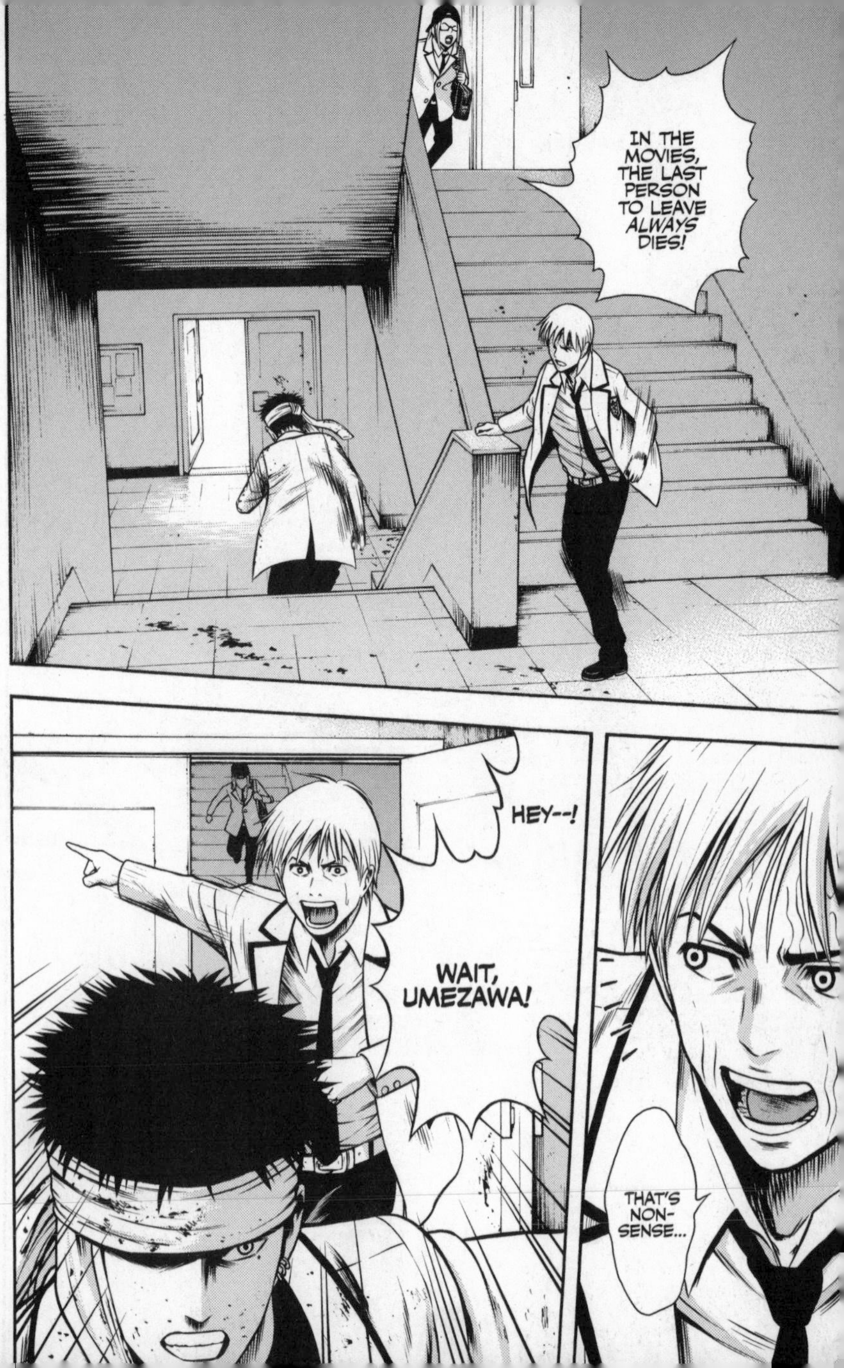
IN THE MOVIES, THE LAST PERSON TO LEAVE ALWAYS DIES!
HEY--!
WAIT, UMEZAWA!
THAT'S NON-SENSE...

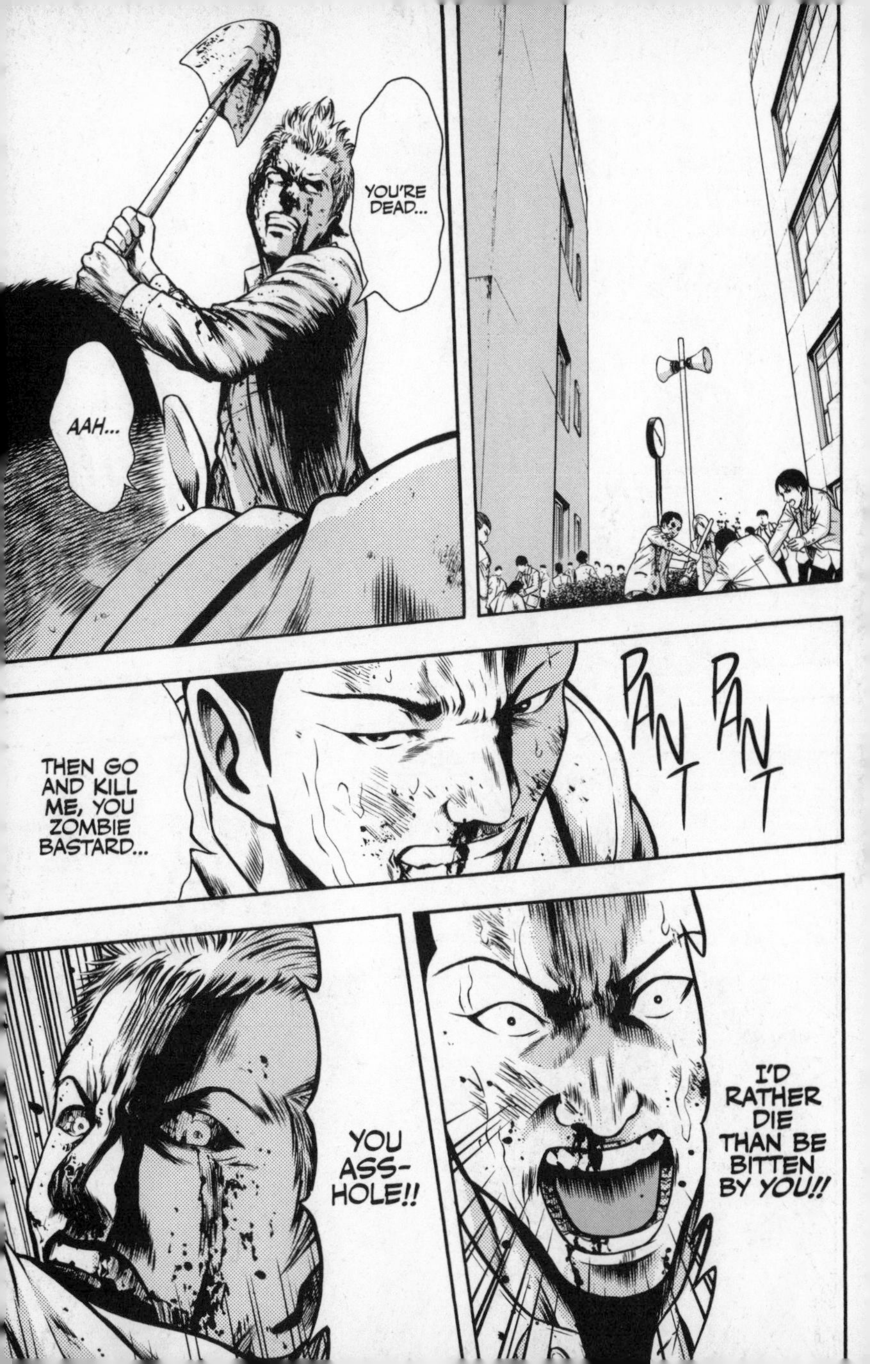
YOU'RE DEAD...
AAH...
PANT PANT
THEN GO AND KILL ME, YOU ZOMBIE BASTARD...
I'D RATHER DIE THAN BE BITTEN BY YOU!!
YOU ASS-HOLE!!

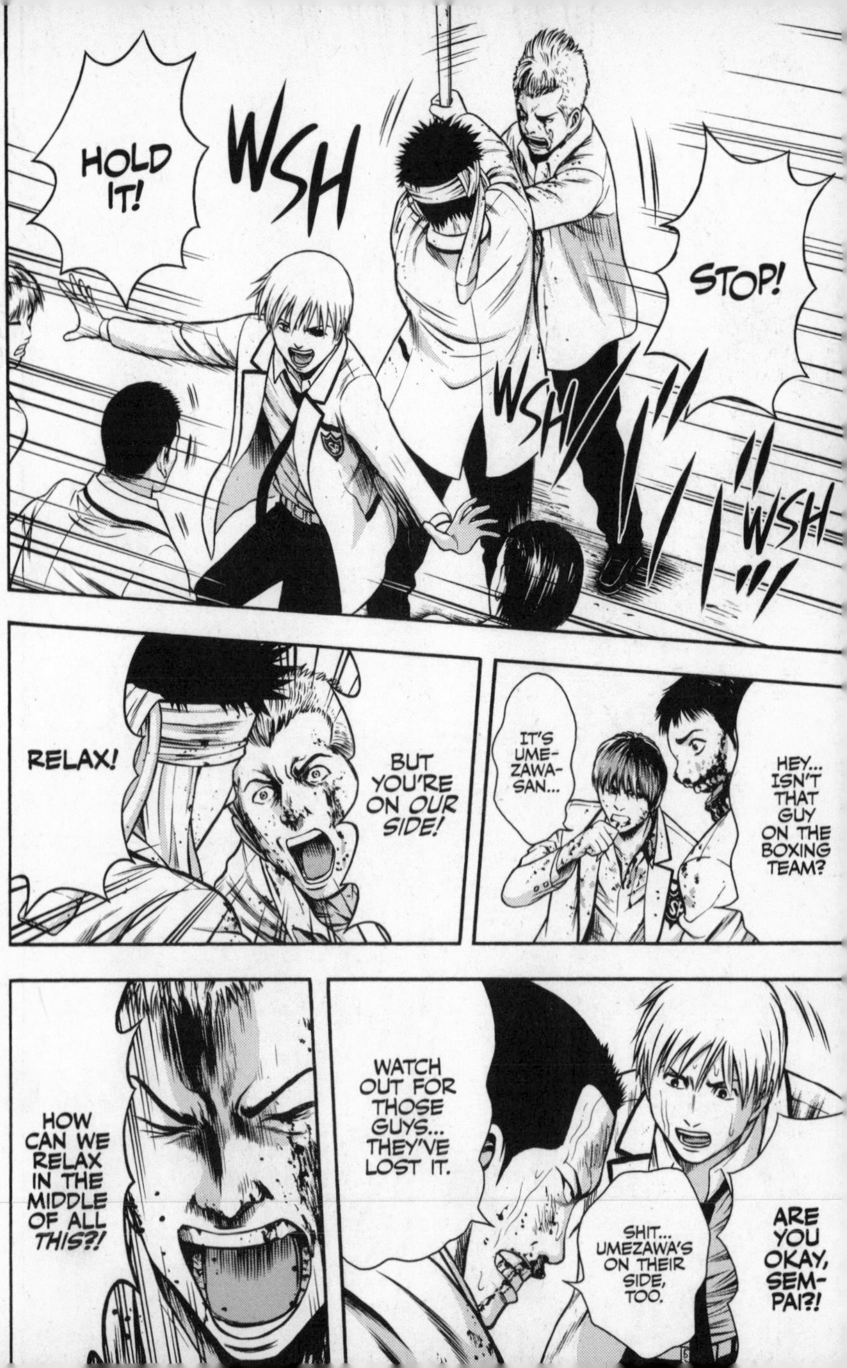
STOP!
WSH
WSH
WSH
HOLD IT!
HEY... ISN'T THAT GUY ON THE BOXING TEAM?
IT'S UMEZAWA-SAN...
BUT YOU'RE ON *OUR* SIDE!
RELAX!
ARE YOU OKAY, SEMPAI?!
SHIT... UMEZAWA'S ON THEIR SIDE, TOO.
WATCH OUT FOR THOSE GUYS... THEY'VE LOST IT.
HOW CAN WE RELAX IN THE MIDDLE OF ALL *THIS?!*

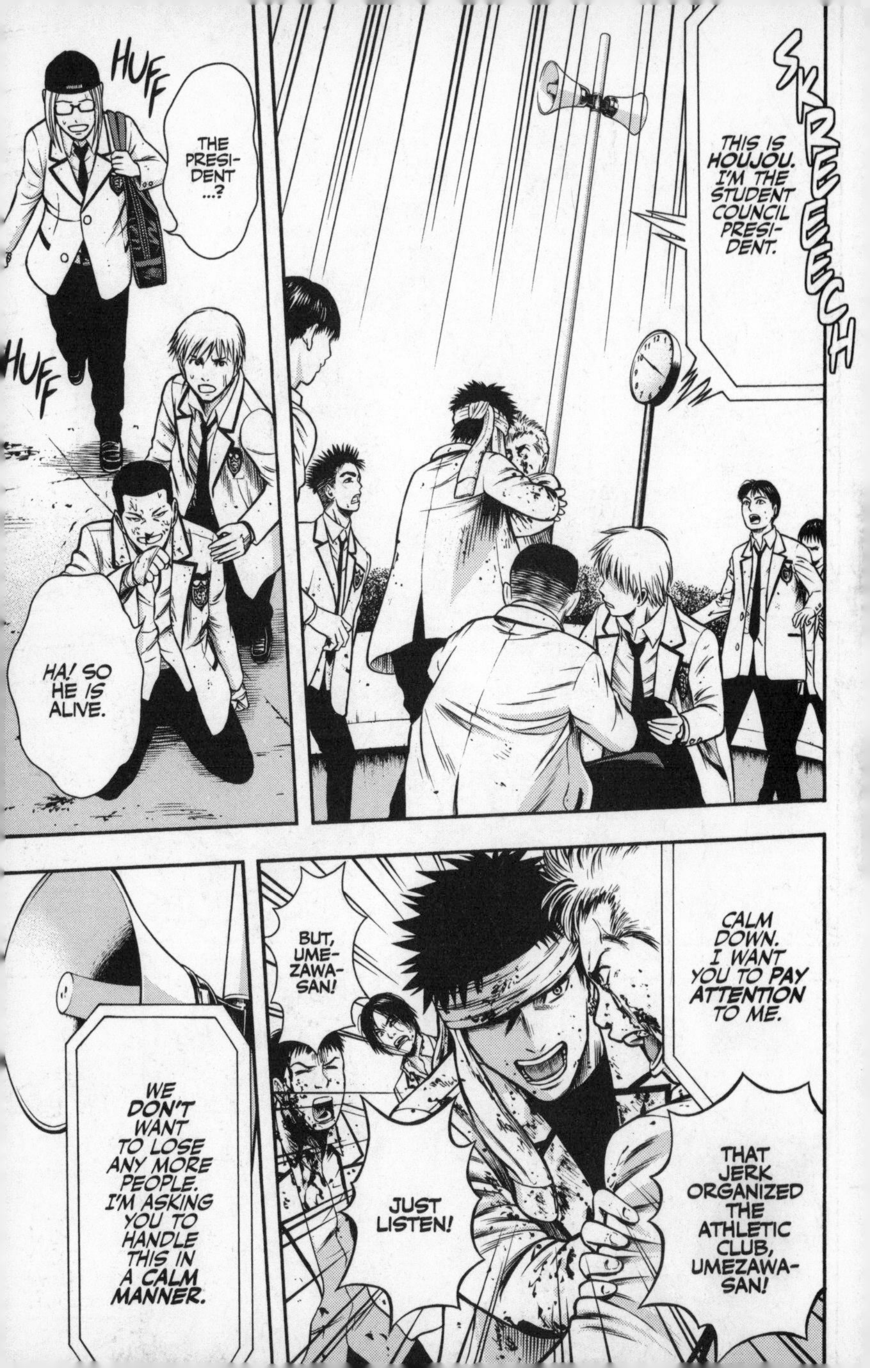
SKREEECH
THIS IS HOUJOU. I'M THE STUDENT COUNCIL PRESIDENT.
HUFF
THE PRESIDENT...?
HUFF
HA! SO HE IS ALIVE.
CALM DOWN. I WANT YOU TO PAY ATTENTION TO ME.
BUT, UMEZAWA-SAN!
THAT JERK ORGANIZED THE ATHLETIC CLUB, UMEZAWA-SAN!
JUST LISTEN!
WE DON'T WANT TO LOSE ANY MORE PEOPLE. I'M ASKING YOU TO HANDLE THIS IN A CALM MANNER.

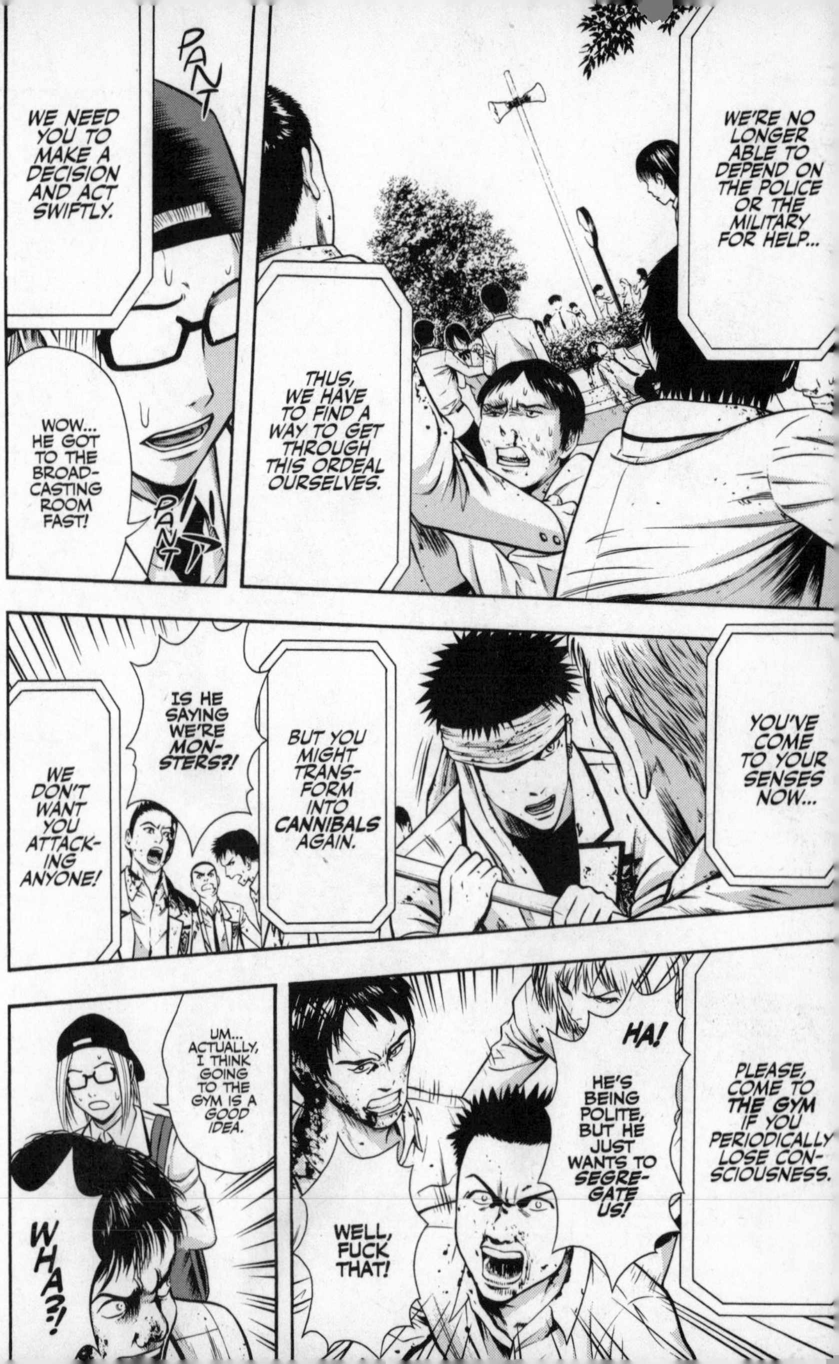
WE'RE NO LONGER ABLE TO DEPEND ON THE POLICE OR THE MILITARY FOR HELP...
THUS, WE HAVE TO FIND A WAY TO GET THROUGH THIS ORDEAL OURSELVES.
WE NEED YOU TO MAKE A DECISION AND ACT SWIFTLY.
PANT
WOW... HE GOT TO THE BROAD-CASTING ROOM FAST!
PANT PANT
YOU'VE COME TO YOUR SENSES NOW...
BUT YOU MIGHT TRANS-FORM INTO CANNIBALS AGAIN.
IS HE SAYING WE'RE MON-STERS?!
WE DON'T WANT YOU ATTACK-ING ANYONE!
PLEASE, COME TO THE GYM IF YOU PERIODICALLY LOSE CON-SCIOUSNESS.
HA!
HE'S BEING POLITE, BUT HE JUST WANTS TO SEGRE-GATE US!
WELL, FUCK THAT!
UM... ACTUALLY, I THINK GOING TO THE GYM IS A GOOD IDEA.
WHA?!

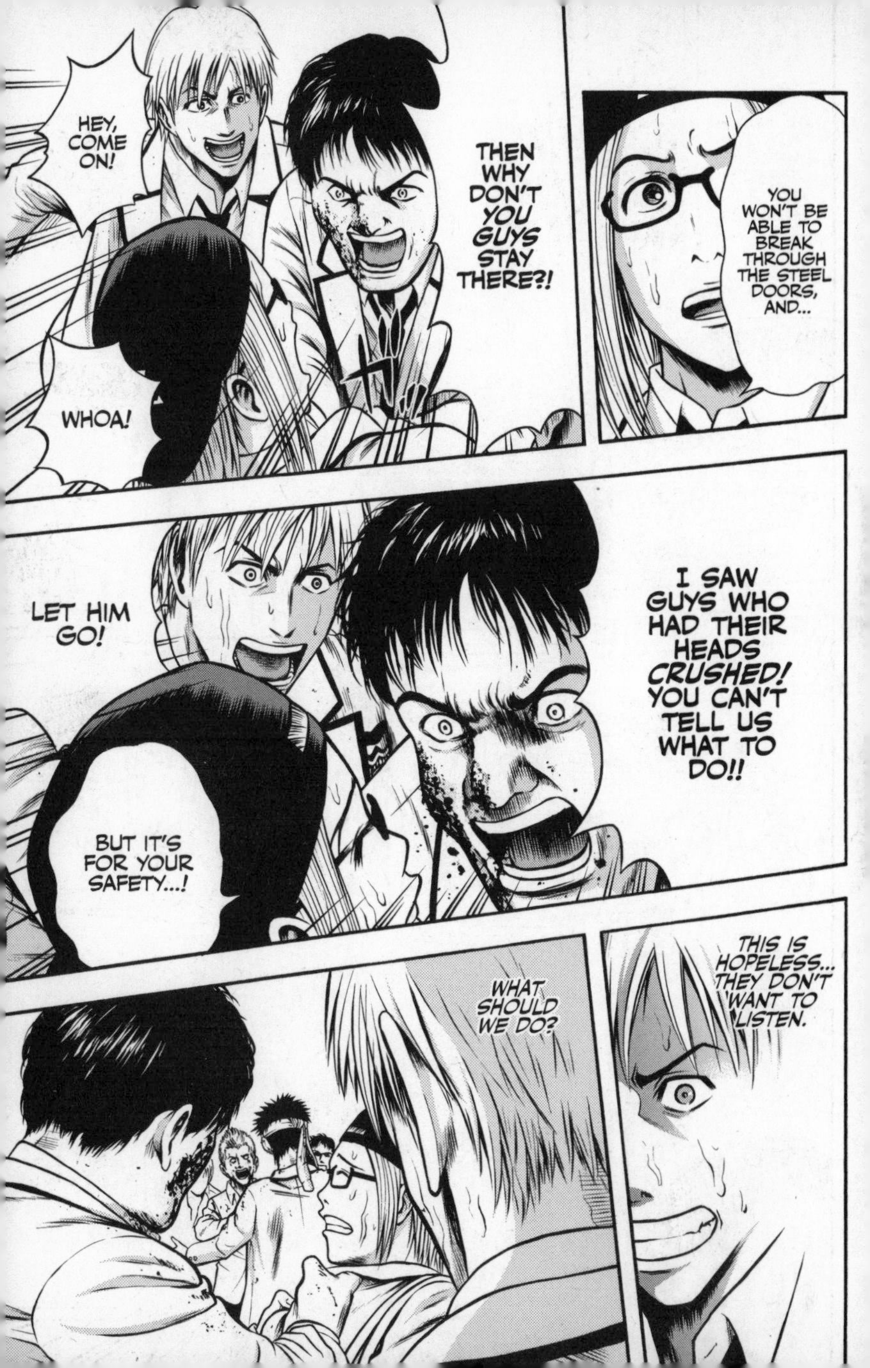
YOU WON'T BE ABLE TO BREAK THROUGH THE STEEL DOORS, AND...
THEN WHY DON'T YOU GUYS STAY THERE?!
HEY, COME ON!
WHOA!
I SAW GUYS WHO HAD THEIR HEADS CRUSHED! YOU CAN'T TELL US WHAT TO DO!!
LET HIM GO!
BUT IT'S FOR YOUR SAFETY...!
THIS IS HOPELESS... THEY DON'T WANT TO LISTEN.
WHAT SHOULD WE DO?

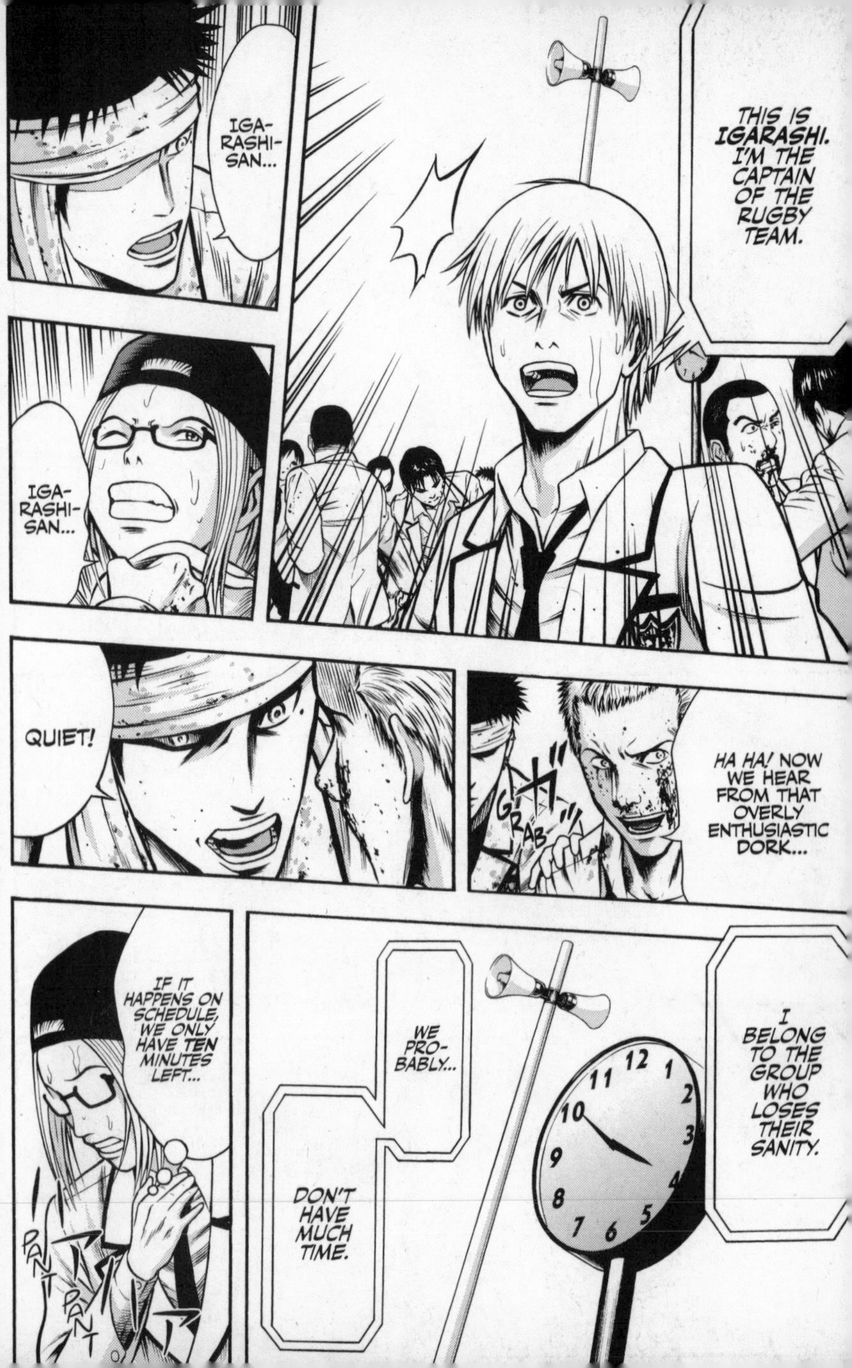
THIS IS IGARASHI. I'M THE CAPTAIN OF THE RUGBY TEAM.
IGA-RASHI-SAN...
IGA-RASHI-SAN...
HA HA! NOW WE HEAR FROM THAT OVERLY ENTHUSIASTIC DORK...
GRAB
QUIET!
I BELONG TO THE GROUP WHO LOSES THEIR SANITY.
WE PRO-BABLY...
DON'T HAVE MUCH TIME.
IF IT HAPPENS ON SCHEDULE, WE ONLY HAVE TEN MINUTES LEFT...
PANT PANT

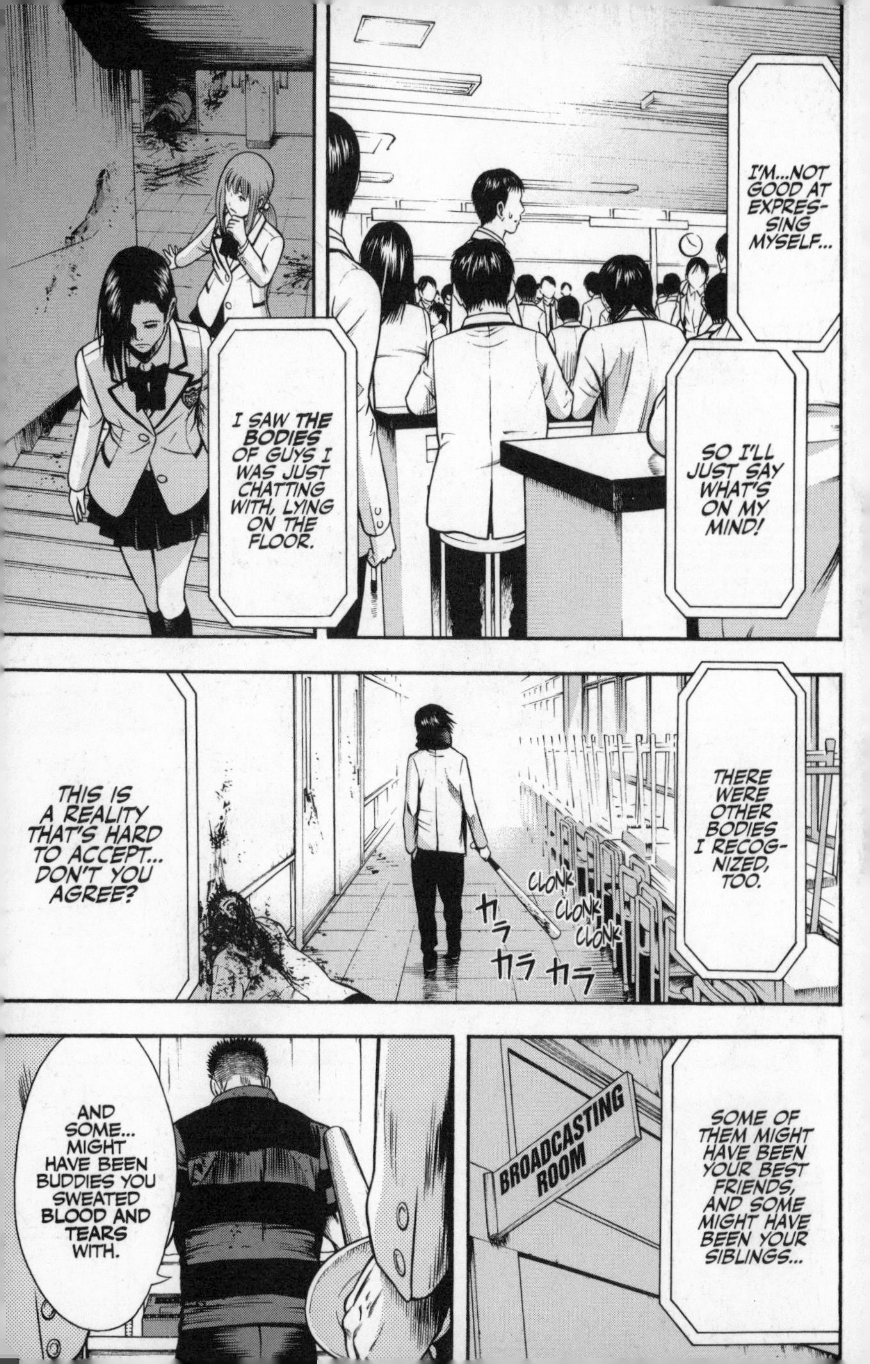
I'M...NOT GOOD AT EXPRES-SING MYSELF...
SO I'LL JUST SAY WHAT'S ON MY MIND!
I SAW THE BODIES OF GUYS I WAS JUST CHATTING WITH, LYING ON THE FLOOR.
THERE WERE OTHER BODIES I RECOG-NIZED, TOO.
CLONK CLONK CLONK
カラ カラ カラ
THIS IS A REALITY THAT'S HARD TO ACCEPT... DON'T YOU AGREE?
BROADCASTING ROOM
SOME OF THEM MIGHT HAVE BEEN YOUR BEST FRIENDS, AND SOME MIGHT HAVE BEEN YOUR SIBLINGS...
AND SOME... MIGHT HAVE BEEN BUDDIES YOU SWEATED BLOOD AND TEARS WITH.

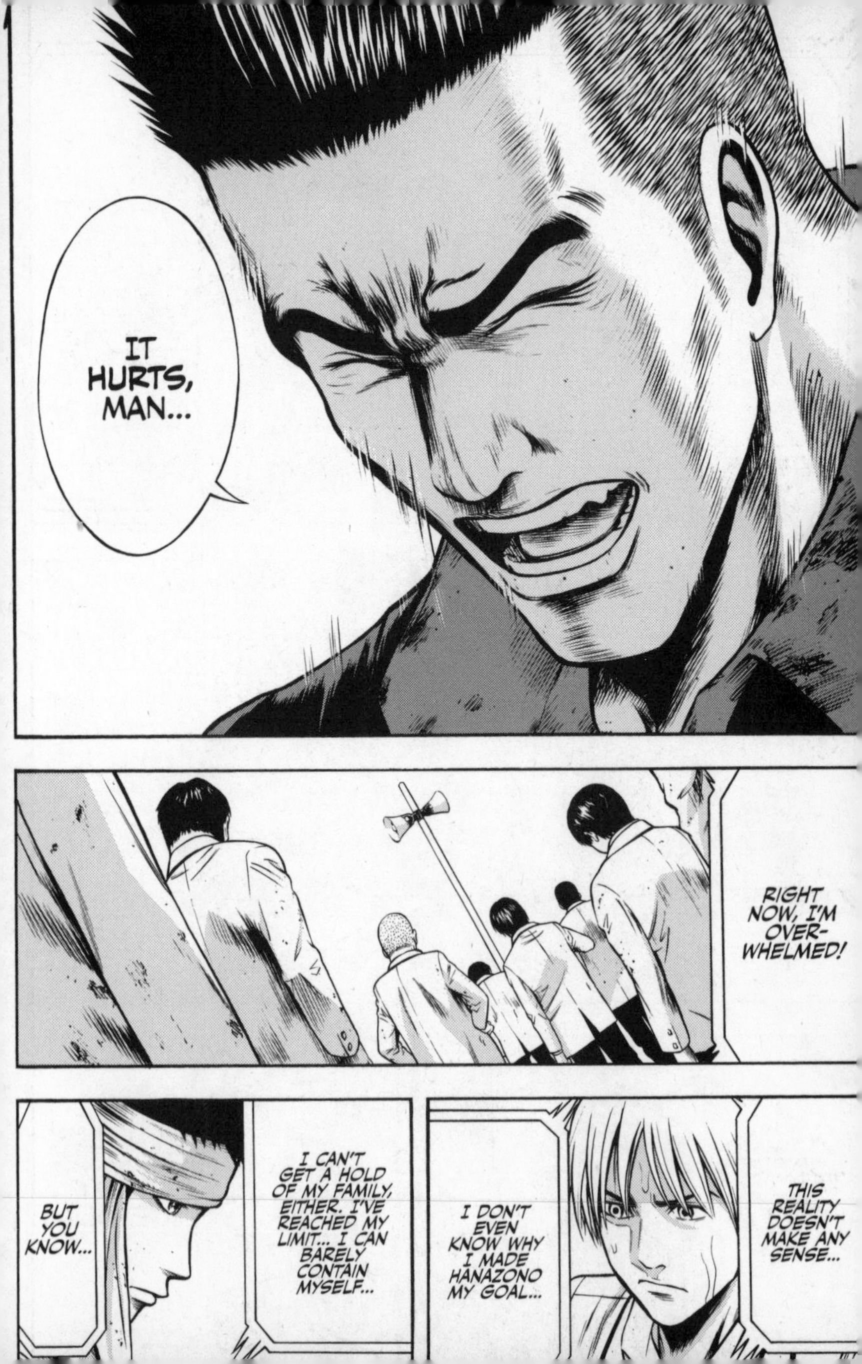
IT HURTS, MAN...
RIGHT NOW, I'M OVER-WHELMED!
THIS REALITY DOESN'T MAKE ANY SENSE...
I DON'T EVEN KNOW WHY I MADE HANAZONO MY GOAL...
I CAN'T GET A HOLD OF MY FAMILY, EITHER. I'VE REACHED MY LIMIT... I CAN BARELY CONTAIN MYSELF...
BUT YOU KNOW...

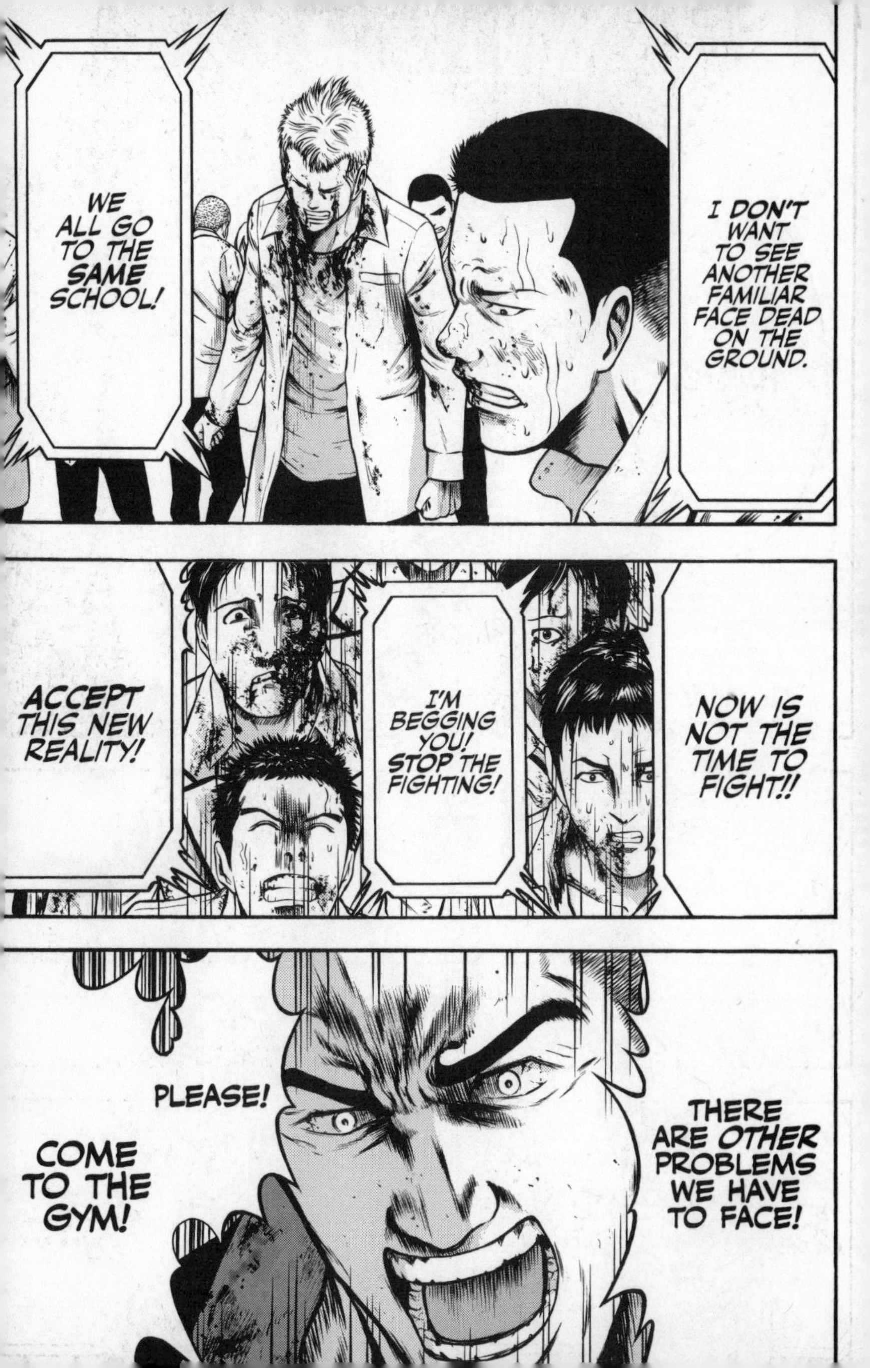
I DON'T WANT TO SEE ANOTHER FAMILIAR FACE DEAD ON THE GROUND.
WE ALL GO TO THE SAME SCHOOL!
NOW IS NOT THE TIME TO FIGHT!!
I'M BEGGING YOU! STOP THE FIGHTING!
ACCEPT THIS NEW REALITY!
THERE ARE OTHER PROBLEMS WE HAVE TO FACE!
PLEASE!
COME TO THE GYM!

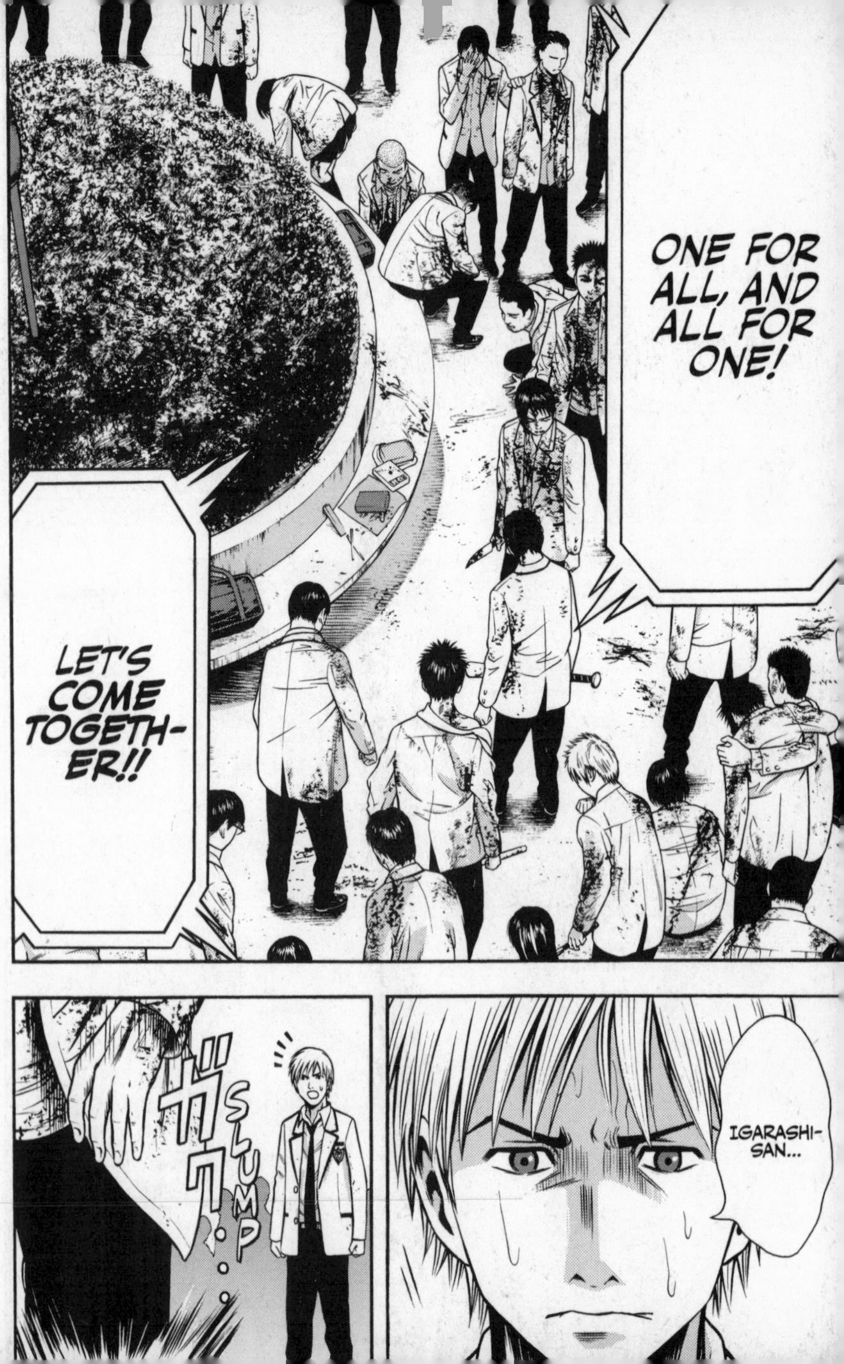
ONE FOR ALL, AND ALL FOR ONE!
LET'S COME TOGETH-ER!!
ガク
SLUMP
IGARASHI-SAN...

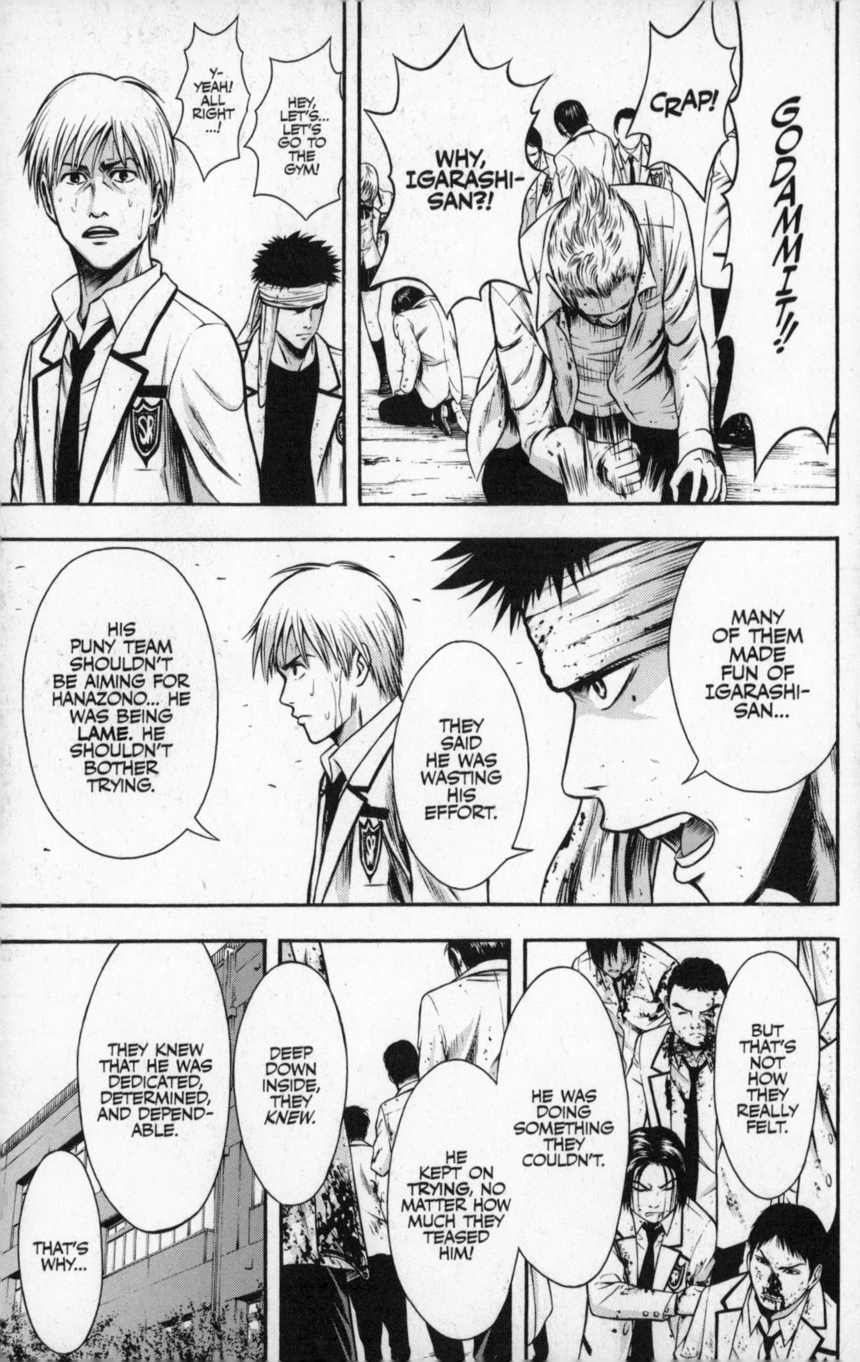
GODAMMIT!!
CRAP!
WHY, IGARASHI-SAN?!
HEY, LET'S... LET'S GO TO THE GYM!
Y-YEAH! ALL RIGHT ...!
MANY OF THEM MADE FUN OF IGARASHI-SAN...
THEY SAID HE WAS WASTING HIS EFFORT.
HIS PUNY TEAM SHOULDN'T BE AIMING FOR HANAZONO... HE WAS BEING LAME. HE SHOULDN'T BOTHER TRYING.
BUT THAT'S NOT HOW THEY REALLY FELT.
HE WAS DOING SOMETHING THEY COULDN'T.
HE KEPT ON TRYING, NO MATTER HOW MUCH THEY TEASED HIM!
DEEP DOWN INSIDE, THEY *KNEW*.
THEY KNEW THAT HE WAS DEDICATED, DETERMINED, AND DEPEND-ABLE.
THAT'S WHY...

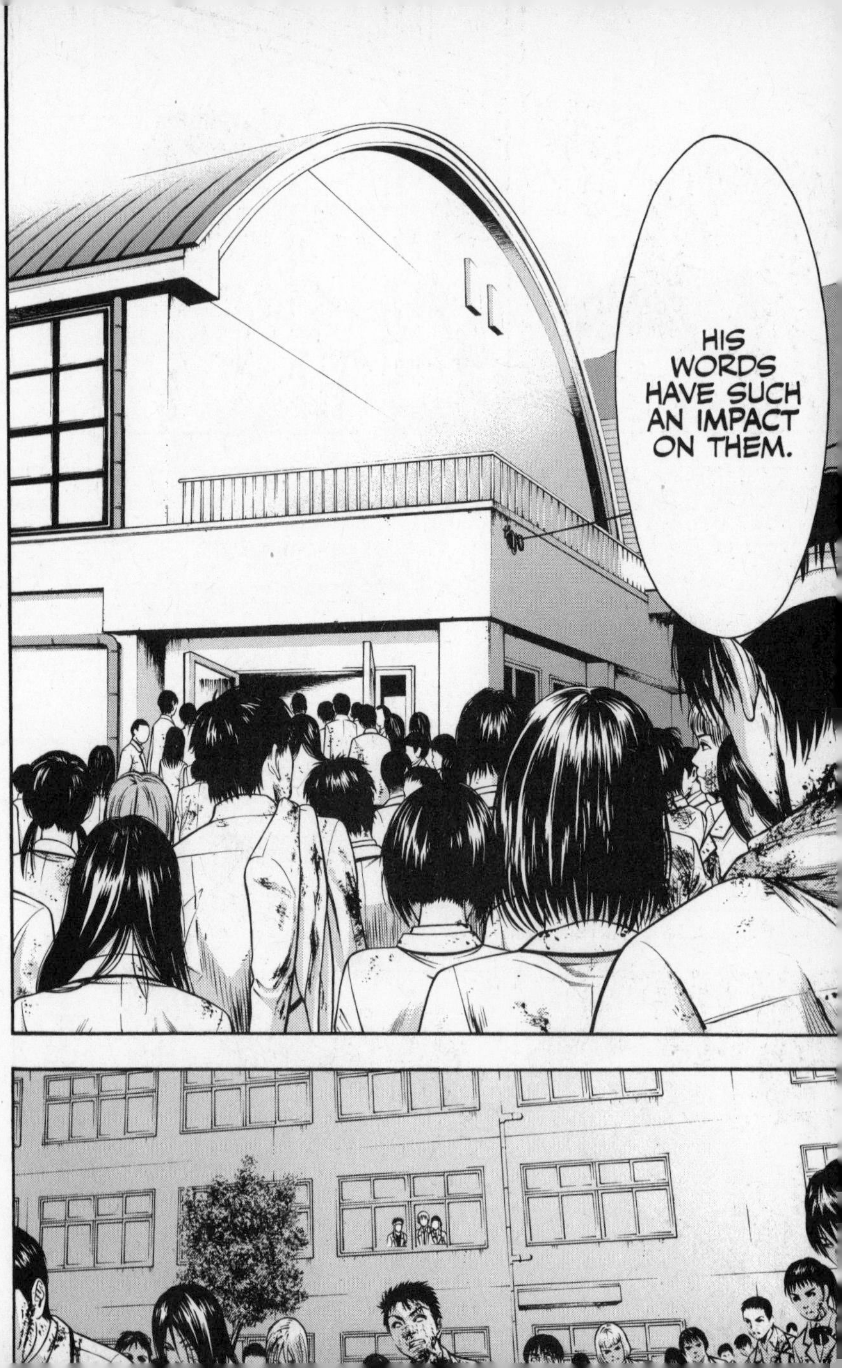
HIS WORDS HAVE SUCH AN IMPACT ON THEM.

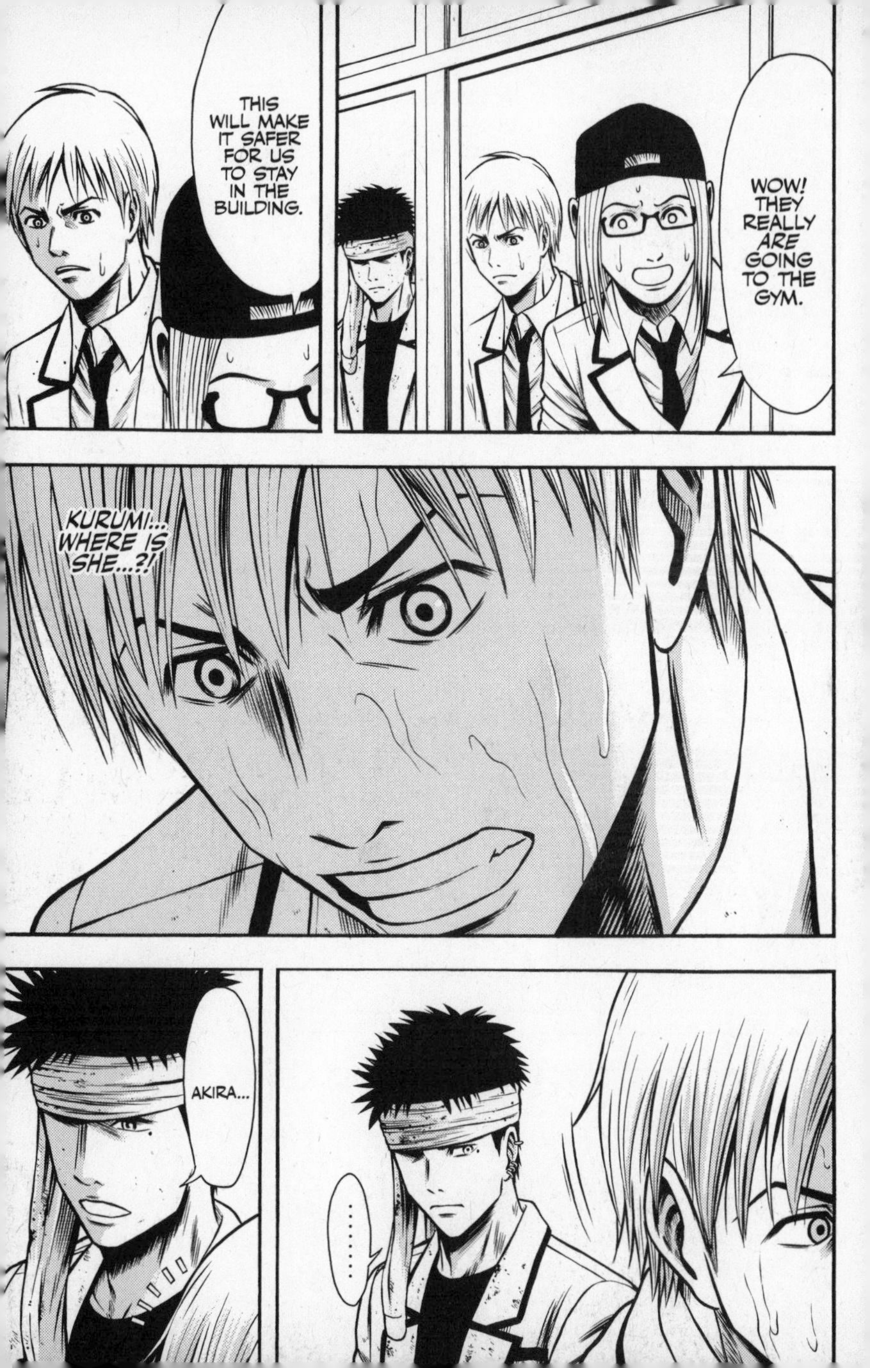
WOW! THEY REALLY ARE GOING TO THE GYM.
THIS WILL MAKE IT SAFER FOR US TO STAY IN THE BUILDING.
KURUMI... WHERE IS SHE...?!
......
AKIRA...

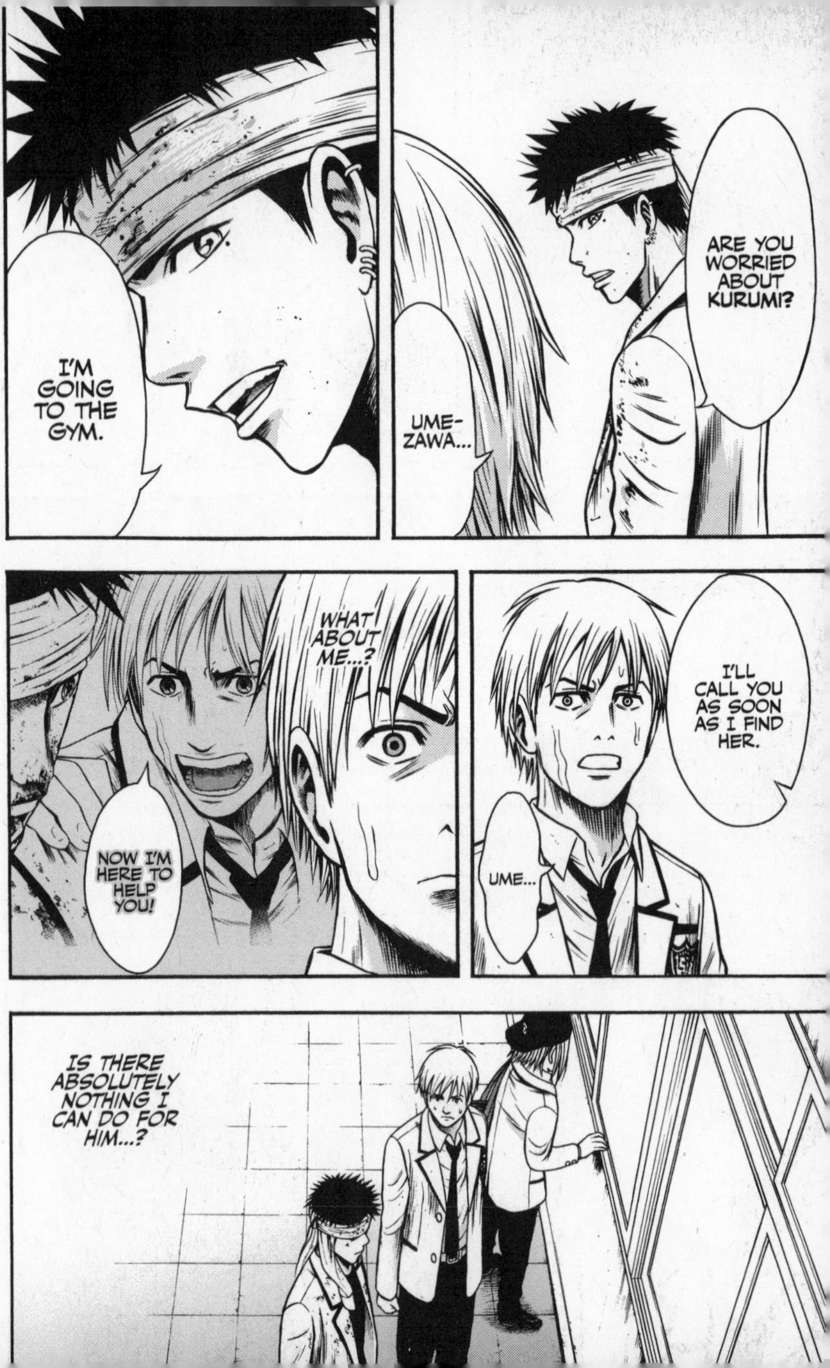
ARE YOU WORRIED ABOUT KURUMI?
UME-ZAWA...
I'M GOING TO THE GYM.
I'LL CALL YOU AS SOON AS I FIND HER.
UME...
WHAT ABOUT ME...?
NOW I'M HERE TO HELP YOU!
IS THERE ABSOLUTELY NOTHING I CAN DO FOR HIM...?

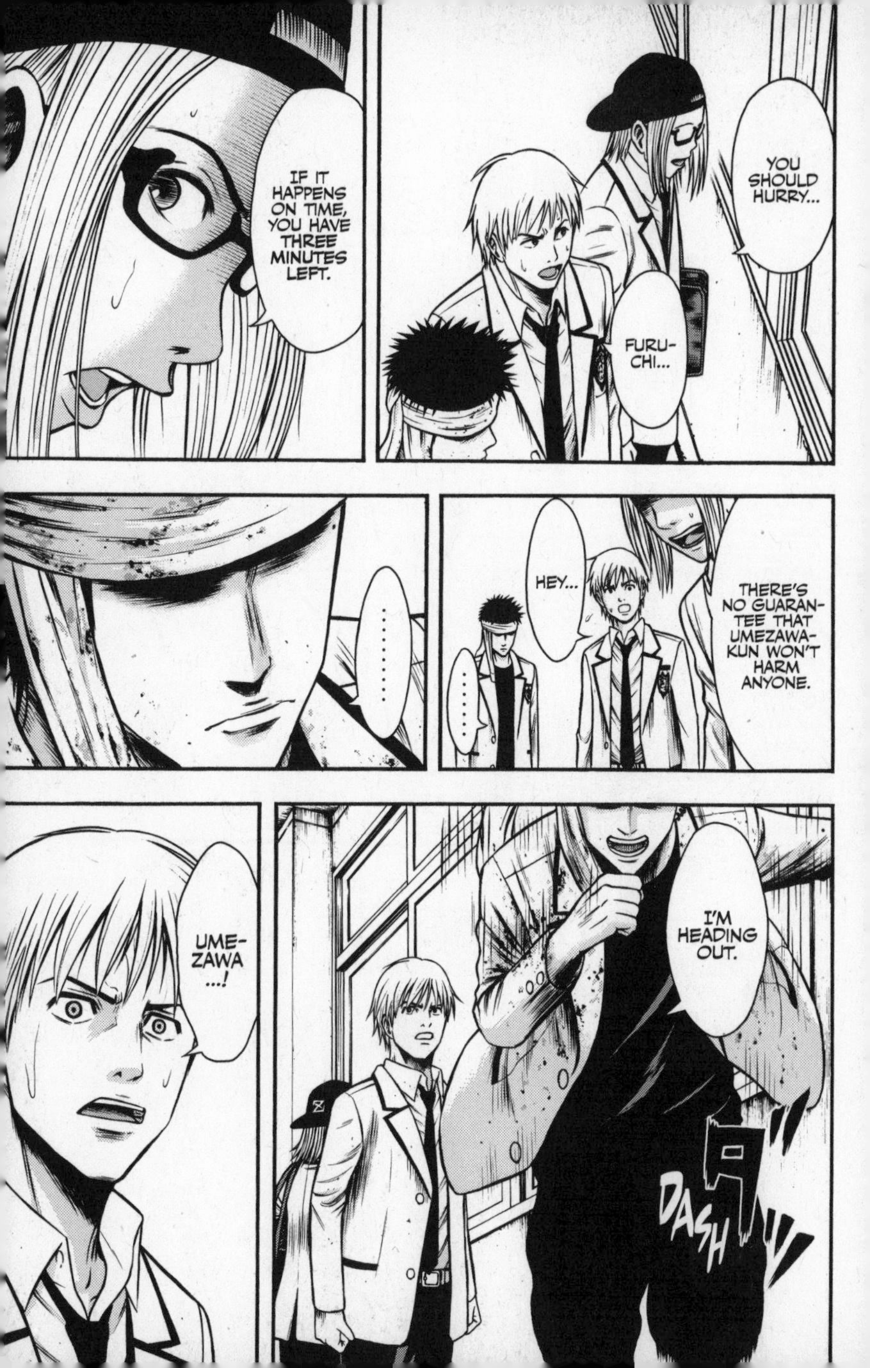
YOU SHOULD HURRY...
FURU-CHI...
IF IT HAPPENS ON TIME, YOU HAVE THREE MINUTES LEFT.
THERE'S NO GUARAN-TEE THAT UMEZAWA-KUN WON'T HARM ANYONE.
HEY...
......
......
I'M HEADING OUT.
DASH
UME-ZAWA...!

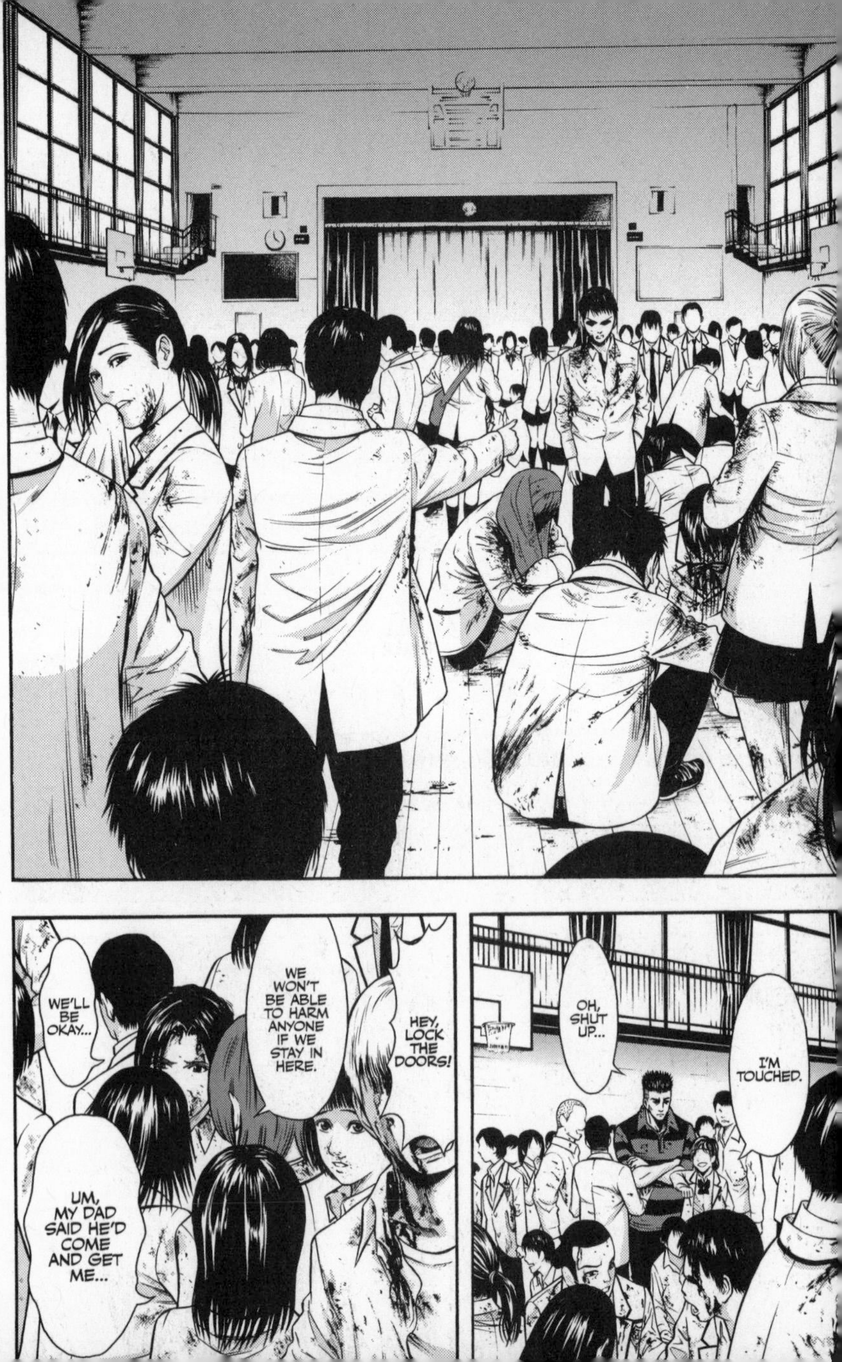
I'M TOUCHED.
OH, SHUT UP...
HEY, LOCK THE DOORS!
WE WON'T BE ABLE TO HARM ANYONE IF WE STAY IN HERE.
WE'LL BE OKAY...
UM, MY DAD SAID HE'D COME AND GET ME...

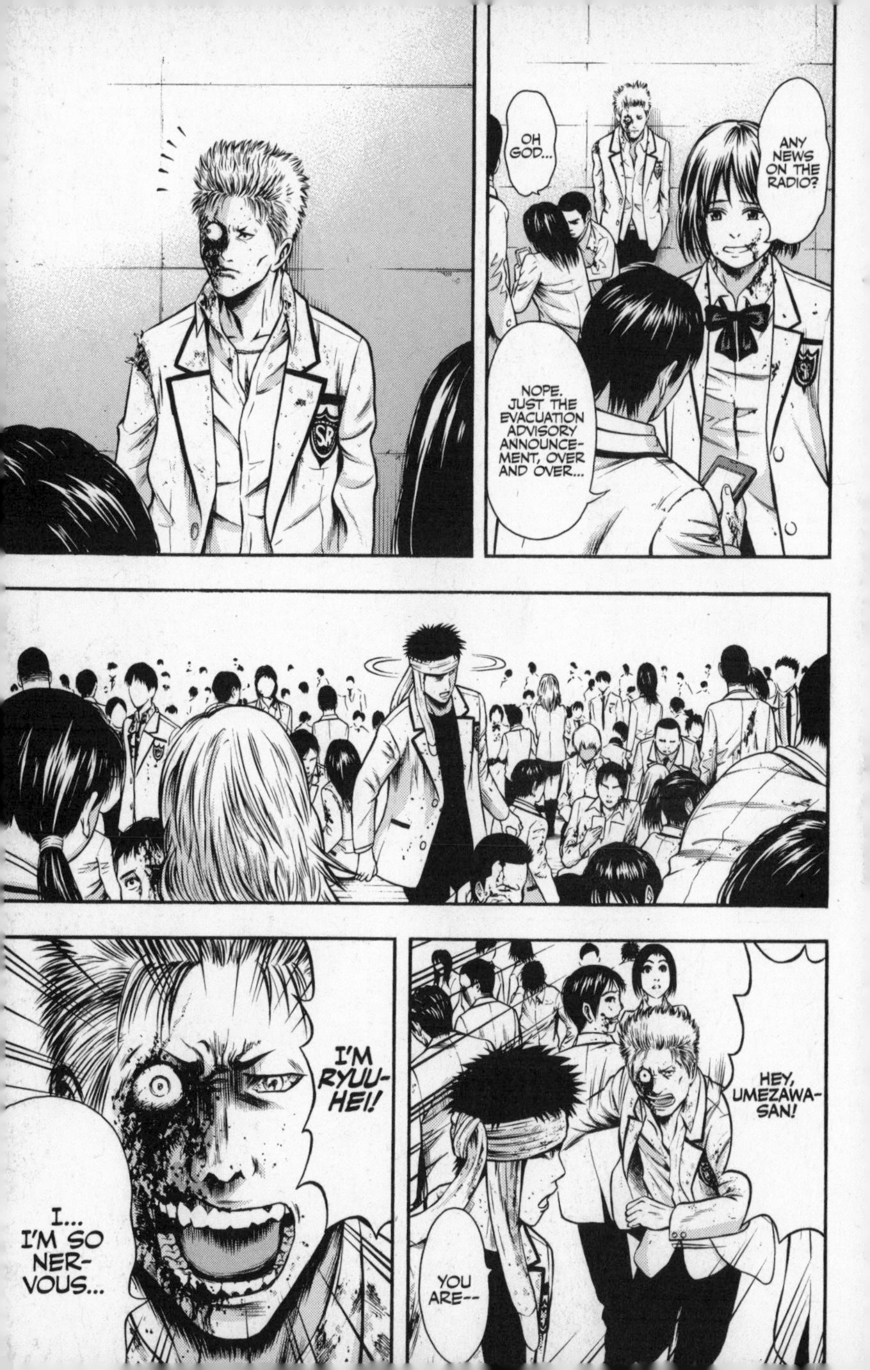
ANY NEWS ON THE RADIO?
OH GOD...
NOPE. JUST THE EVACUATION ADVISORY ANNOUNCE-MENT, OVER AND OVER...
HEY, UMEZAWA-SAN!
YOU ARE--
I'M RYUU-HEI!
I... I'M SO NER-VOUS...

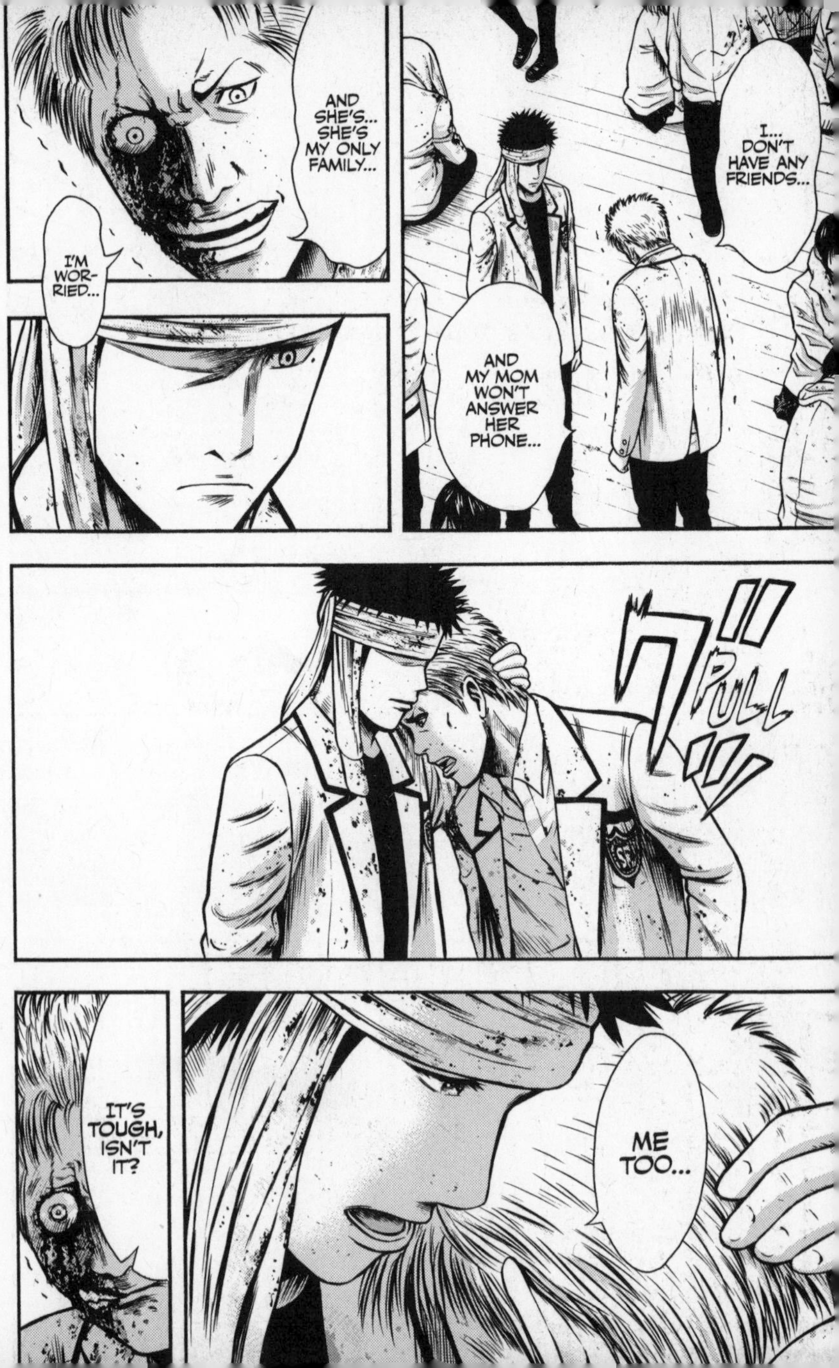
I... DON'T HAVE ANY FRIENDS...
AND MY MOM WON'T ANSWER HER PHONE...
AND SHE'S... SHE'S MY ONLY FAMILY...
I'M WOR-RIED...
PULL
ME TOO...
IT'S TOUGH, ISN'T IT?

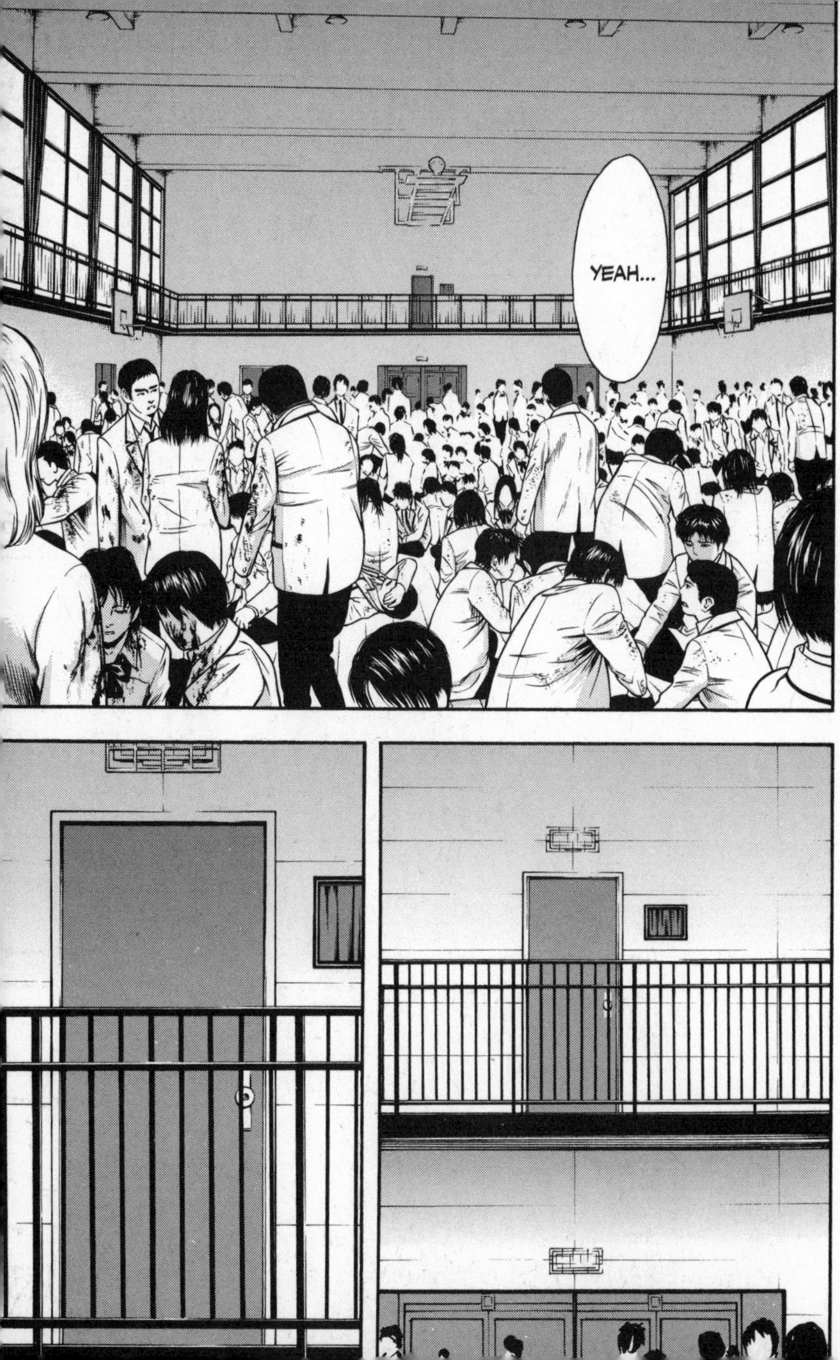
YEAH...

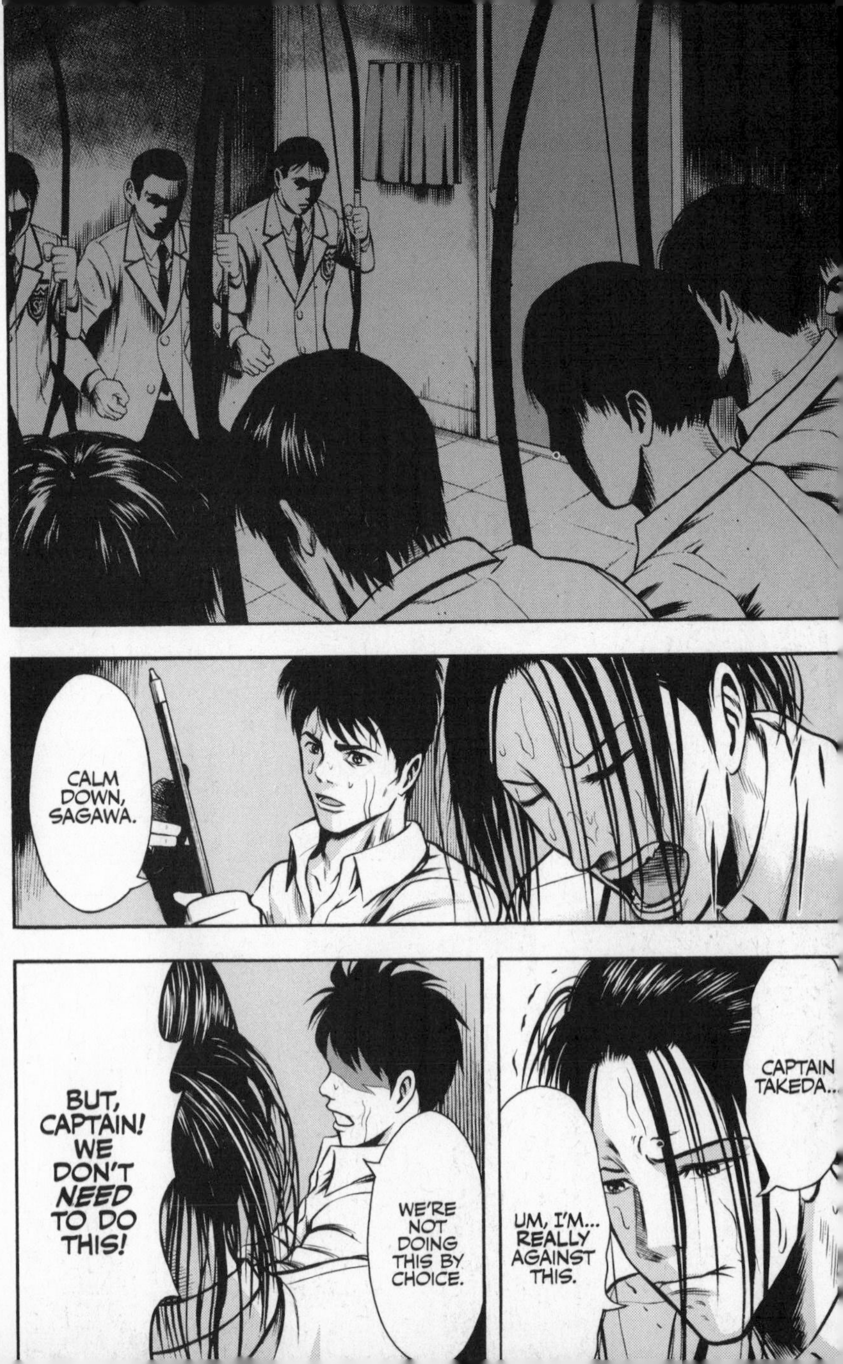
CALM DOWN, SAGAWA.
CAPTAIN TAKEDA...
UM, I'M... REALLY AGAINST THIS.
WE'RE NOT DOING THIS BY CHOICE.
BUT, CAPTAIN! WE DON'T NEED TO DO THIS!

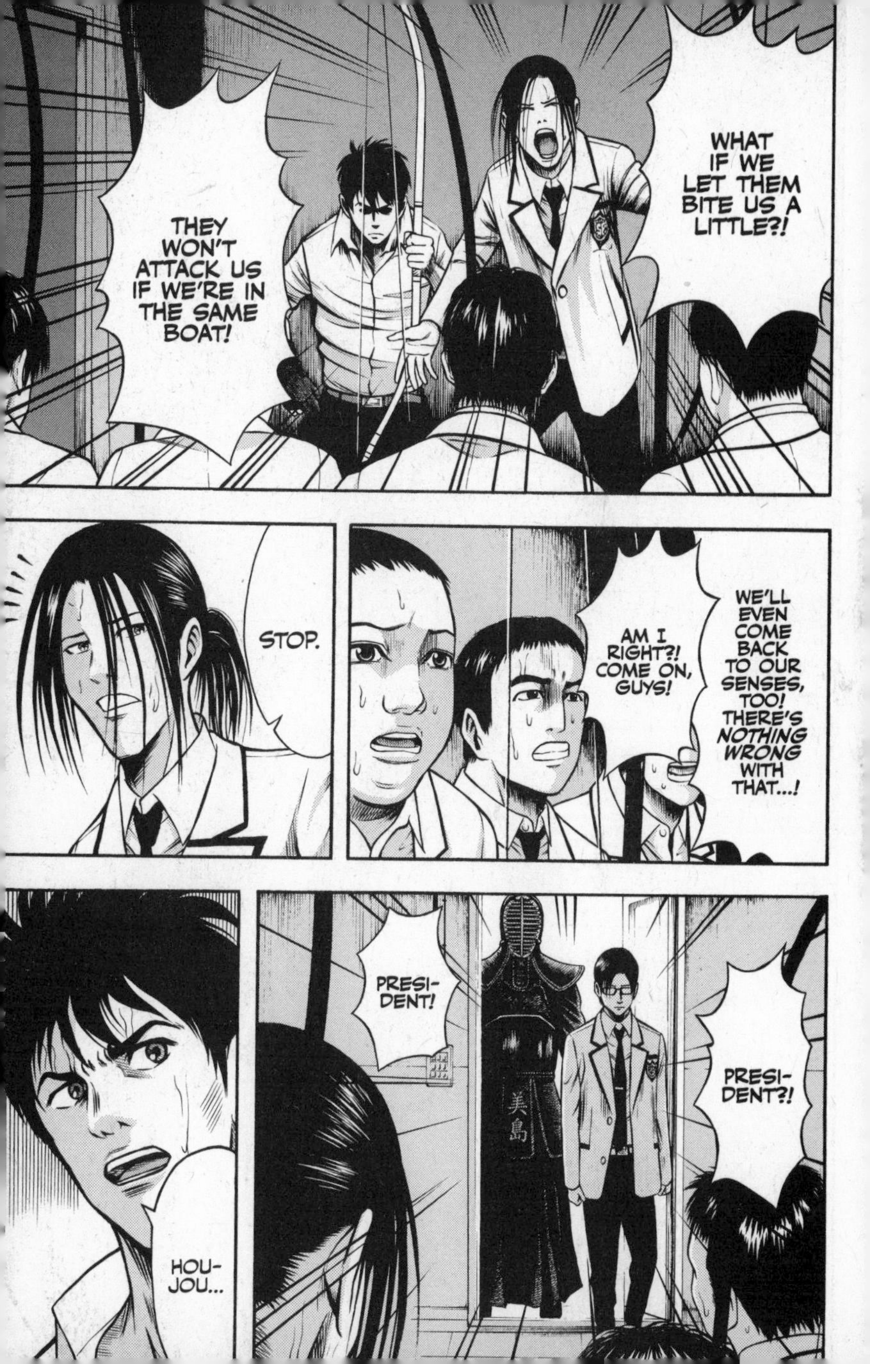
WHAT IF WE LET THEM BITE US A LITTLE?!
THEY WON'T ATTACK US IF WE'RE IN THE SAME BOAT!
WE'LL EVEN COME BACK TO OUR SENSES, TOO! THERE'S *NOTHING WRONG* WITH THAT...!
AM I RIGHT?! COME ON, GUYS!
STOP.
PRESI-DENT?!
PRESI-DENT!
美島
HOU-JOU...

HOUJOU, AROUND FIVE HUNDRED PEOPLE SHOWED UP.

SMALL
BUBO
PLAGUE,
CHOLER
THE SP
FLU... TH
THEY WE
DEADLY D
THEY DID
ANYONE
THE FIRS
HOU

THAT MEANS LESS OF THEM REMAIN OUTSIDE THE GYM.

NOW STOP WITH THESE SILLY THOUGHTS.

KILL ANYONE WHO TRIES TO ESCAPE.

GOC

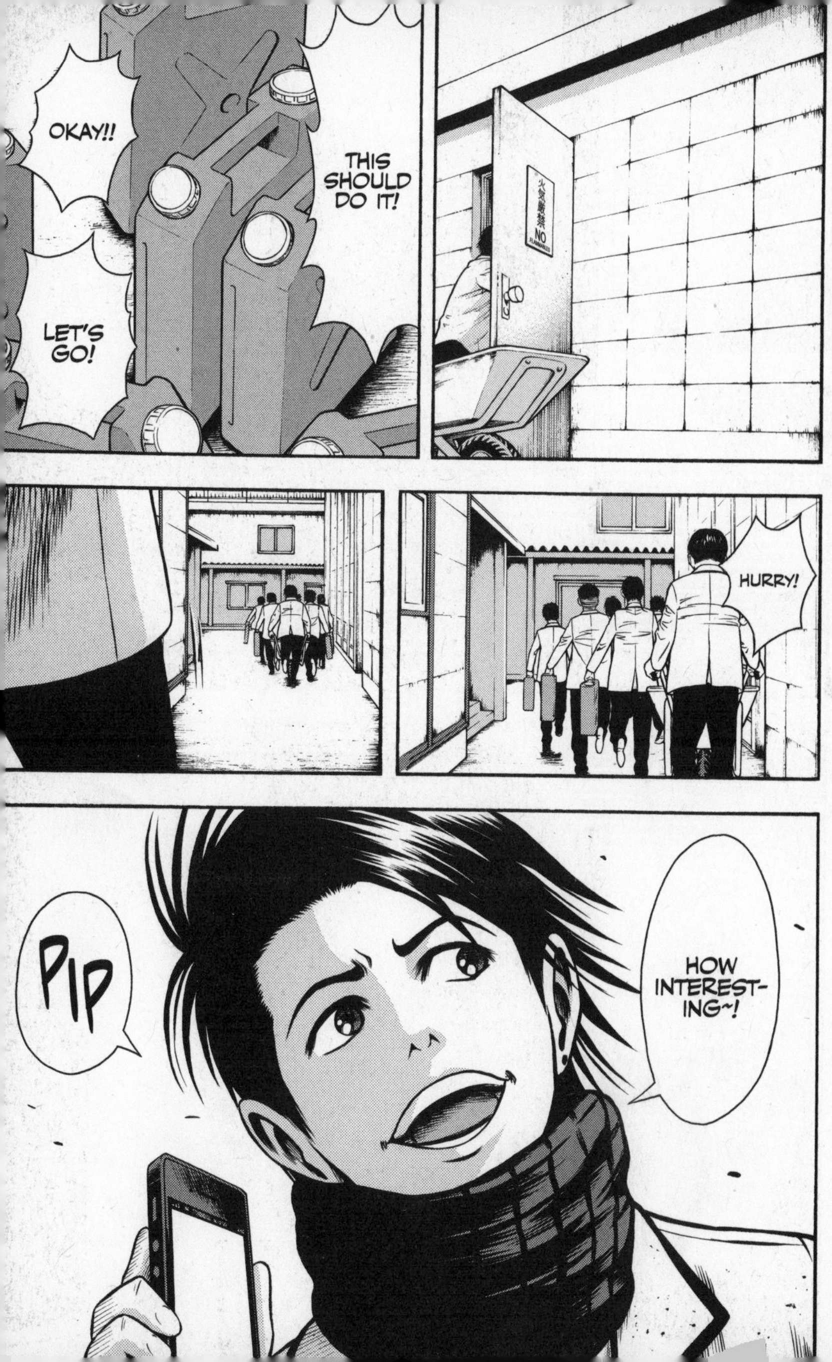
火気厳禁
NO FLAMMABLES
THIS SHOULD DO IT!
OKAY!!
LET'S GO!
HURRY!
HOW INTERESTING~!
PIP

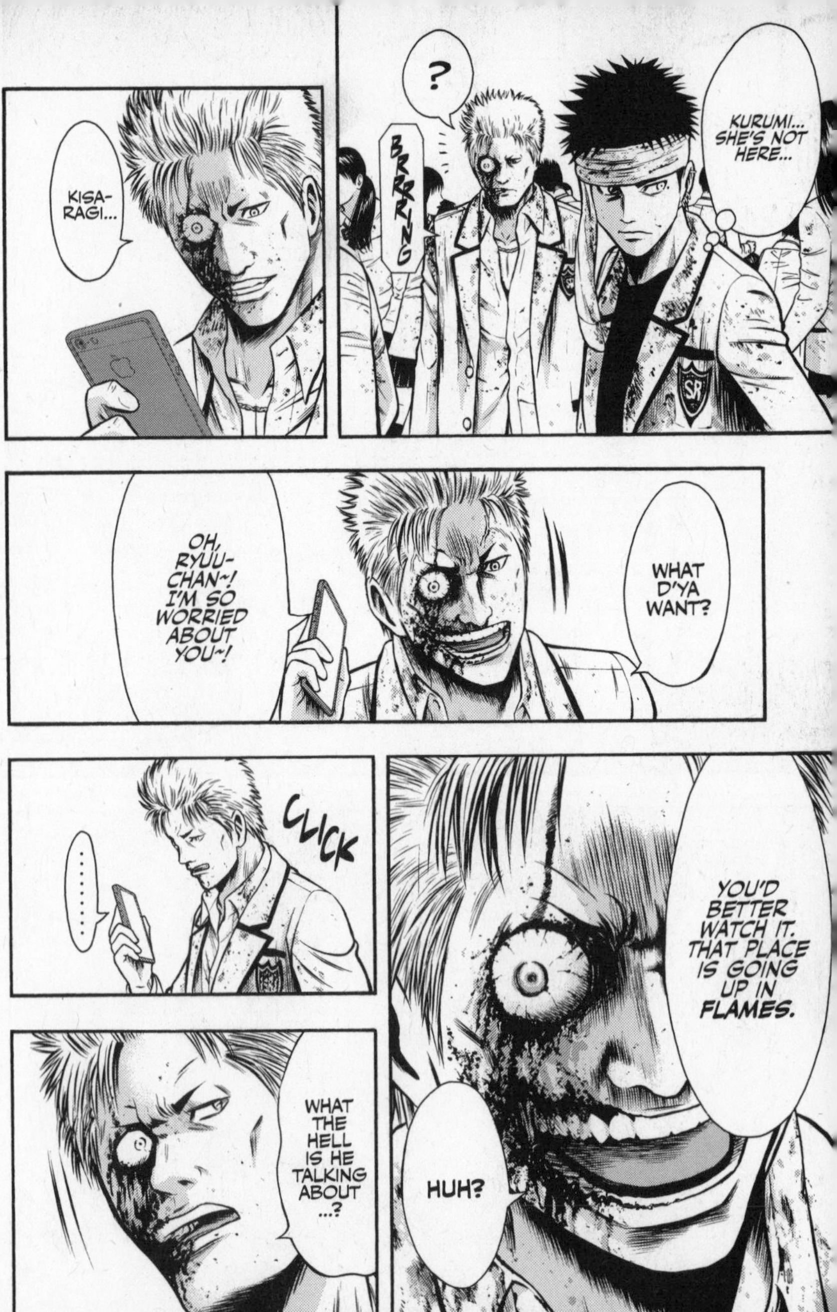
KURUMI... SHE'S NOT HERE...
?
BRRRRING
KISA-RAGI...
WHAT D'YA WANT?
OH, RYUU-CHAN~! I'M SO WORRIED ABOUT YOU~!
YOU'D BETTER WATCH IT. THAT PLACE IS GOING UP IN **FLAMES.**
CLICK
....
HUH?
WHAT THE HELL IS HE TALKING ABOUT ...?

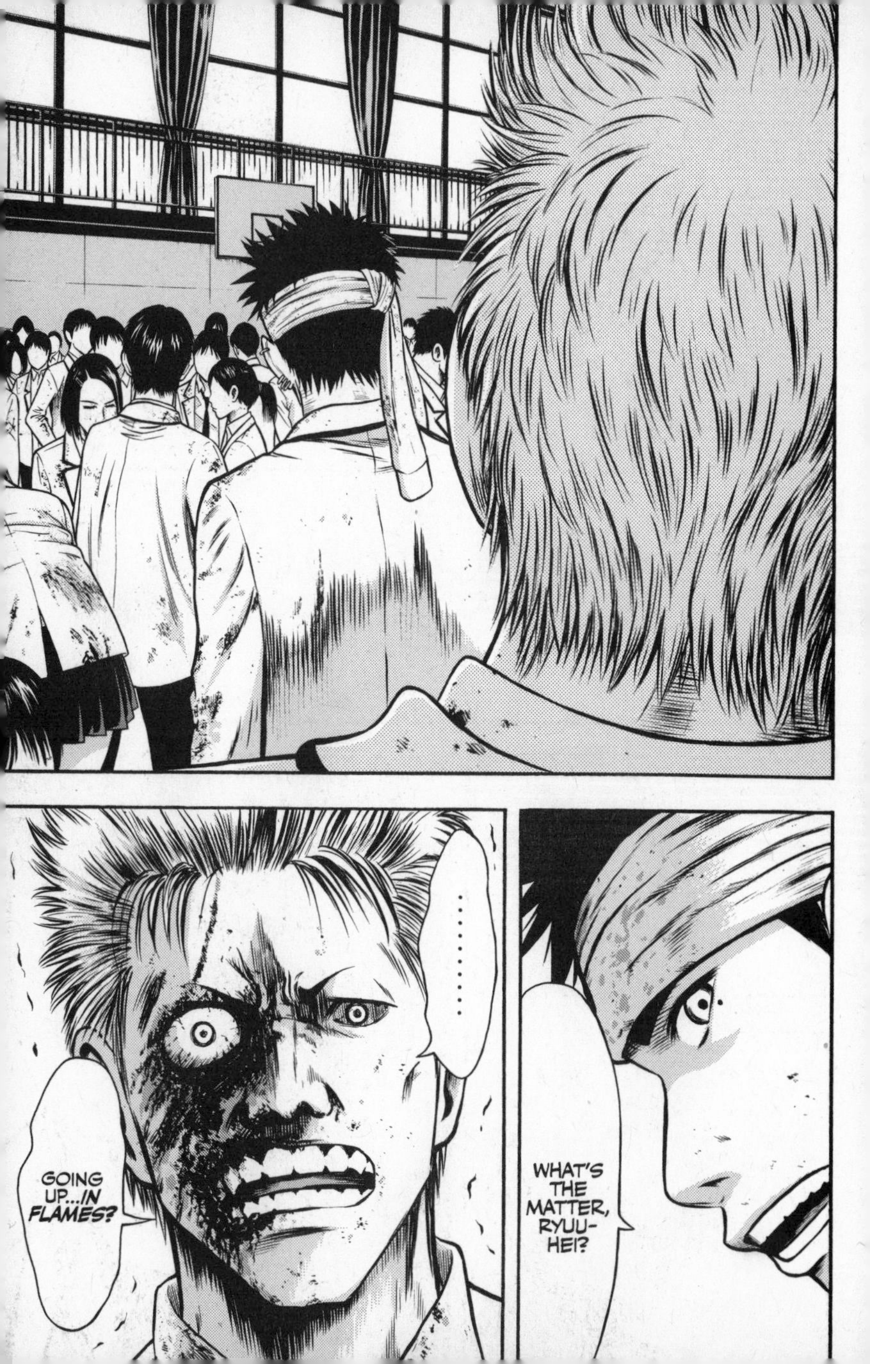
WHAT'S THE MATTER, RYUU-HEI?
......
GOING UP...*IN FLAMES?*

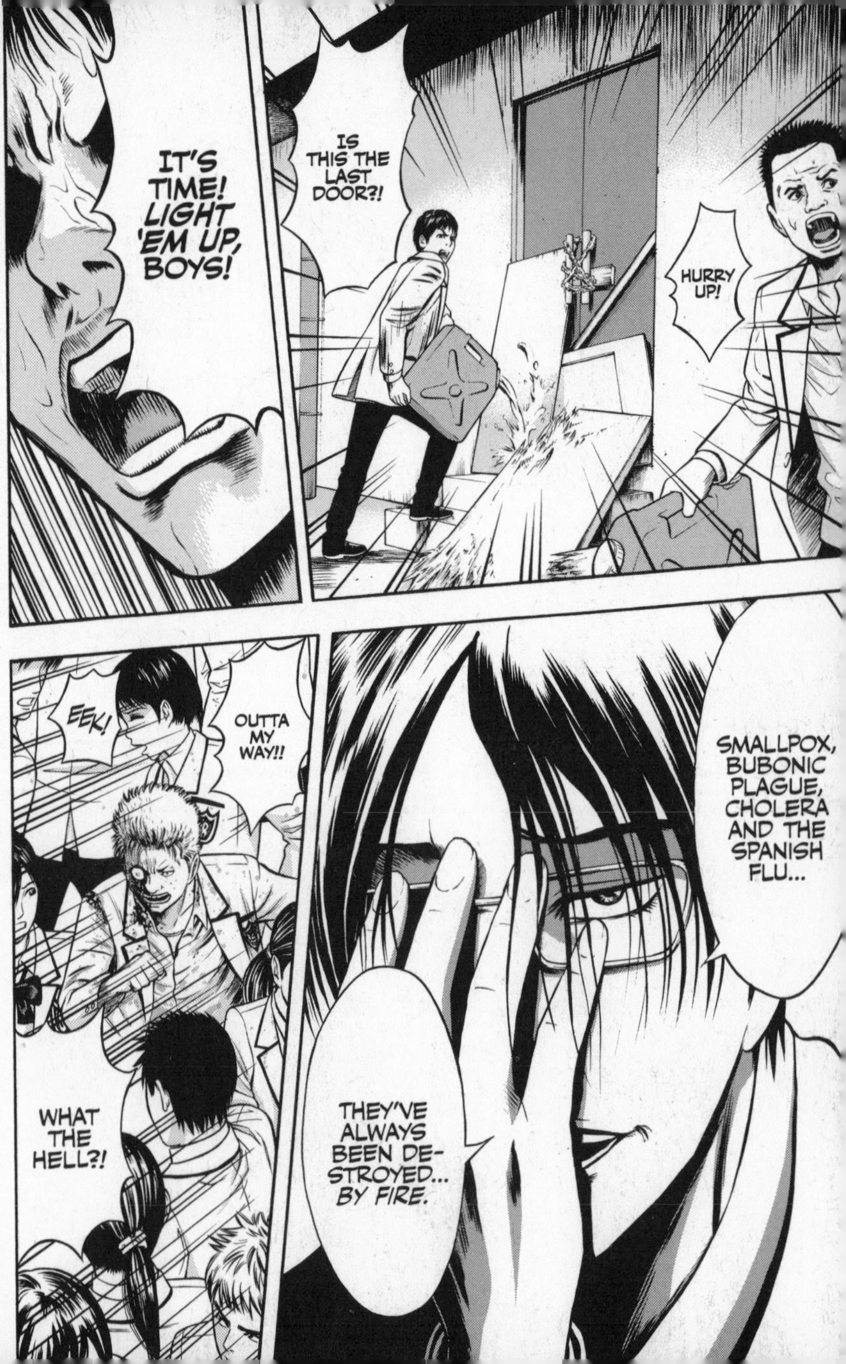
HURRY UP!
IS THIS THE LAST DOOR?!
IT'S TIME! LIGHT 'EM UP, BOYS!
SMALLPOX, BUBONIC PLAGUE, CHOLERA AND THE SPANISH FLU...
THEY'VE ALWAYS BEEN DE-STROYED... BY FIRE.
OUTTA MY WAY!!
EEK!
WHAT THE HELL?!

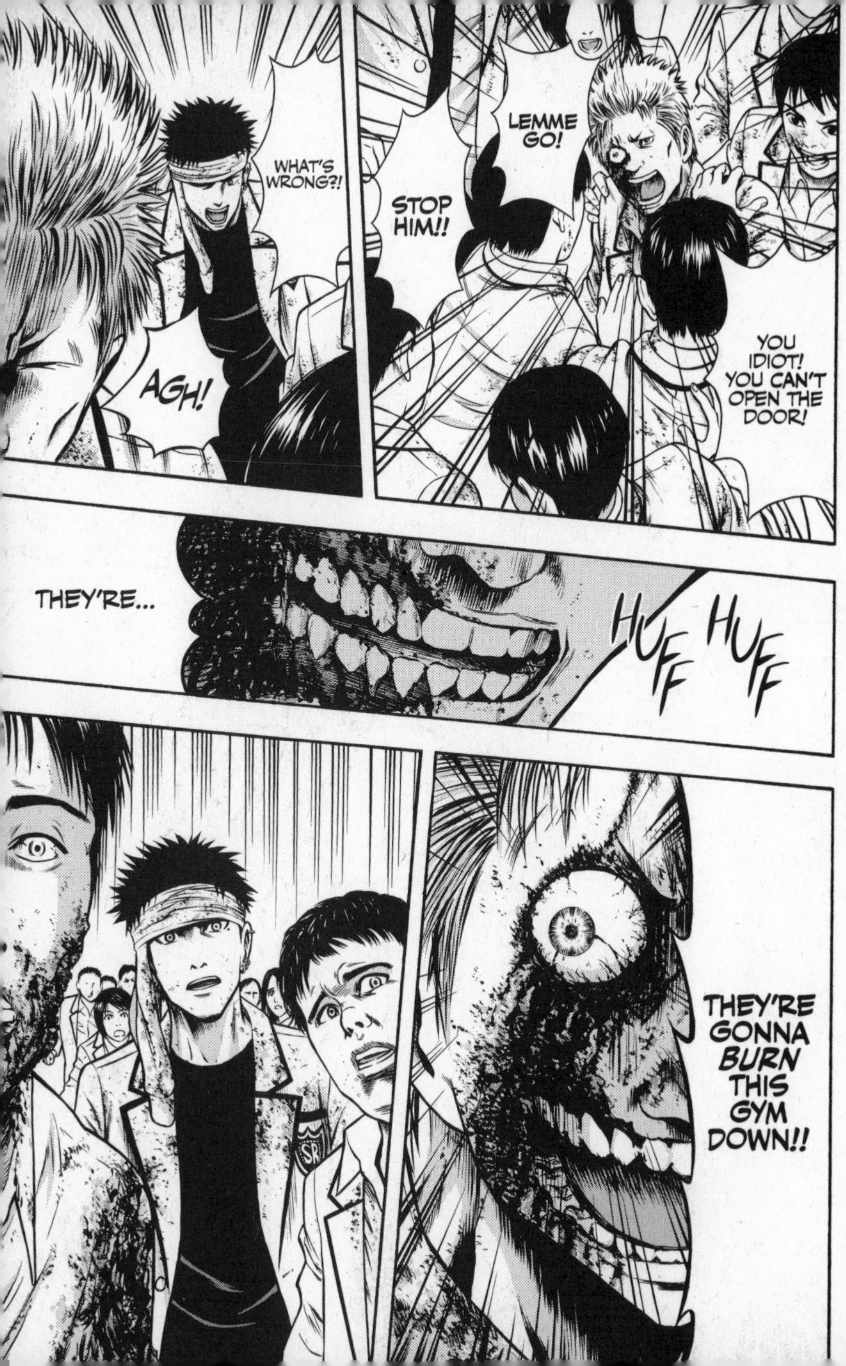
LEMME GO!
STOP HIM!!
YOU IDIOT! YOU CAN'T OPEN THE DOOR!
WHAT'S WRONG?!
AGH!
THEY'RE...
HUFF HUFF
THEY'RE GONNA BURN THIS GYM DOWN!!

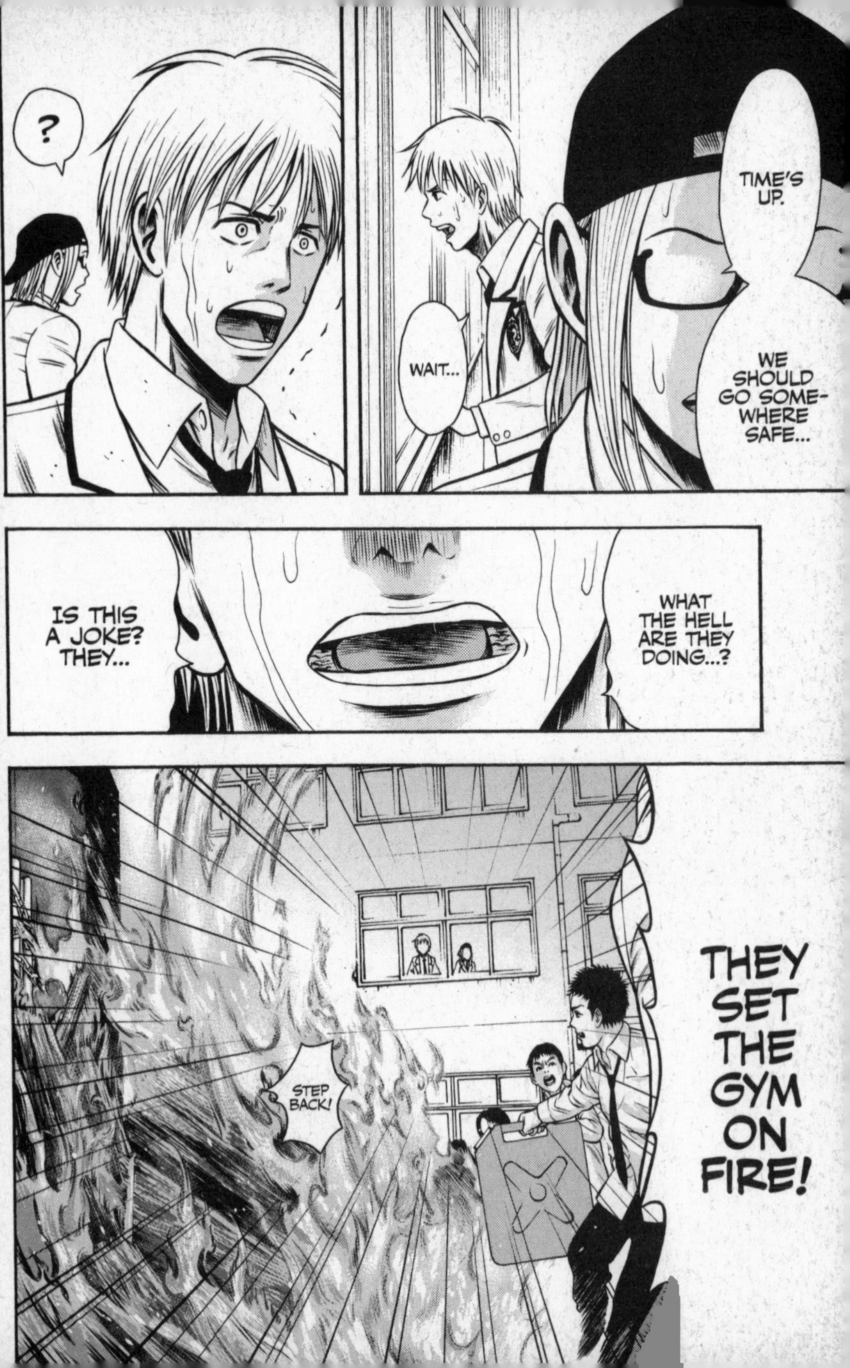
TIME'S UP.
WE SHOULD GO SOME-WHERE SAFE...
WAIT...
?
WHAT THE HELL ARE THEY DOING...?
IS THIS A JOKE? THEY...
THEY SET THE GYM ON FIRE!
STEP BACK!

HOUR OF THE ZOMBIE

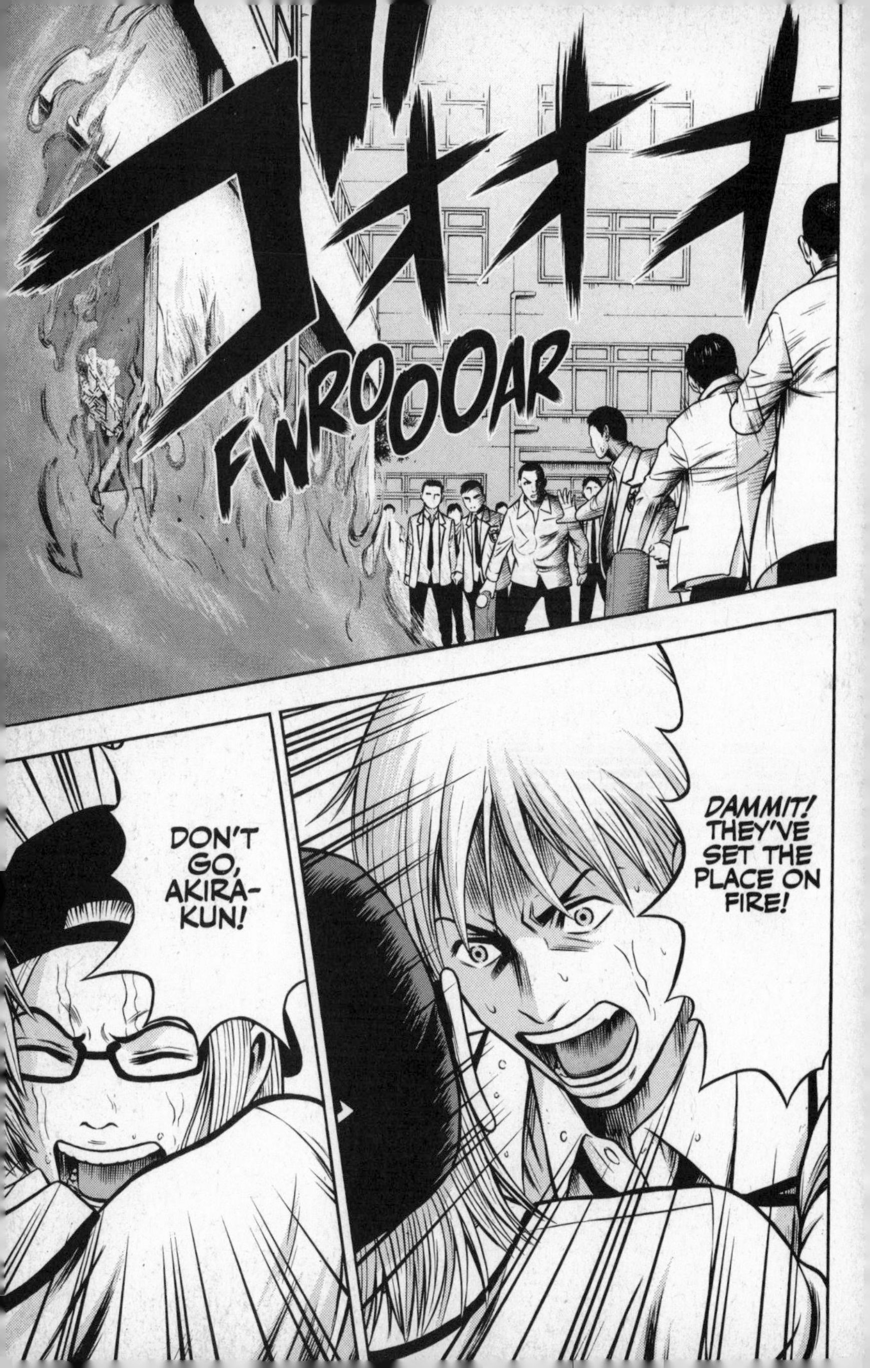
FWROOOAR
DAMMIT! THEY'VE SET THE PLACE ON FIRE!
DON'T GO, AKIRA-KUN!

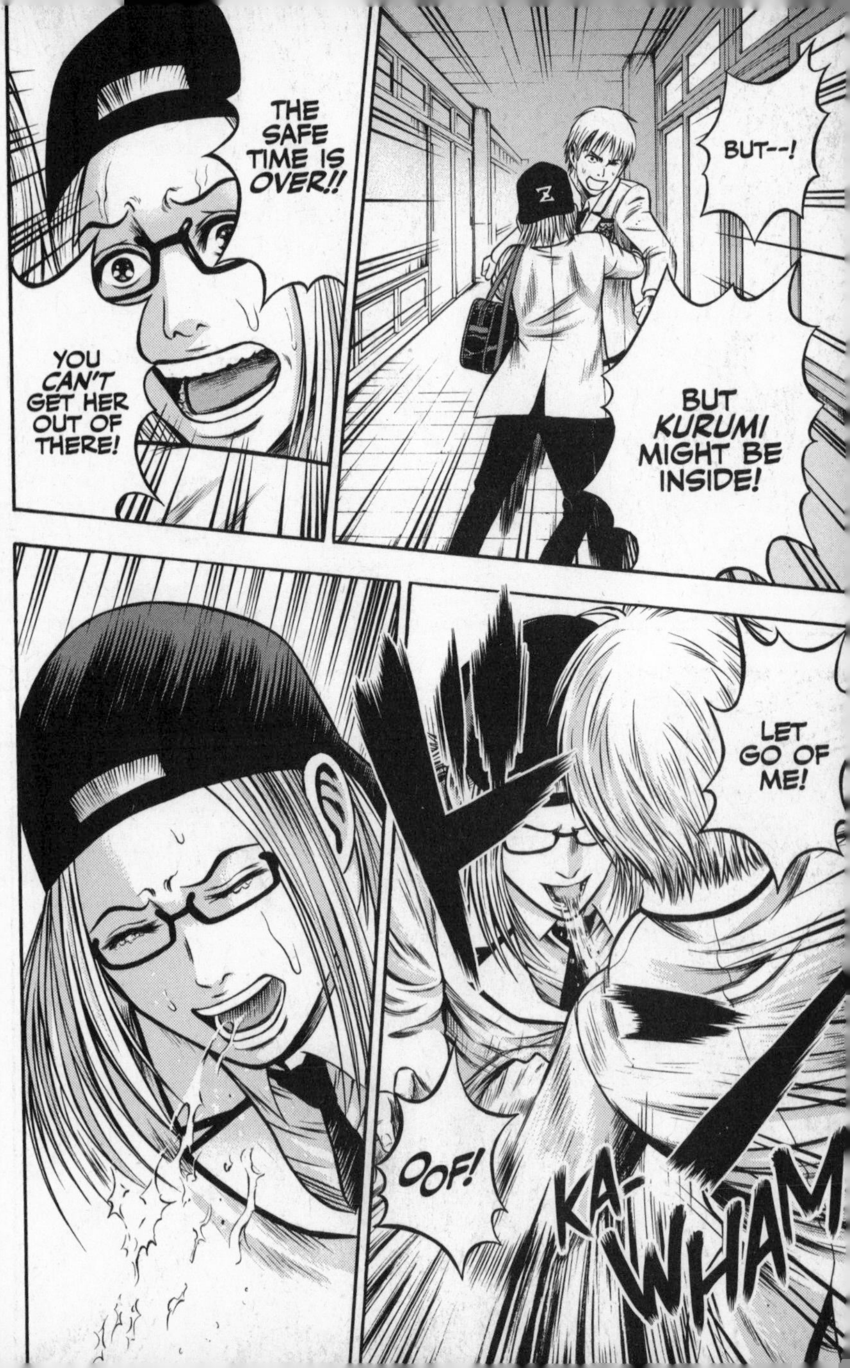
BUT--!
THE SAFE TIME IS OVER!!
BUT KURUMI MIGHT BE INSIDE!
YOU CAN'T GET HER OUT OF THERE!
LET GO OF ME!
KA-WHAM
OOF!

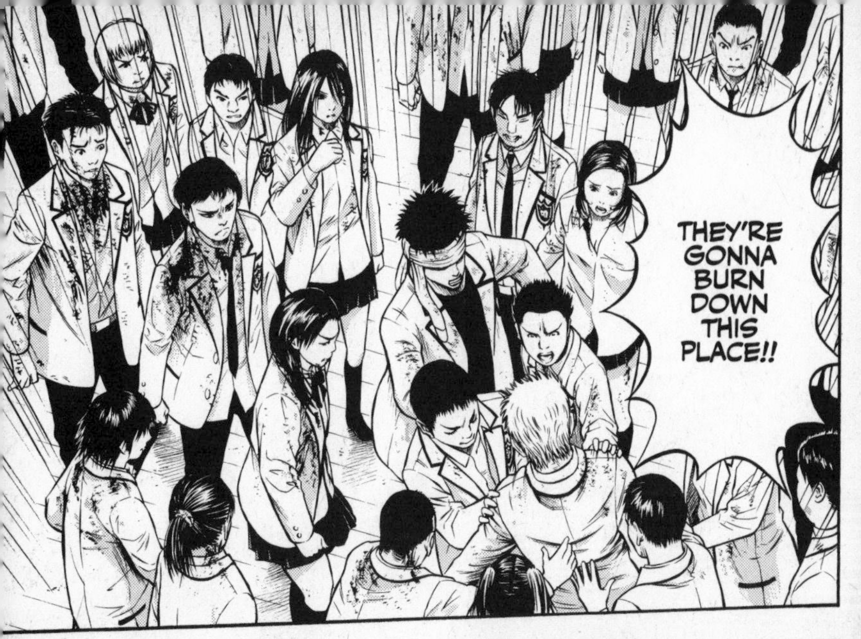
THEY'RE GONNA BURN DOWN THIS PLACE!!

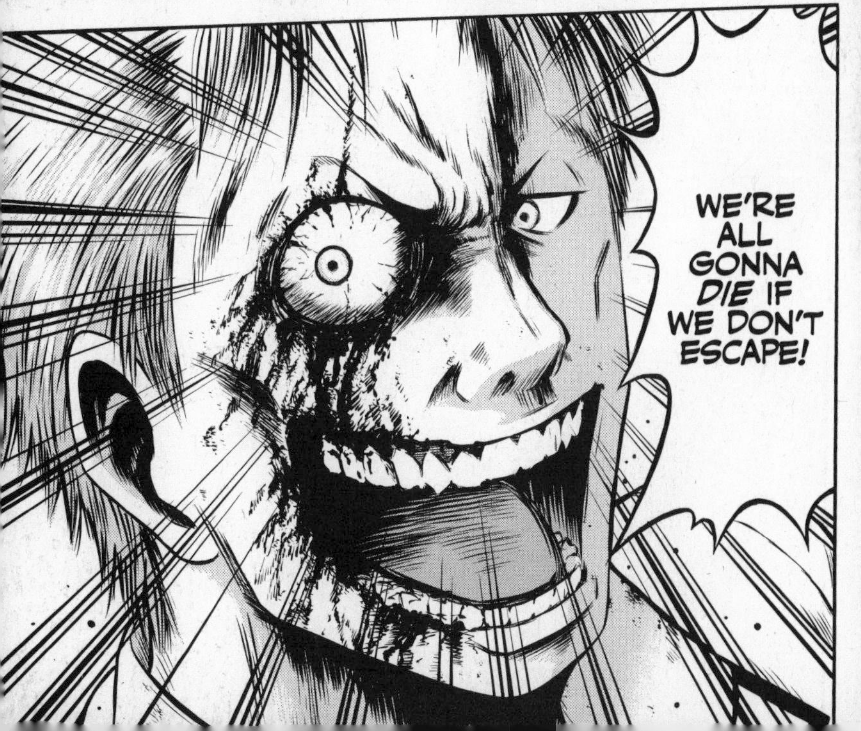
WE'RE ALL GONNA *DIE* IF WE DON'T ESCAPE!

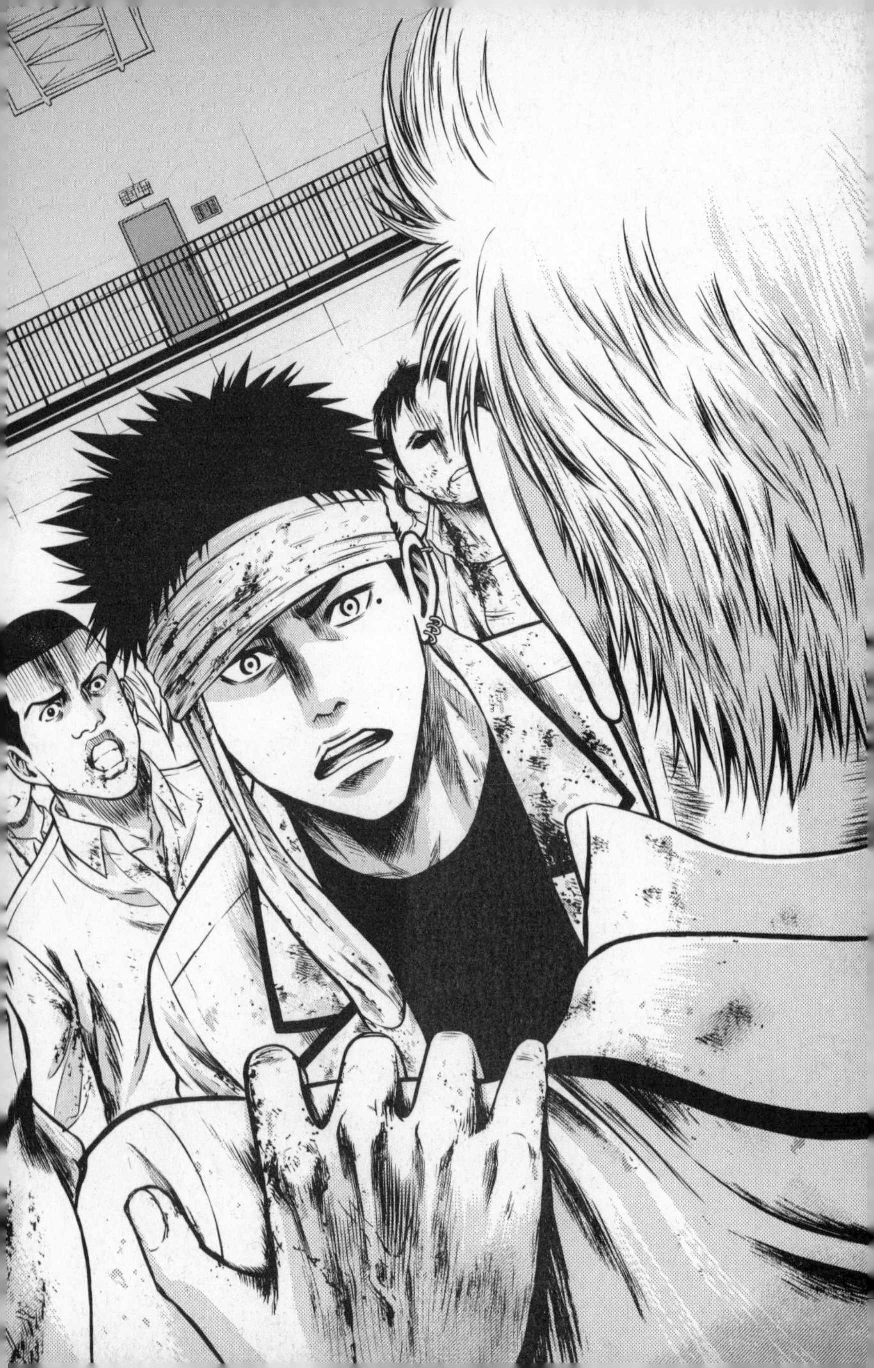

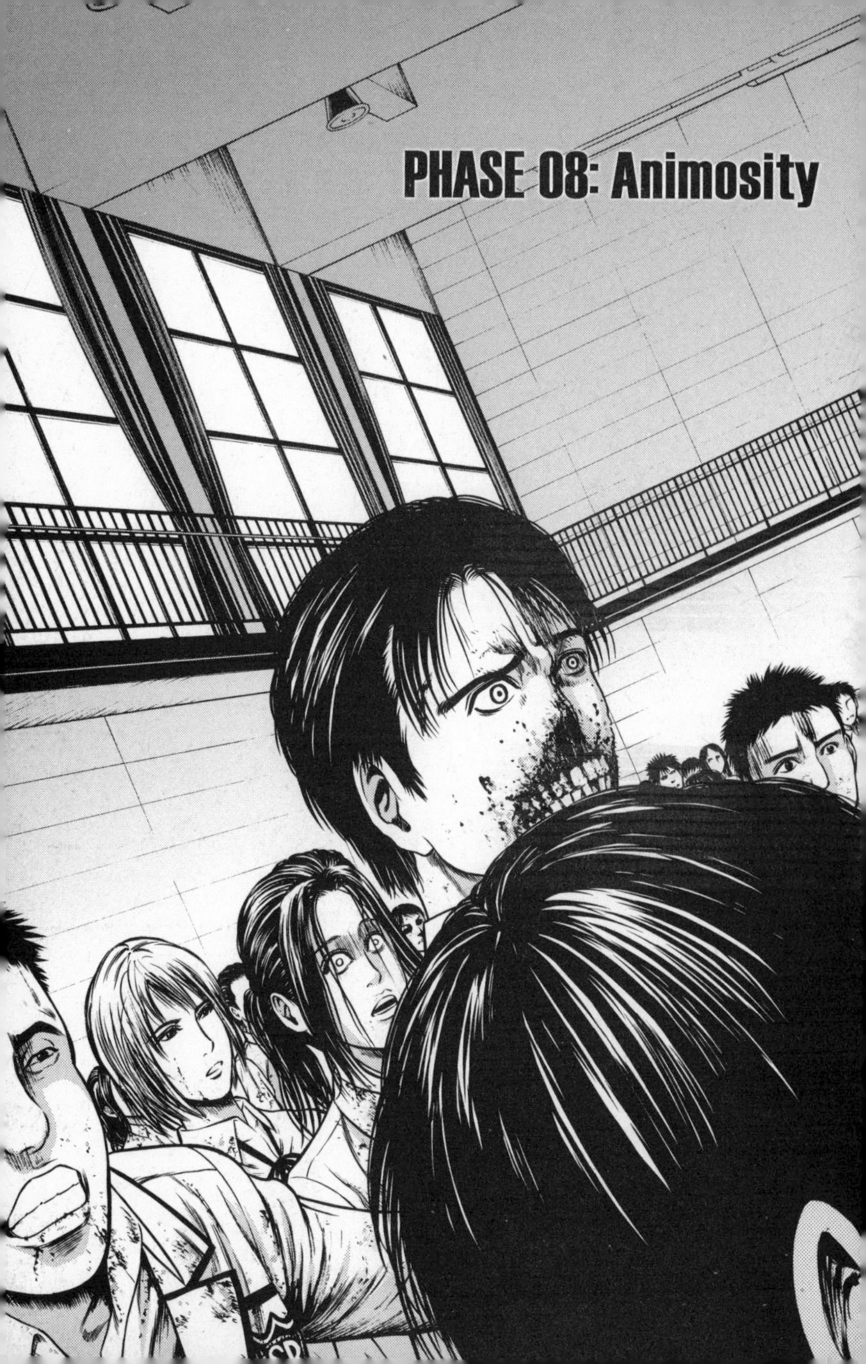
PHASE 08: Animosity

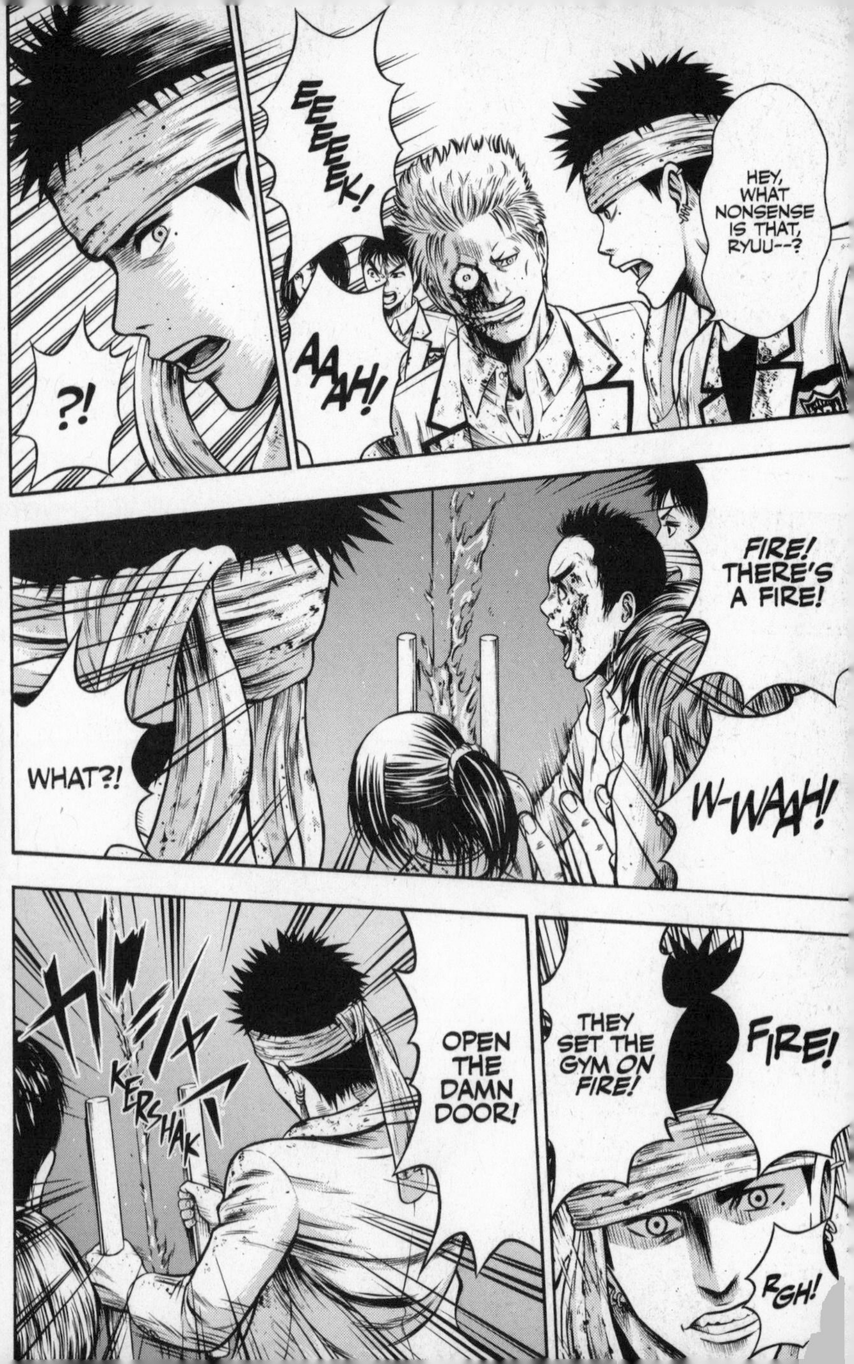
HEY, WHAT NONSENSE IS THAT, RYUU--?
EEEEEK!
AAAH!
?!
FIRE! THERE'S A FIRE!
W-WAAH!
WHAT?!
FIRE!
THEY SET THE GYM ON FIRE!
RGH!
OPEN THE DAMN DOOR!
KERSHAK

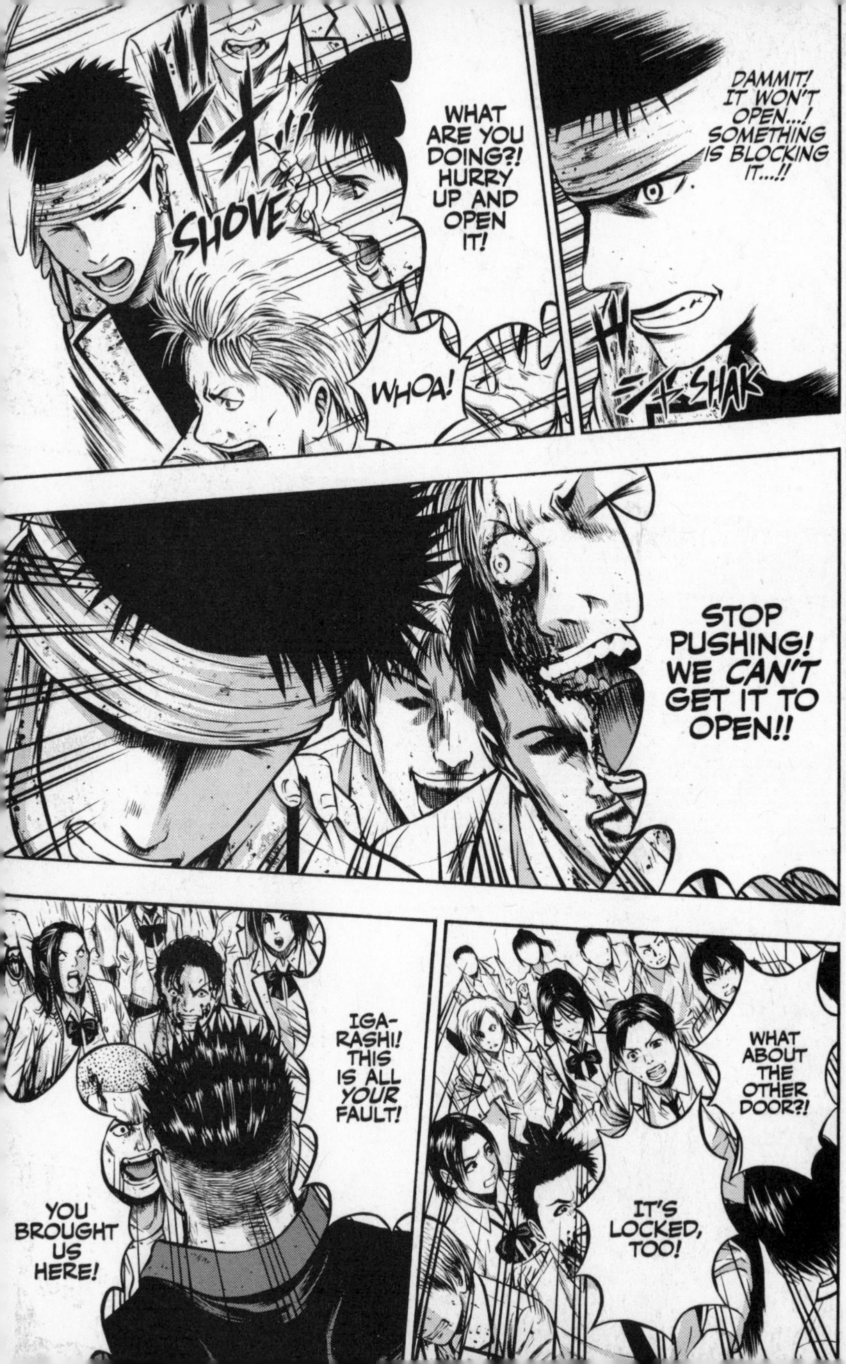
DAMMIT! IT WON'T OPEN...! SOMETHING IS BLOCKING IT...!!
SHAK
WHAT ARE YOU DOING?! HURRY UP AND OPEN IT!
SHOVE
WHOA!
STOP PUSHING! WE *CAN'T* GET IT TO OPEN!!
WHAT ABOUT THE OTHER DOOR?!
IT'S LOCKED, TOO!
IGA-RASHI! THIS IS ALL *YOUR* FAULT!
YOU BROUGHT US HERE!

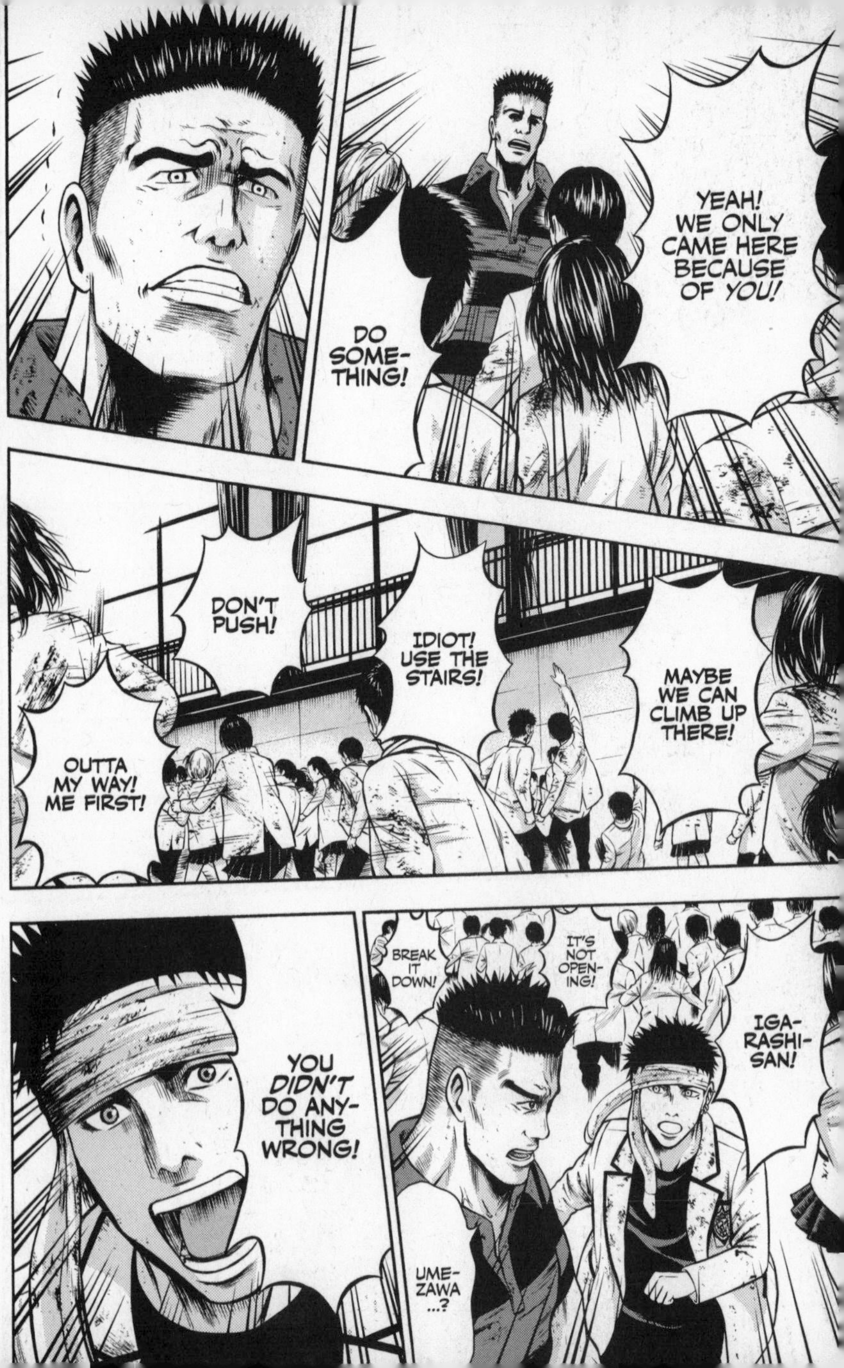
YEAH! WE ONLY CAME HERE BECAUSE OF YOU!
DO SOME-THING!
MAYBE WE CAN CLIMB UP THERE!
IDIOT! USE THE STAIRS!
DON'T PUSH!
OUTTA MY WAY! ME FIRST!
IGA-RASHI-SAN!
IT'S NOT OPEN-ING!
BREAK IT DOWN!
UME-ZAWA ...?
YOU DIDN'T DO ANY-THING WRONG!

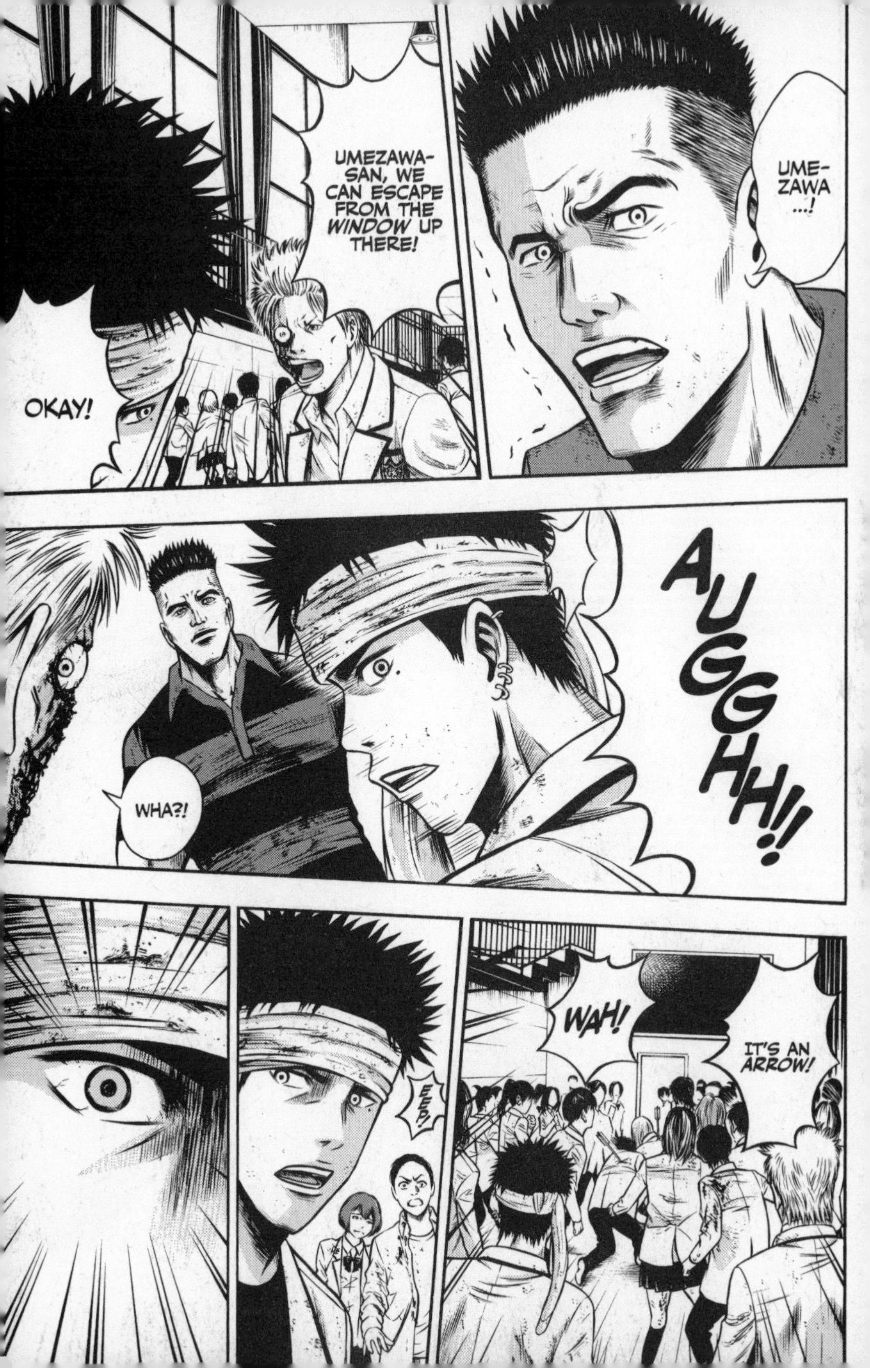
UME-
ZAWA
...!
UMEZAWA-SAN, WE CAN ESCAPE FROM THE *WINDOW* UP THERE!
OKAY!
AUGGHH!!
WHA?!
IT'S AN ARROW!
WAH!
EEP!

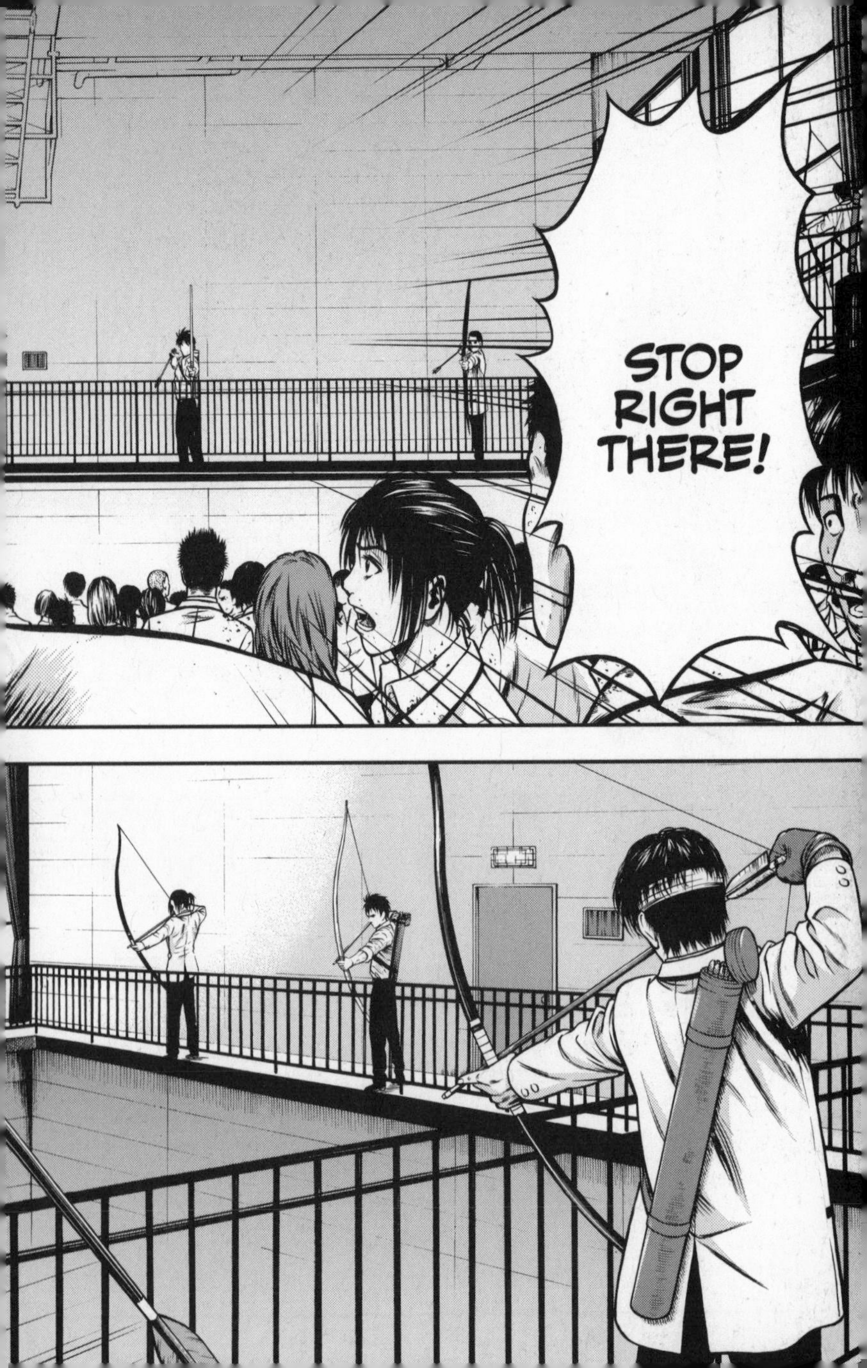
STOP RIGHT THERE!

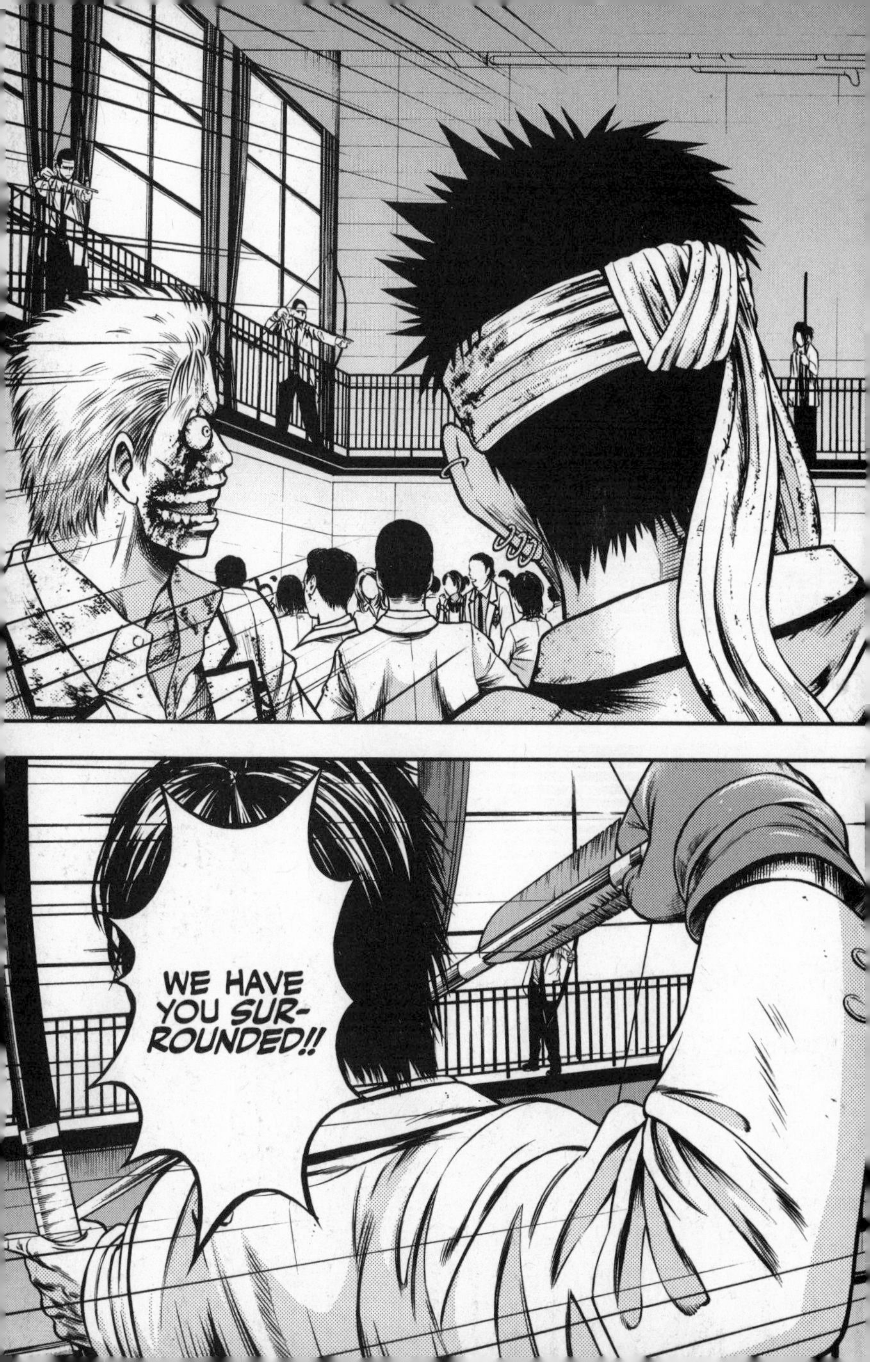
WE HAVE YOU SUR-ROUNDED!!

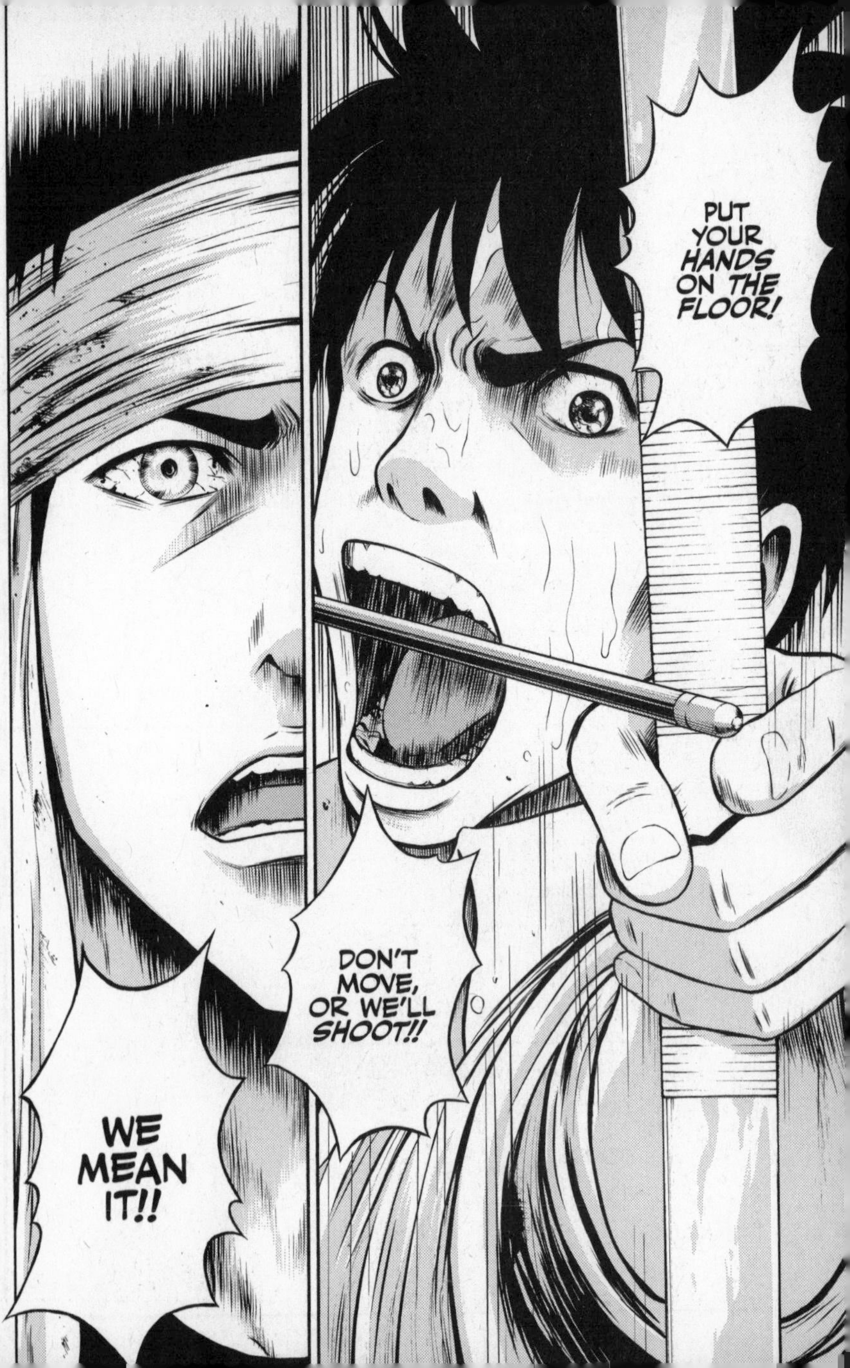
PUT YOUR HANDS ON THE FLOOR!
DON'T MOVE, OR WE'LL SHOOT!!
WE MEAN IT!!

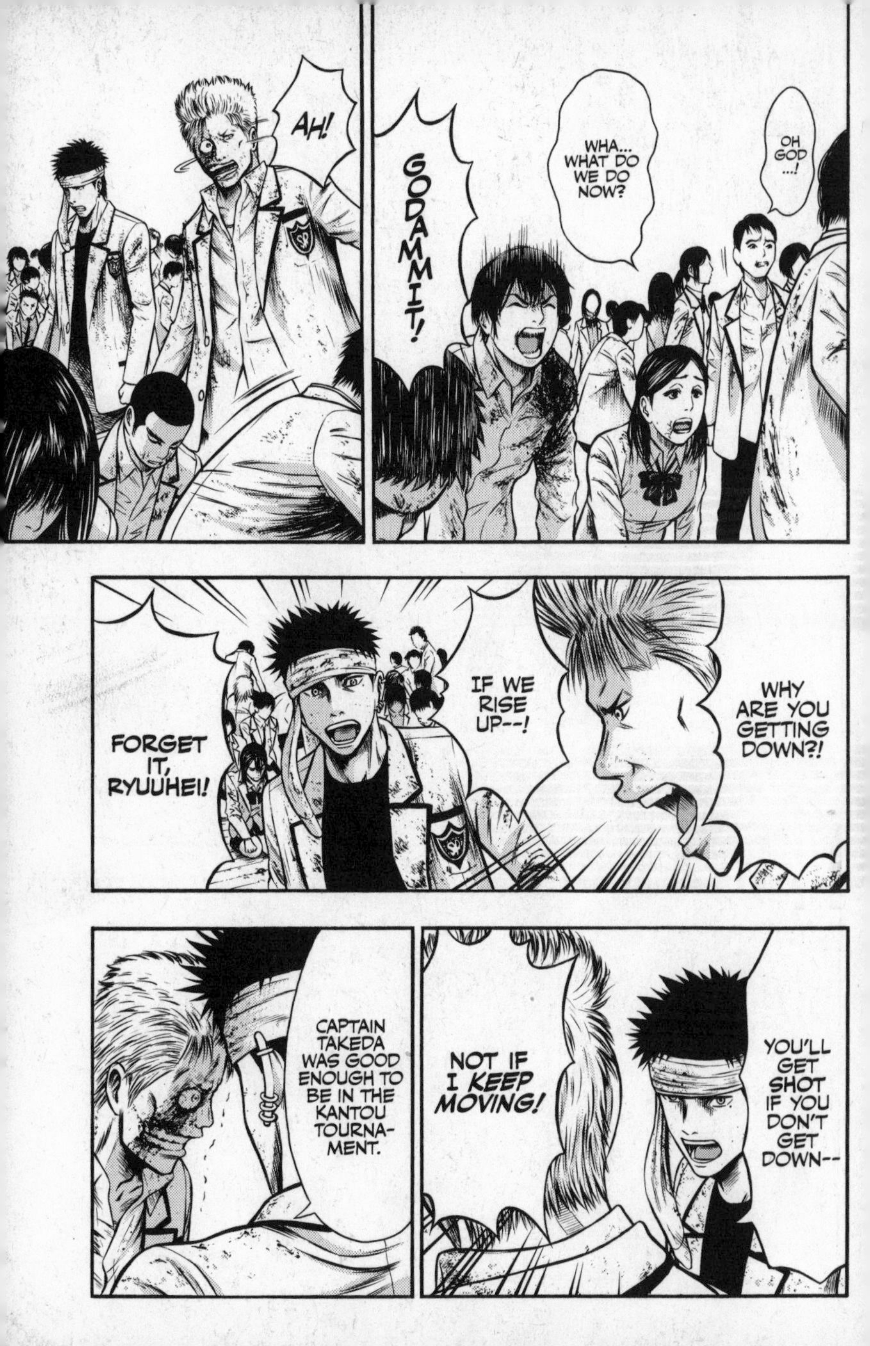
OH GOD ...!
WHA... WHAT DO WE DO NOW?
GODAMMIT!
AH!
WHY ARE YOU GETTING DOWN?!
IF WE RISE UP--!
FORGET IT, RYUUHEI!
YOU'LL GET SHOT IF YOU DON'T GET DOWN--
NOT IF I *KEEP MOVING!*
CAPTAIN TAKEDA WAS GOOD ENOUGH TO BE IN THE KANTOU TOURNA-MENT.

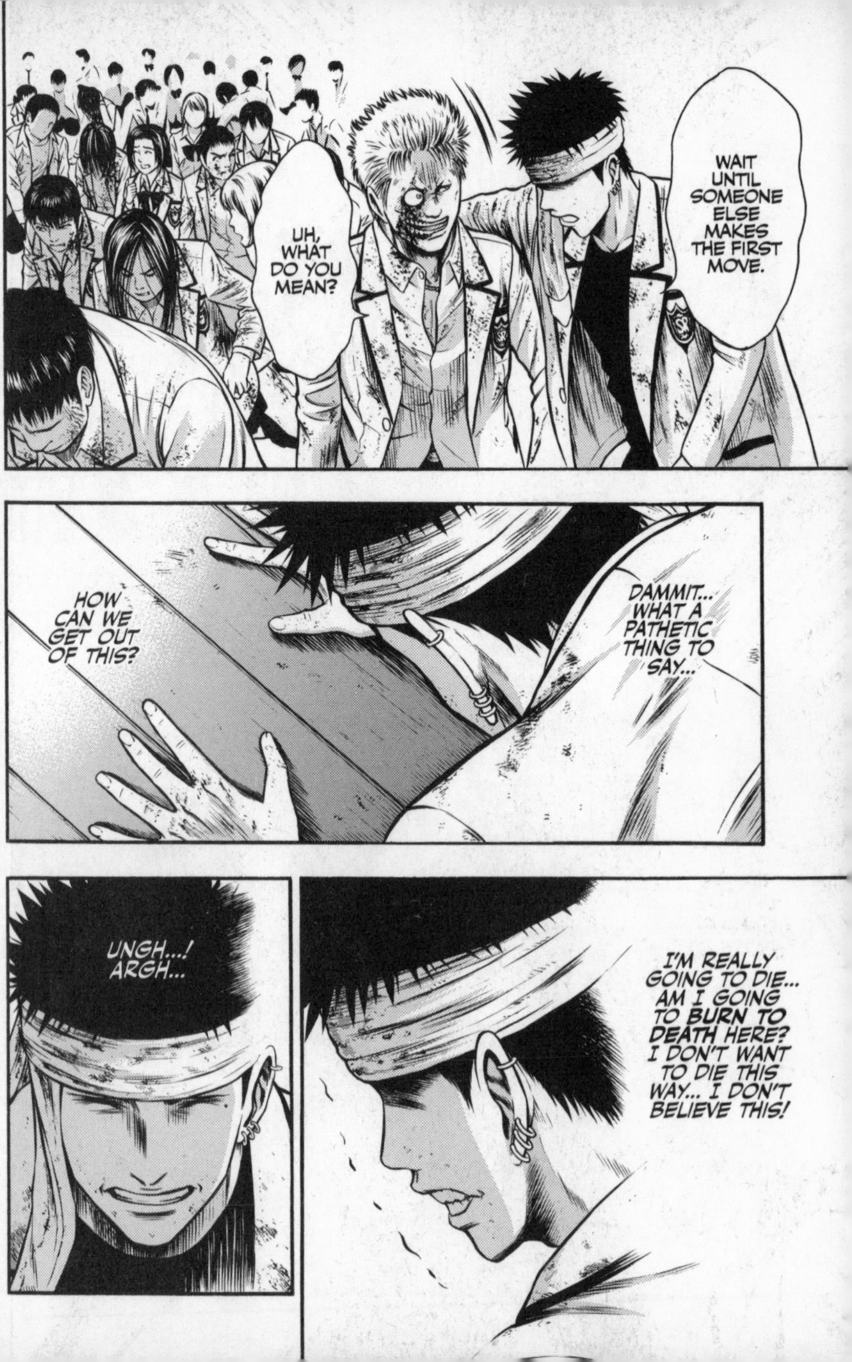
WAIT UNTIL SOMEONE ELSE MAKES THE FIRST MOVE.
UH, WHAT DO YOU MEAN?
DAMMIT... WHAT A PATHETIC THING TO SAY...
HOW CAN WE GET OUT OF THIS?
I'M REALLY GOING TO DIE... AM I GOING TO BURN TO DEATH HERE? I DON'T WANT TO DIE THIS WAY... I DON'T BELIEVE THIS!
UNGH...! ARGH...

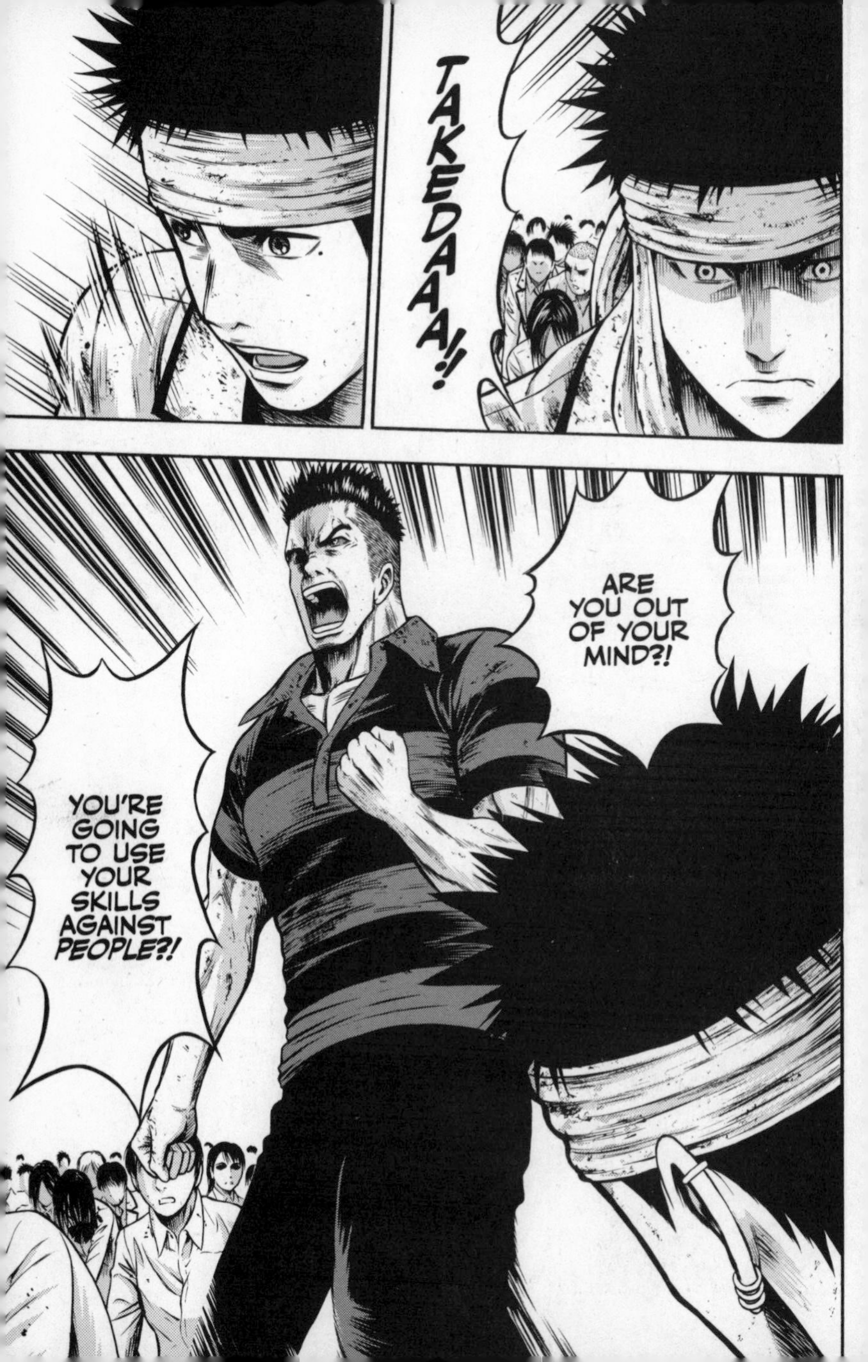
TAKEDAAA!!
ARE YOU OUT OF YOUR MIND?!
YOU'RE GOING TO USE YOUR SKILLS AGAINST PEOPLE?!

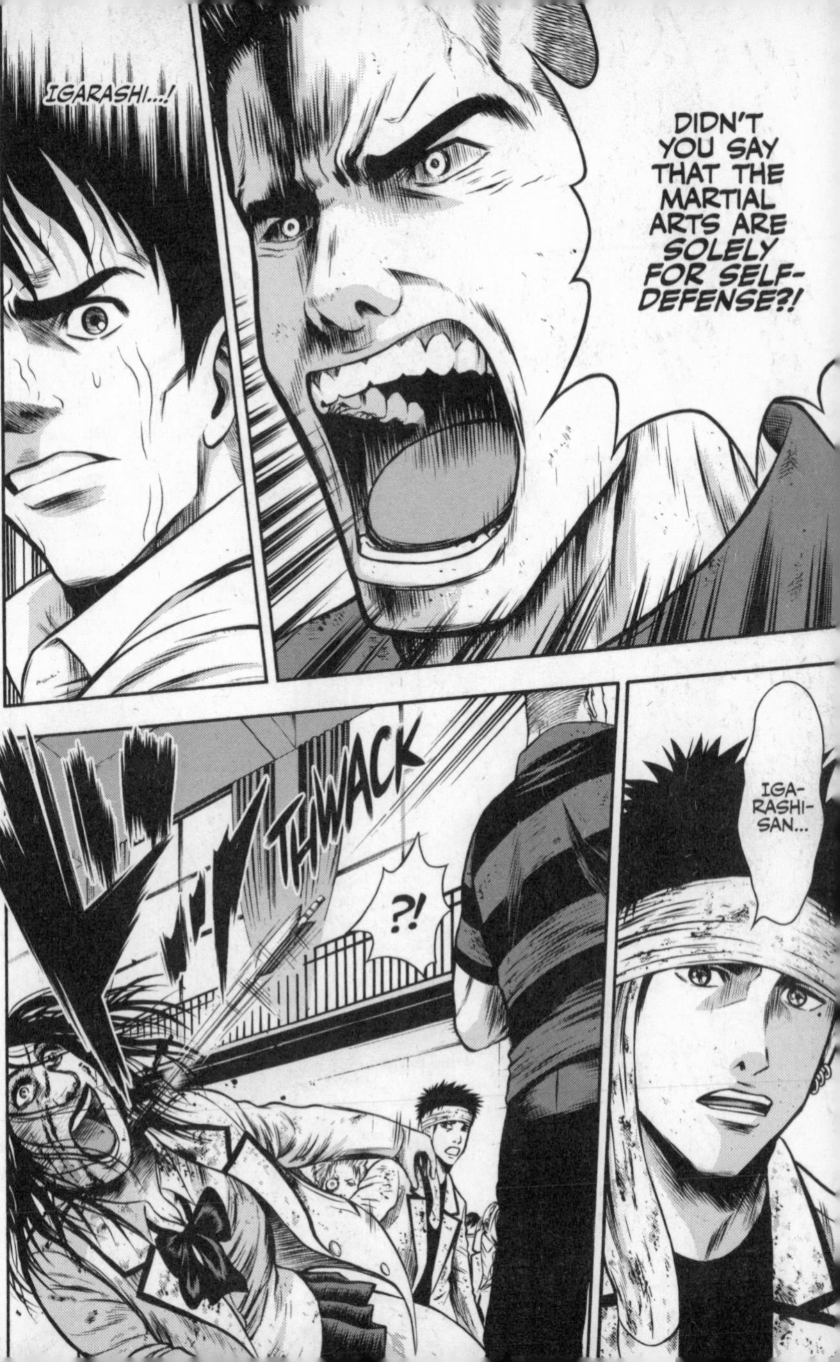
DIDN'T YOU SAY THAT THE MARTIAL ARTS ARE SOLELY FOR SELF-DEFENSE?!
IGARASHI...!
IGA-RASHI-SAN...
?!
THWACK

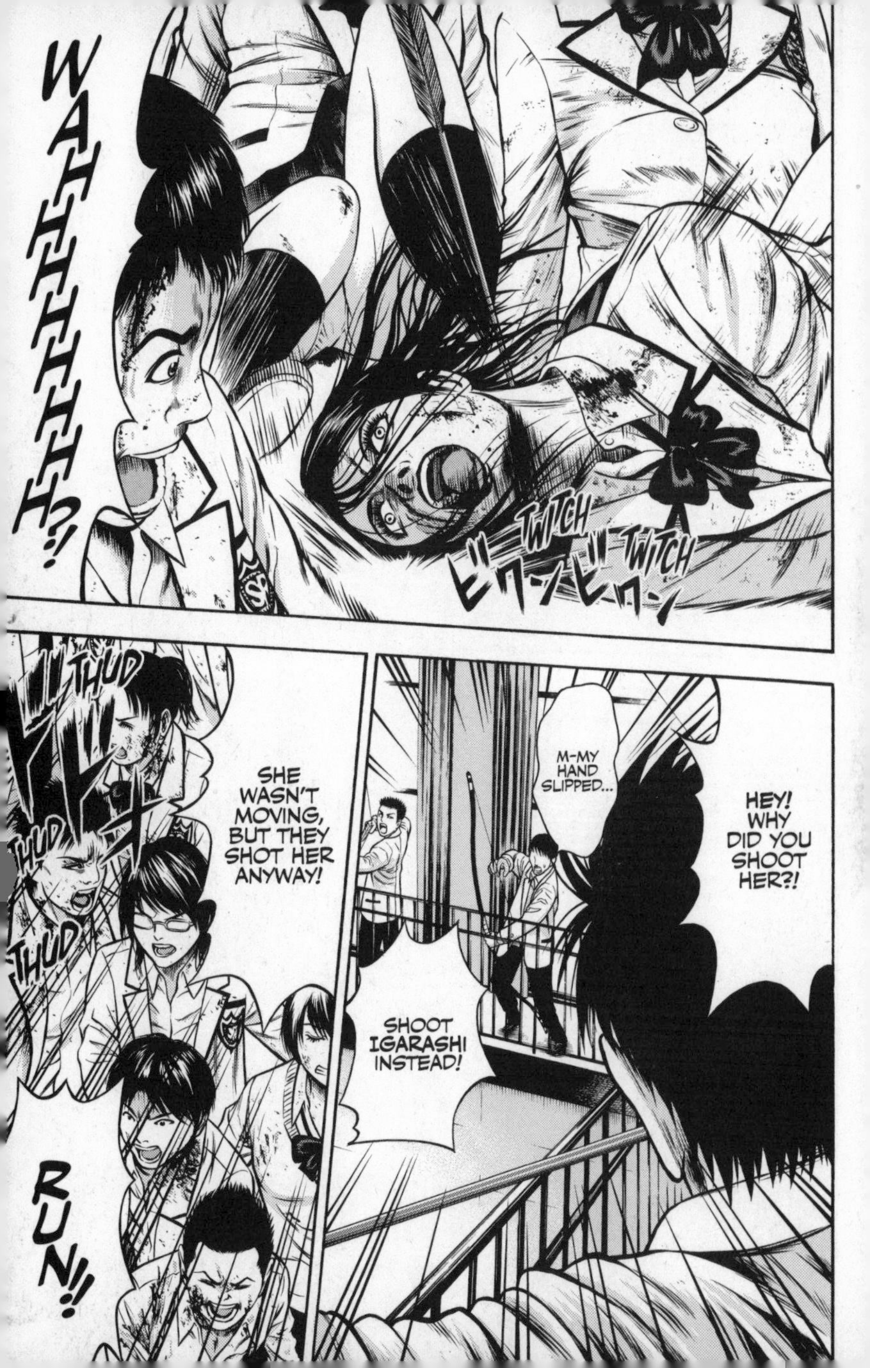
TWITCH TWITCH
WAHHHHHHHHH?!
HEY! WHY DID YOU SHOOT HER?!
M-MY HAND SLIPPED...
SHOOT IGARASHI INSTEAD!
SHE WASN'T MOVING, BUT THEY SHOT HER ANYWAY!
THUD
THUD
THUD
RUN!!

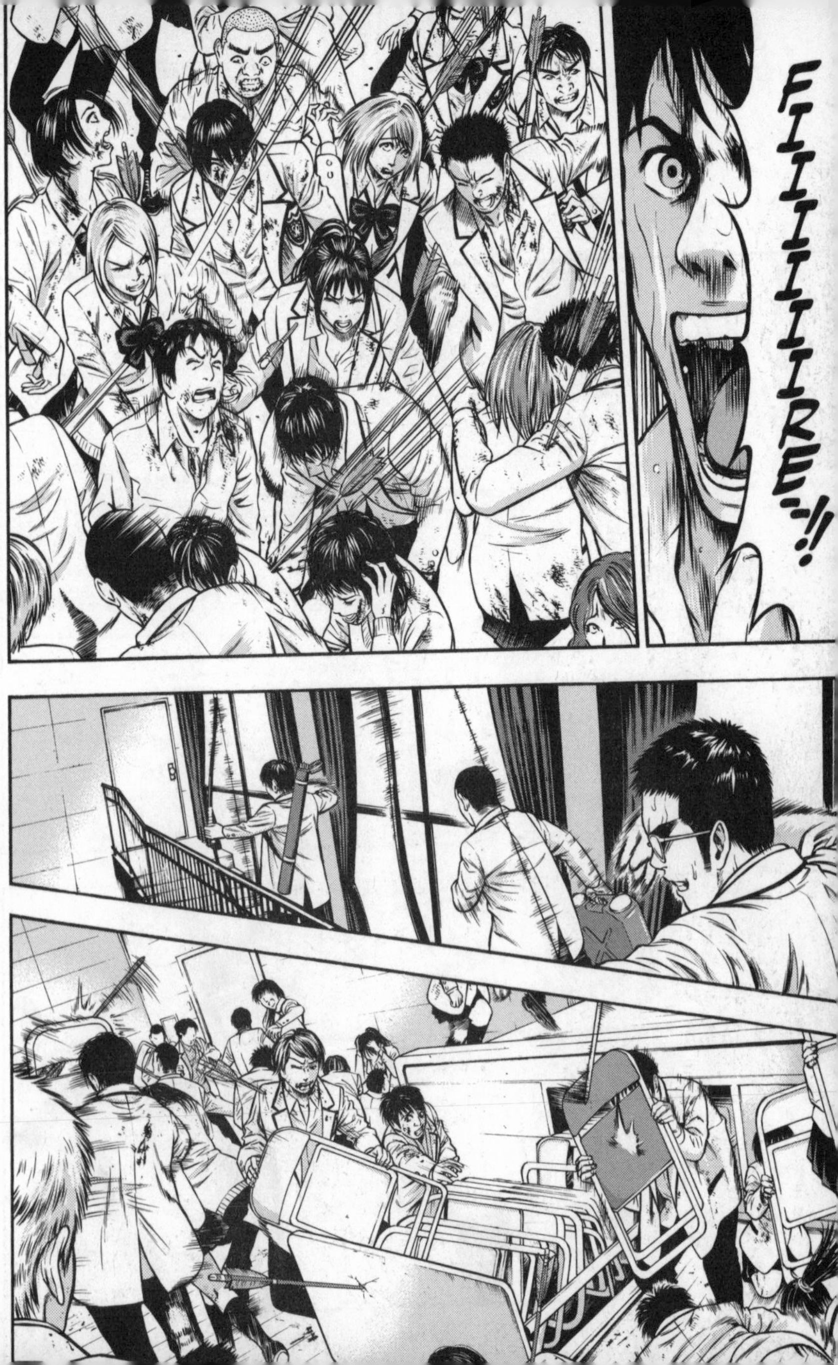
FIIIIIIRE--!!

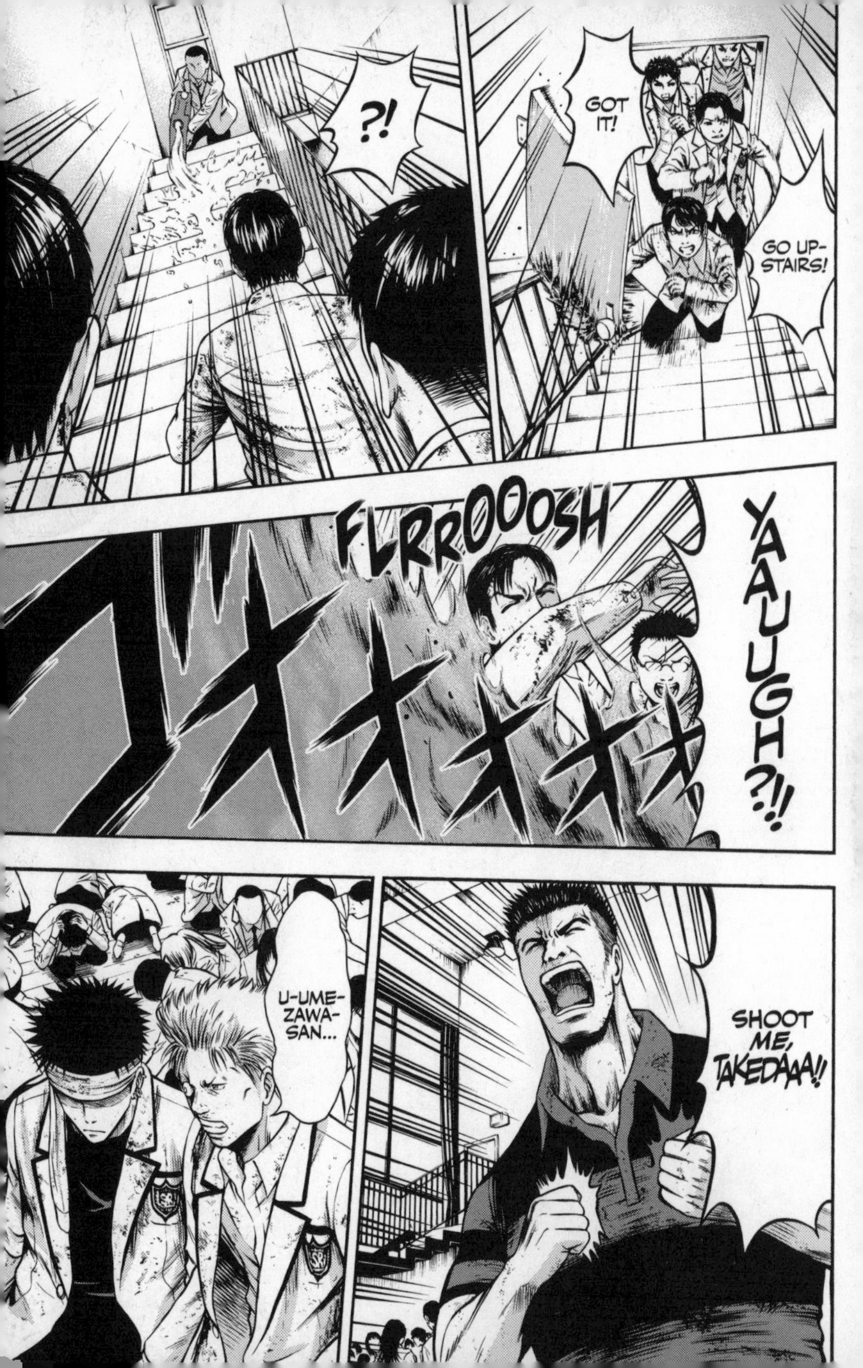
GO UP-STAIRS!
GOT IT!
?!
YAAUUGH?!!
FLRROOOSH
SHOOT ME, TAKEDAAA!!
U-UME-ZAWA-SAN...

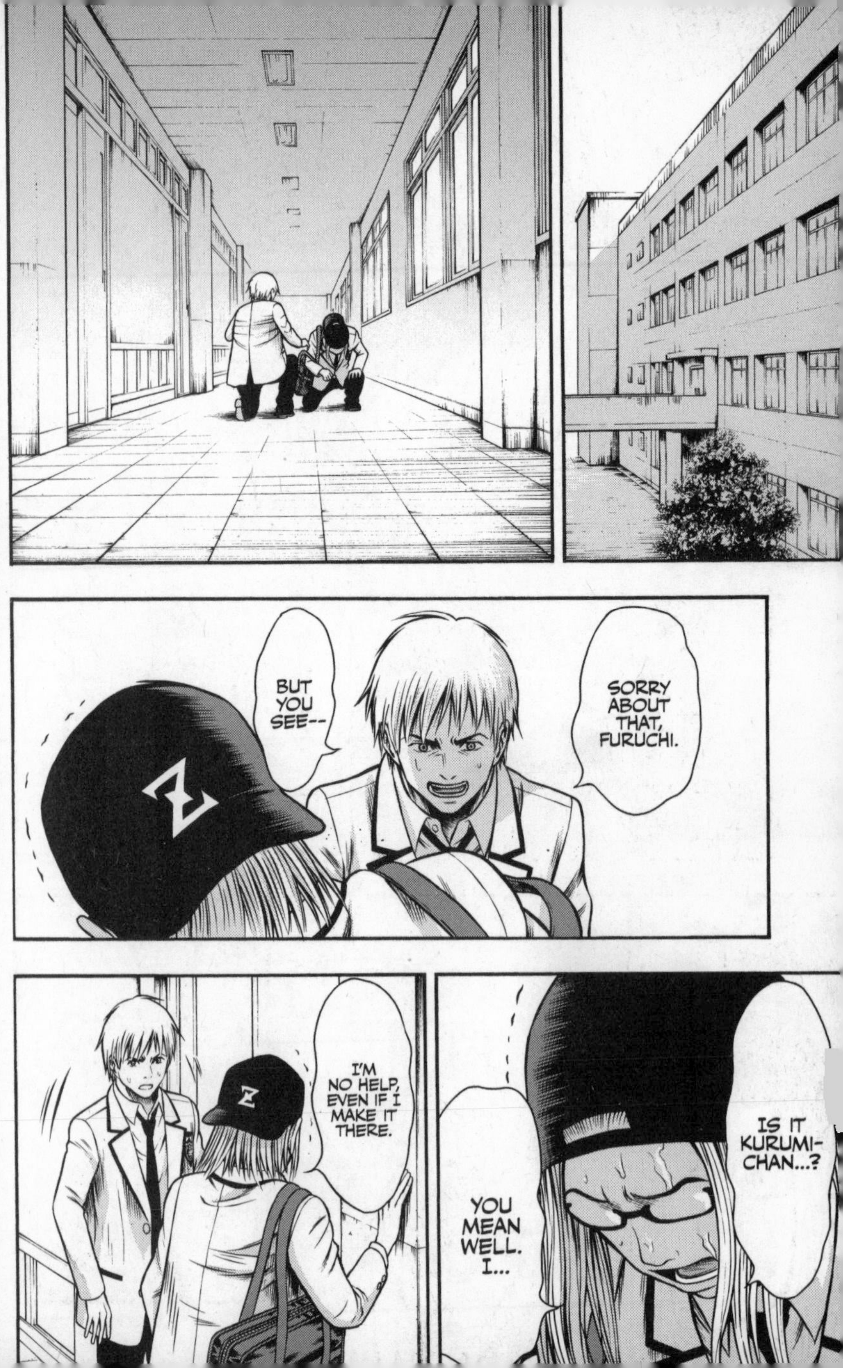
SORRY ABOUT THAT, FURUCHI.
BUT YOU SEE--
IS IT KURUMI-CHAN...?
YOU MEAN WELL. I...
I'M NO HELP, EVEN IF I MAKE IT THERE.

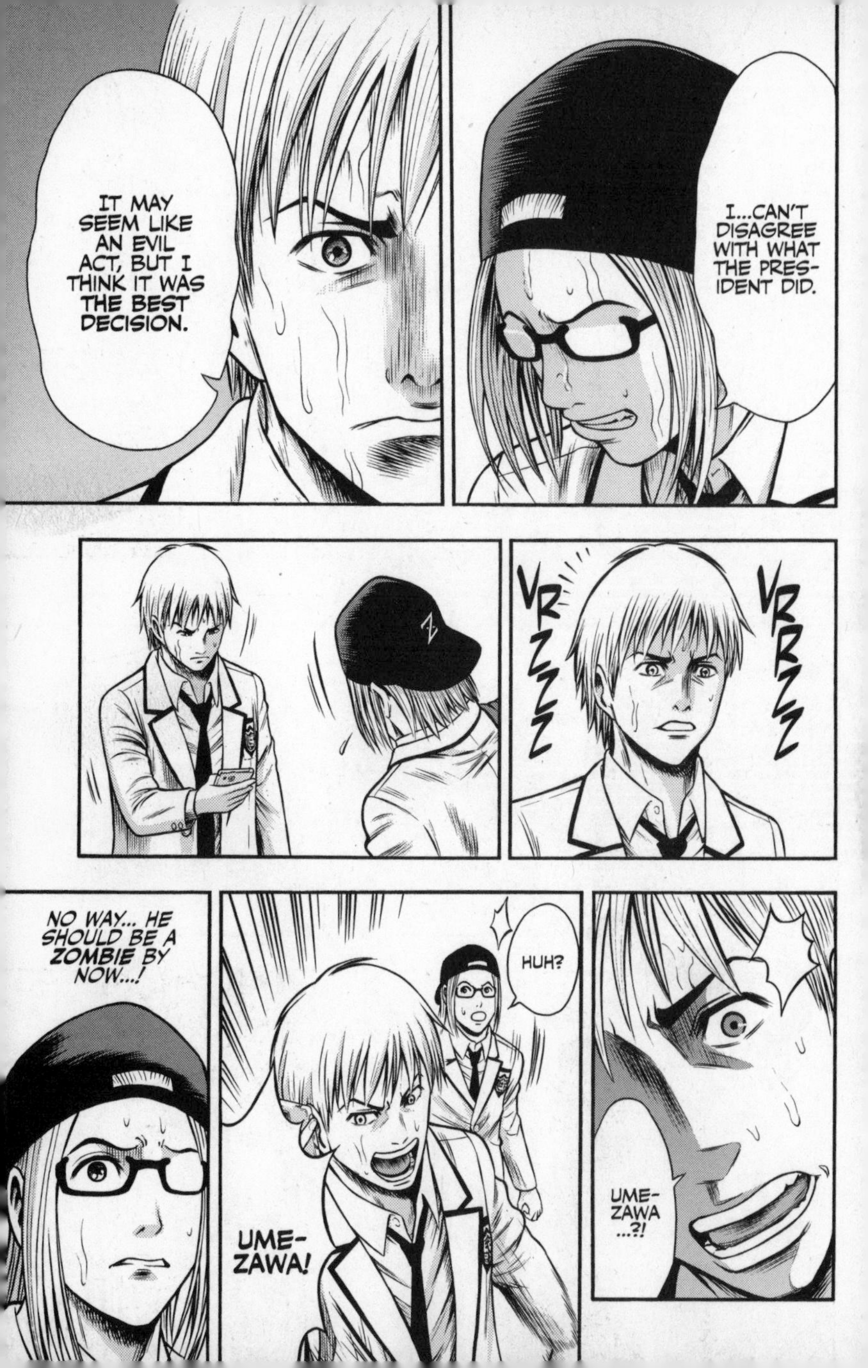
I...CAN'T DISAGREE WITH WHAT THE PRES-IDENT DID.
IT MAY SEEM LIKE AN EVIL ACT, BUT I THINK IT WAS THE BEST DECISION.
VRRZZZ
VRZZZZ
UME-ZAWA ...?!
HUH?
UME-ZAWA!
NO WAY... HE SHOULD BE A ZOMBIE BY NOW...!

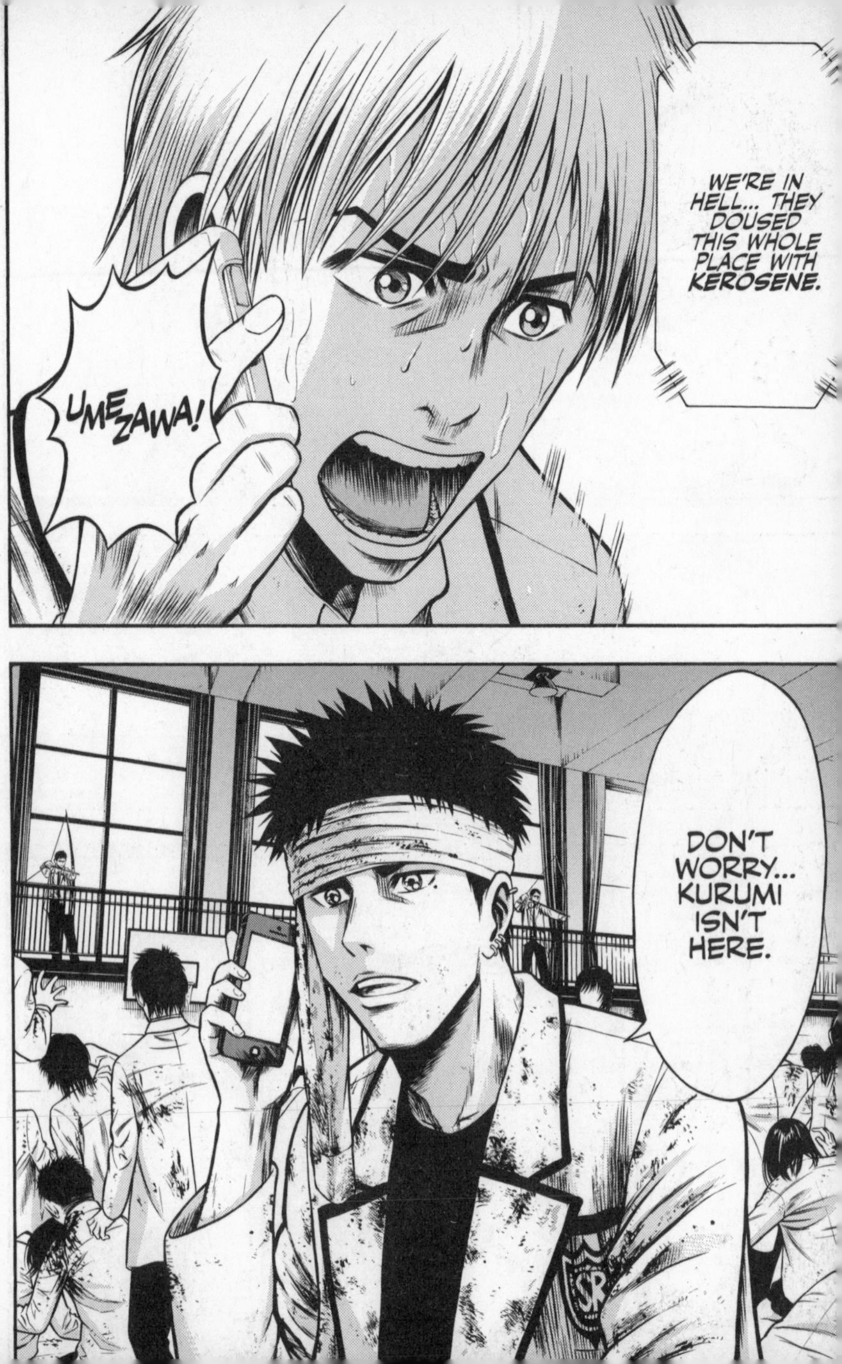
WE'RE IN HELL... THEY DOUSED THIS WHOLE PLACE WITH KEROSENE.
UMEZAWA!
DON'T WORRY... KURUMI ISN'T HERE.

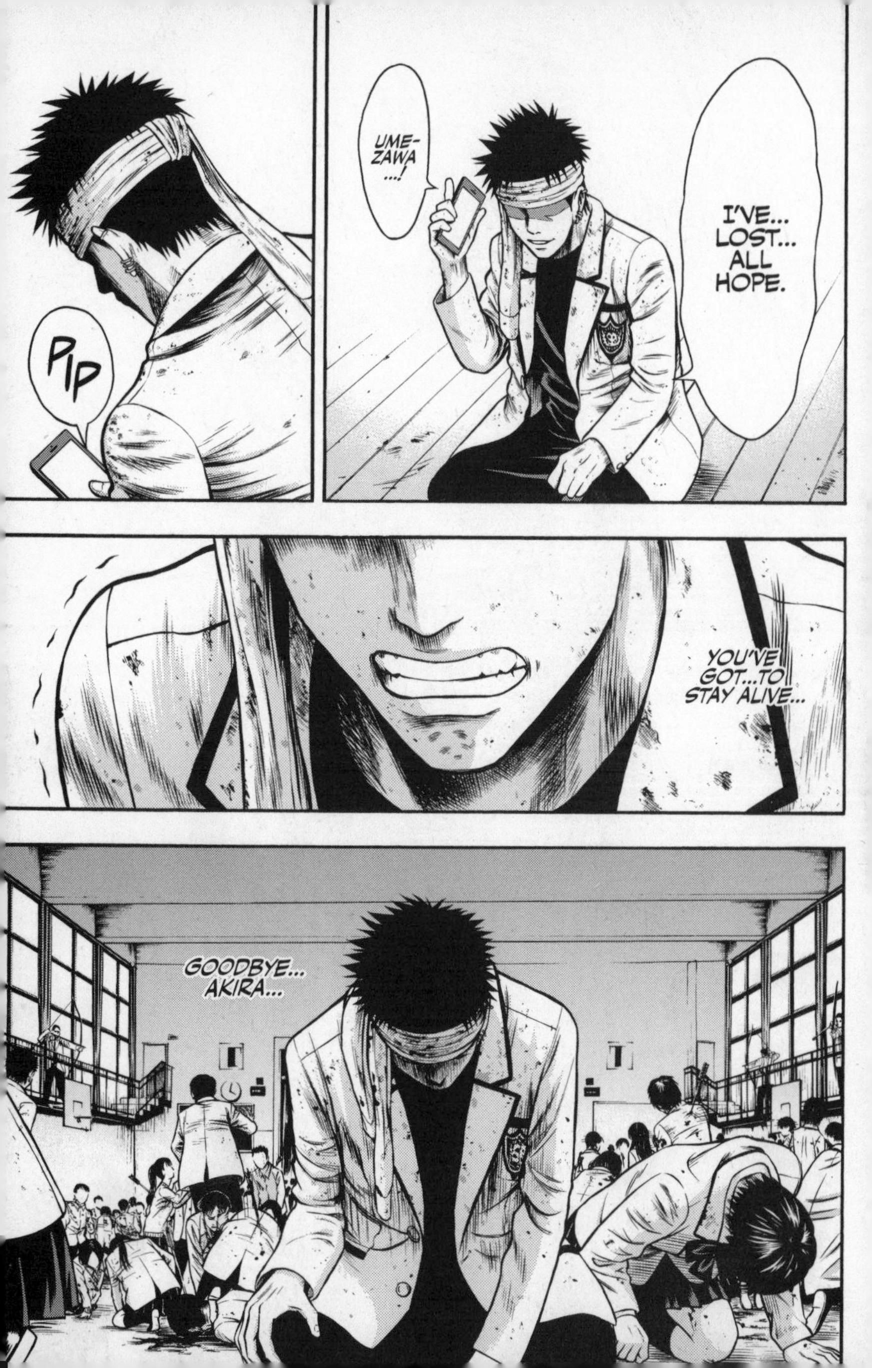
I'VE... LOST... ALL HOPE.
UME-ZAWA ...!
PIP
YOU'VE GOT...TO STAY ALIVE...
GOODBYE... AKIRA...

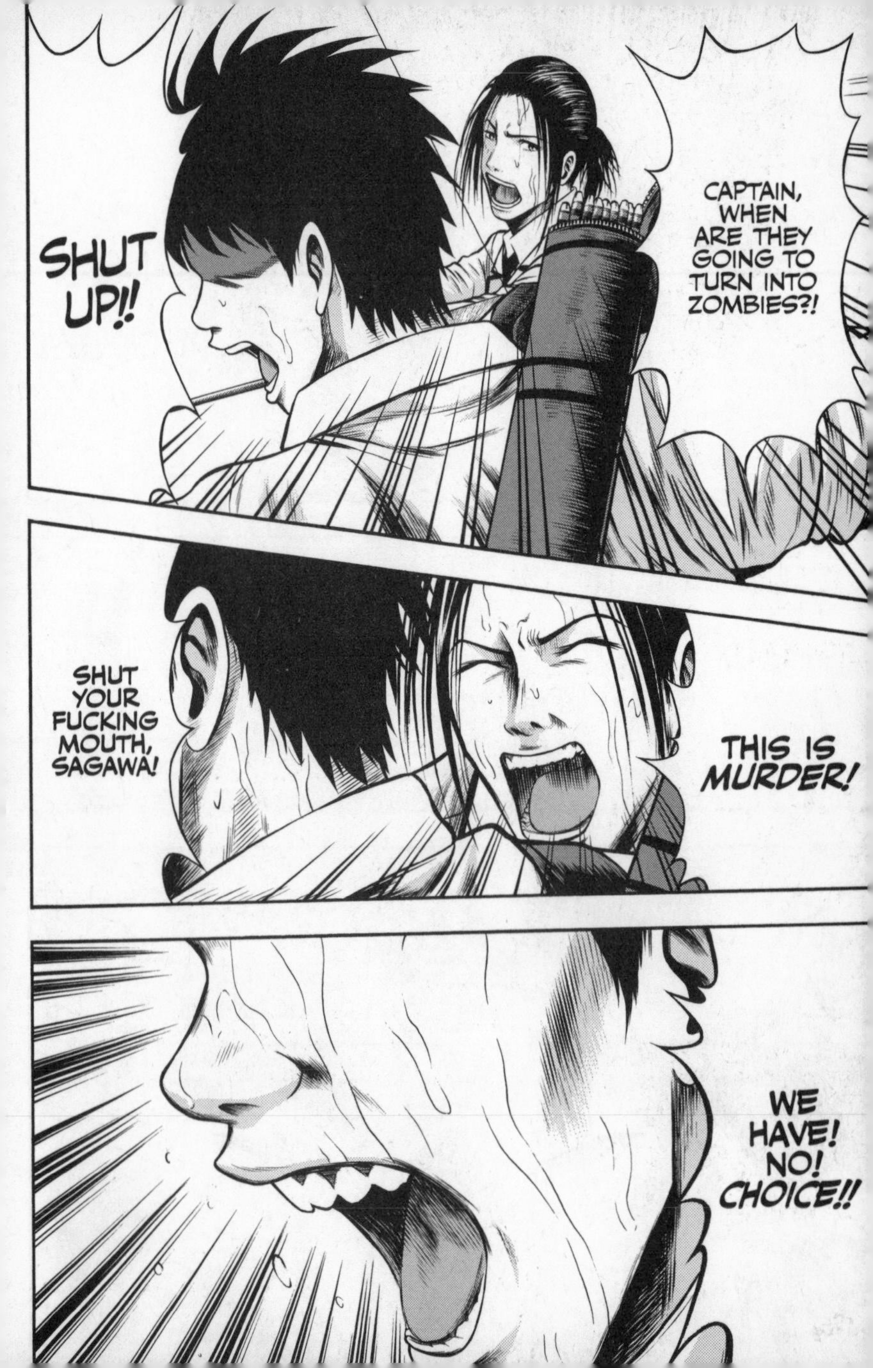
CAPTAIN, WHEN ARE THEY GOING TO TURN INTO ZOMBIES?!
SHUT UP!!
THIS IS MURDER!
SHUT YOUR FUCKING MOUTH, SAGAWA!
WE HAVE! NO! CHOICE!!

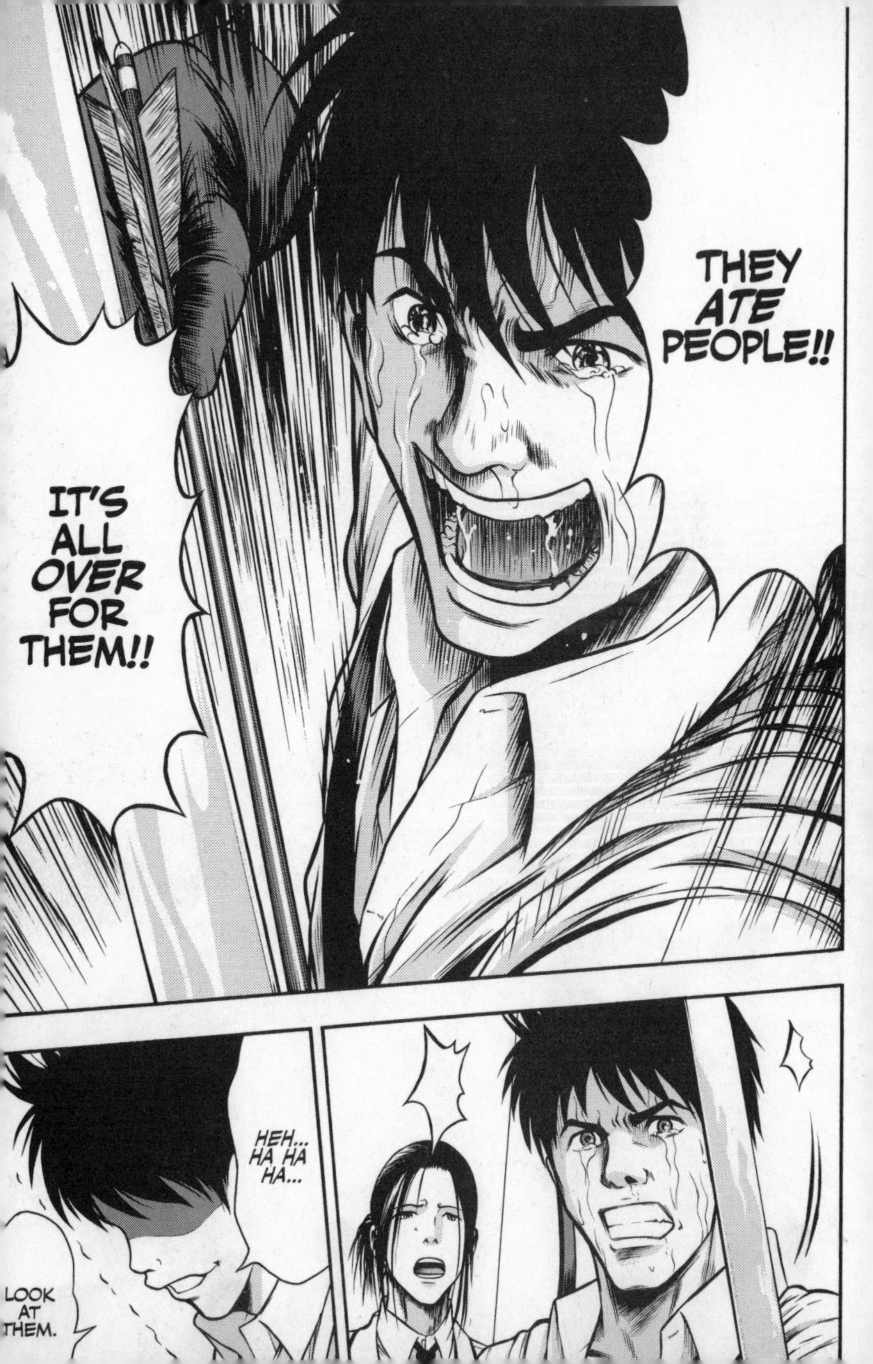
THEY ATE PEOPLE!!
IT'S ALL OVER FOR THEM!!
HEH... HA HA HA...
LOOK AT THEM.

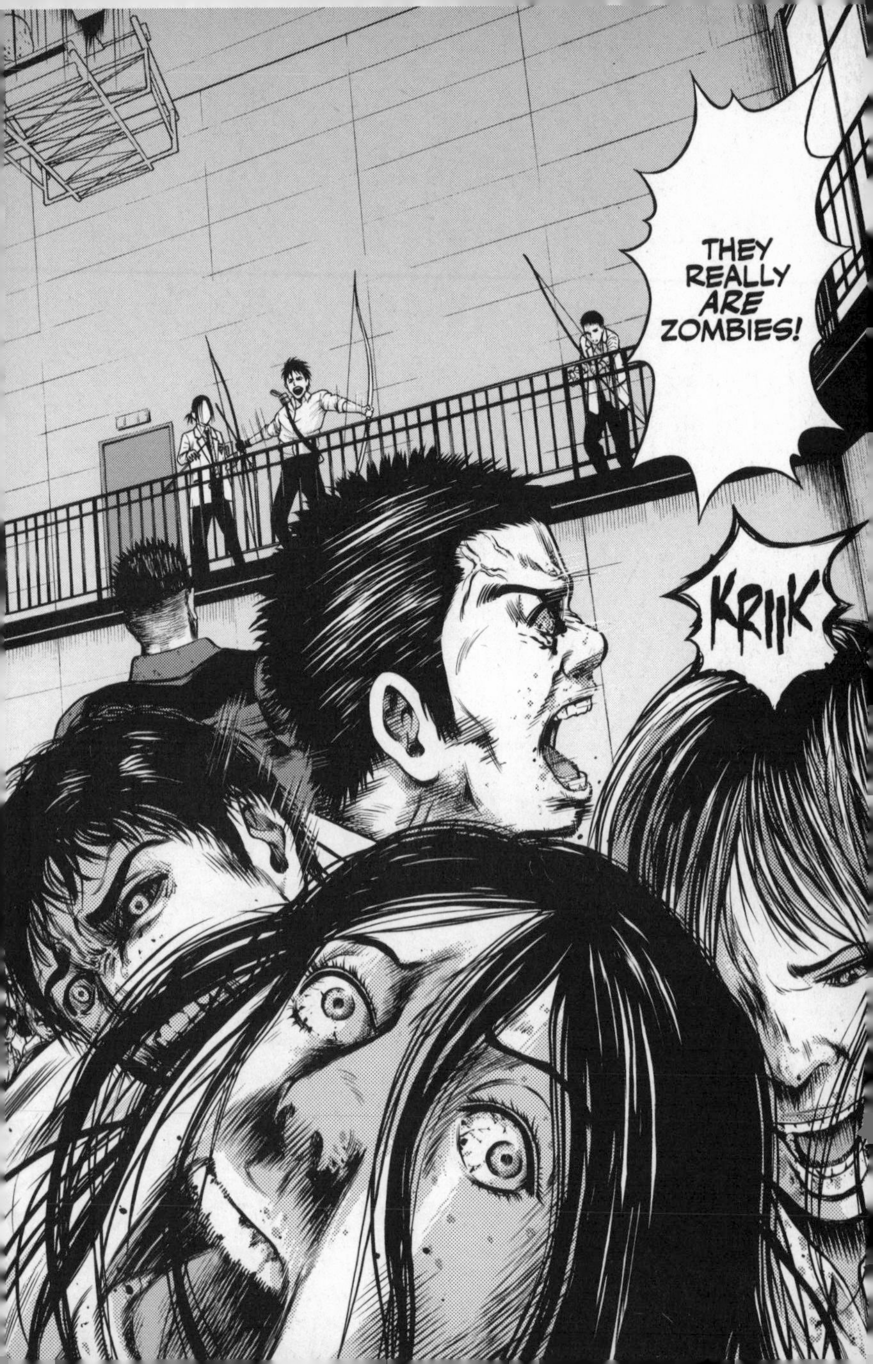
THEY REALLY *ARE* ZOMBIES!
KRIIK

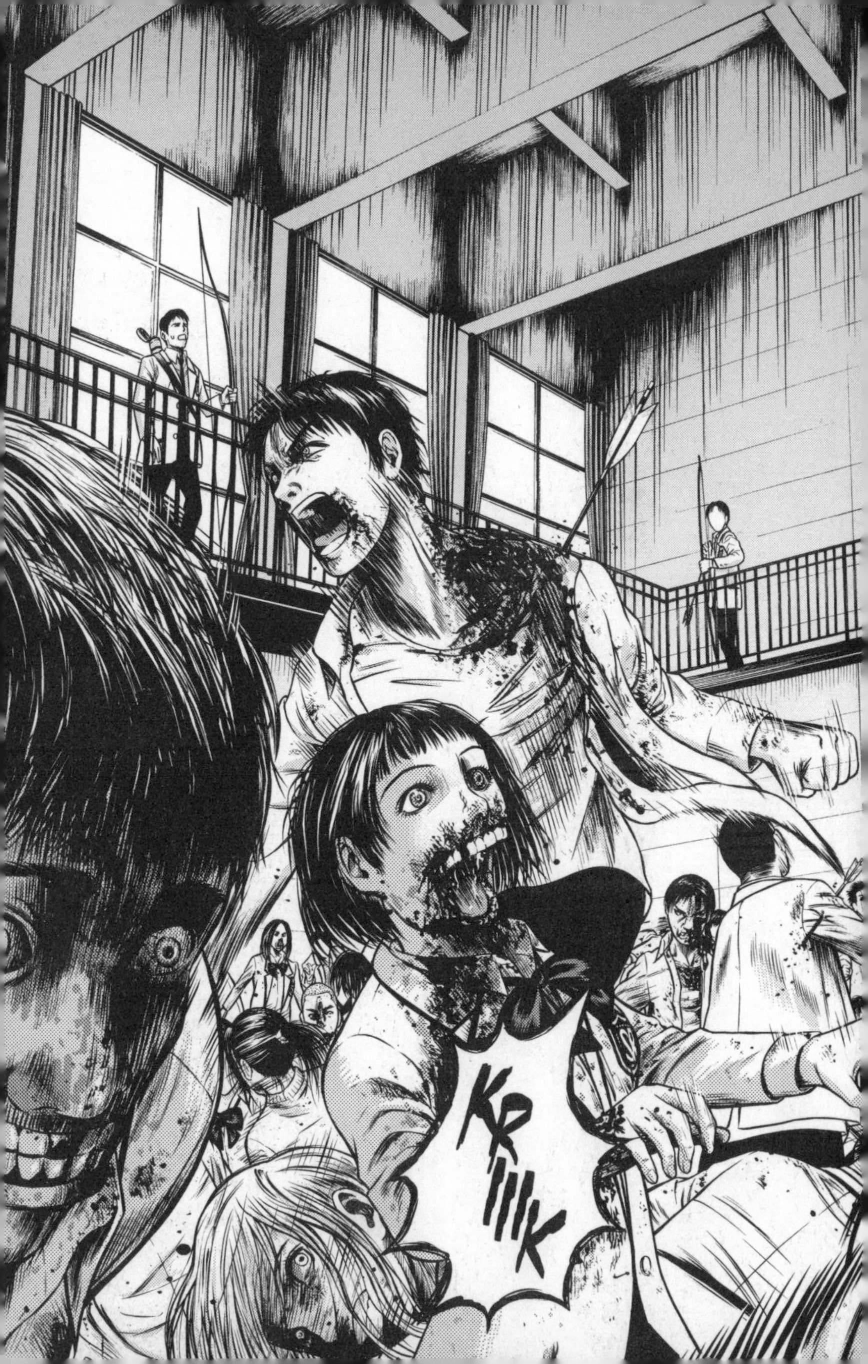
KRIIIK

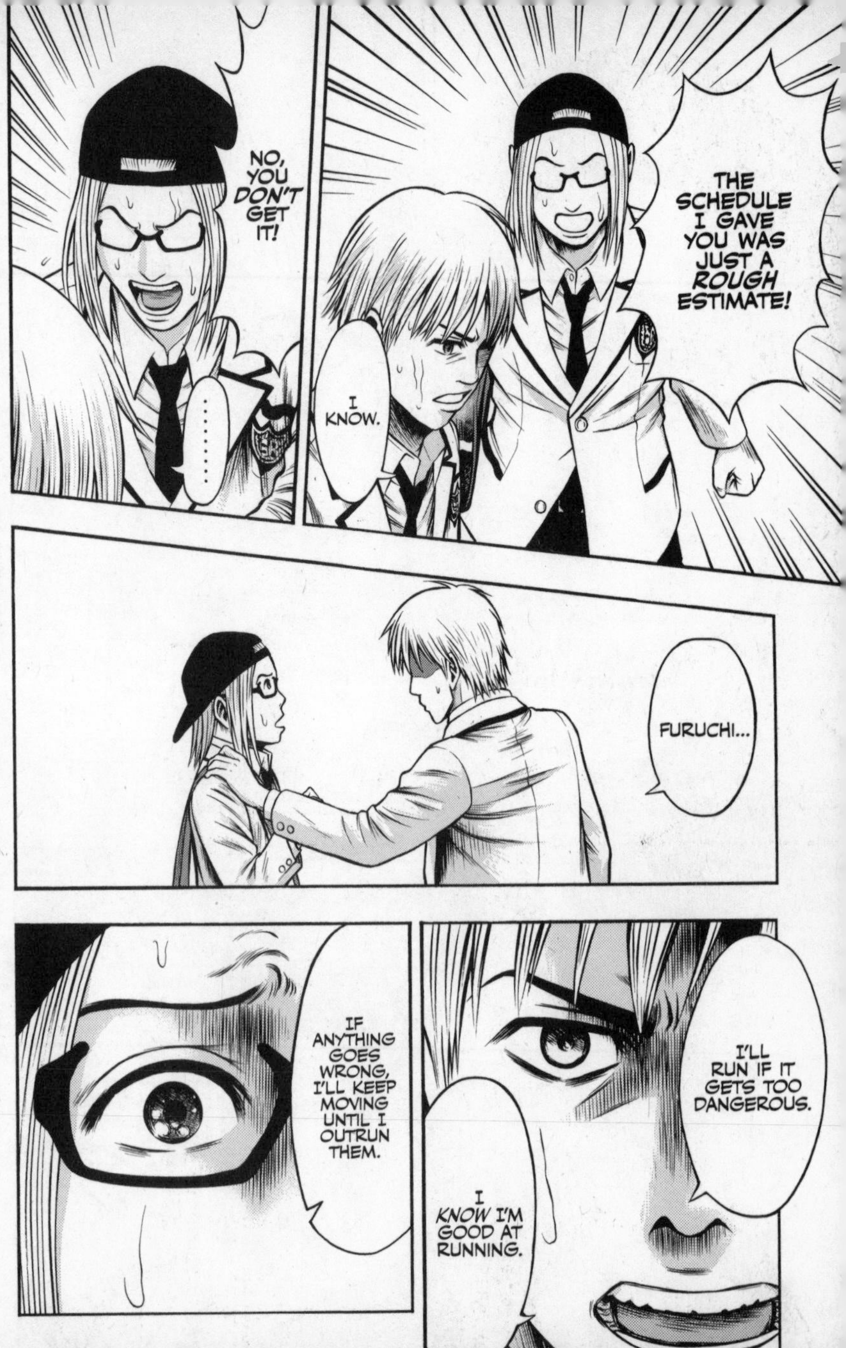
THE SCHEDULE I GAVE YOU WAS JUST A *ROUGH* ESTIMATE!
I KNOW.
NO, YOU *DON'T* GET IT!
......
FURUCHI...
I'LL RUN IF IT GETS TOO DANGEROUS.
I *KNOW* I'M GOOD AT RUNNING.
IF ANYTHING GOES WRONG, I'LL KEEP MOVING UNTIL I OUTRUN THEM.

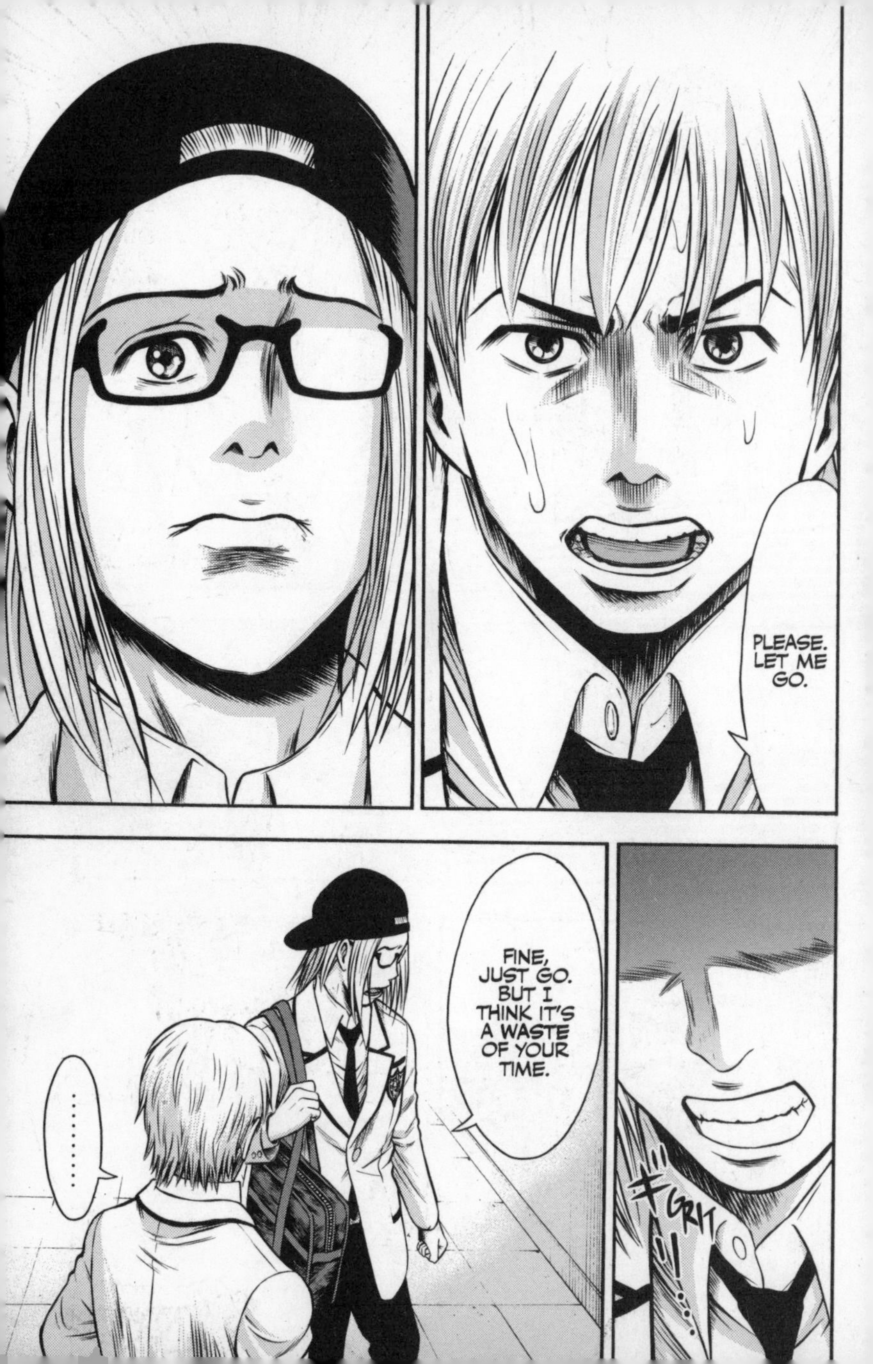
PLEASE. LET ME GO.
FINE, JUST GO. BUT I THINK IT'S A WASTE OF YOUR TIME.
GRIT
......

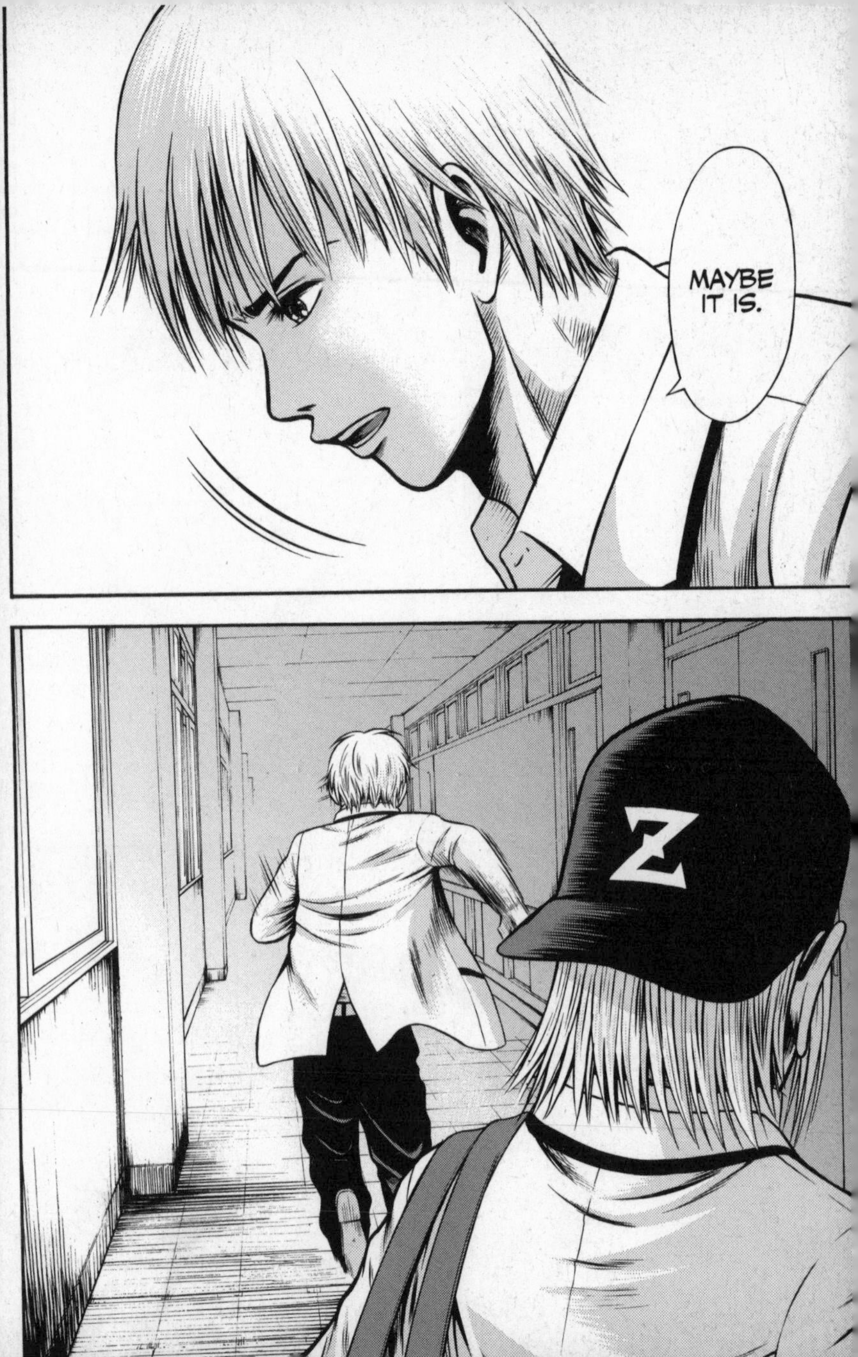
MAYBE IT IS.

HOUR OF THE ZOMBIE

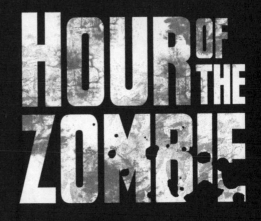

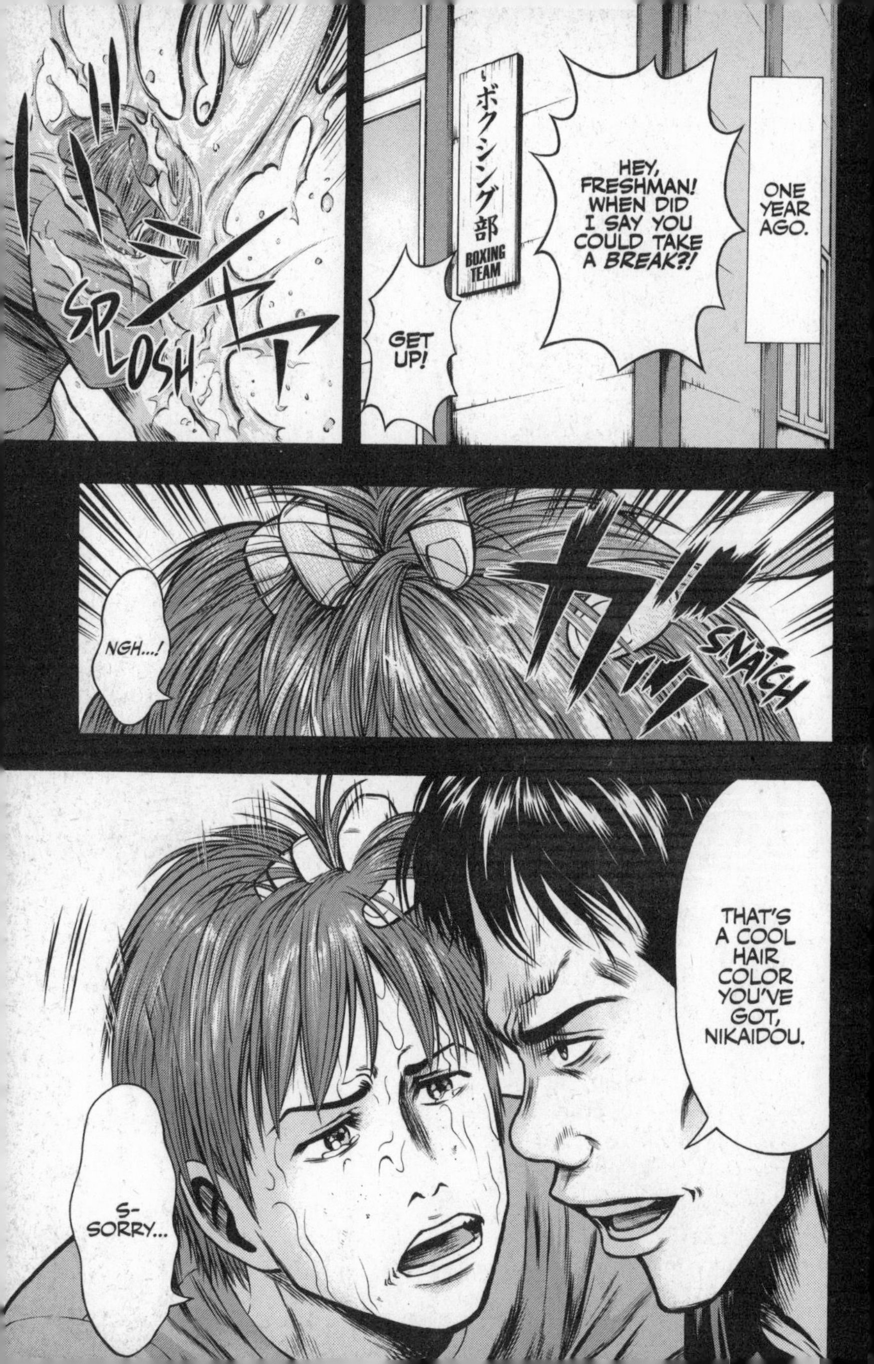
ONE YEAR AGO.
HEY, FRESHMAN! WHEN DID I SAY YOU COULD TAKE A *BREAK*?!
ボクシング部
BOXING TEAM
GET UP!
SPLOSH
SNATCH
NGH...!
THAT'S A COOL HAIR COLOR YOU'VE GOT, NIKAIDOU.
S-SORRY...

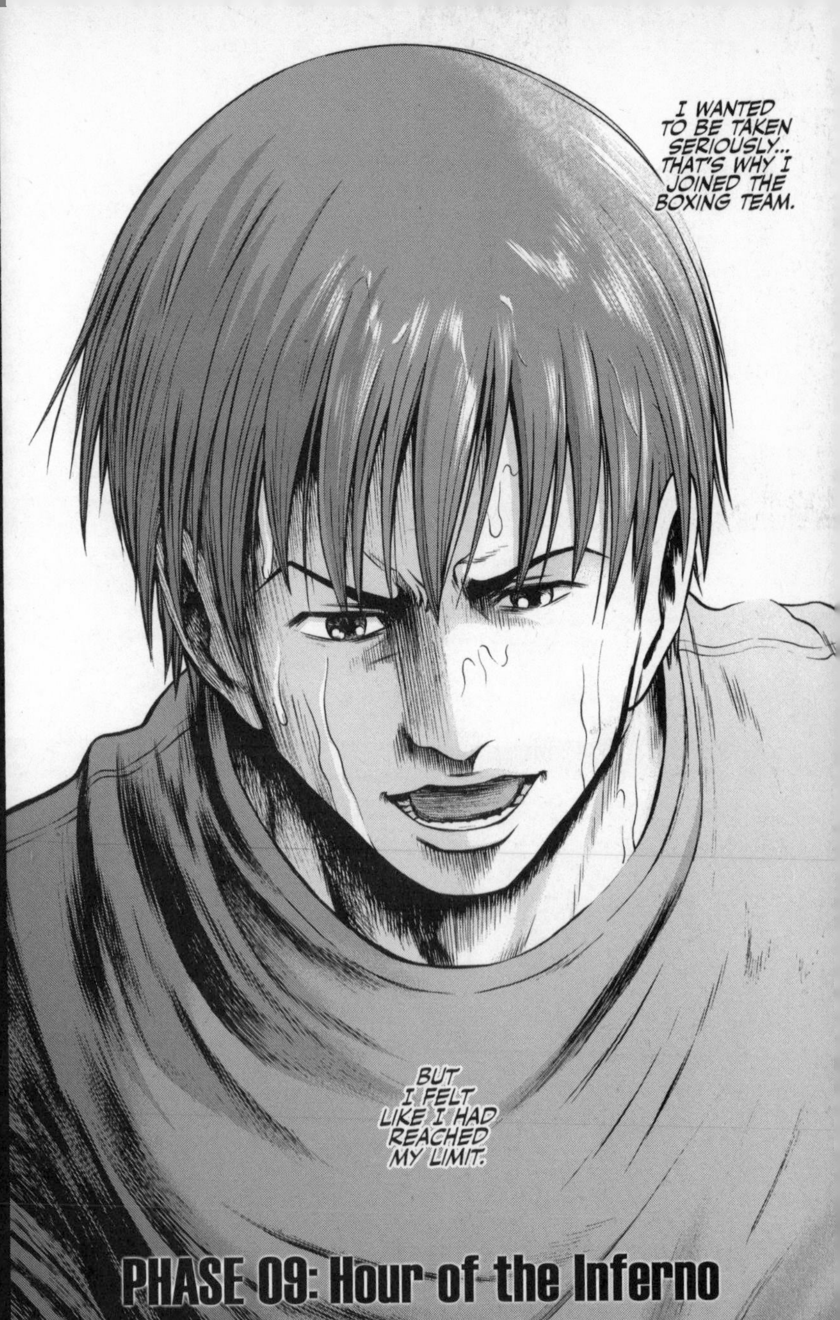
I WANTED TO BE TAKEN SERIOUSLY... THAT'S WHY I JOINED THE BOXING TEAM.
BUT I FELT LIKE I HAD REACHED MY LIMIT.

PHASE 09: Hour of the Inferno

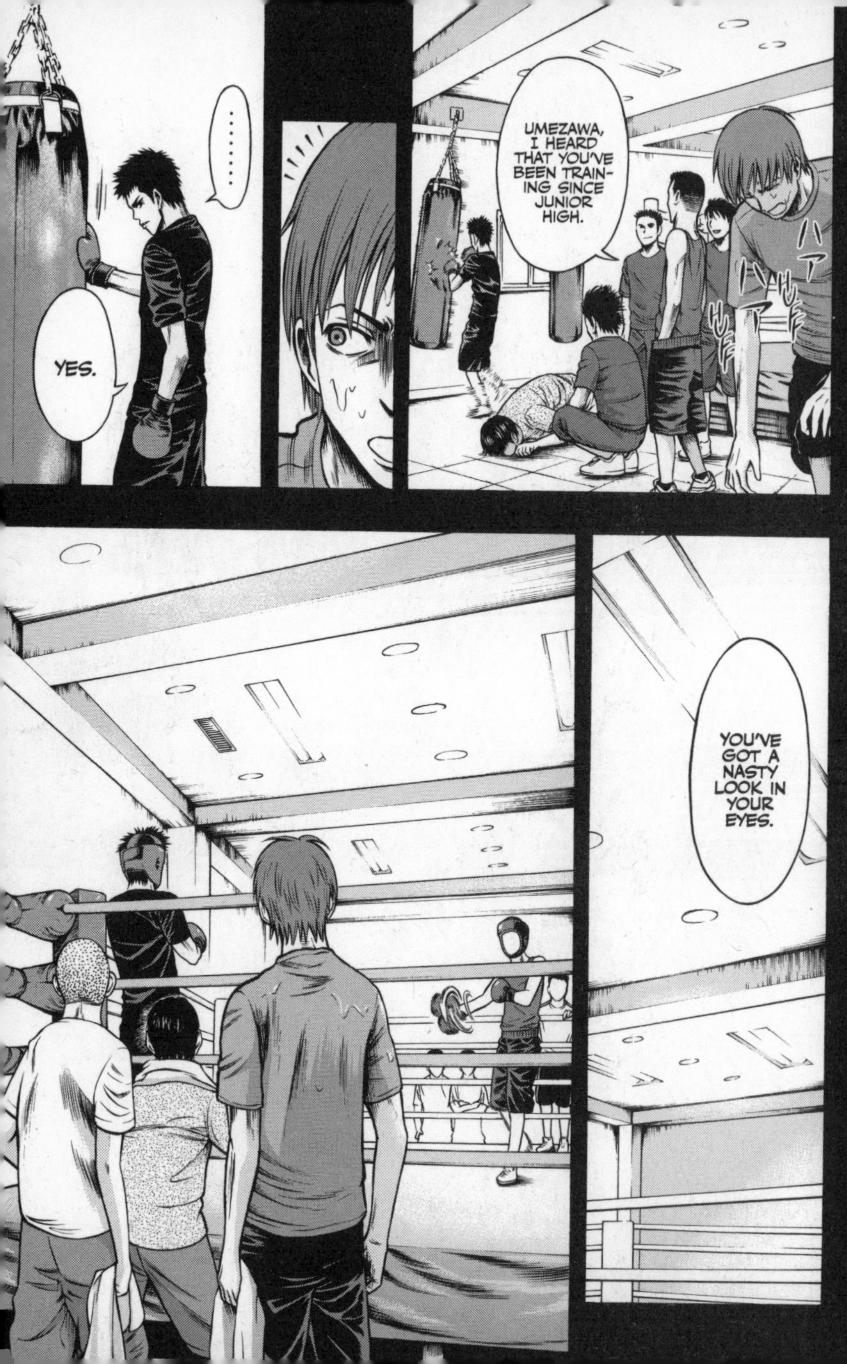
UMEZAWA, I HEARD THAT YOU'VE BEEN TRAINING SINCE JUNIOR HIGH.
......
YES.
YOU'VE GOT A NASTY LOOK IN YOUR EYES.

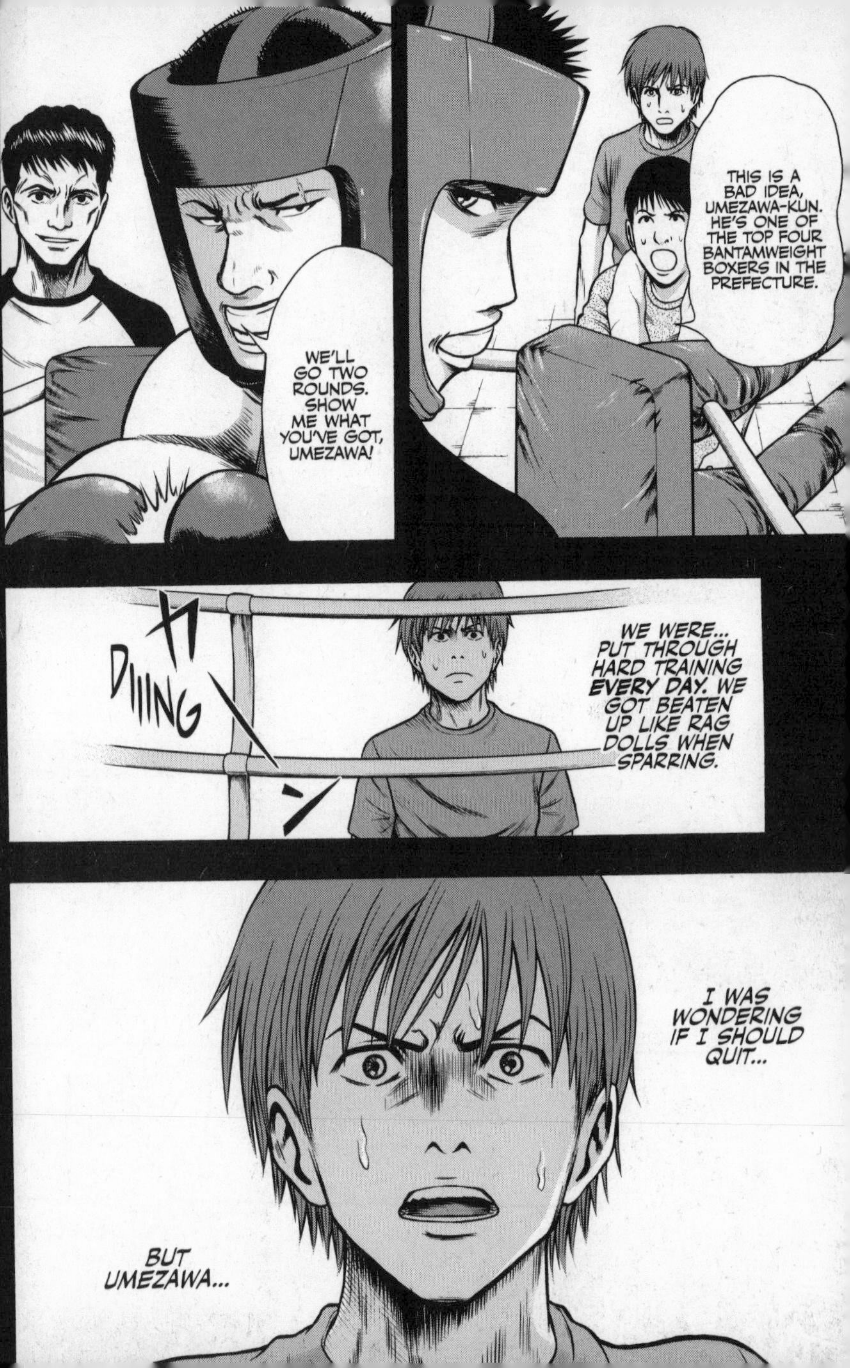
THIS IS A BAD IDEA, UMEZAWA-KUN. HE'S ONE OF THE TOP FOUR BANTAMWEIGHT BOXERS IN THE PREFECTURE.
WE'LL GO TWO ROUNDS. SHOW ME WHAT YOU'VE GOT, UMEZAWA!
WE WERE... PUT THROUGH HARD TRAINING EVERY DAY. WE GOT BEATEN UP LIKE RAG DOLLS WHEN SPARRING.
DIIING
I WAS WONDERING IF I SHOULD QUIT...
BUT UMEZAWA...

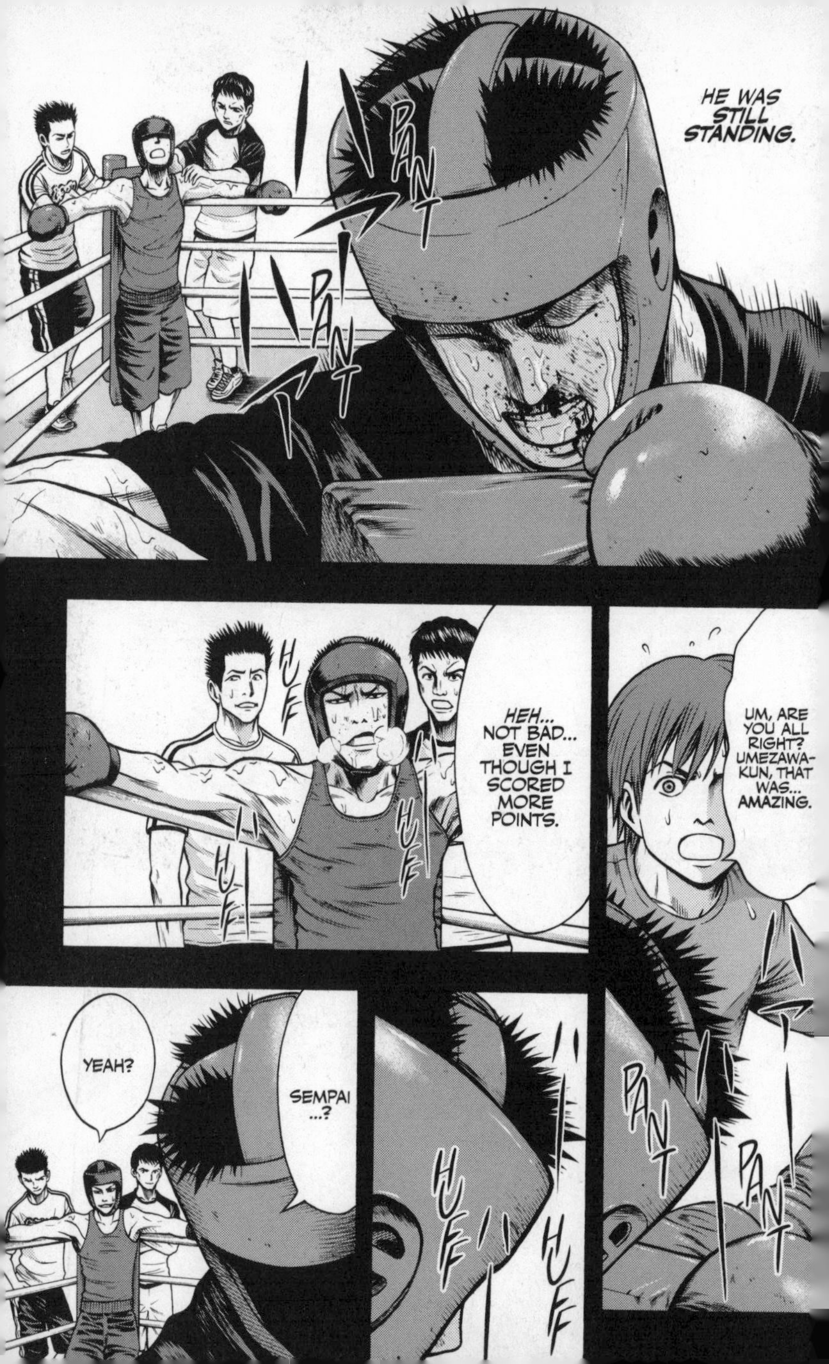
HE WAS STILL STANDING.
PANT
PANT
UM, ARE YOU ALL RIGHT? UMEZAWA-KUN, THAT WAS... AMAZING.
HEH... NOT BAD... EVEN THOUGH I SCORED MORE POINTS.
HUFF
HUFF
HUFF
PANT
PANT
HUFF
HUFF
SEMPAI ...?
YEAH?

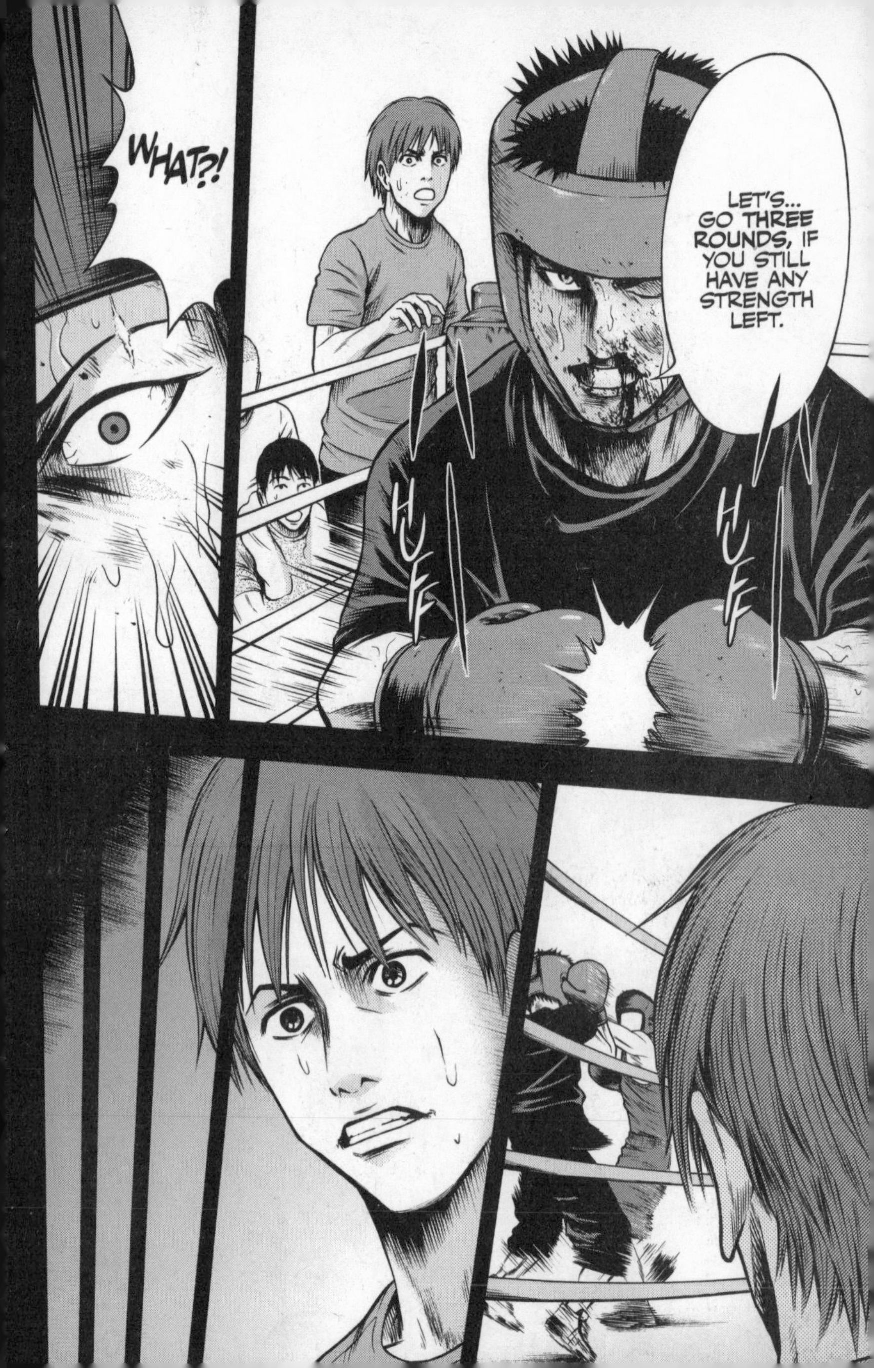
LET'S... GO THREE ROUNDS, IF YOU STILL HAVE ANY STRENGTH LEFT.
HUFF
HUFF
WHAT?!

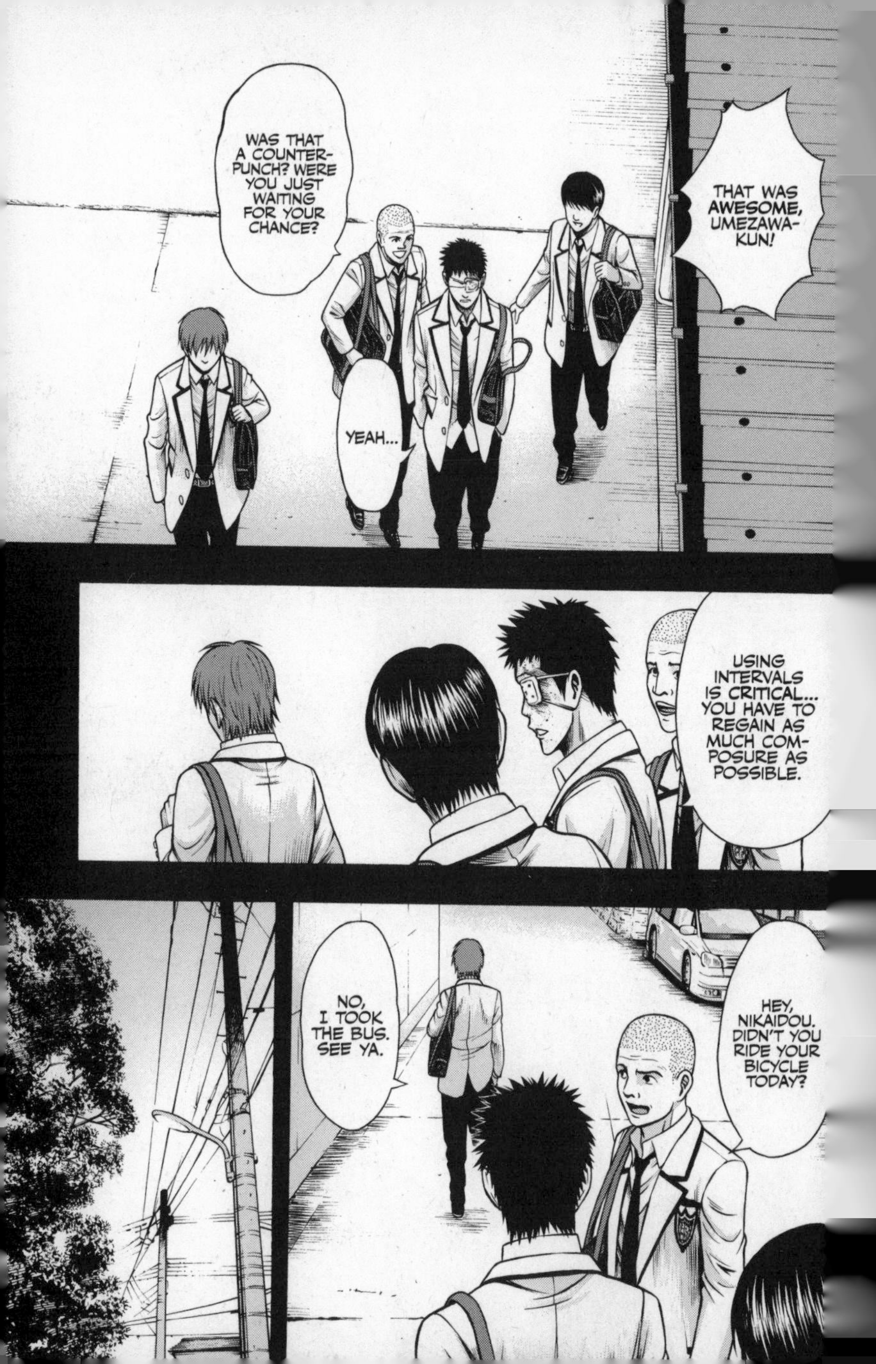
THAT WAS AWESOME, UMEZAWA-KUN!
WAS THAT A COUNTER-PUNCH? WERE YOU JUST WAITING FOR YOUR CHANCE?
YEAH...
USING INTERVALS IS CRITICAL... YOU HAVE TO REGAIN AS MUCH COM-POSURE AS POSSIBLE.
HEY, NIKAIDOU. DIDN'T YOU RIDE YOUR BICYCLE TODAY?
NO, I TOOK THE BUS. SEE YA.

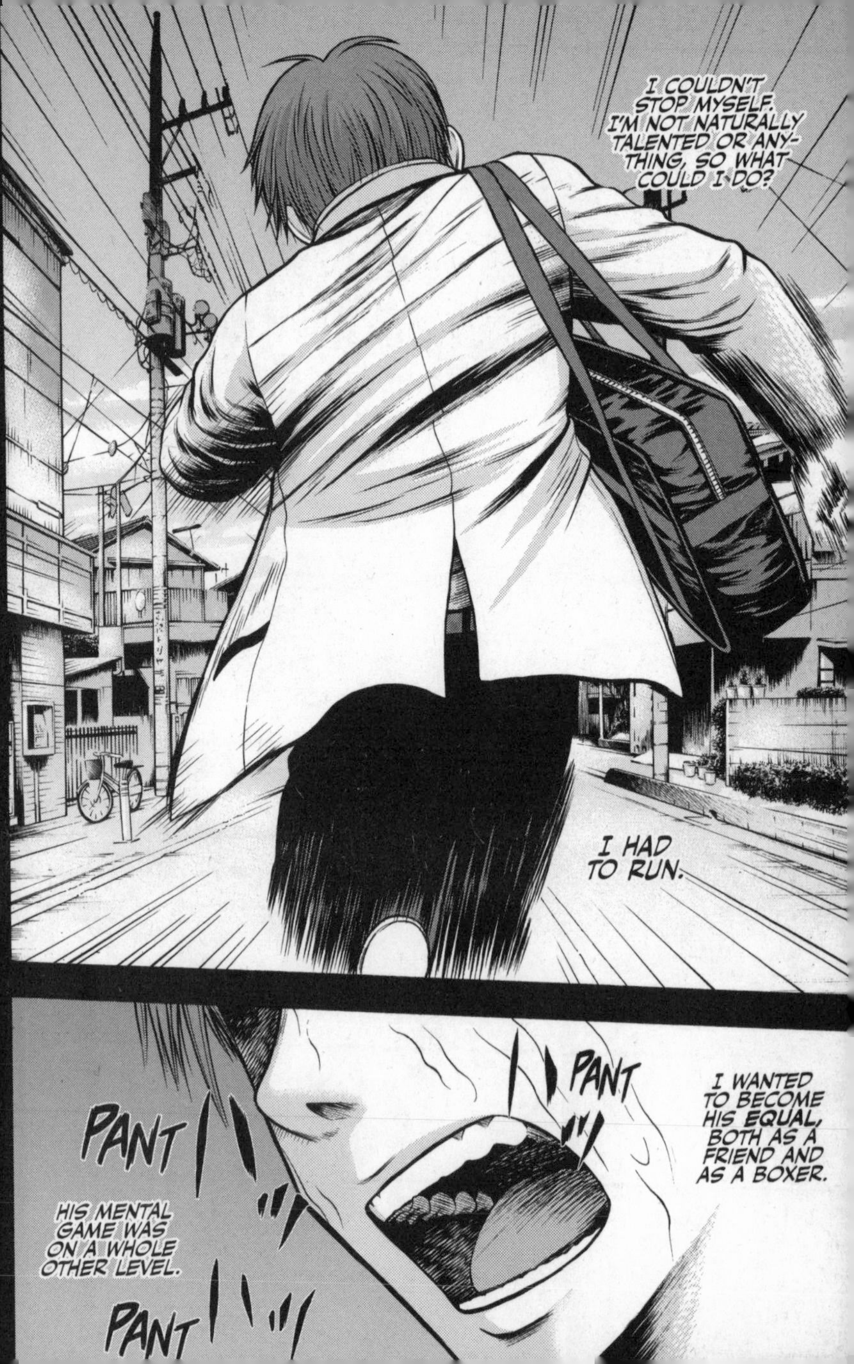
I COULDN'T STOP MYSELF. I'M NOT NATURALLY TALENTED OR ANY-THING, SO WHAT COULD I DO?
I HAD TO RUN.
I WANTED TO BECOME HIS EQUAL, BOTH AS A FRIEND AND AS A BOXER.
PANT
PANT
HIS MENTAL GAME WAS ON A WHOLE OTHER LEVEL.
PANT

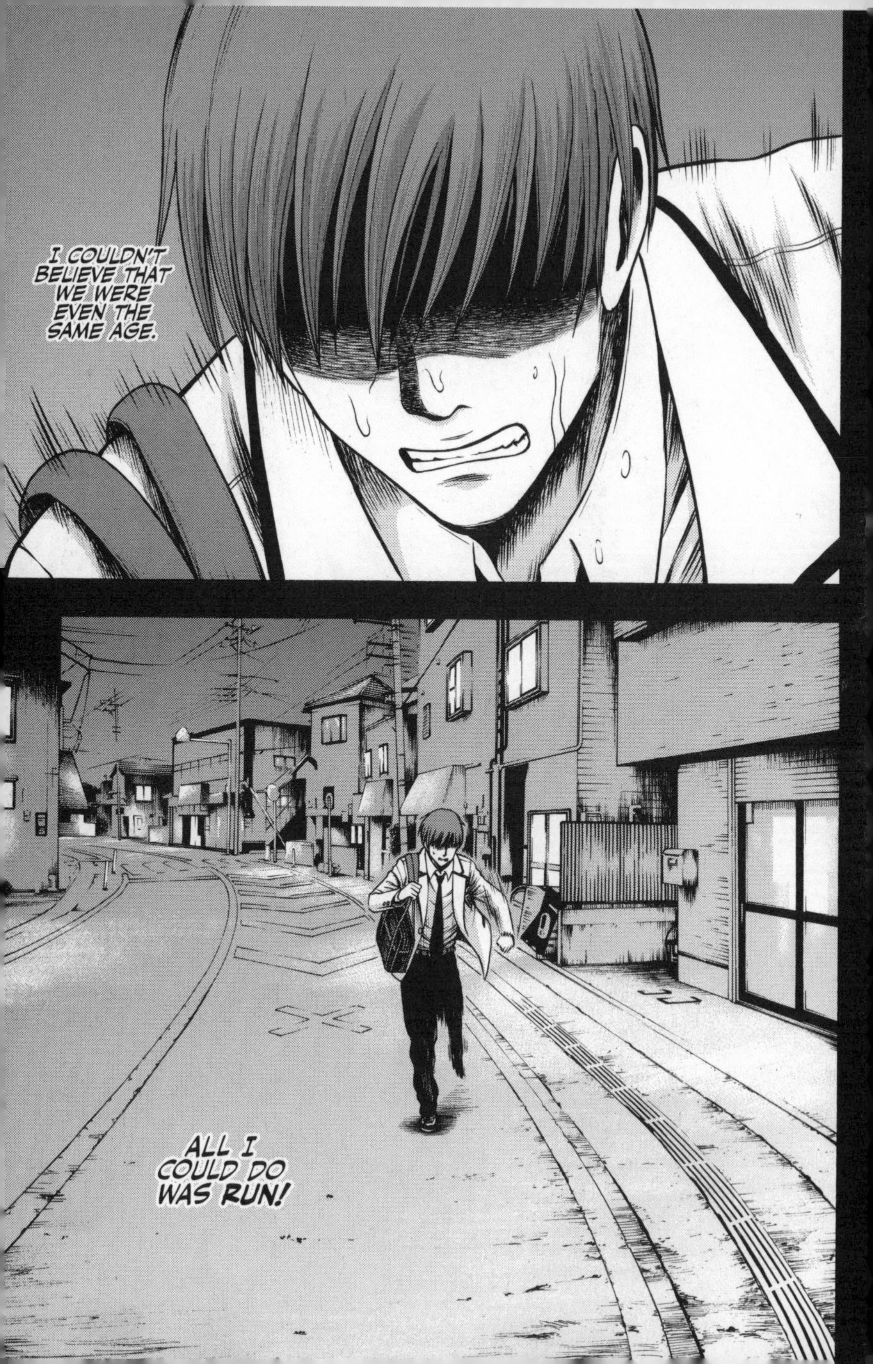
I COULDN'T BELIEVE THAT WE WERE EVEN THE SAME AGE.
ALL I COULD DO WAS RUN!

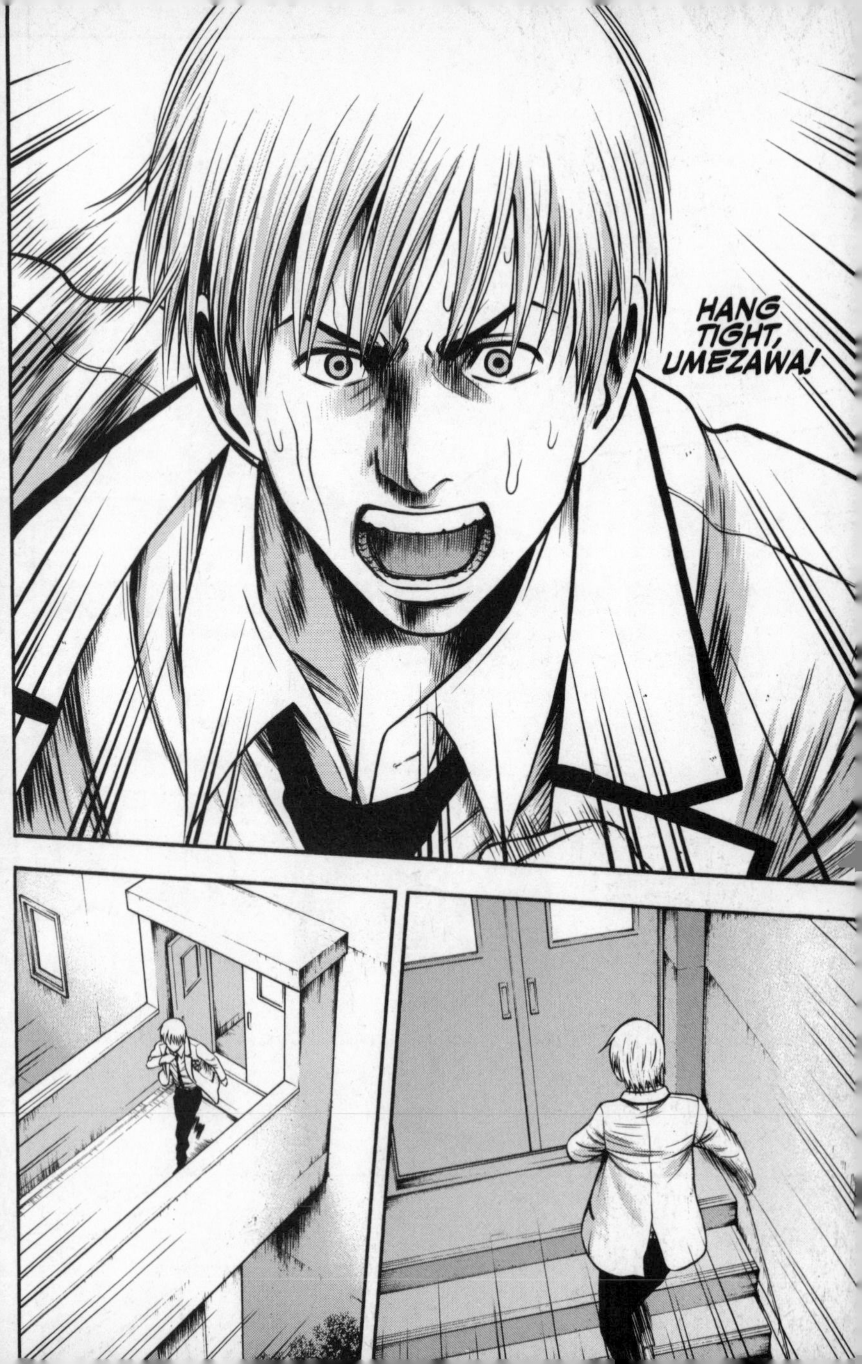
HANG TIGHT, UMEZAWA!

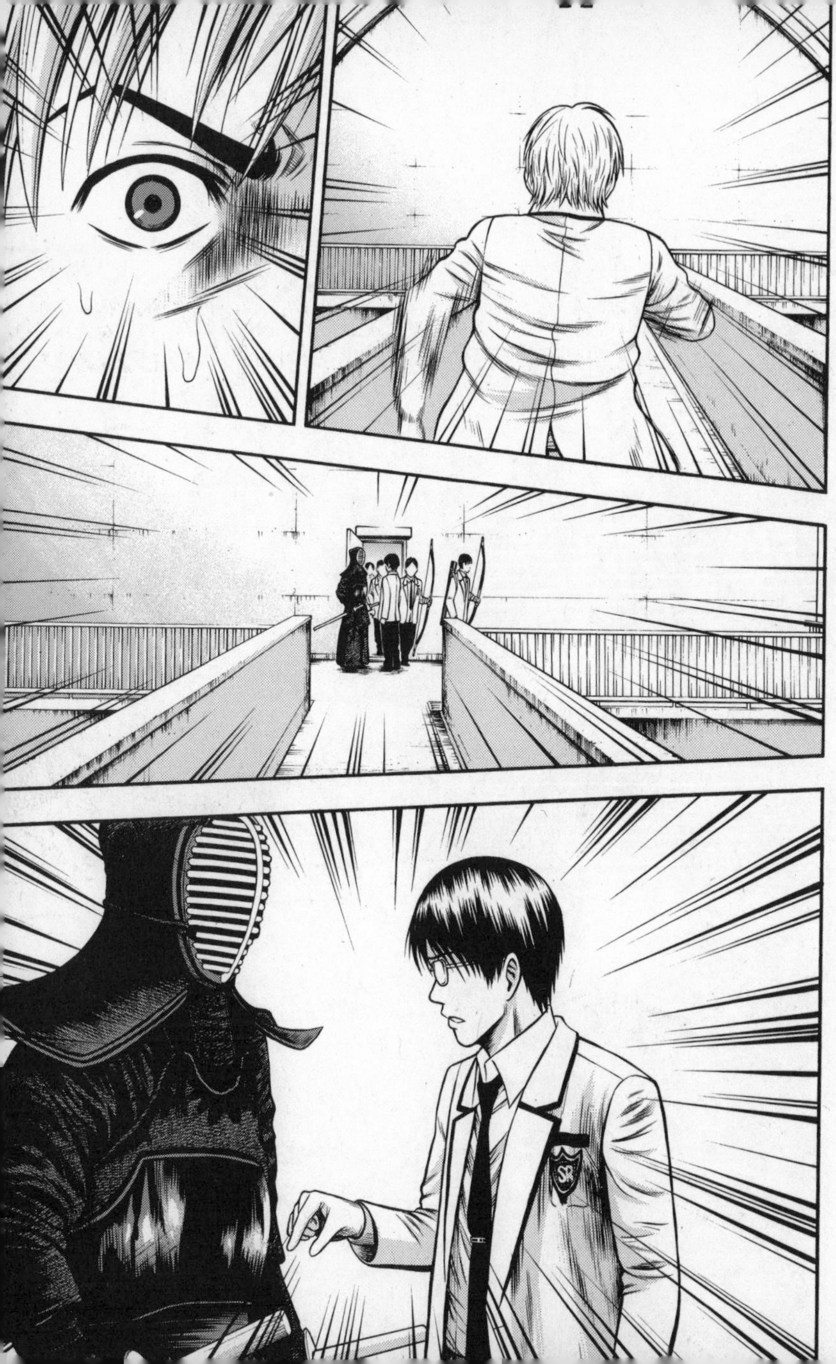

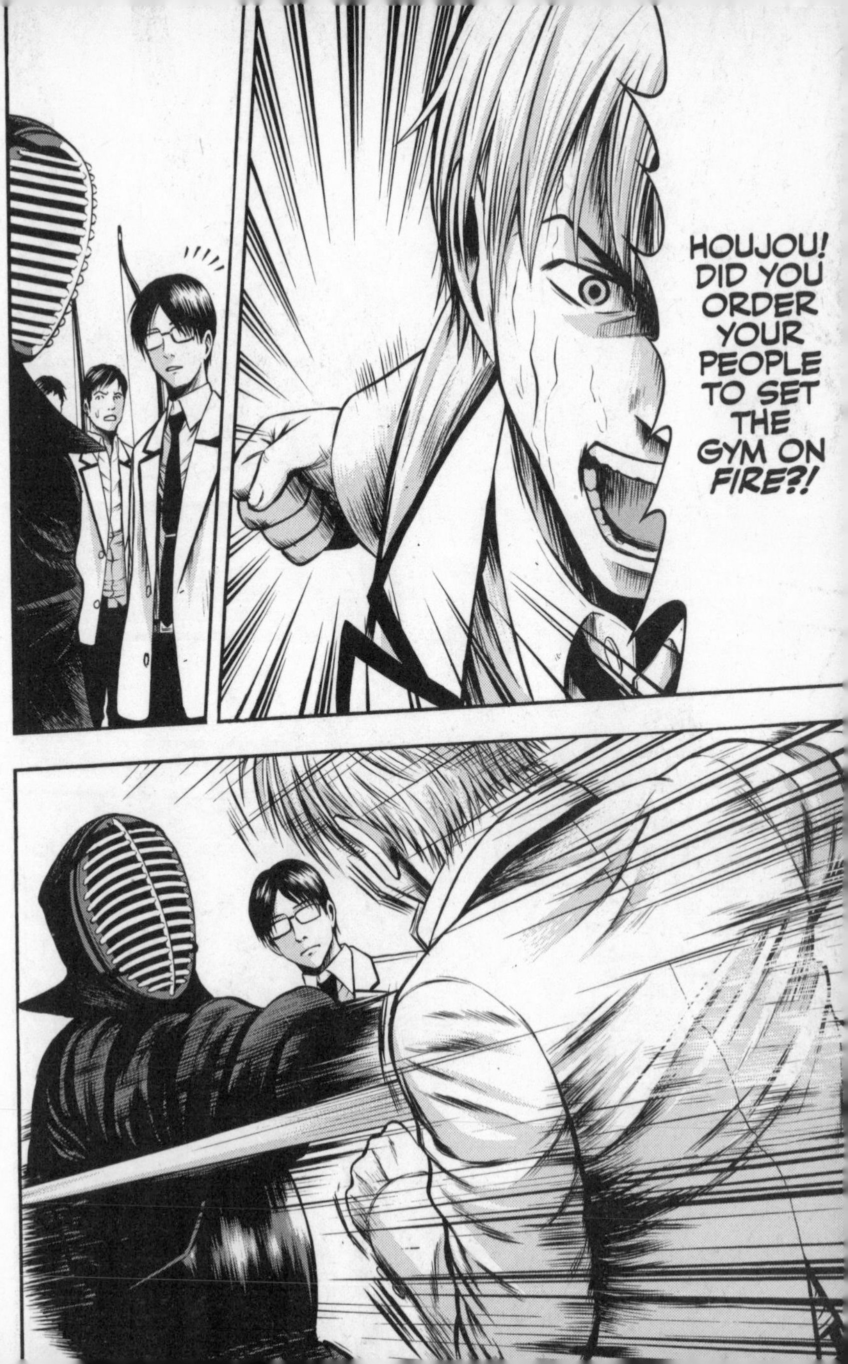
HOUJOU! DID YOU ORDER YOUR PEOPLE TO SET THE GYM ON FIRE?!

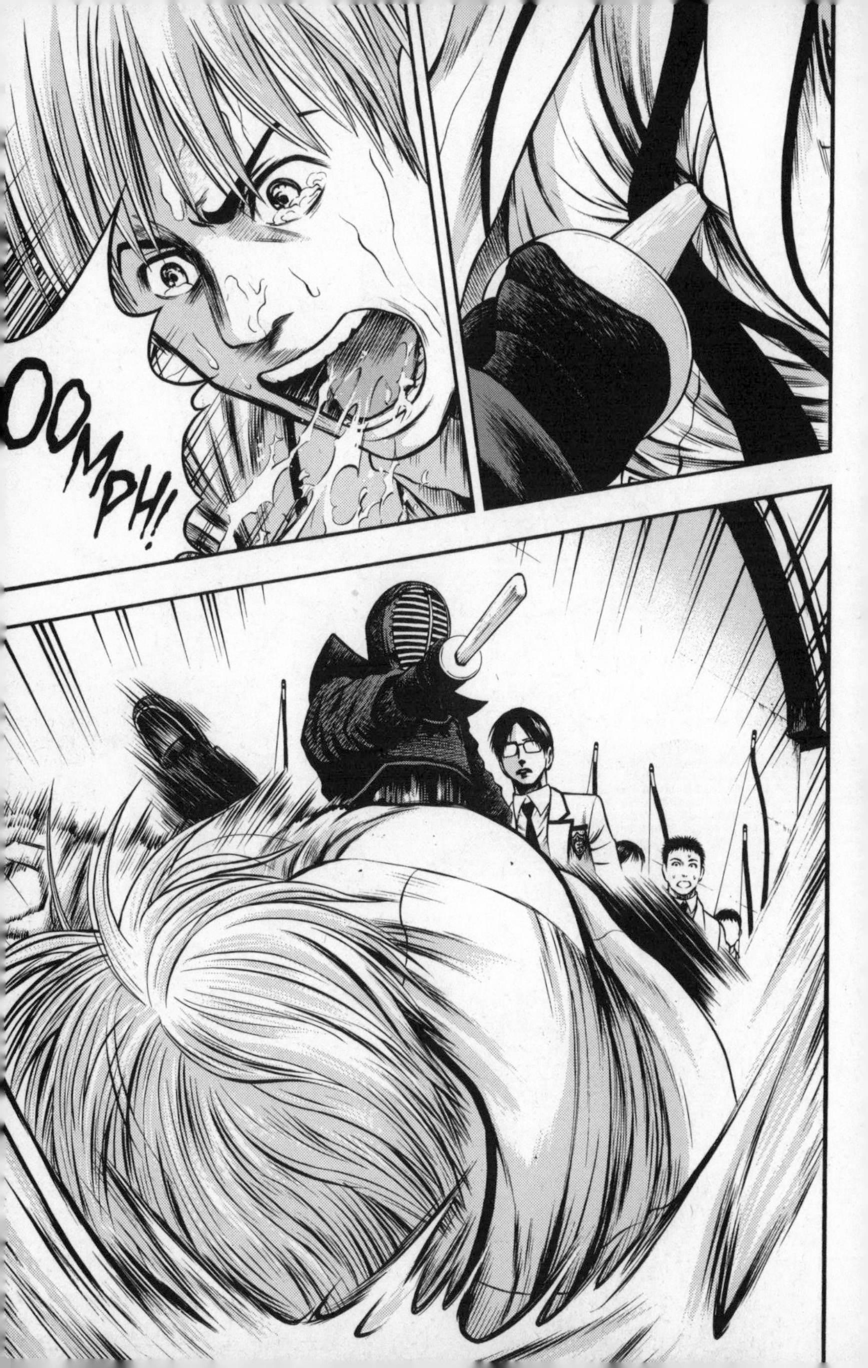
OOMPH!!

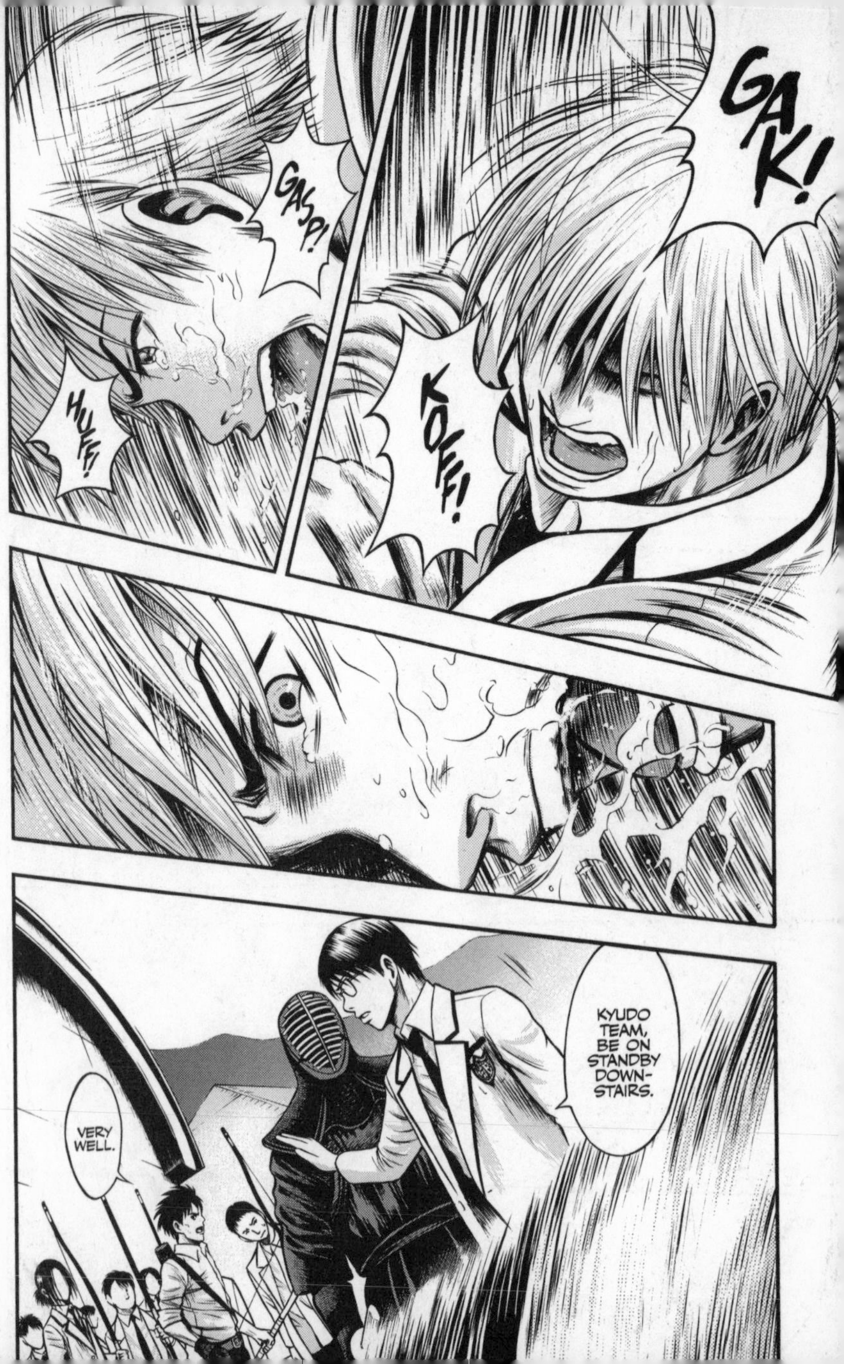
GAK!
KOFF!
GASP!
HUFF!
KYUDO TEAM, BE ON STANDBY DOWN-STAIRS.
VERY WELL.

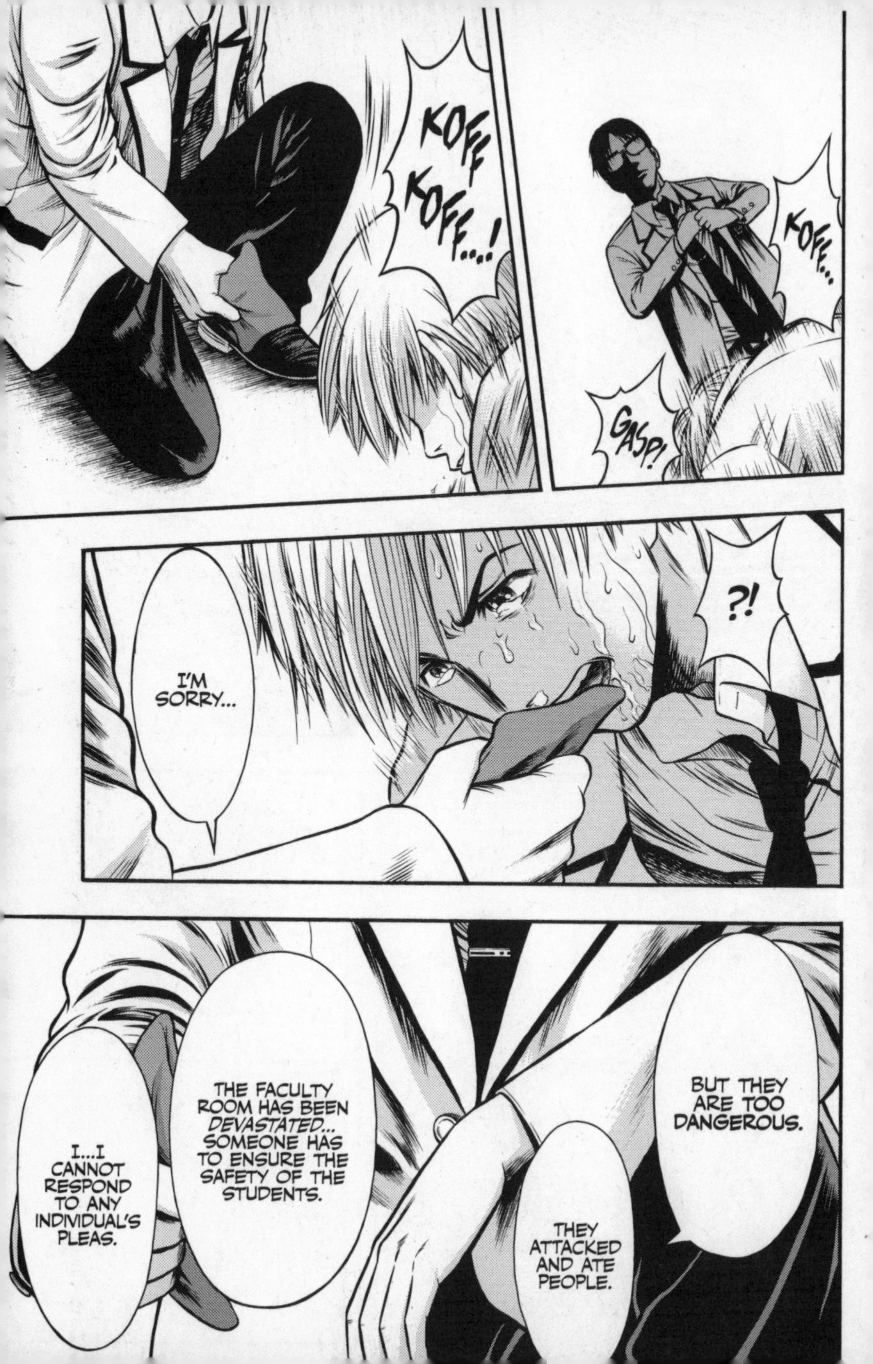
KOFF...
GASP!
KOFF KOFF...!
?!
I'M SORRY...
BUT THEY ARE TOO DANGEROUS.
THEY ATTACKED AND ATE PEOPLE.
THE FACULTY ROOM HAS BEEN *DEVASTATED*... SOMEONE HAS TO ENSURE THE SAFETY OF THE STUDENTS.
I...I CANNOT RESPOND TO ANY INDIVIDUAL'S PLEAS.

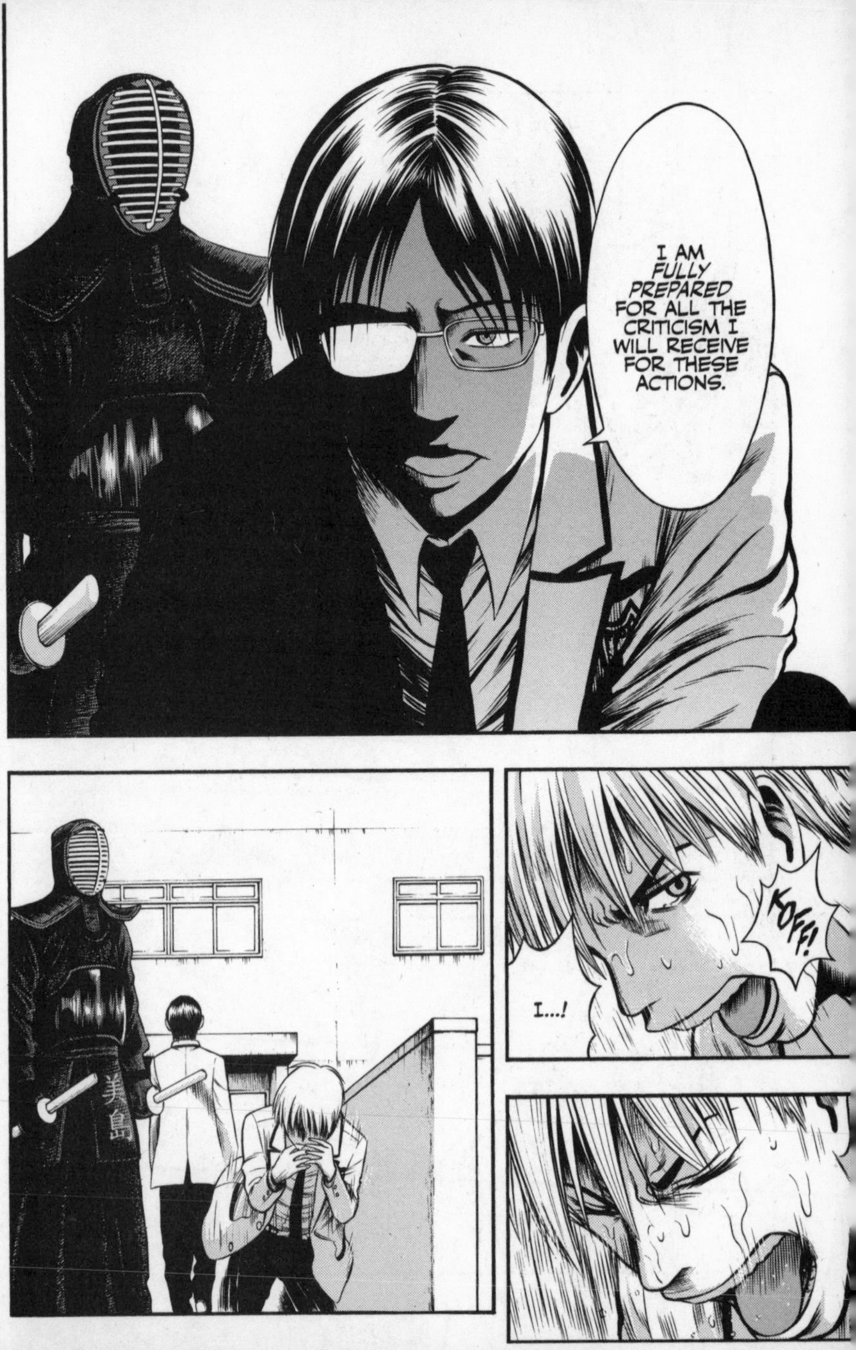
I AM FULLY PREPARED FOR ALL THE CRITICISM I WILL RECEIVE FOR THESE ACTIONS.
KOFF!
I...!
美島

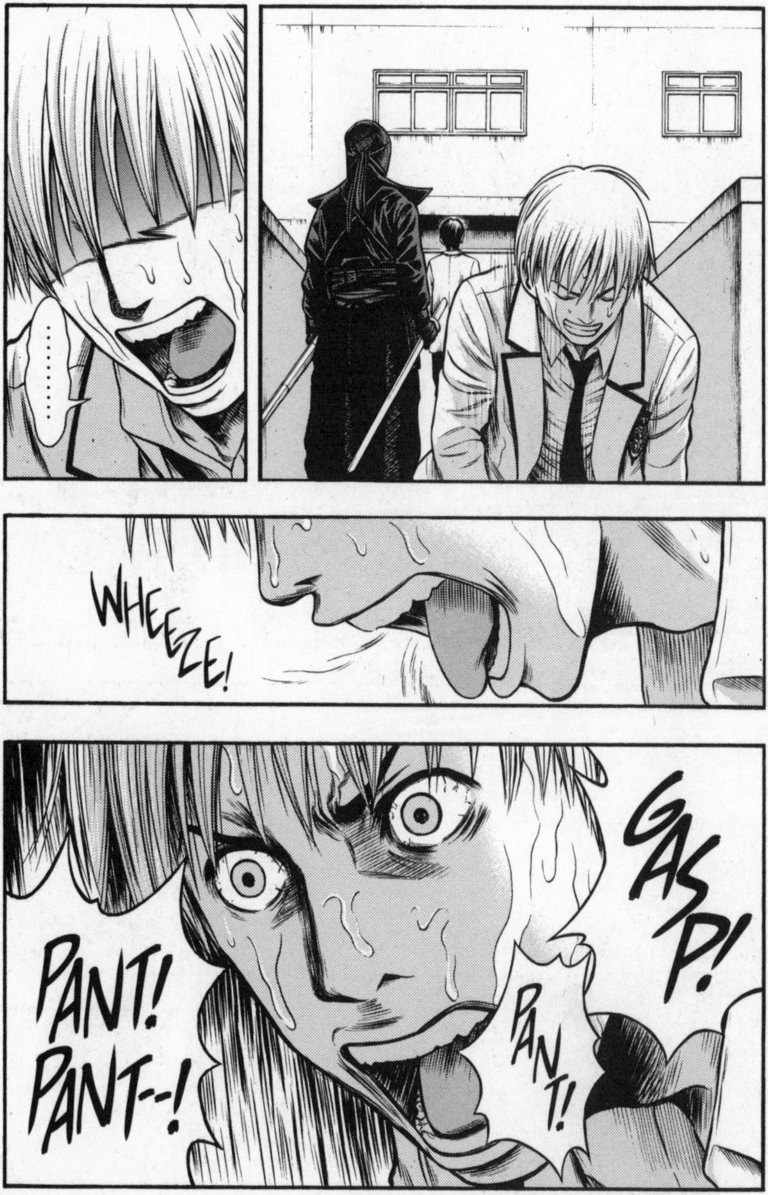
......
WHEEZE!
GASP!
PANT!
PANT! PANT--!

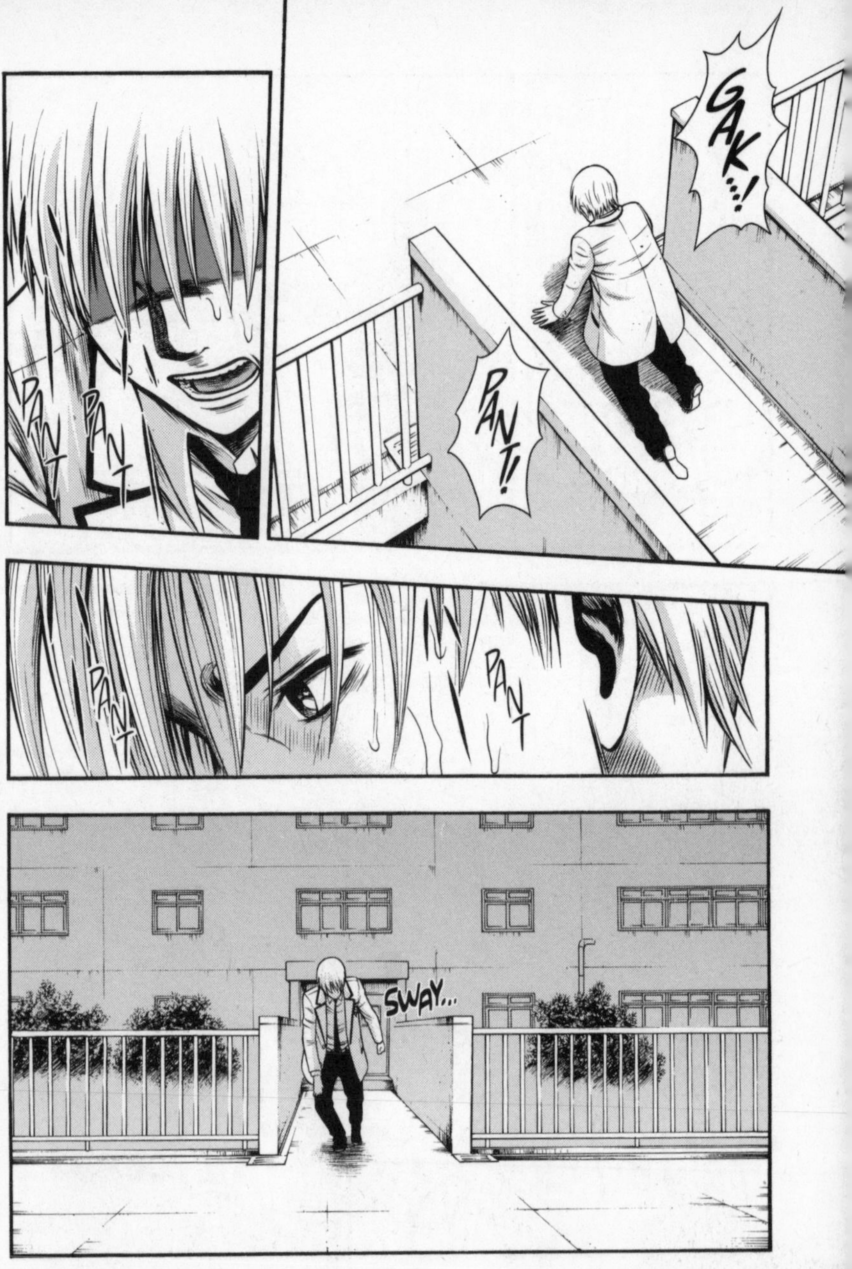

GAK...!
PANT!!
PANT
PANT
PANT
PANT
SWAY...

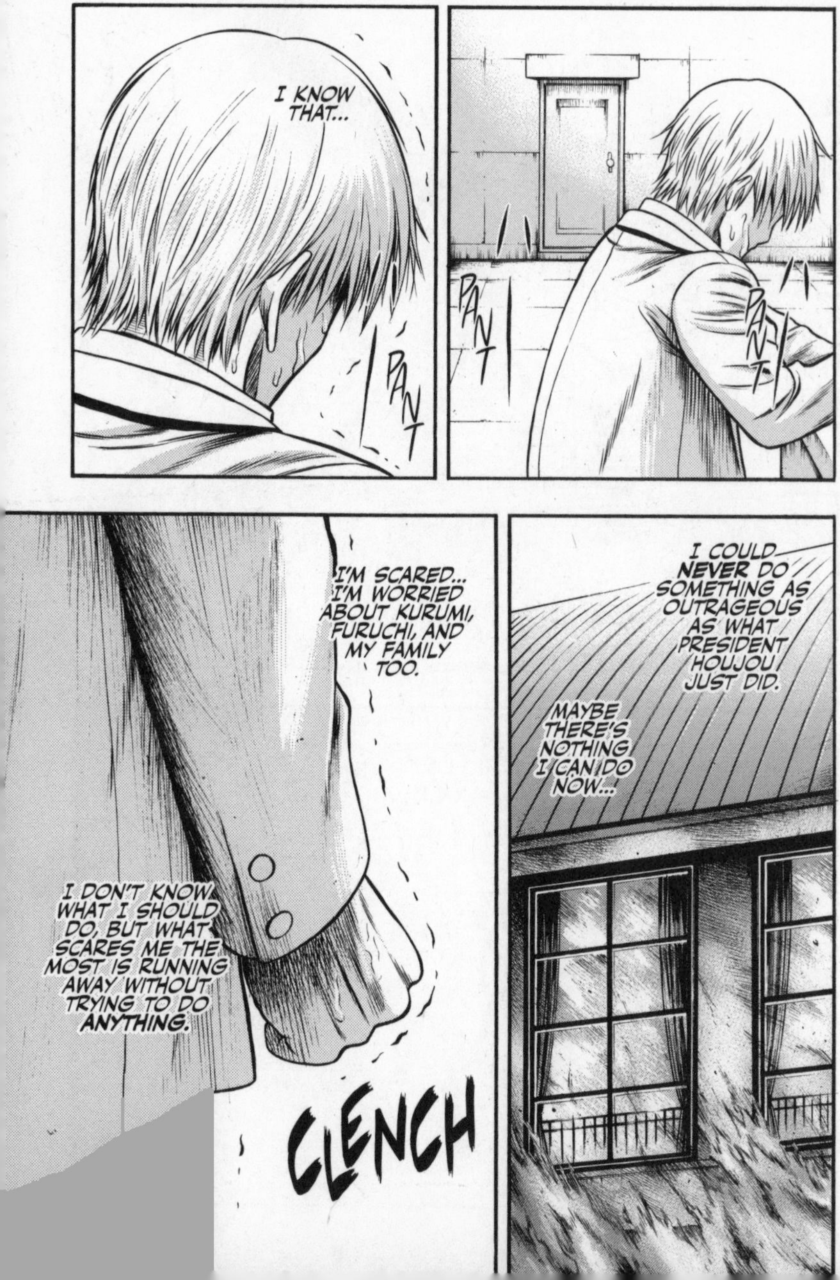
PANT
PANT
I KNOW THAT...
PANT
I COULD NEVER DO SOMETHING AS OUTRAGEOUS AS WHAT PRESIDENT HOUJOU JUST DID.
MAYBE THERE'S NOTHING I CAN DO NOW...
I'M SCARED... I'M WORRIED ABOUT KURUMI, FURUCHI, AND MY FAMILY TOO.
I DON'T KNOW WHAT I SHOULD DO, BUT WHAT SCARES ME THE MOST IS RUNNING AWAY WITHOUT TRYING TO DO ANYTHING.
CLENCH

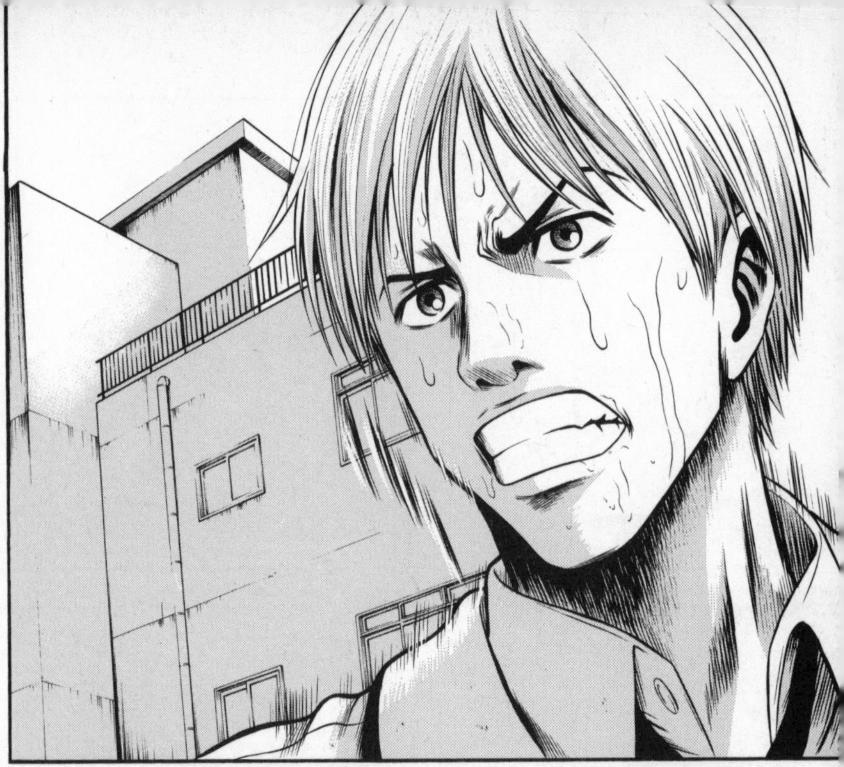
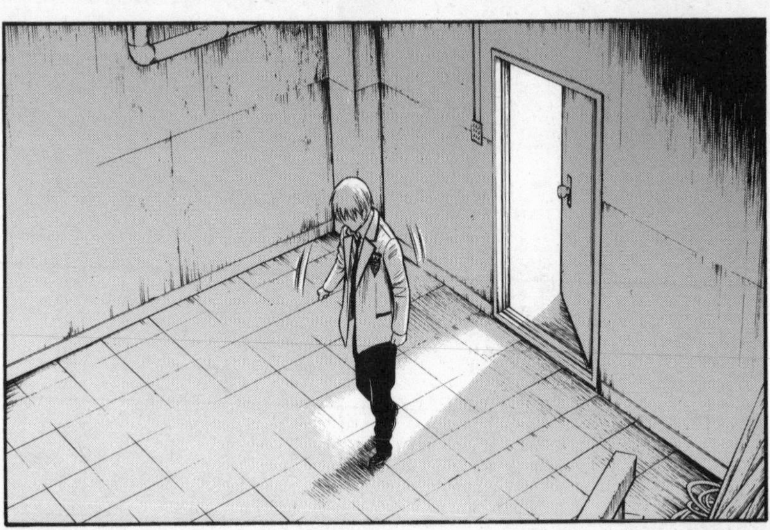

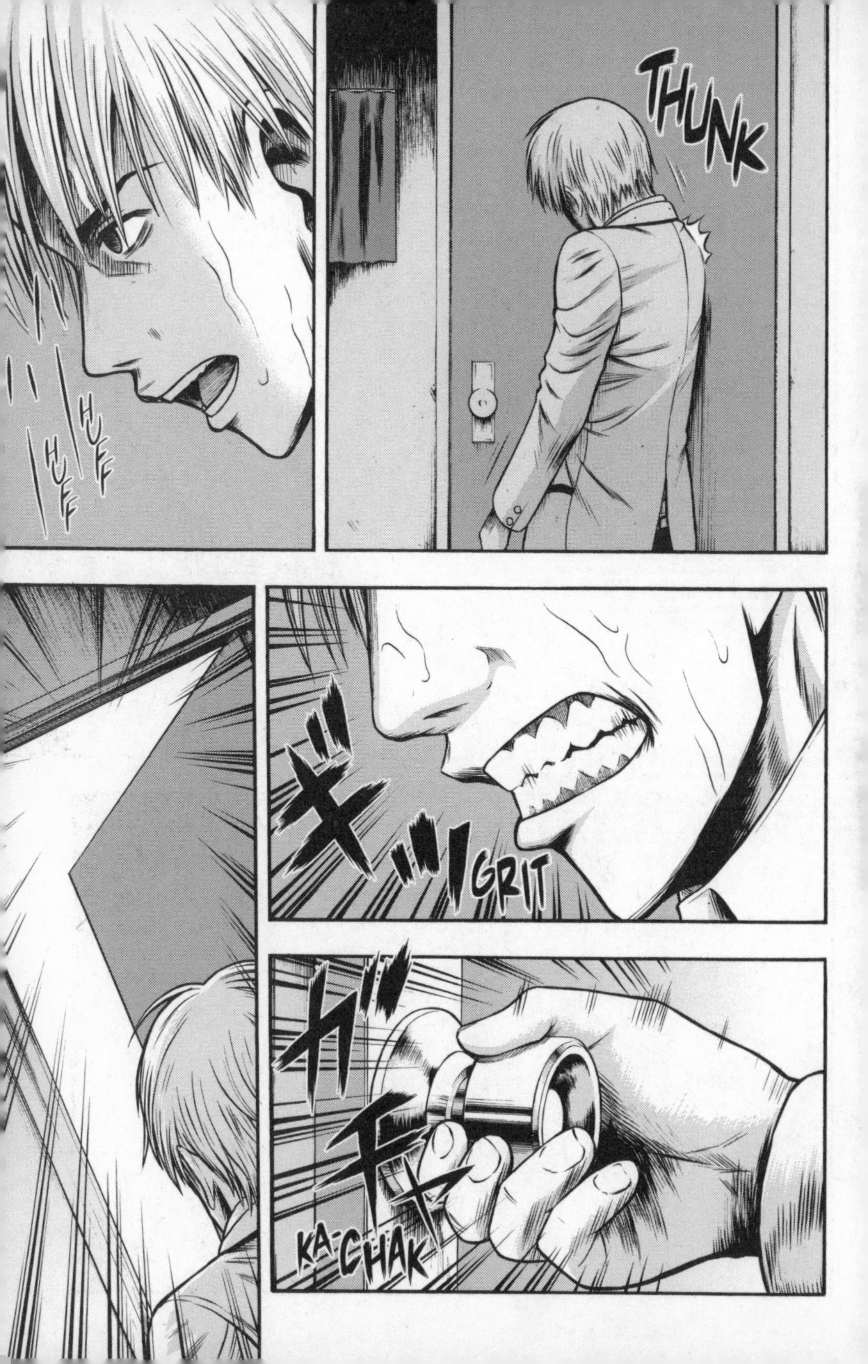
THUNK
HUFF
HUFF
GRIT
KA-CHAK

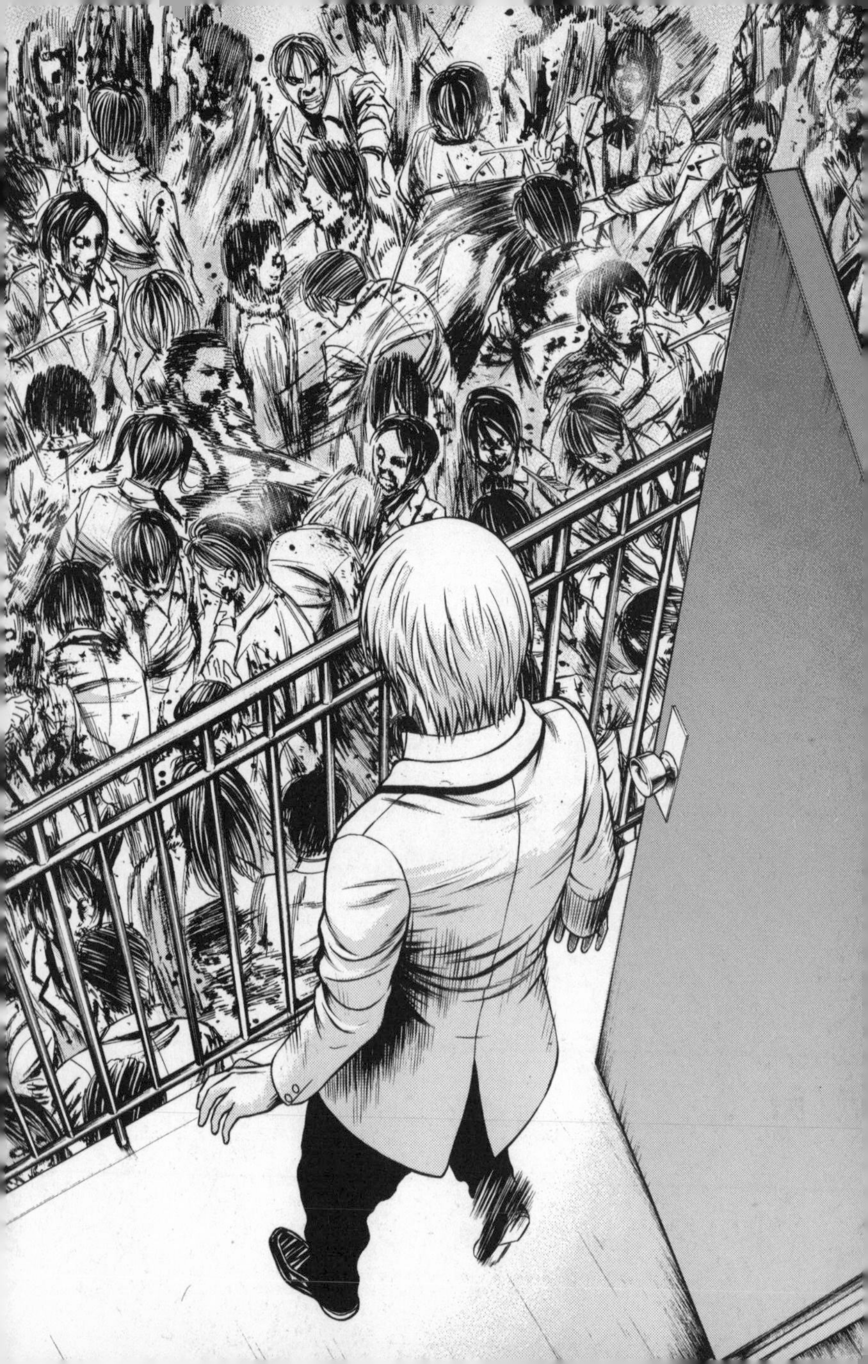

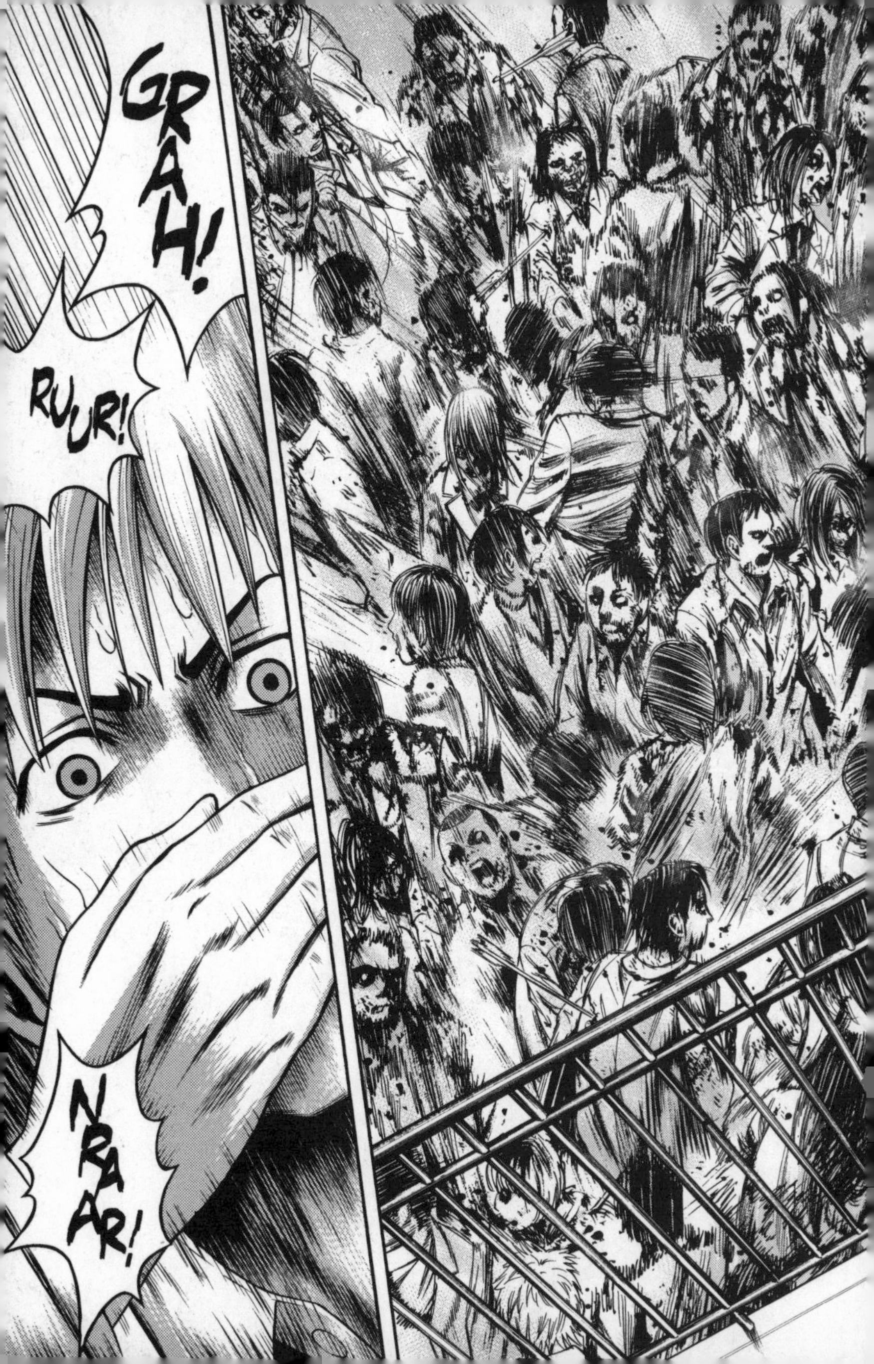
GRAH!
RUUR!
NRAAR!

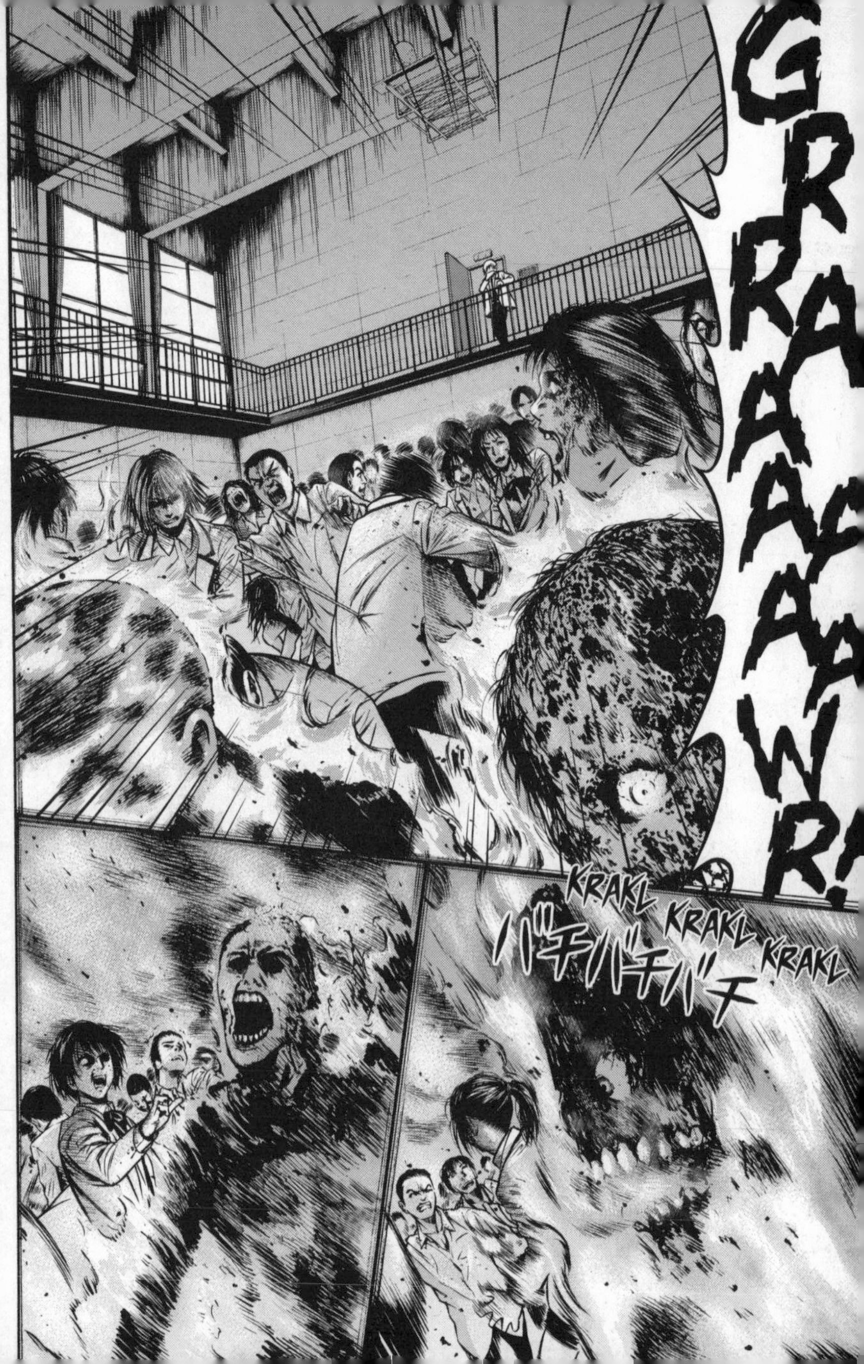
GRRAAAAAAWR!
KRAKL KRAKL KRAKL
バチバチバチ

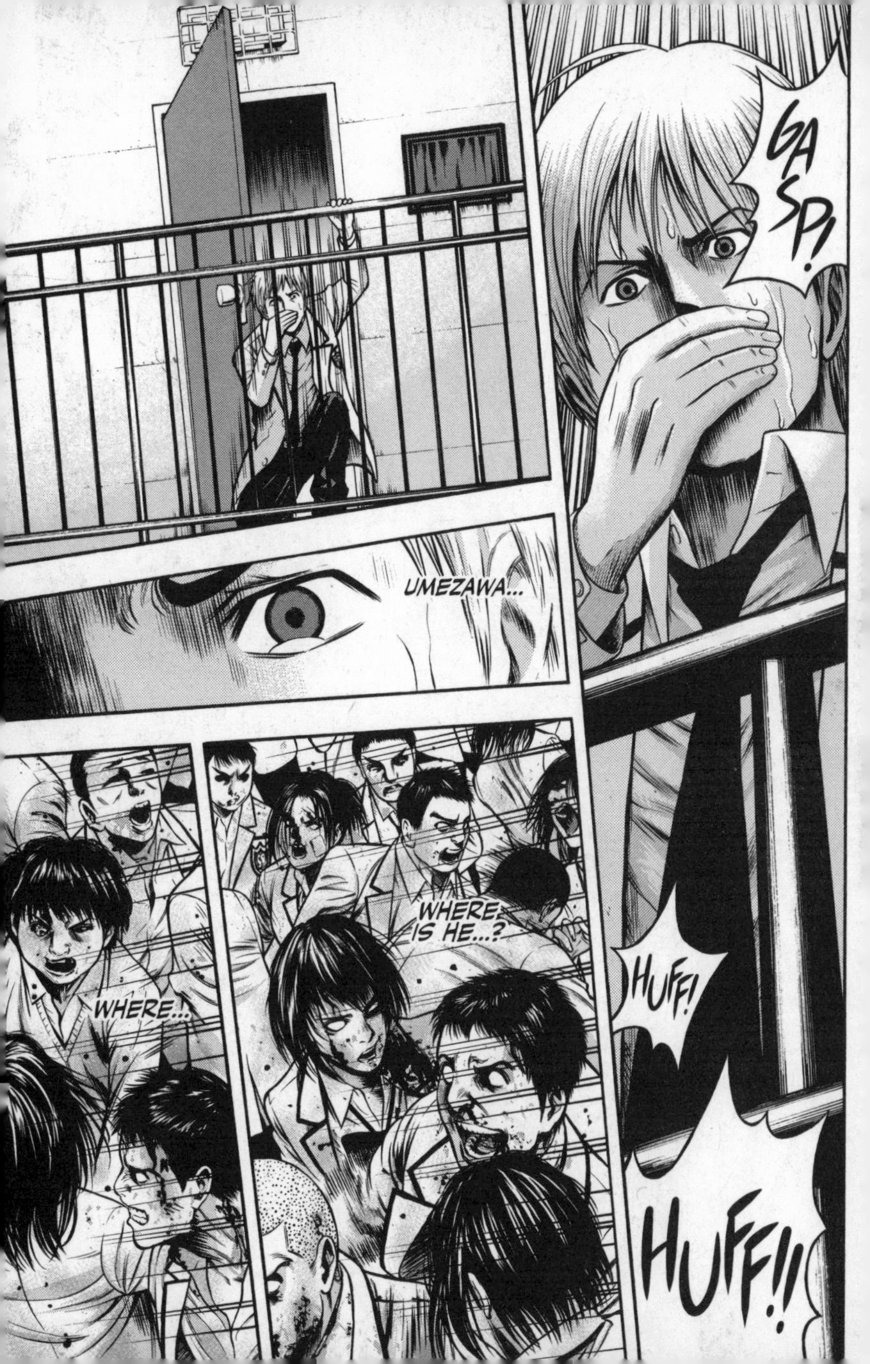
GASP!
UMEZAWA...
HUFF!
HUFF!!
WHERE IS HE...?
WHERE...

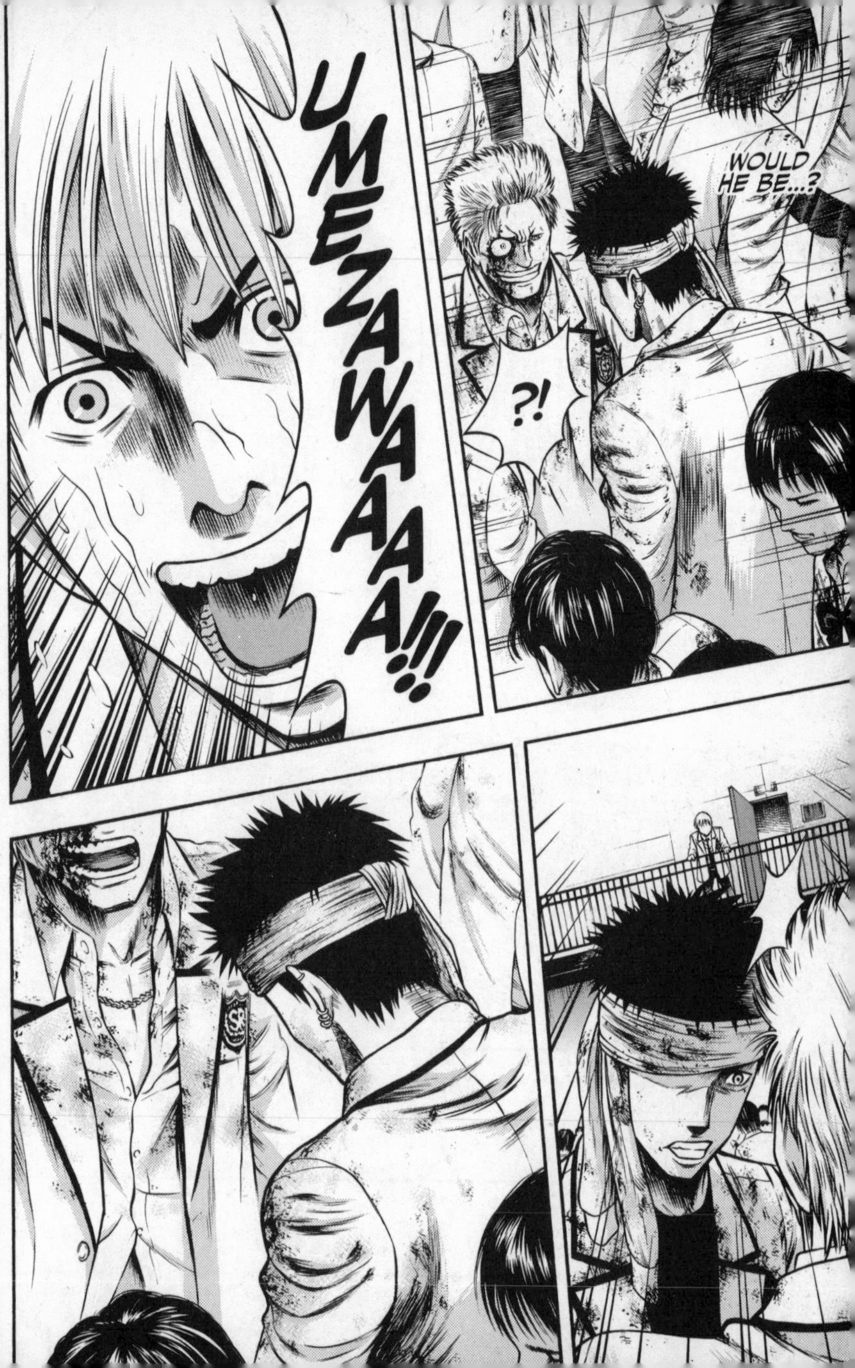
WOULD HE BE...?
?!
UMEZAWAAAAA!!!

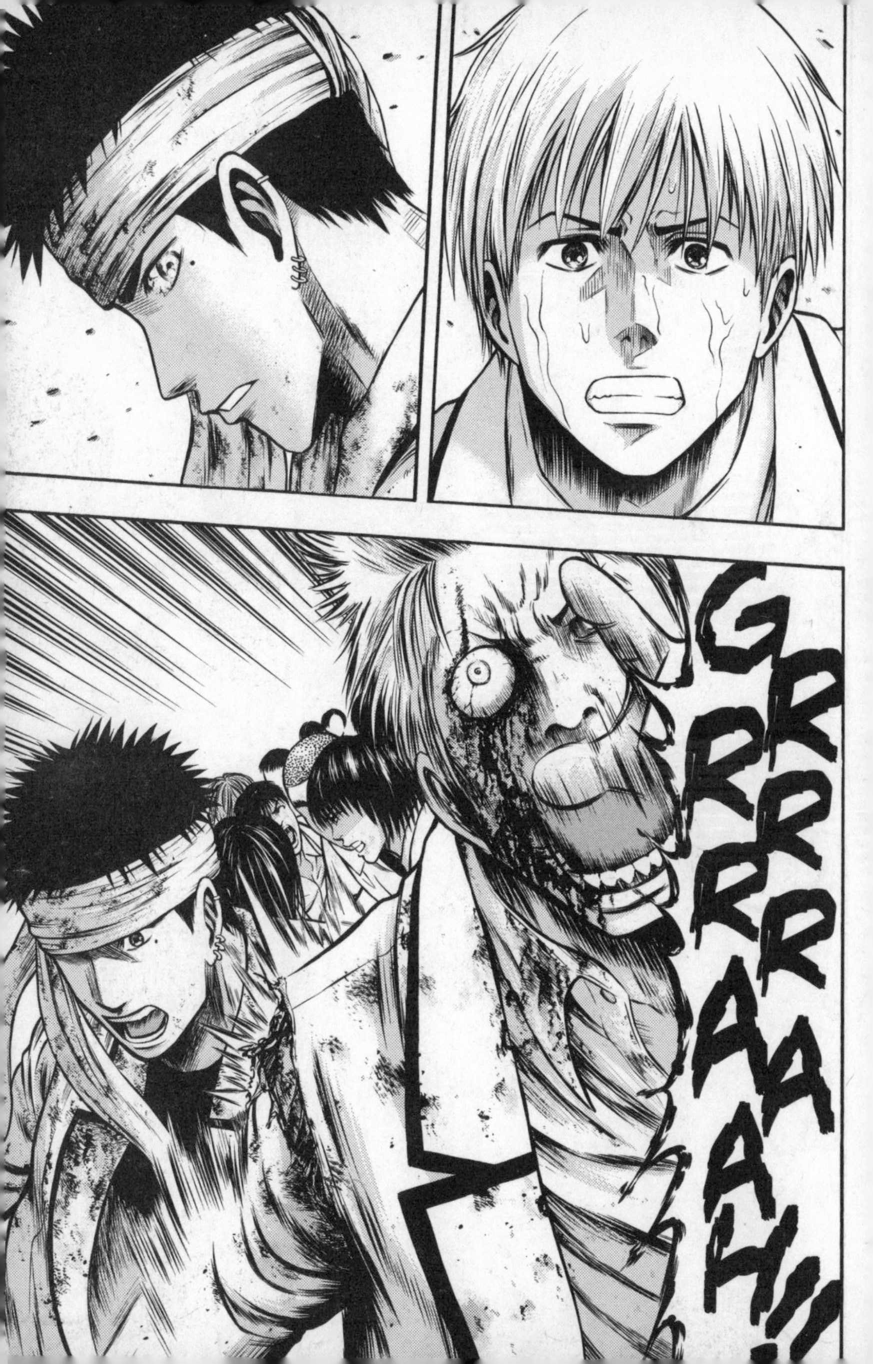
GRRRRRAAAAH!!

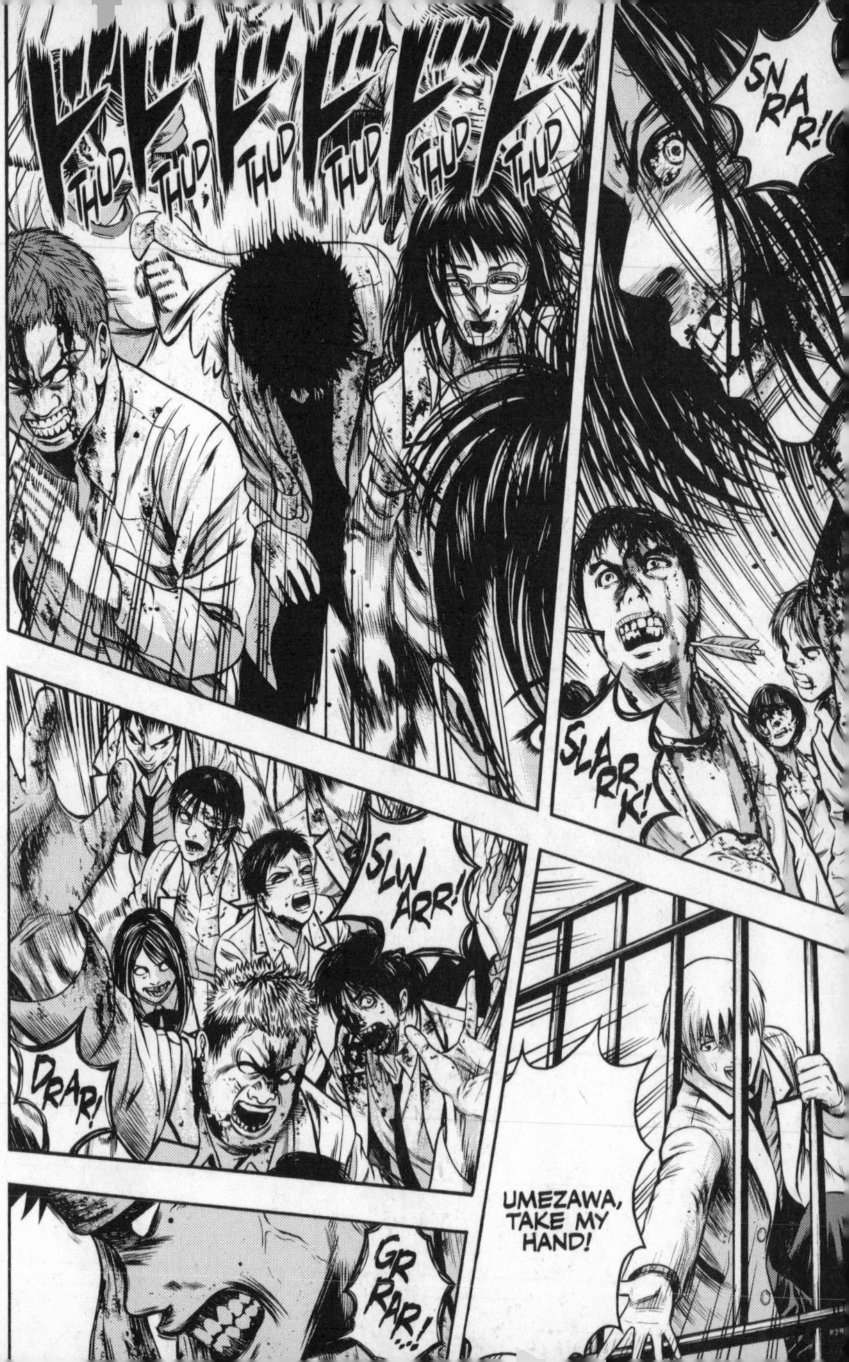

SNARR!
THUD THUD THUD THUD THUD THUD
SLARRK!
SLWARR!
DRAR!
UMEZAWA, TAKE MY HAND!
GRRAR!

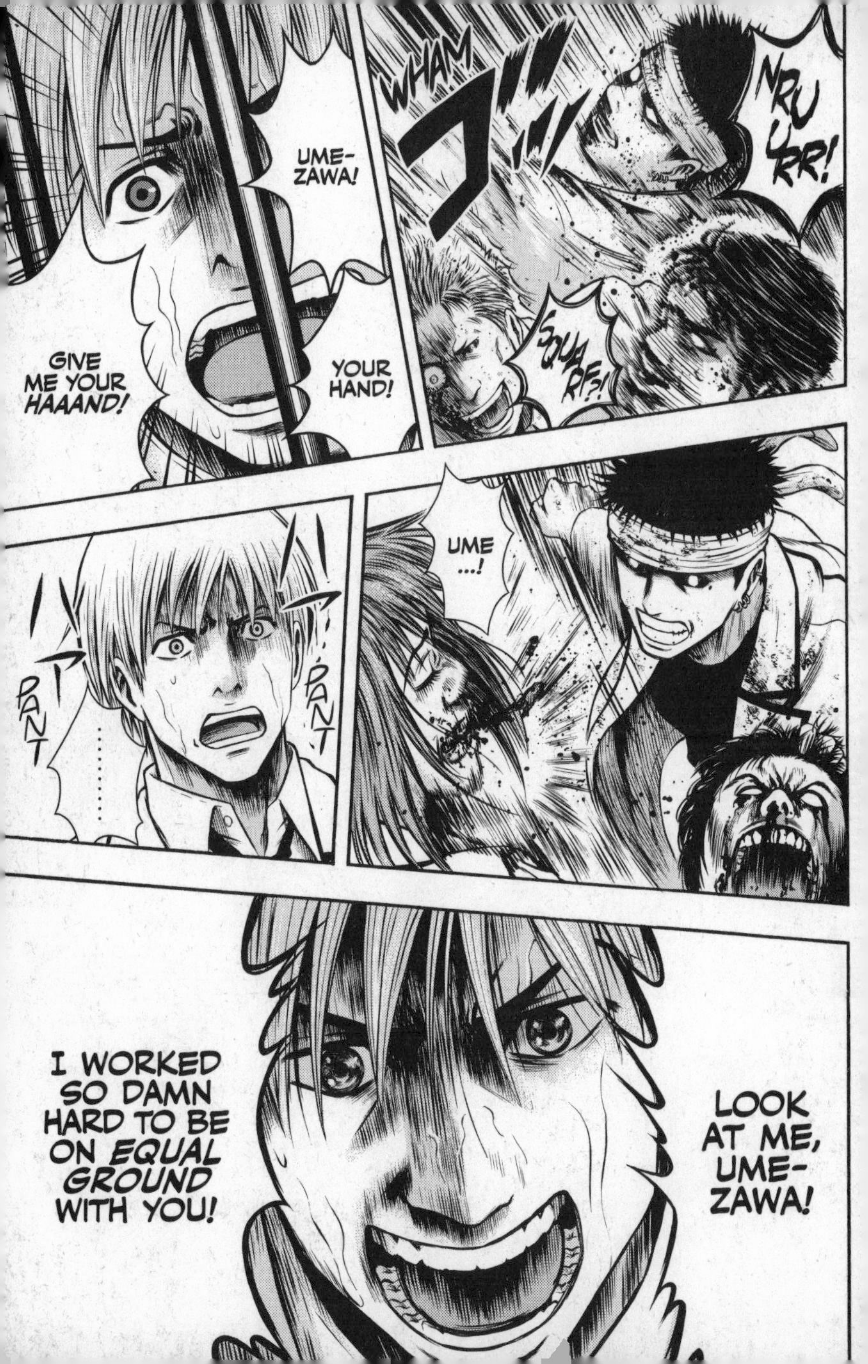
NRUURRR!
WHAM
SQUARF?!
UME-ZAWA!
YOUR HAND!
GIVE ME YOUR HAAAND!
UME ...!
PANT
PANT
LOOK AT ME, UME-ZAWA!
I WORKED SO DAMN HARD TO BE ON EQUAL GROUND WITH YOU!

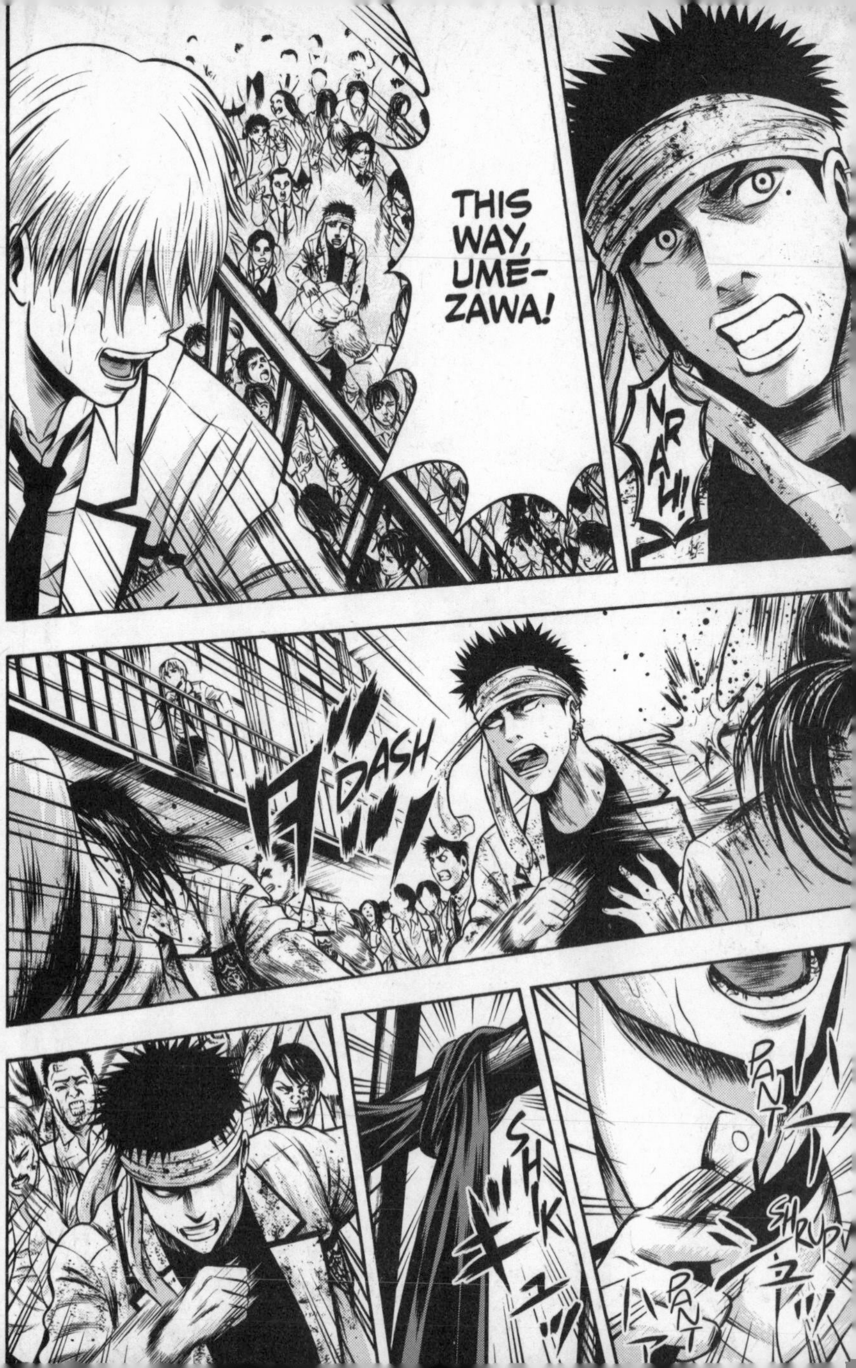
NRAH!
THIS WAY, UME-ZAWA!
DASH
SHIK
SHRUP
PANT
PANT

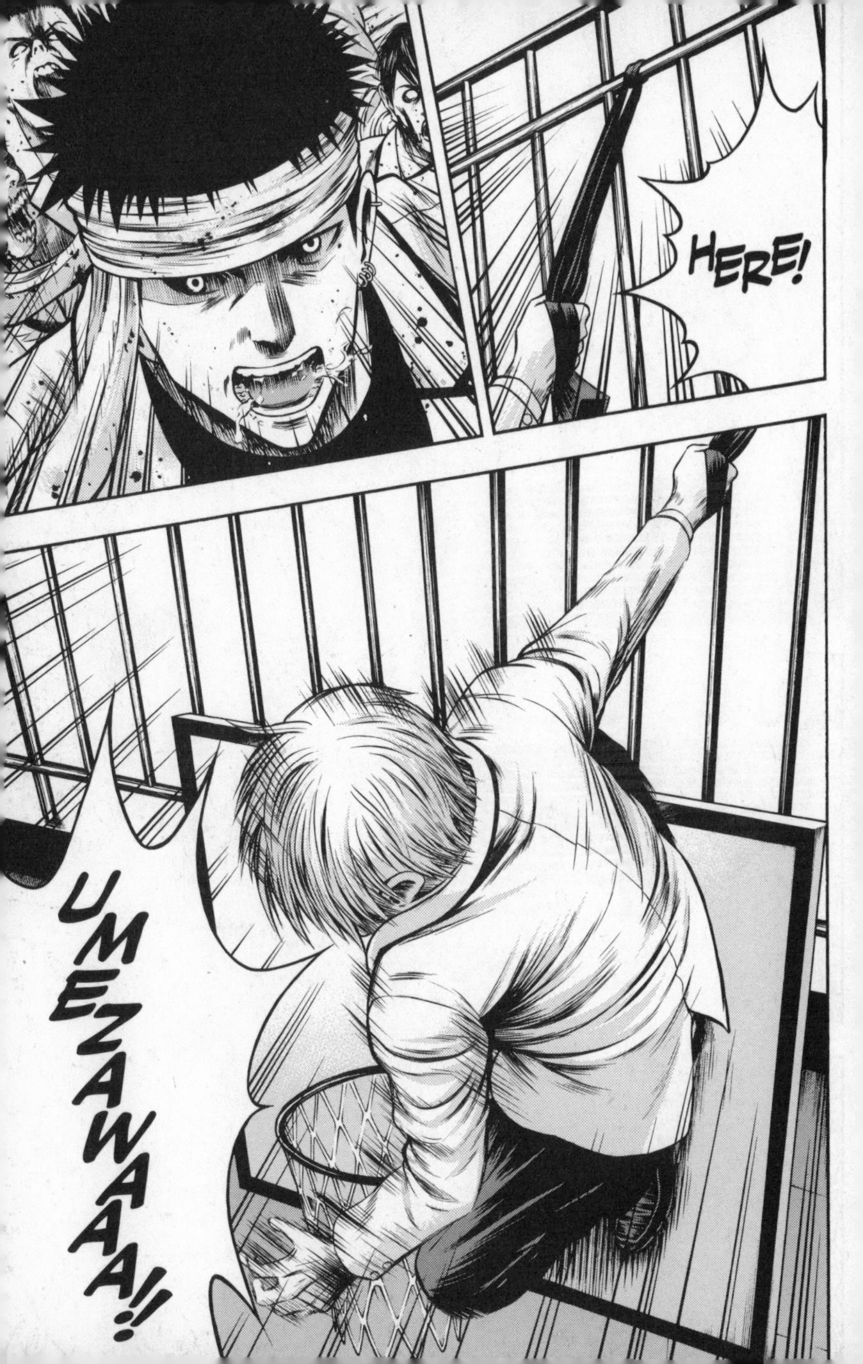
HERE!
UMEZAWAAA!!

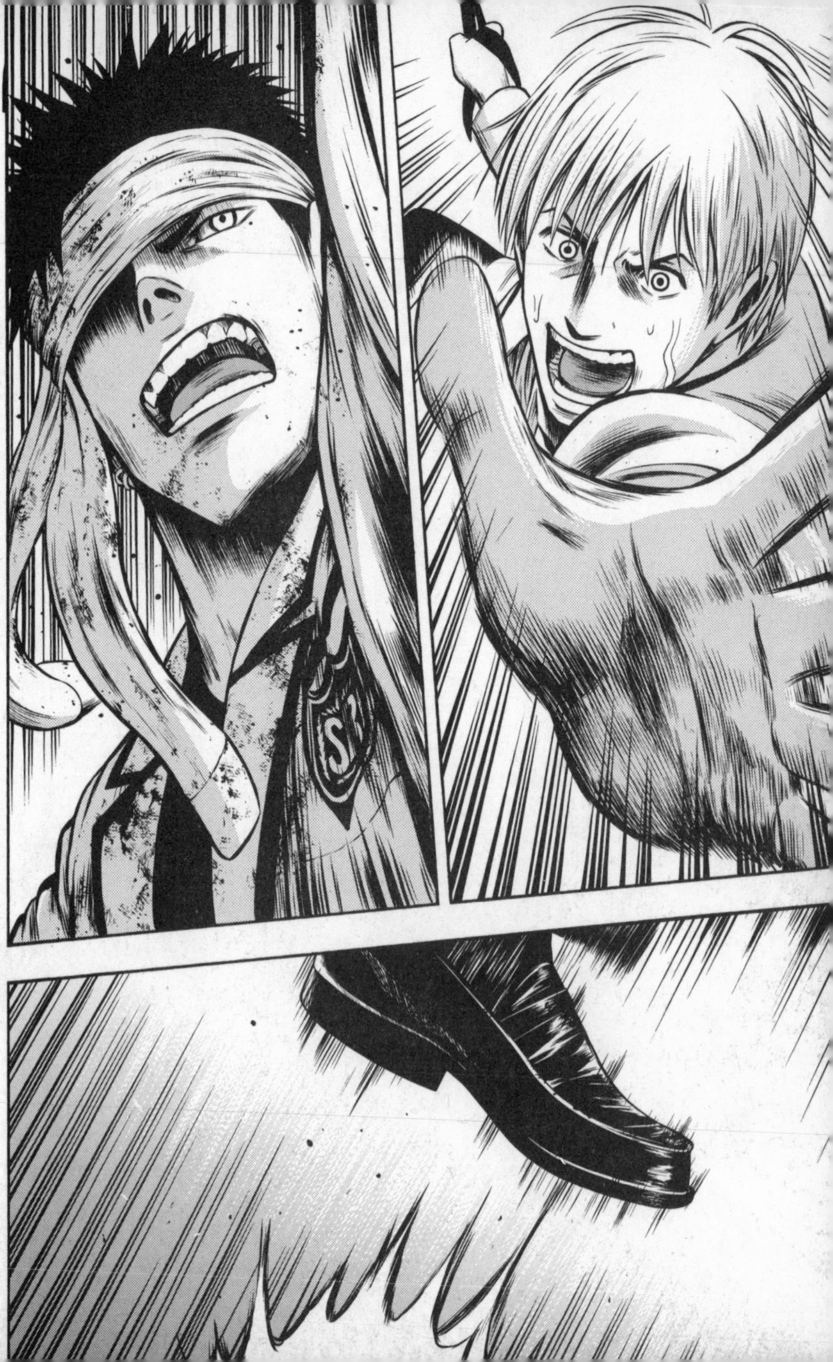

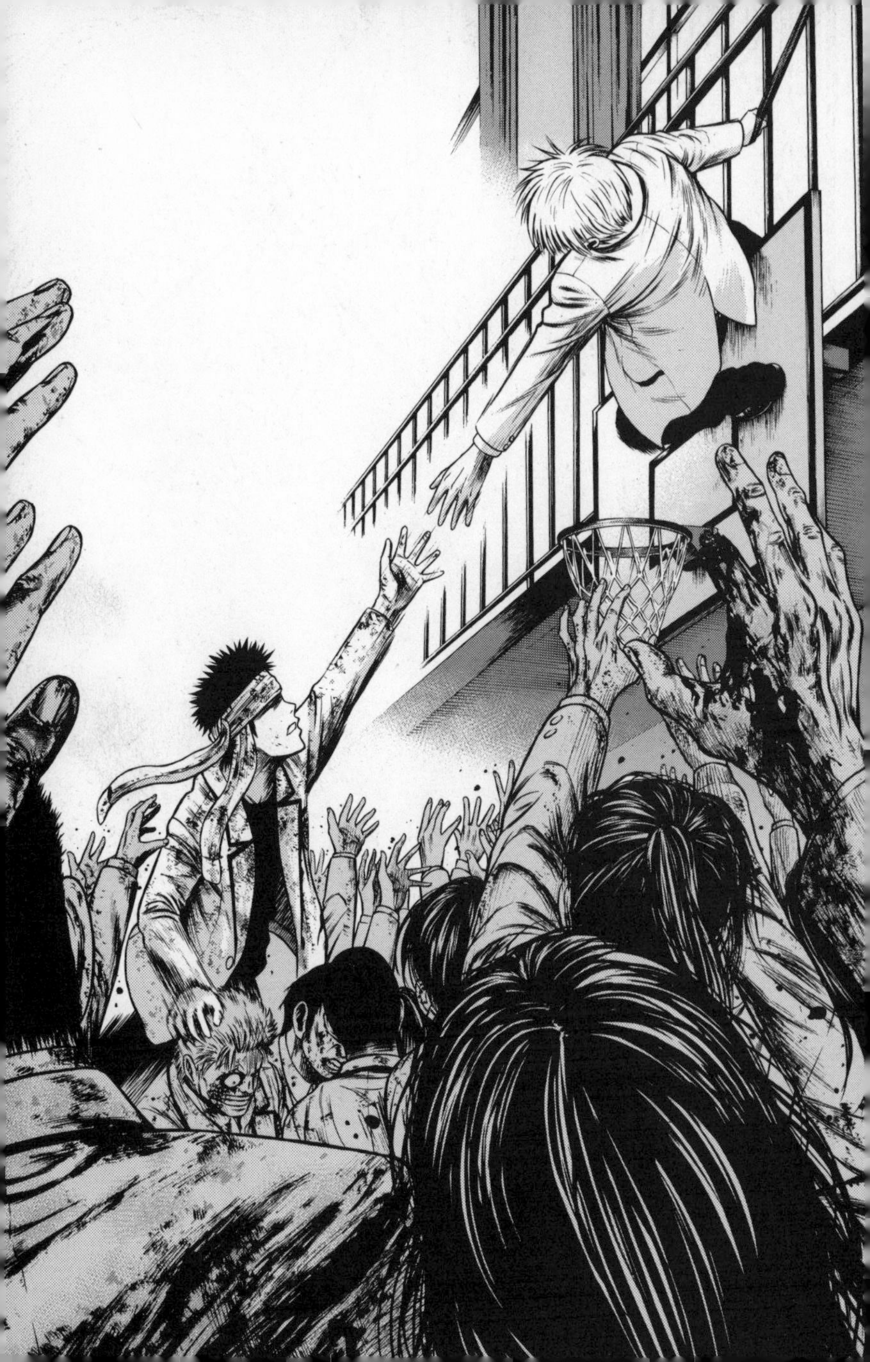

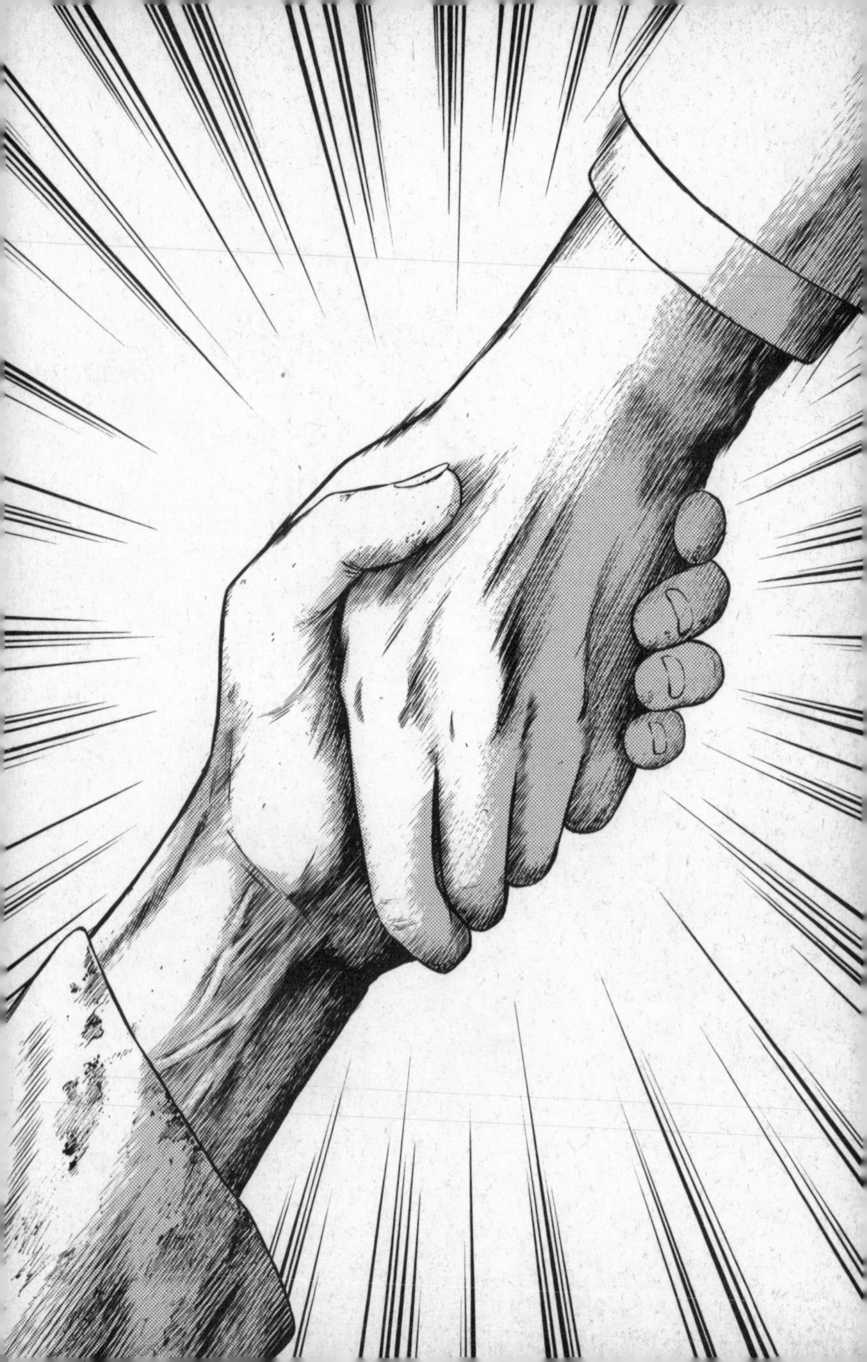

HOUR OF THE ZOMBIE

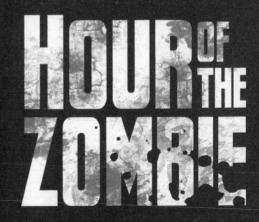

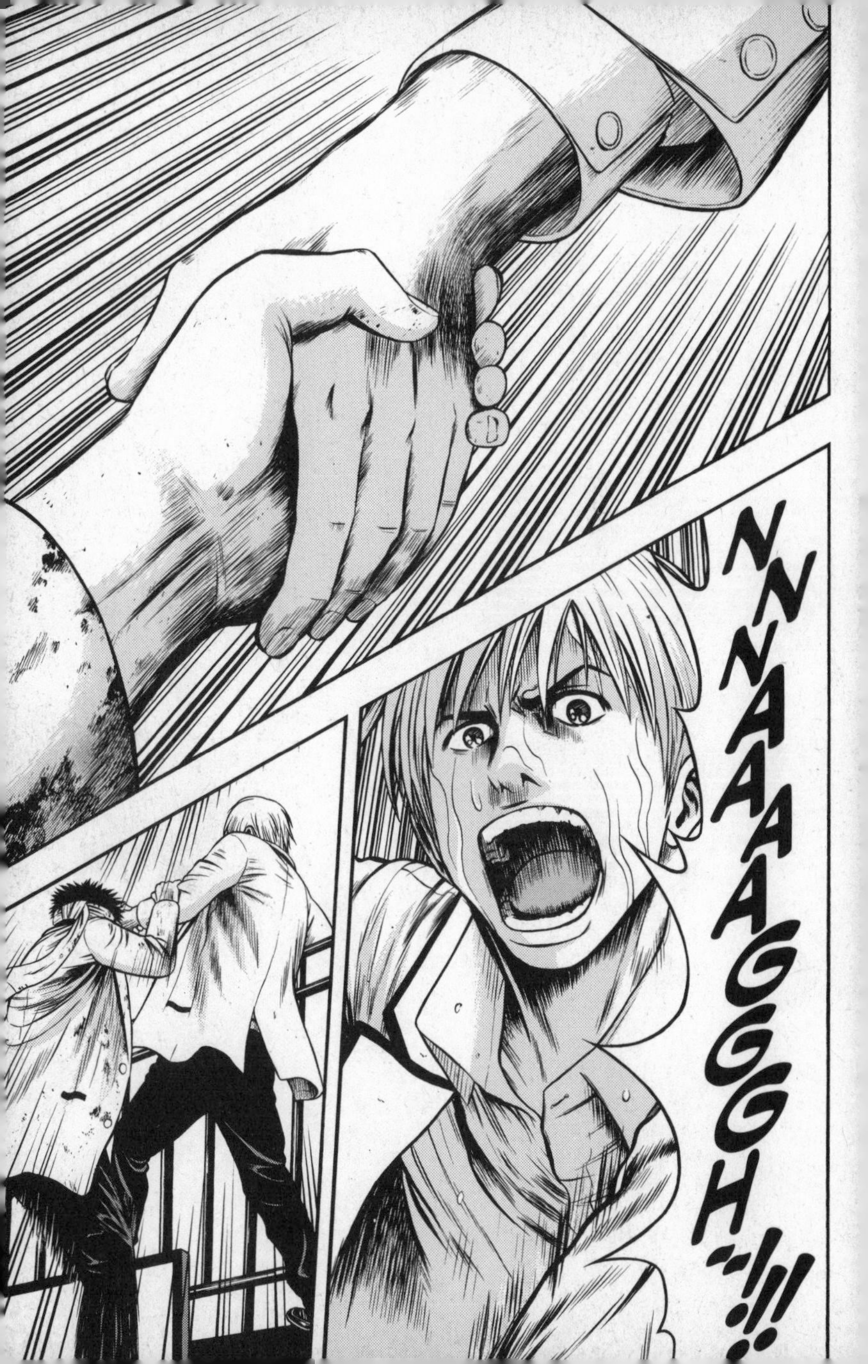
NNNAAAAGGGGH--!!!

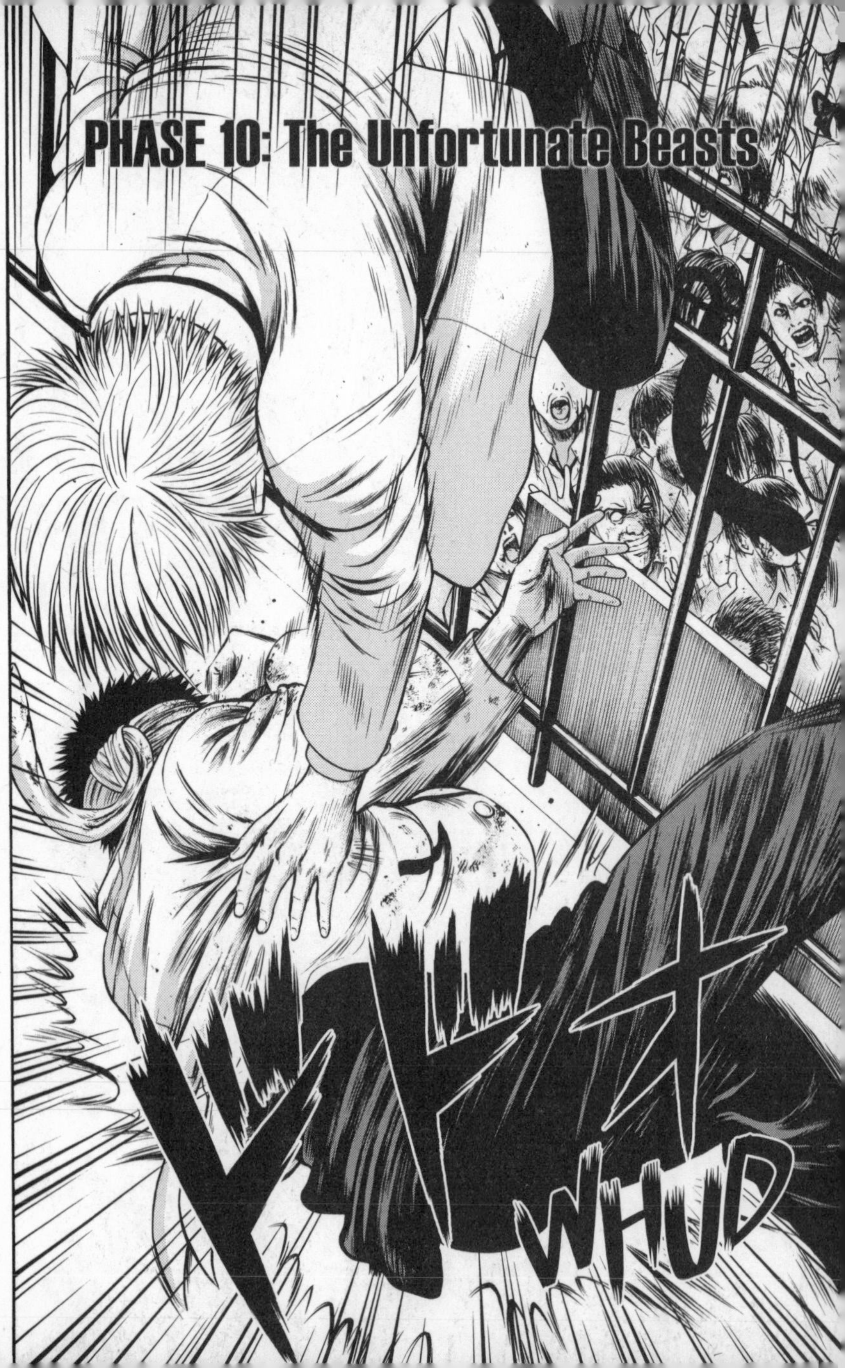
PHASE 10: The Unfortunate Beasts
WHUD

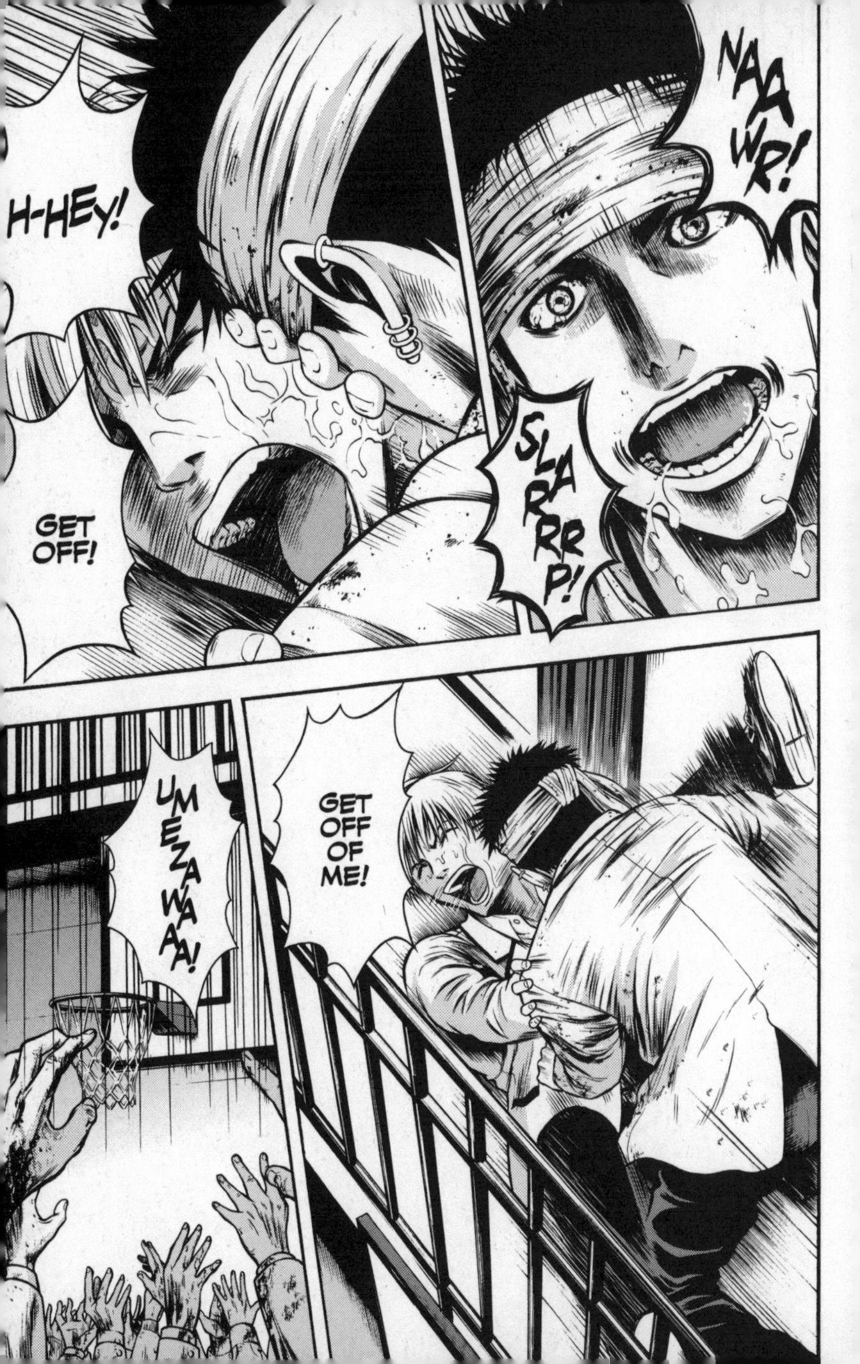
NAAAWR!
SLARRRP!
H-HEY!
GET OFF!
GET OFF OF ME!
UMEZAWAAA!

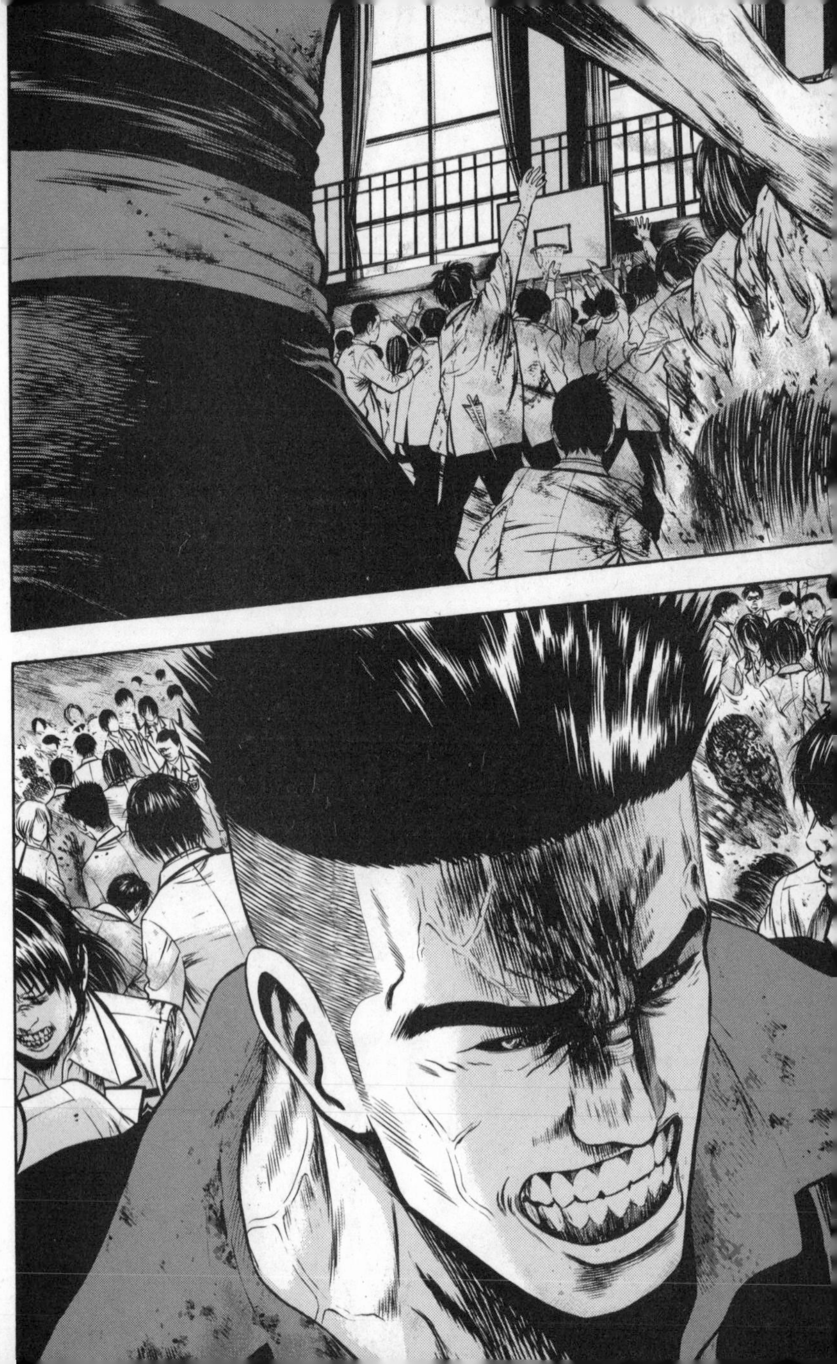

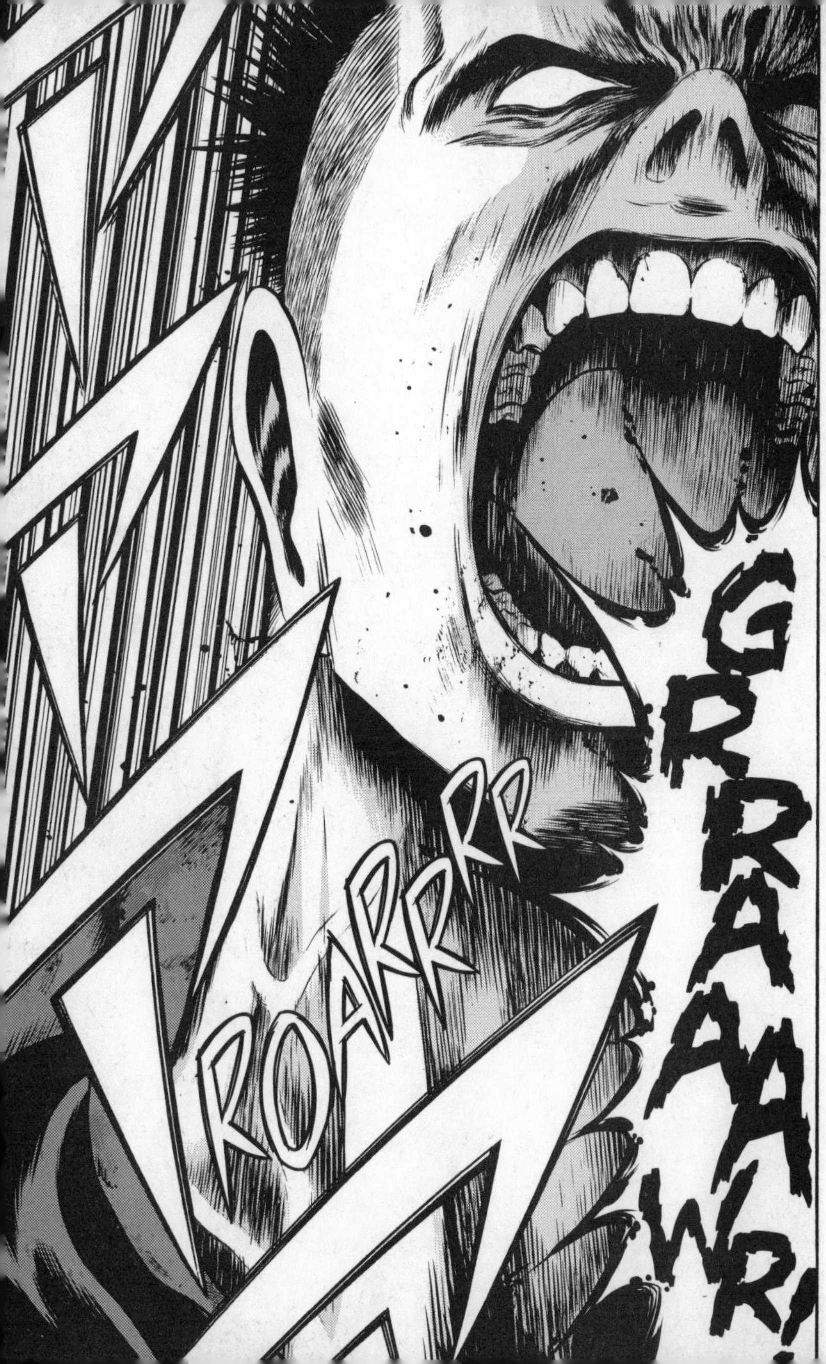
GRRAAAWR!
ROARRRR

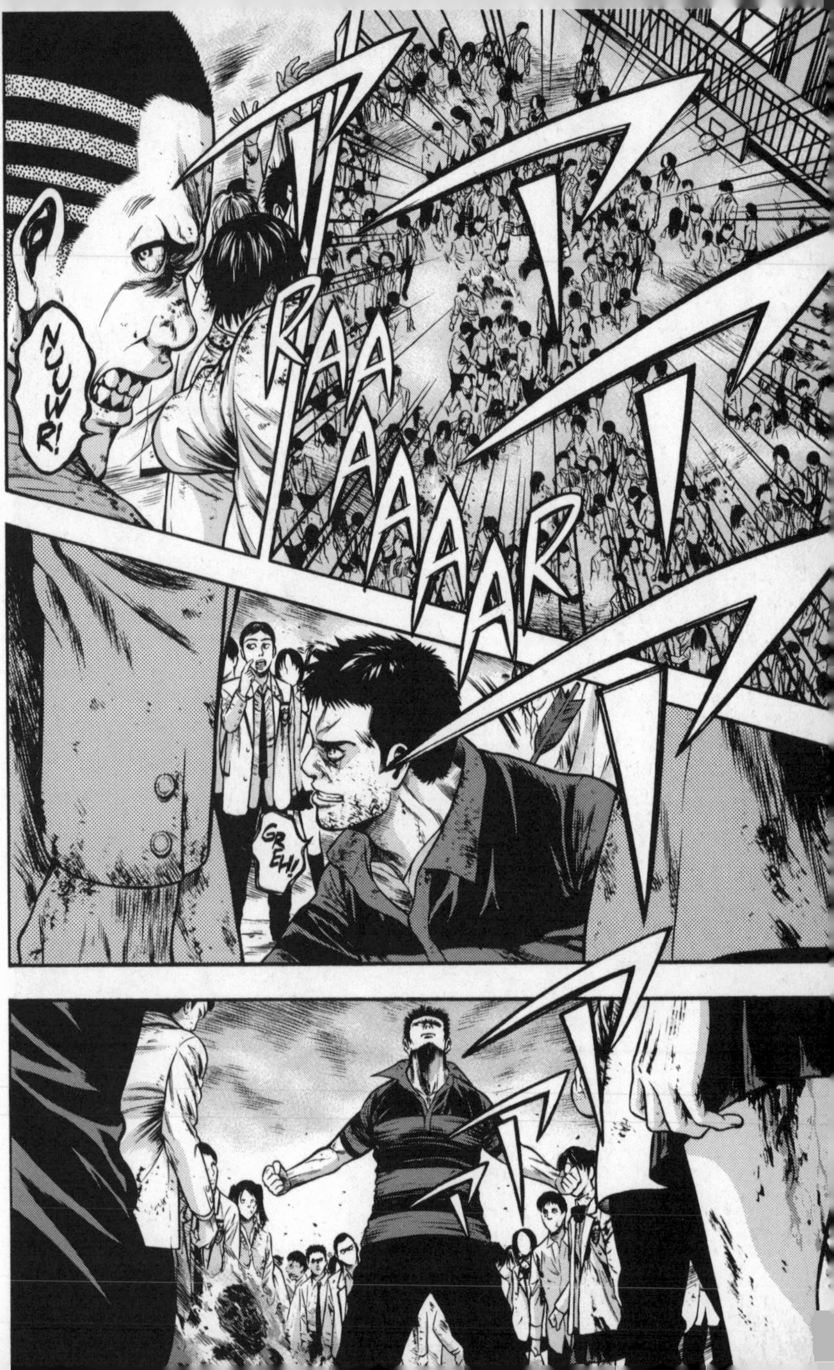
NUUWR!
RAAAAAAR
GREH!!

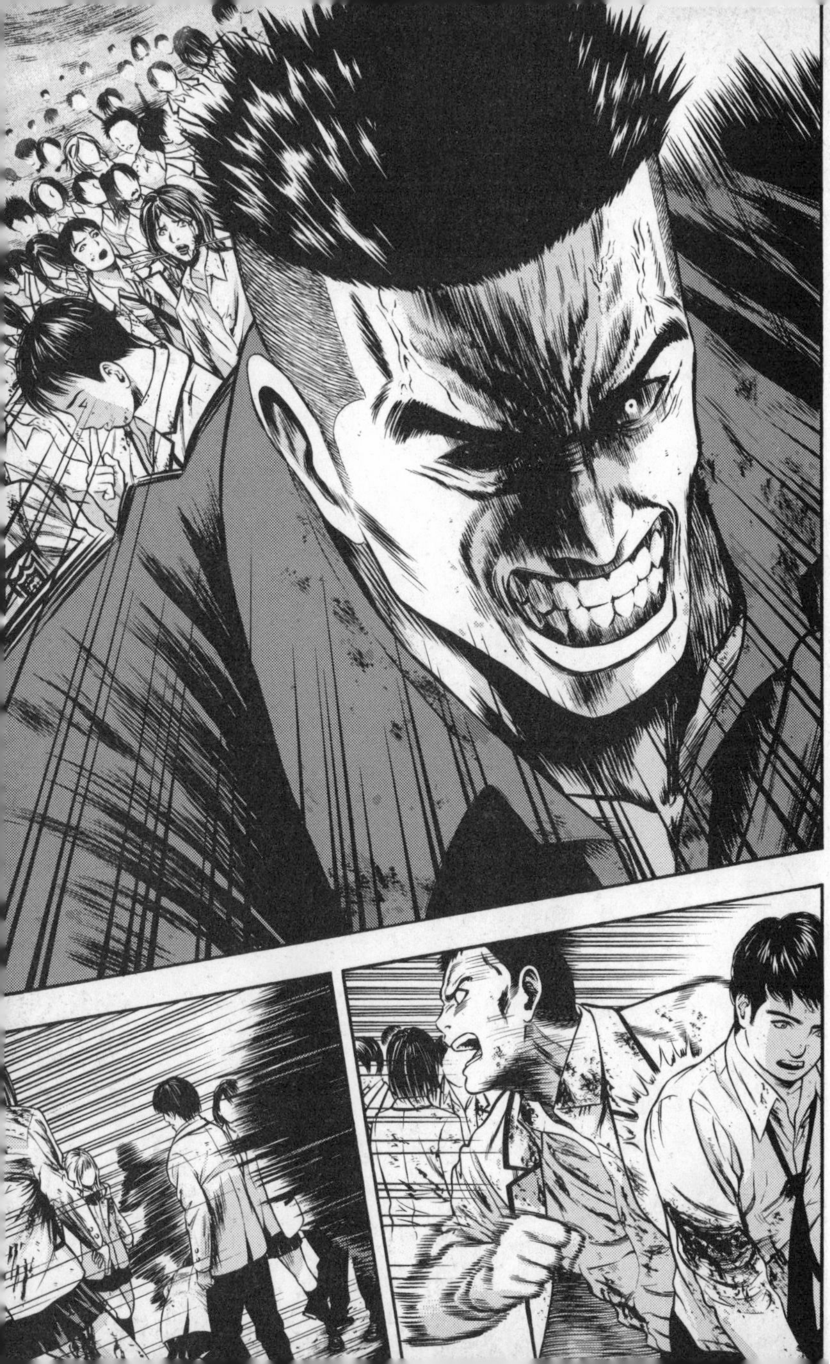

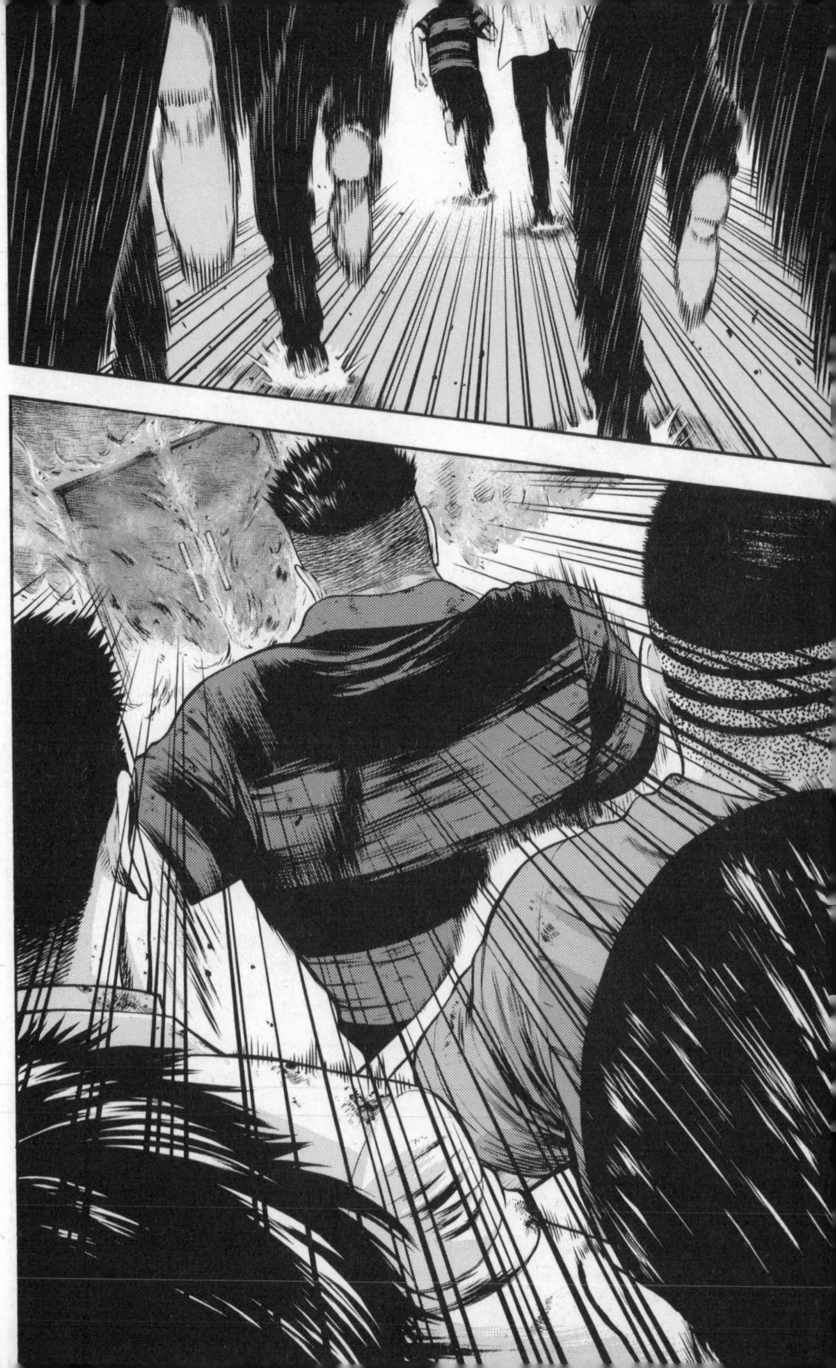

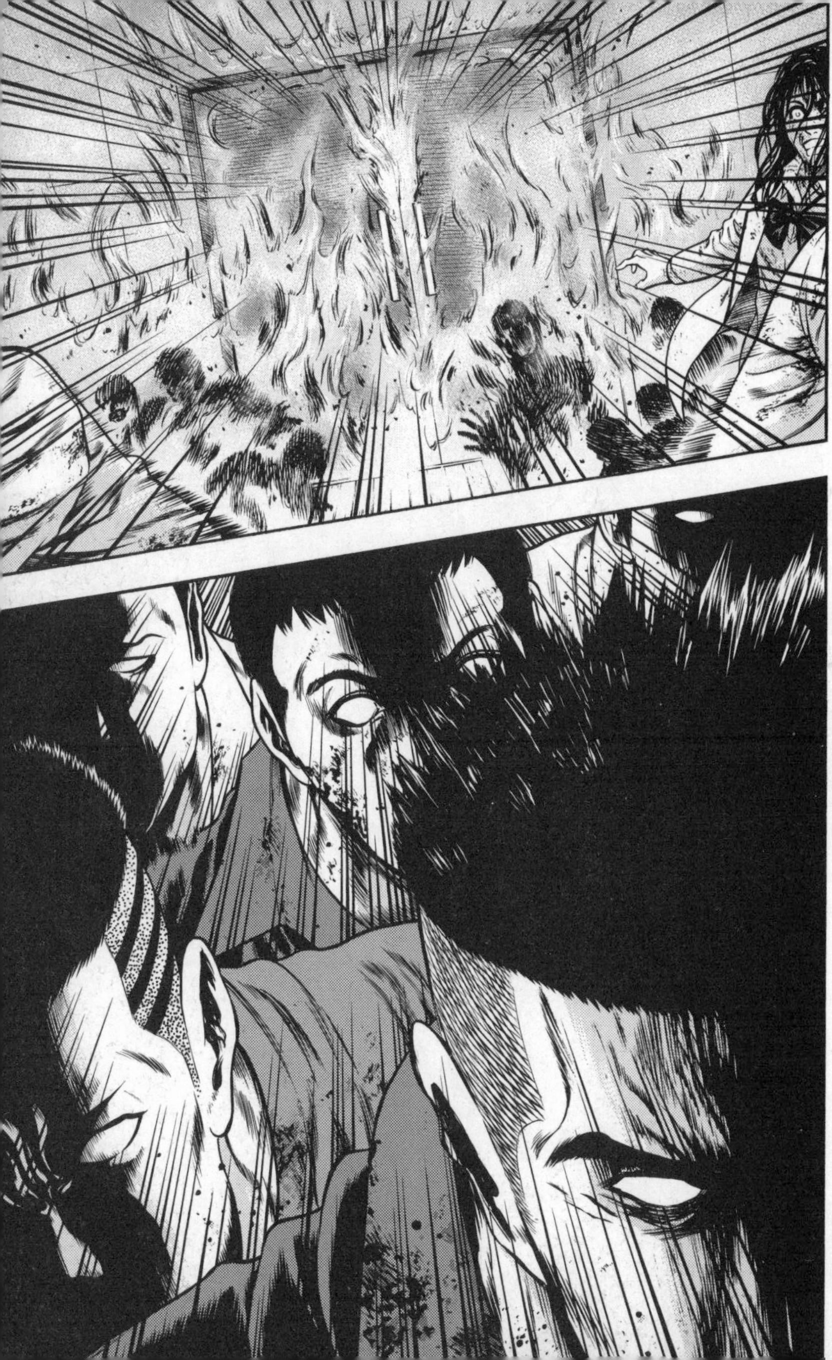

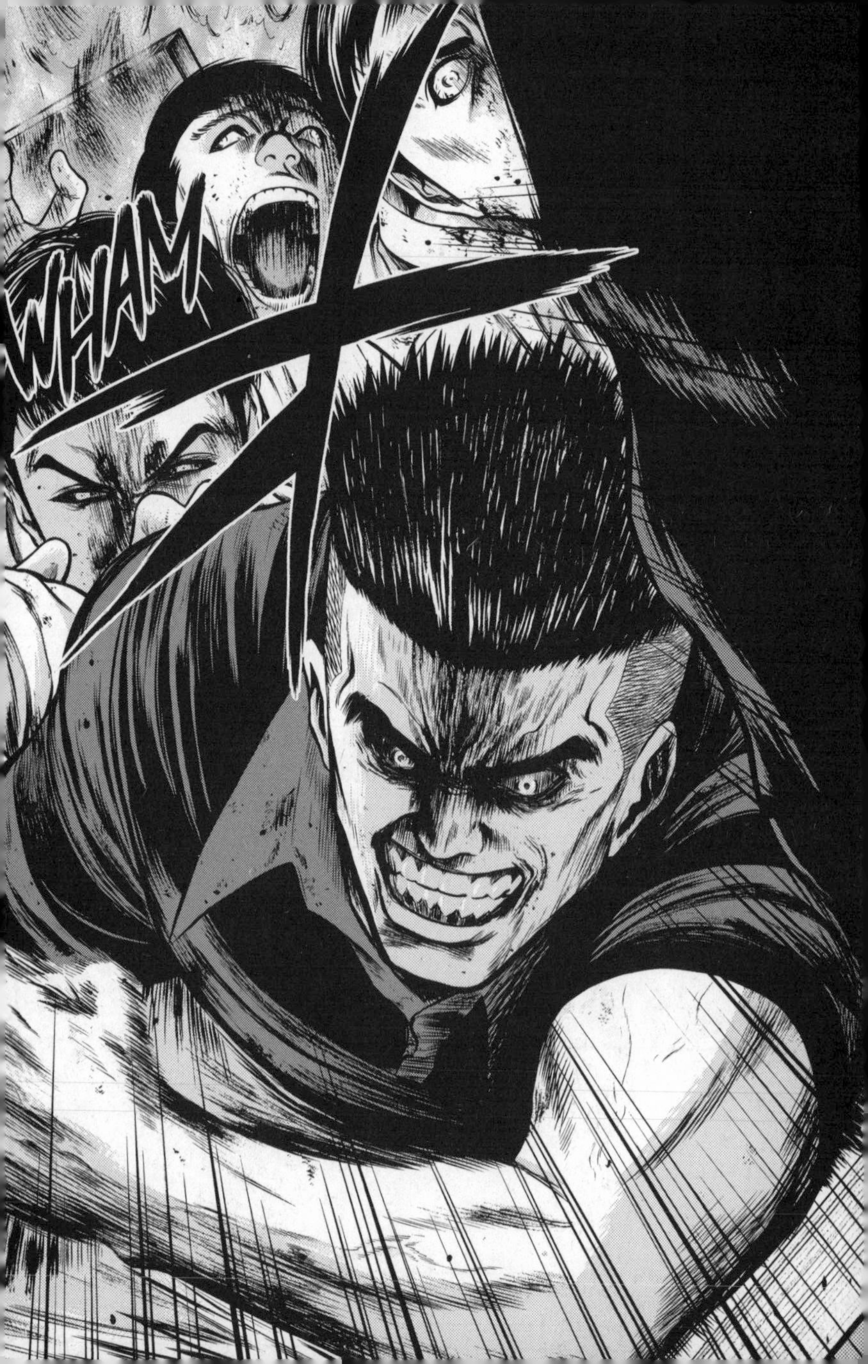
WHAM

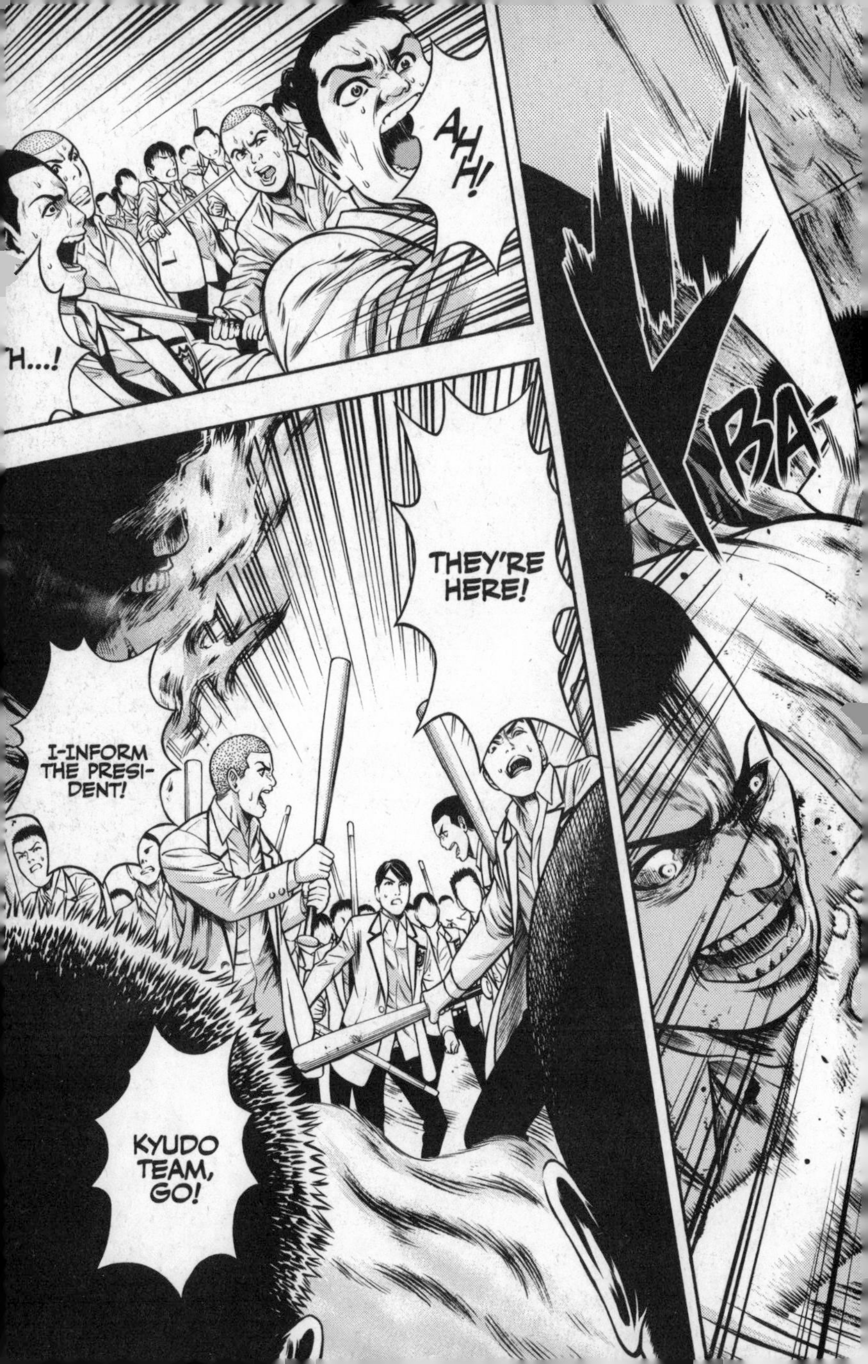

AHH!
H...!
BA-
THEY'RE HERE!
I-INFORM THE PRESI-DENT!
KYUDO TEAM, GO!

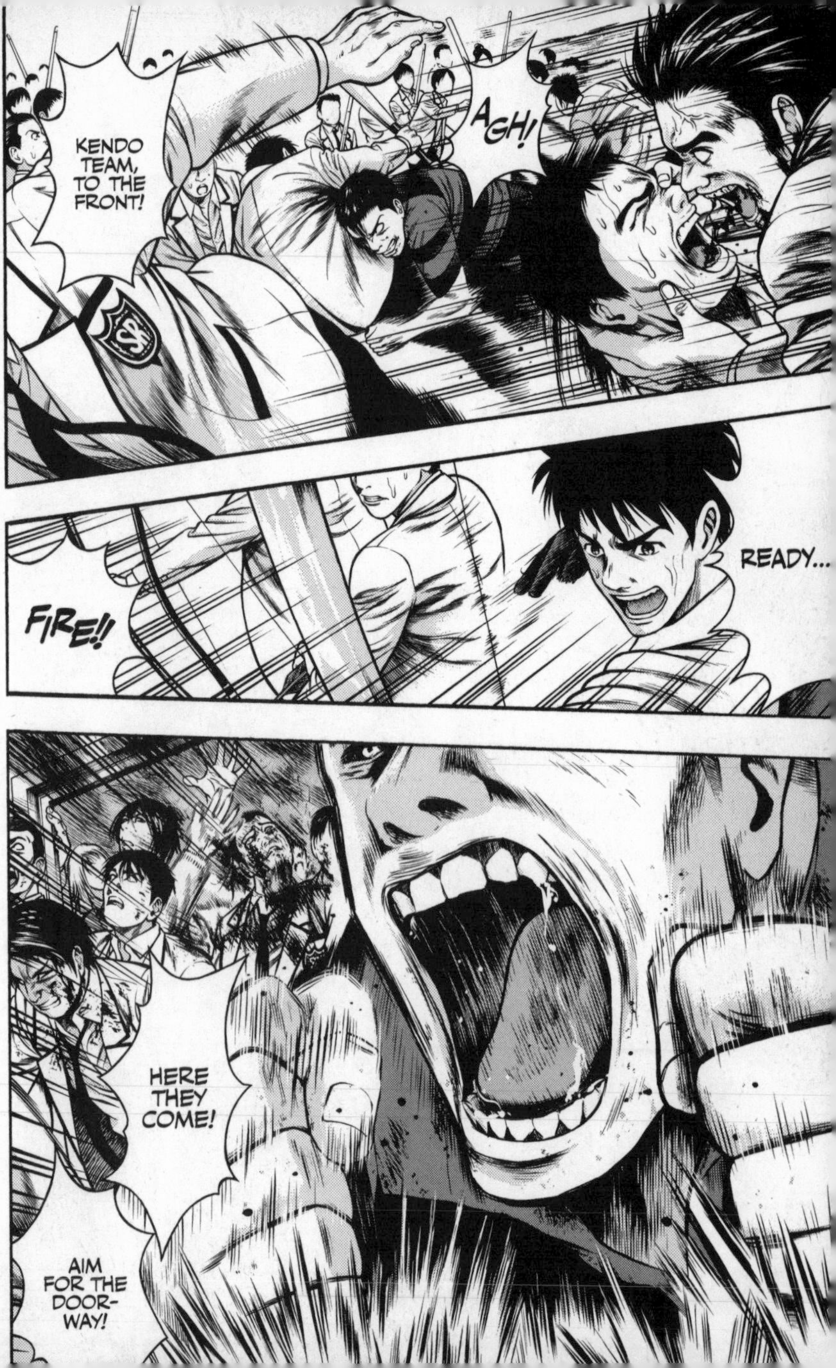
AGH!
KENDO TEAM, TO THE FRONT!
READY...
FIRE!!
HERE THEY COME!
AIM FOR THE DOOR-WAY!

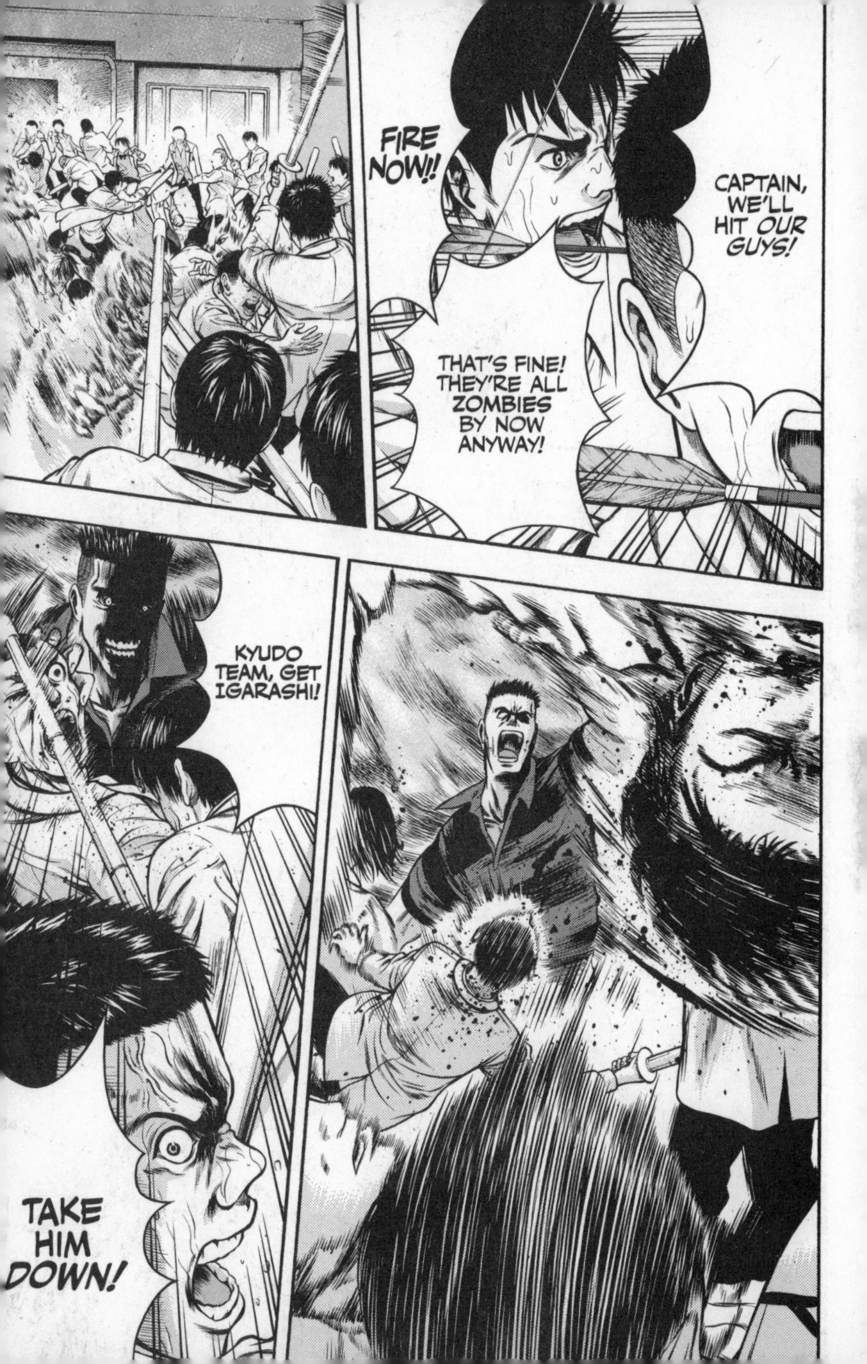
FIRE NOW!!
CAPTAIN, WE'LL HIT *OUR* GUYS!
THAT'S FINE! THEY'RE ALL ZOMBIES BY NOW ANYWAY!
KYUDO TEAM, GET IGARASHI!
TAKE HIM *DOWN!*

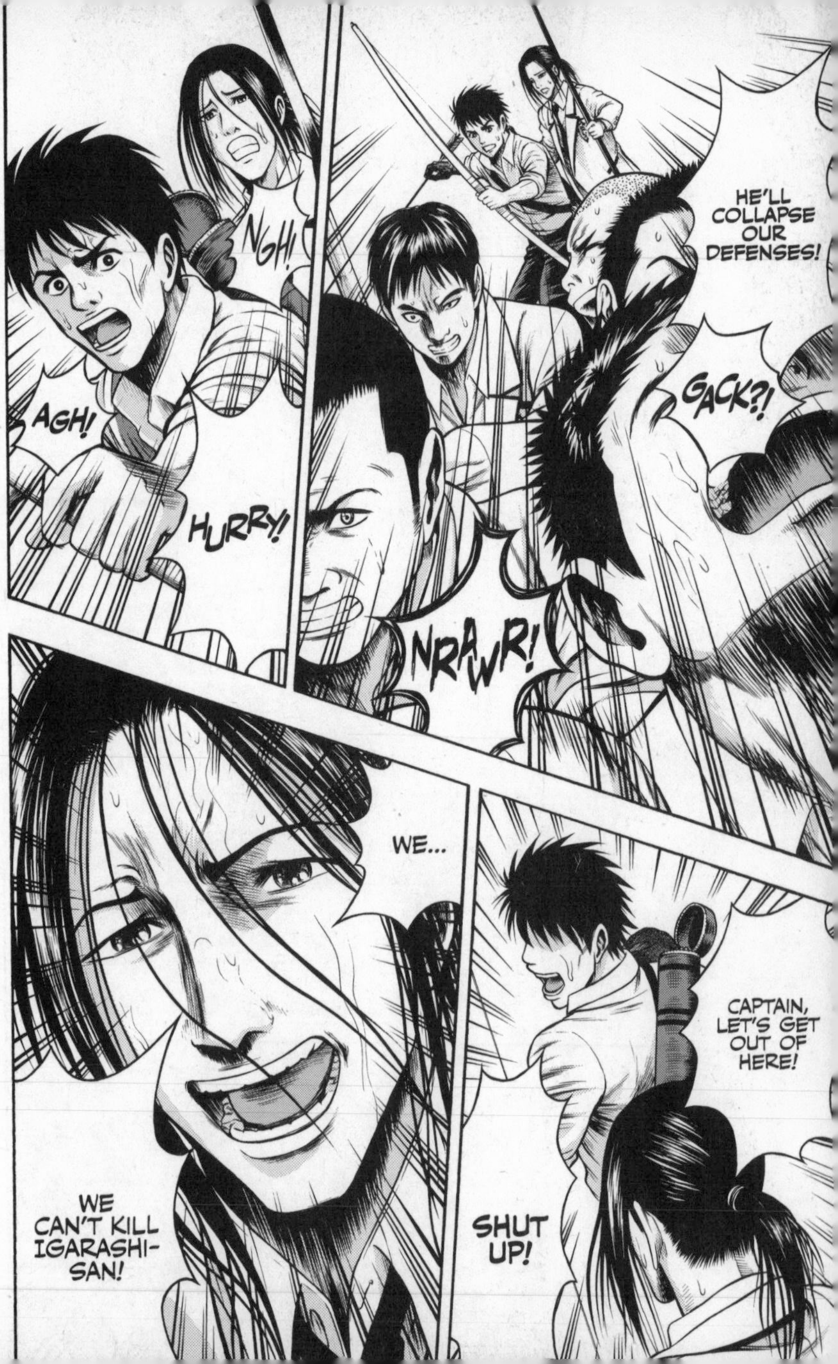
HE'LL COLLAPSE OUR DEFENSES!
GACK?!
NRAWR!
NGH!
AGH!
HURRY!
CAPTAIN, LET'S GET OUT OF HERE!
SHUT UP!
WE...
WE CAN'T KILL IGARASHI-SAN!

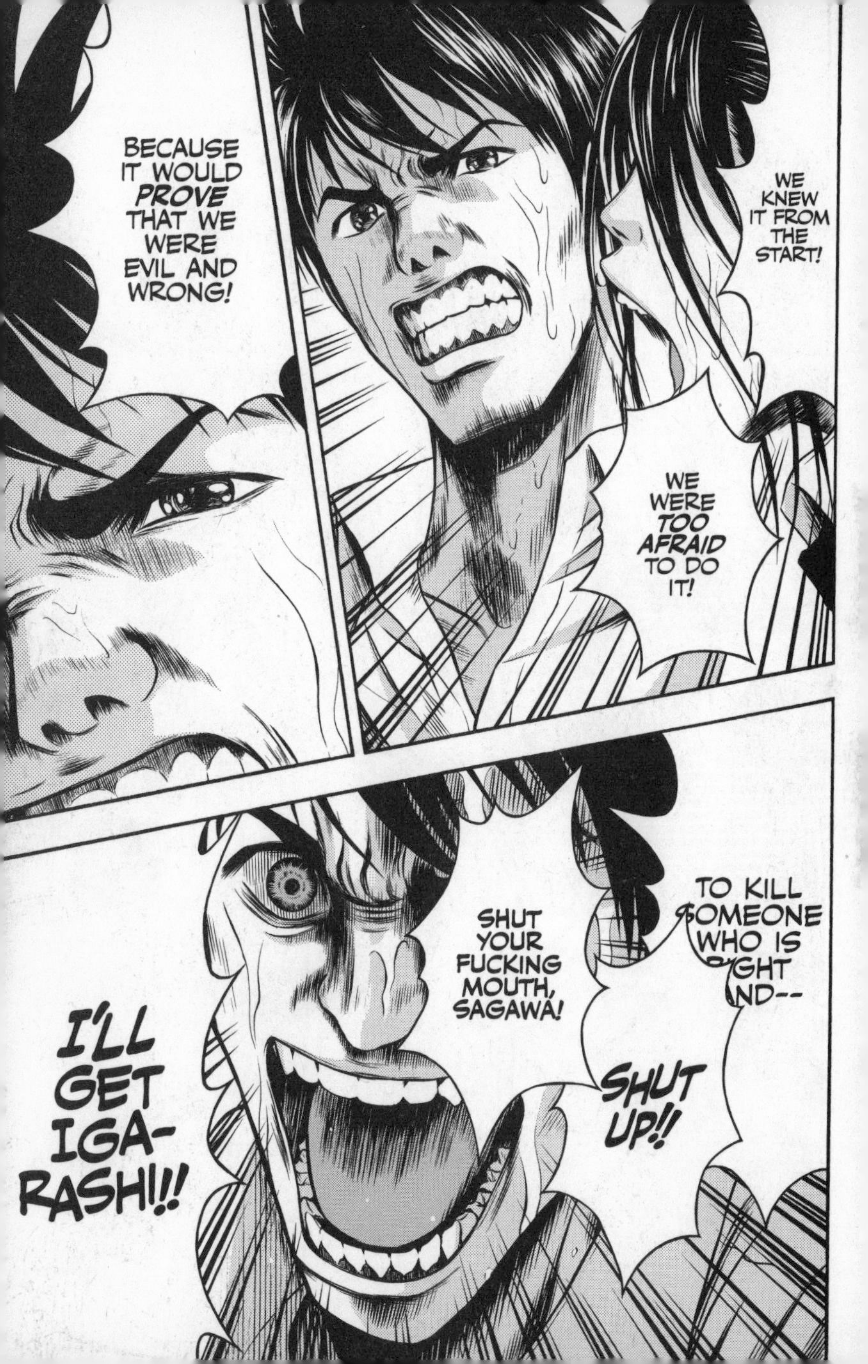
WE KNEW IT FROM THE START!
WE WERE *TOO AFRAID* TO DO IT!
BECAUSE IT WOULD *PROVE* THAT WE WERE EVIL AND WRONG!
TO KILL SOMEONE WHO IS RIGHT AND--
SHUT YOUR FUCKING MOUTH, SAGAWA!
SHUT UP!!
I'LL GET IGA-RASHI!!!

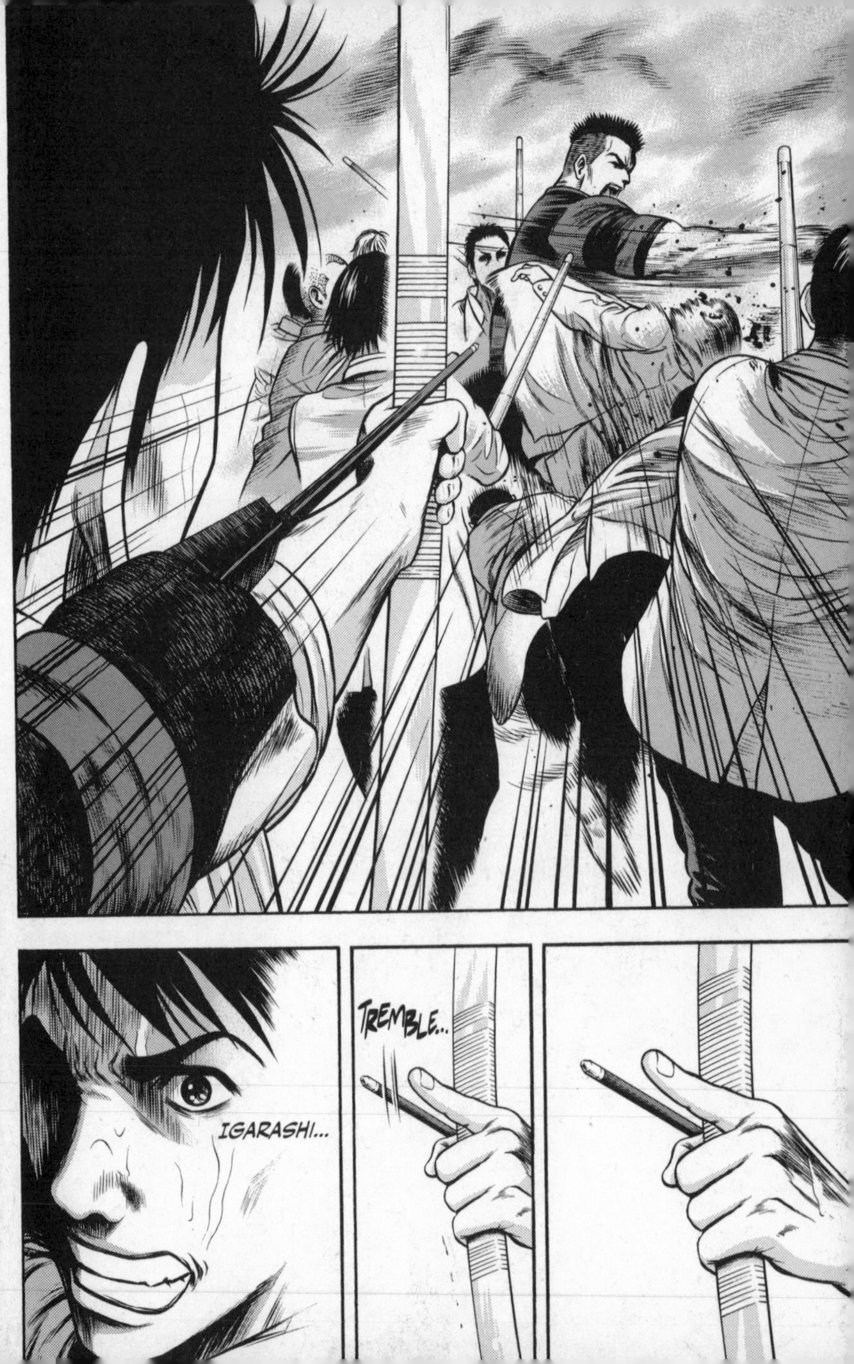
TREMBLE...
IGARASHI...

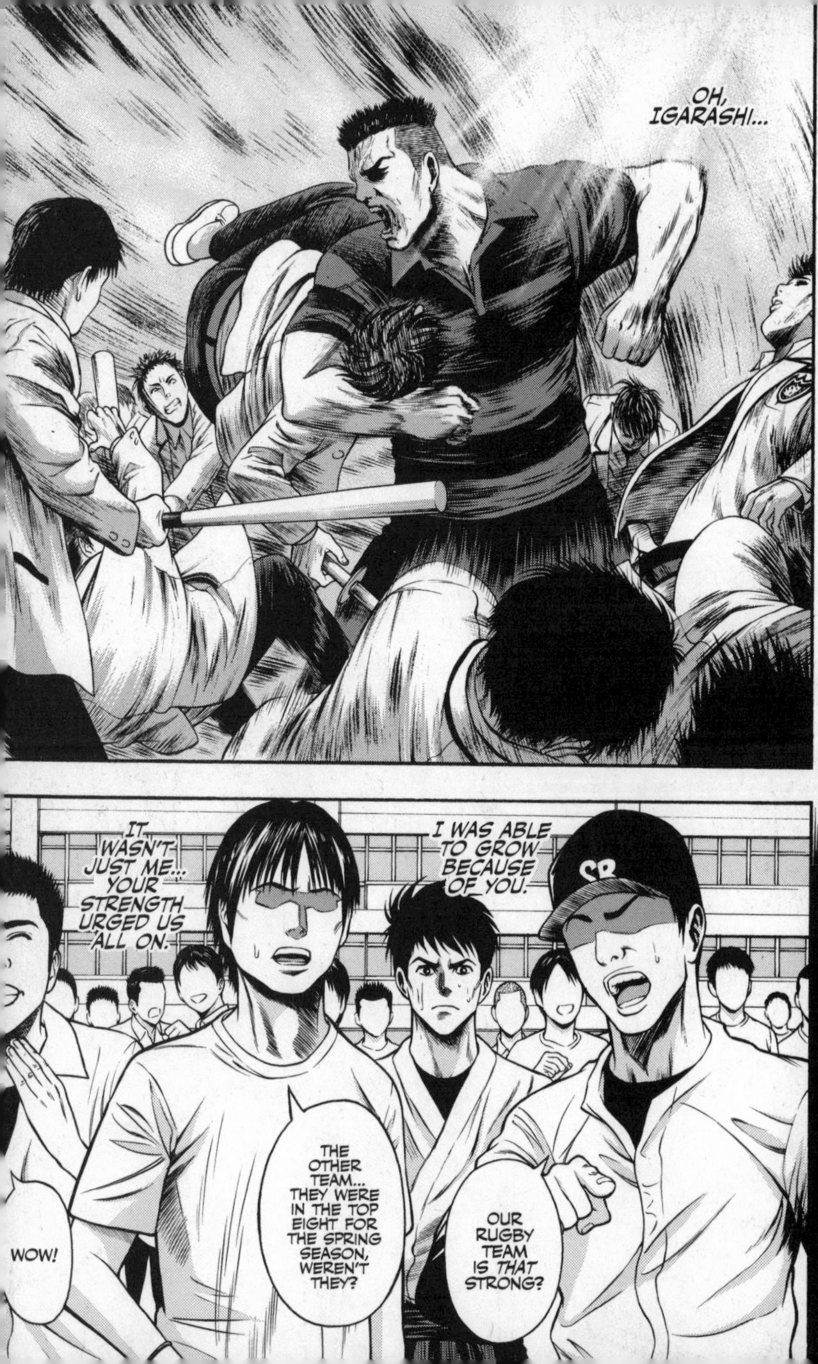
OH, IGARASHI...
I WAS ABLE TO GROW BECAUSE OF YOU.
IT WASN'T JUST ME... YOUR STRENGTH URGED US ALL ON.
OUR RUGBY TEAM IS *THAT* STRONG?
THE OTHER TEAM... THEY WERE IN THE TOP EIGHT FOR THE SPRING SEASON, WEREN'T THEY?
WOW!

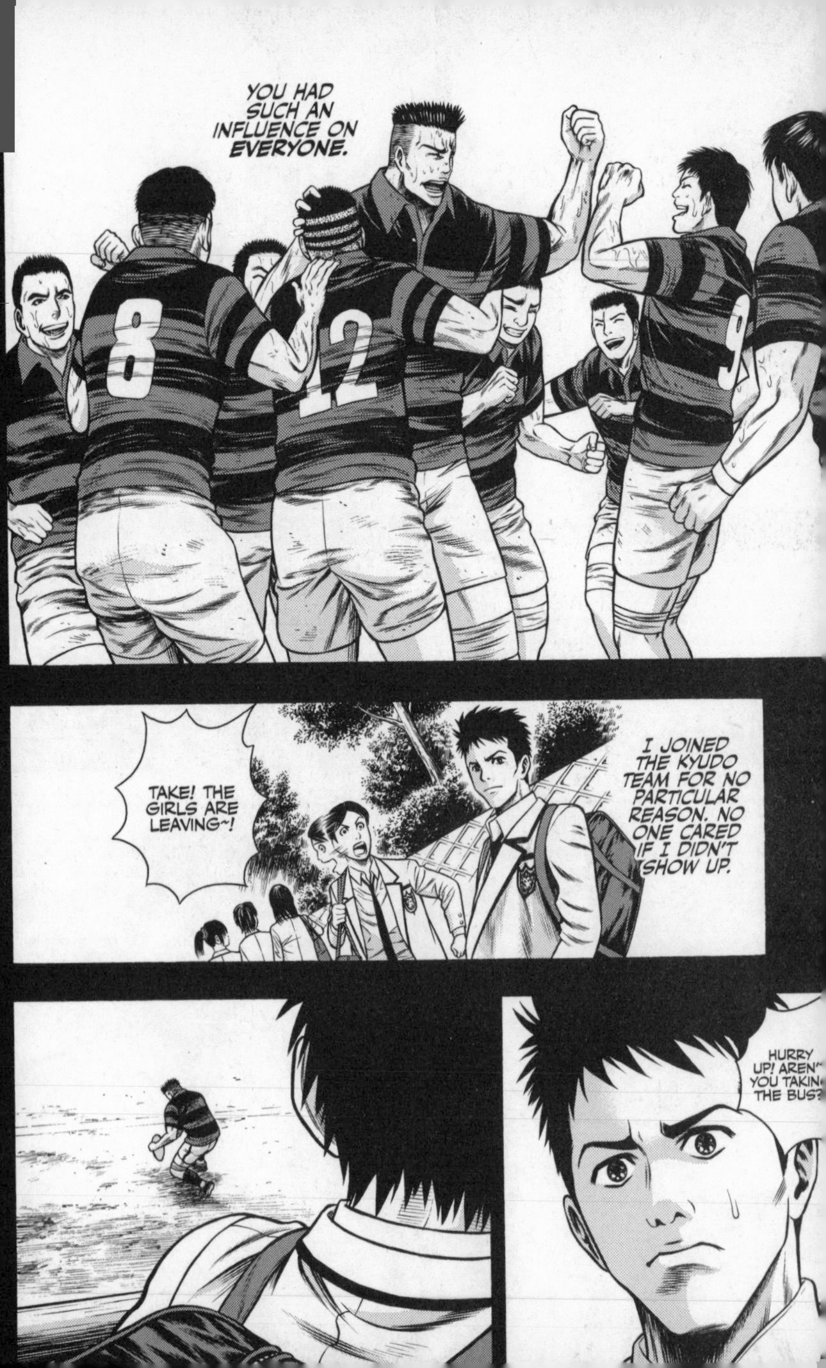
YOU HAD SUCH AN INFLUENCE ON EVERYONE.
I JOINED THE KYUDO TEAM FOR NO PARTICULAR REASON. NO ONE CARED IF I DIDN'T SHOW UP.
TAKE! THE GIRLS ARE LEAVING~!
HURRY UP! AREN'T YOU TAKING THE BUS?

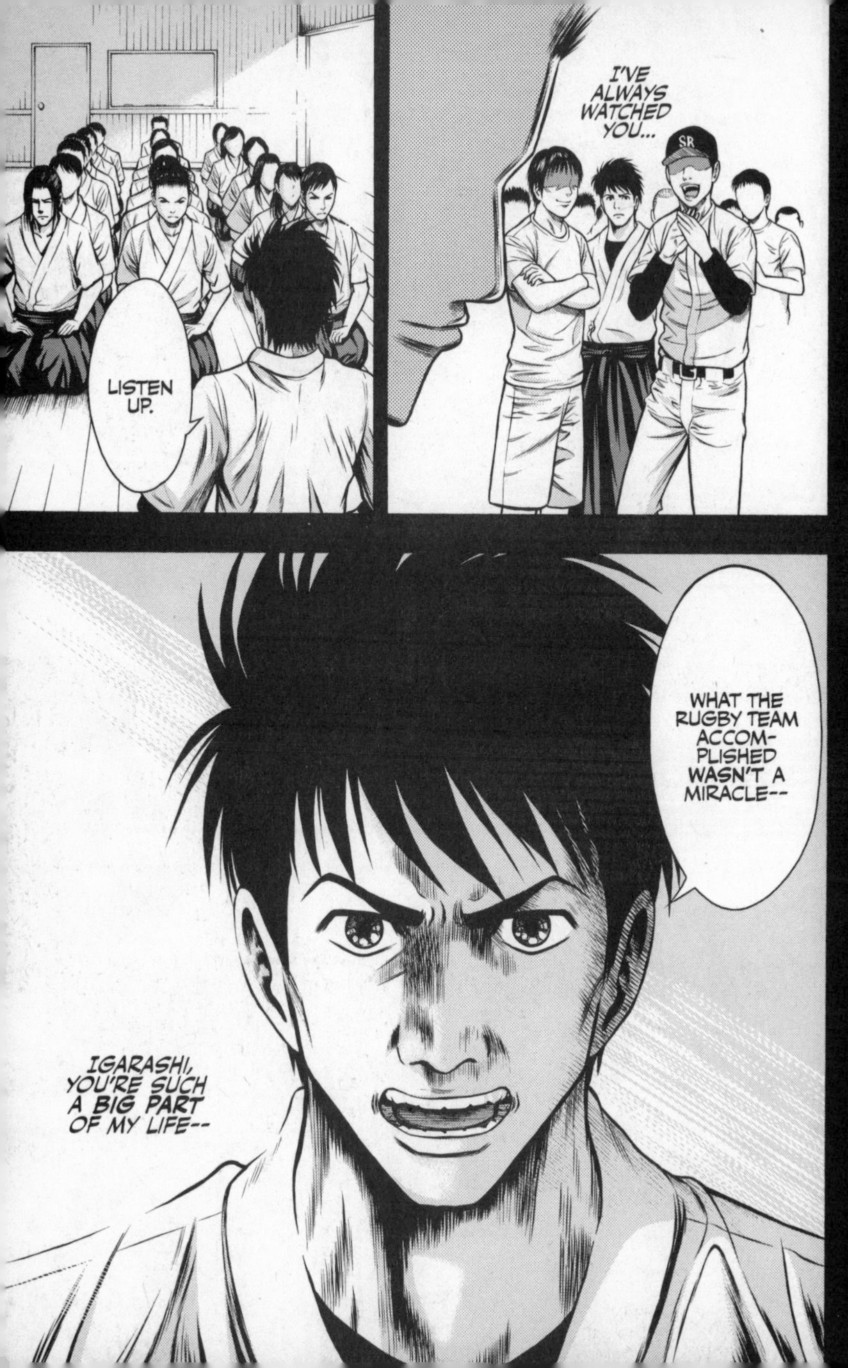
I'VE ALWAYS WATCHED YOU...
LISTEN UP.
WHAT THE RUGBY TEAM ACCOM-PLISHED WASN'T A MIRACLE--
IGARASHI, YOU'RE SUCH A BIG PART OF MY LIFE--

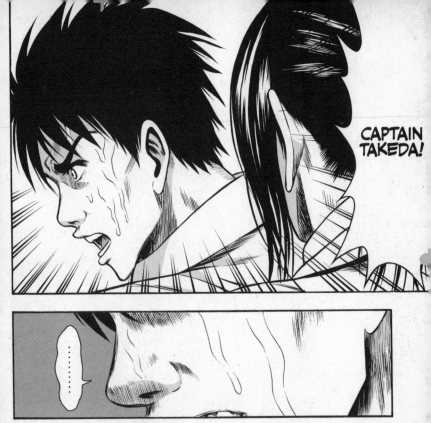

CAPTAIN TAKEDA!

......

?!

SAGAWA, LET'S GO!

SHF...

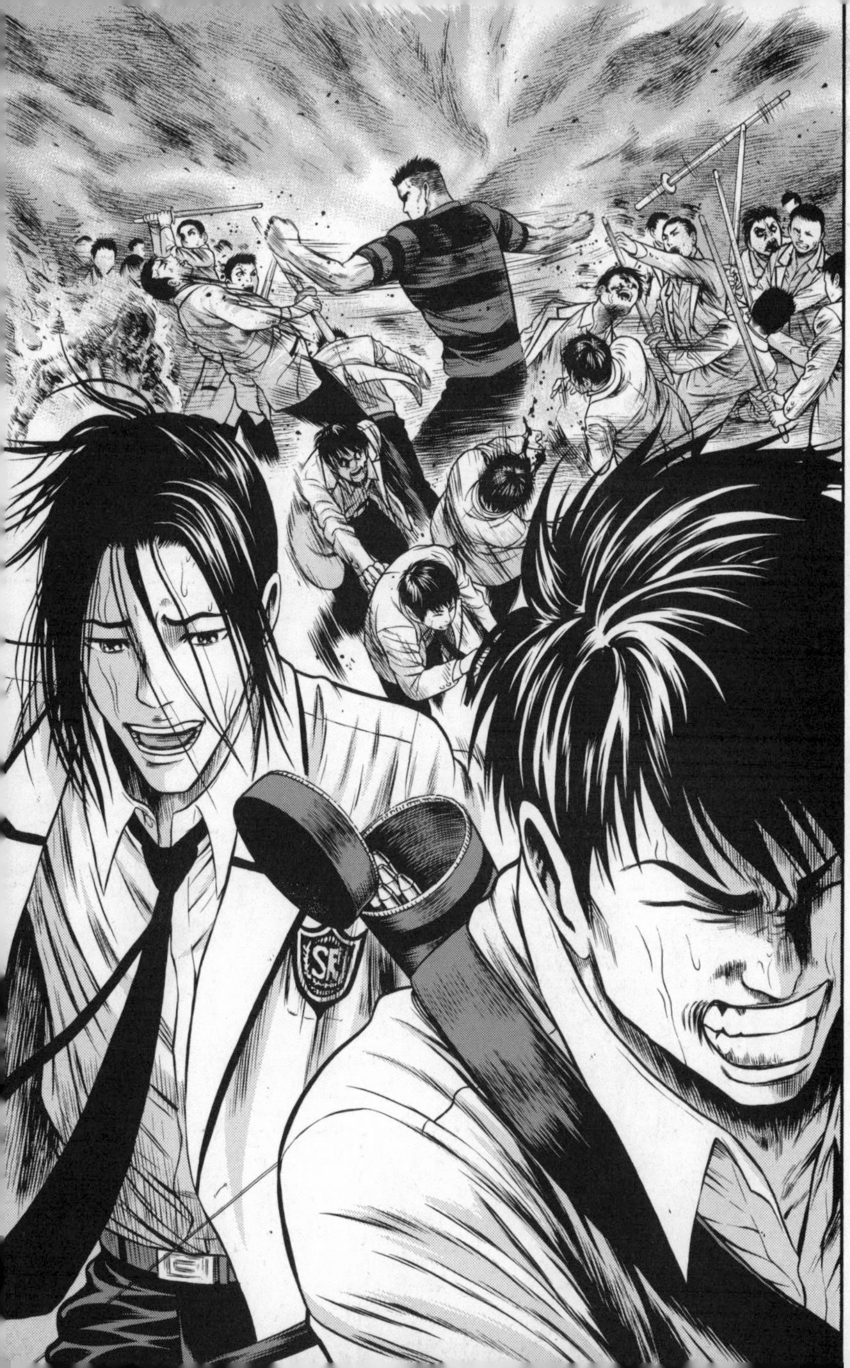

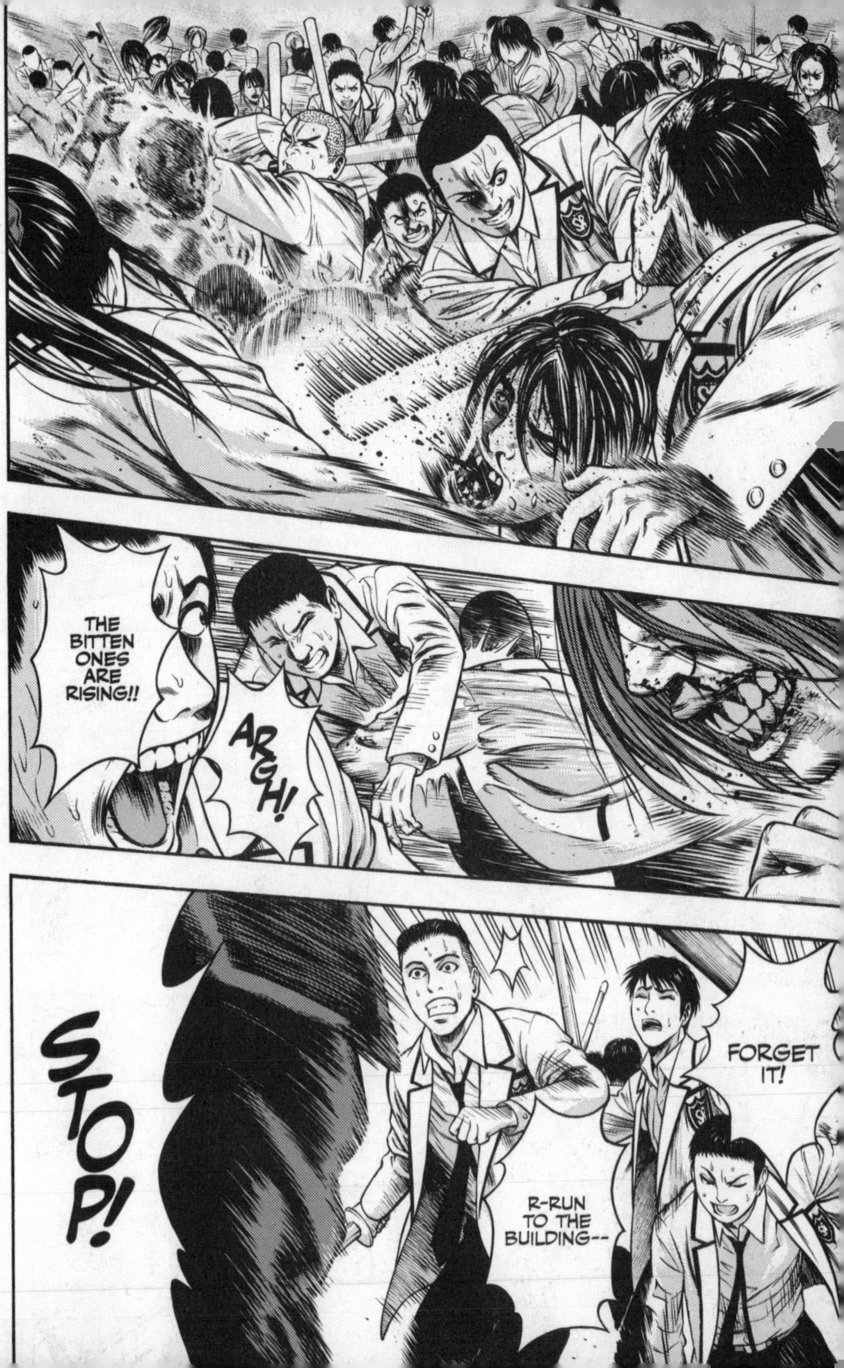
THE BITTEN ONES ARE RISING!!
ARGH!
FORGET IT!
R-RUN TO THE BUILDING--
STOP!

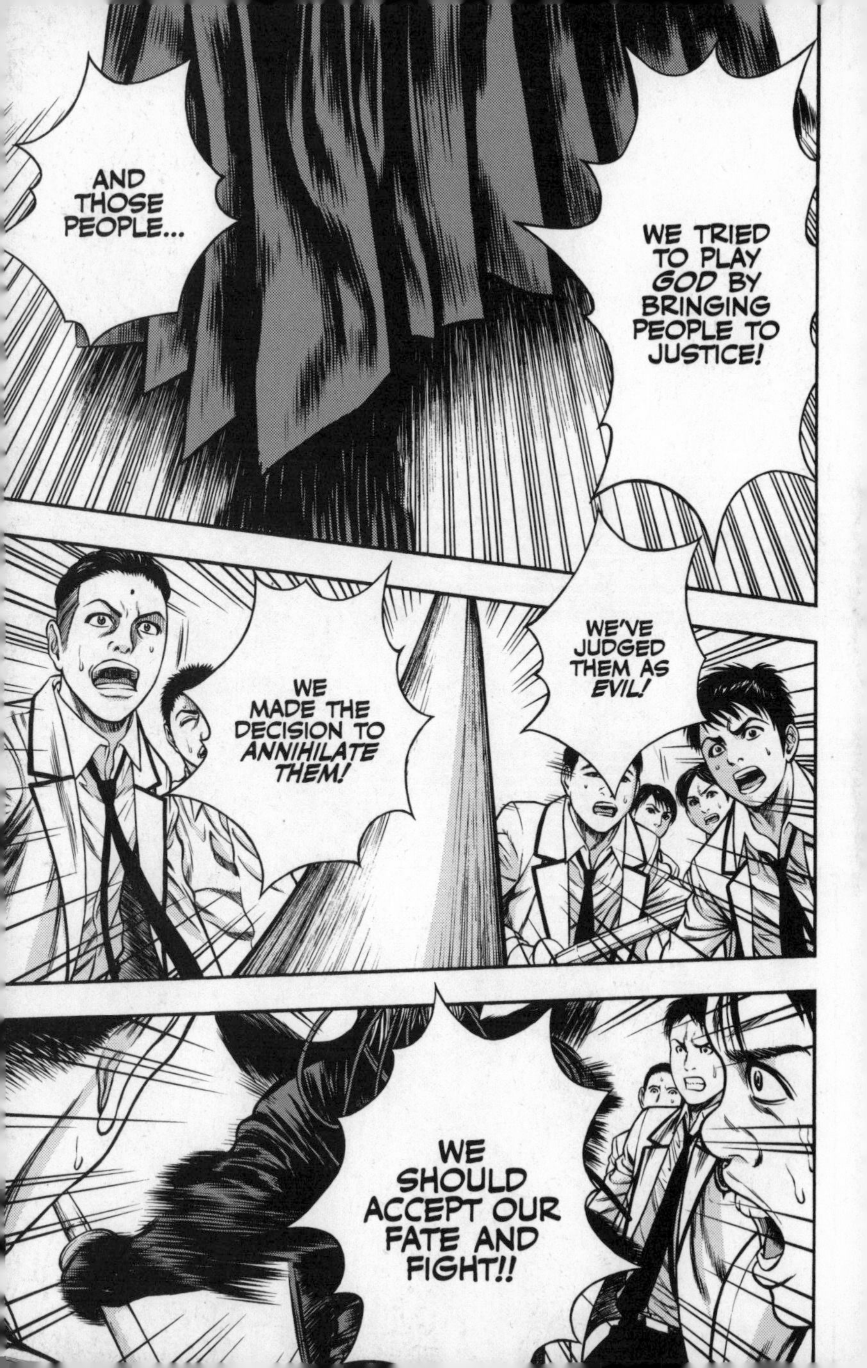
WE TRIED TO PLAY *GOD* BY BRINGING PEOPLE TO JUSTICE!
AND THOSE PEOPLE...
WE'VE JUDGED THEM AS *EVIL!*
WE MADE THE DECISION TO *ANNIHILATE THEM!*
WE SHOULD ACCEPT OUR FATE AND FIGHT!!

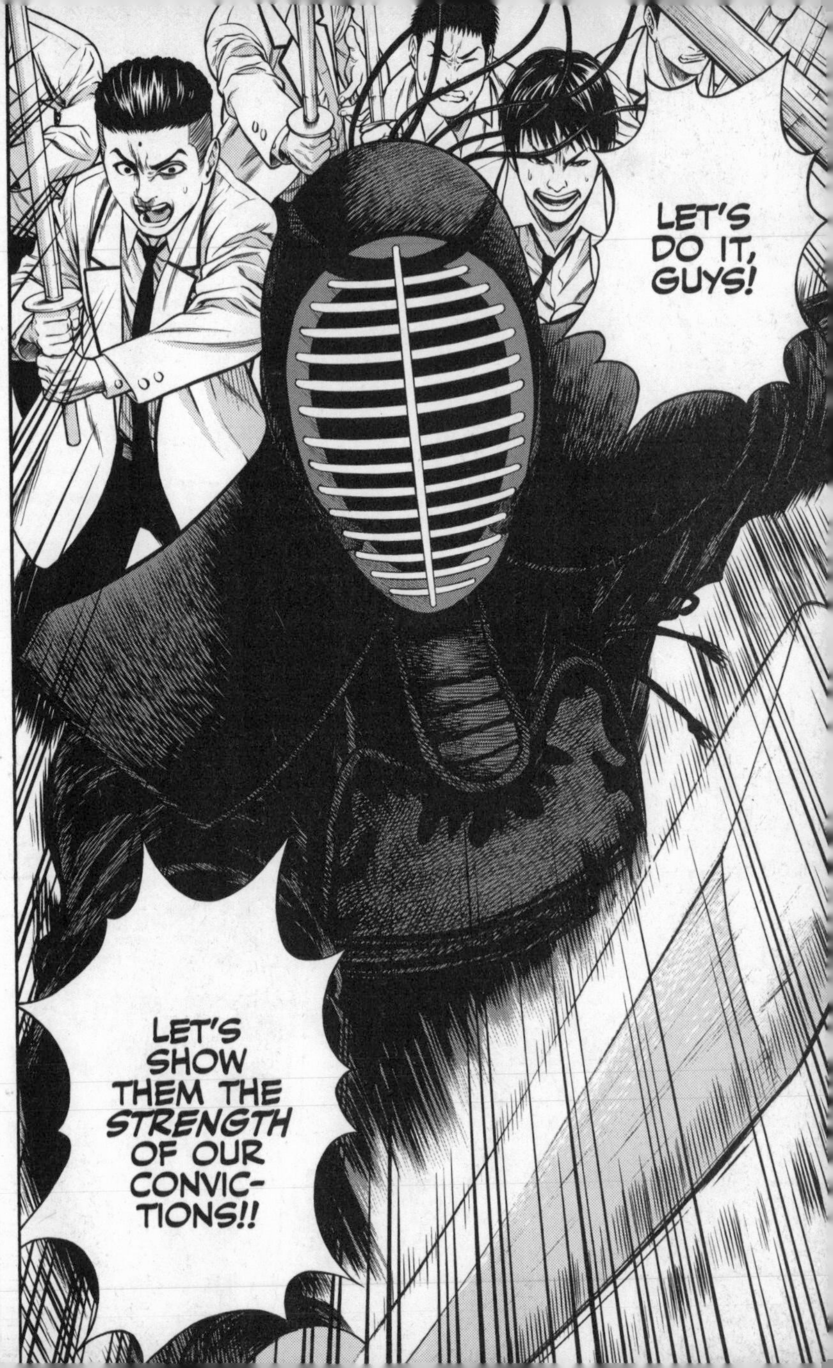
LET'S DO IT, GUYS!
LET'S SHOW THEM THE STRENGTH OF OUR CONVIC-TIONS!!

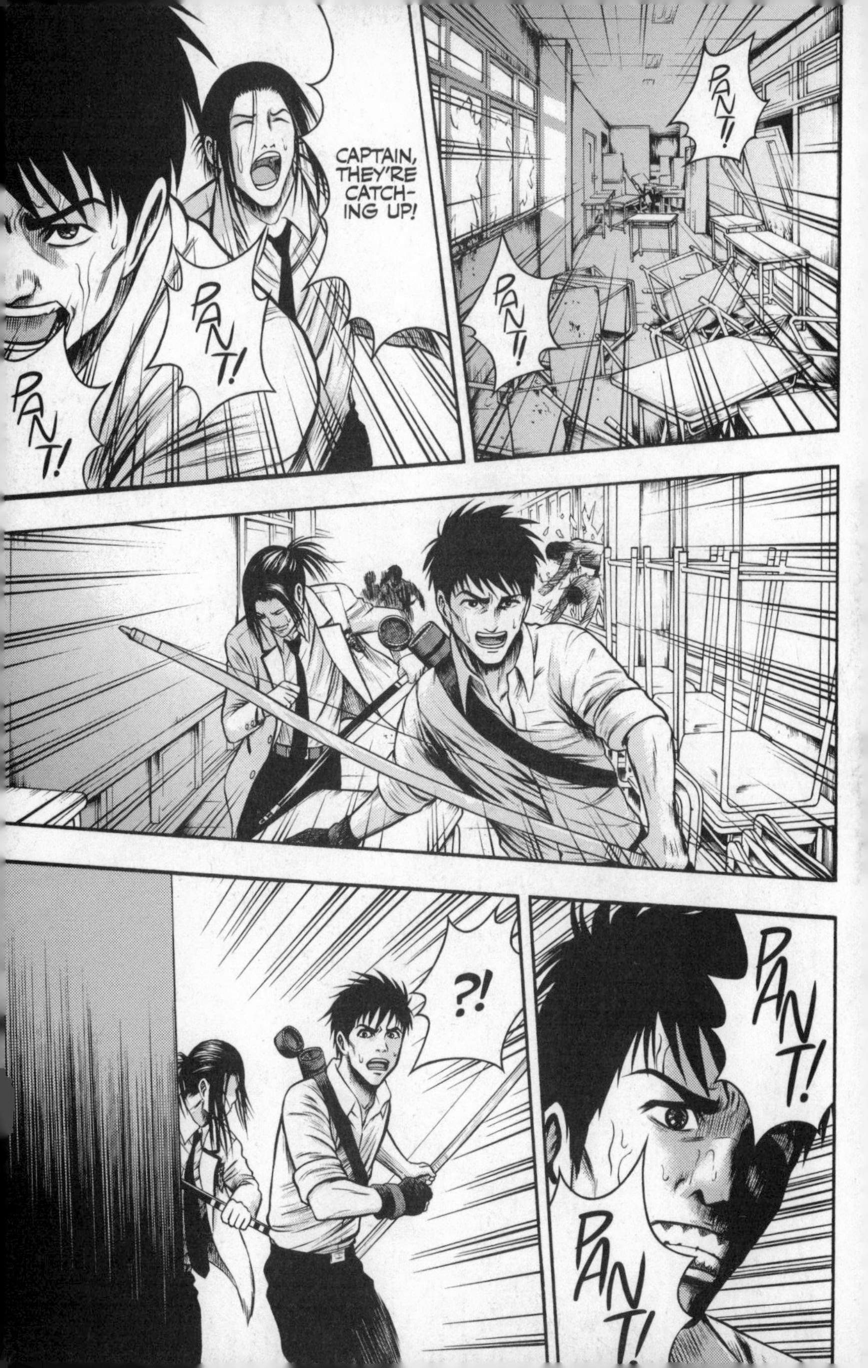
PANT!!
PANT!!
CAPTAIN, THEY'RE CATCHING UP!
PANT!
PANT!
PANT!
PANT!
?!

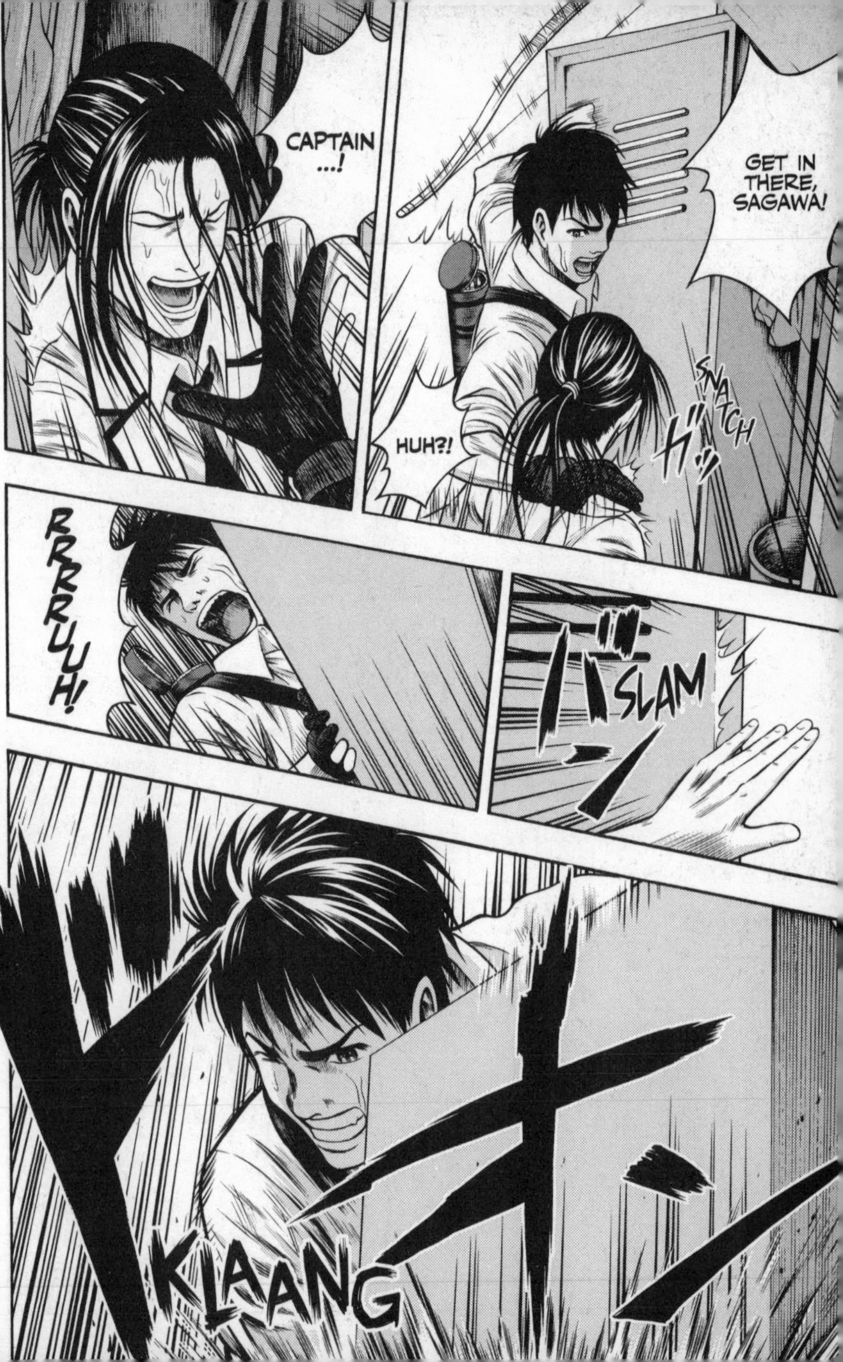
GET IN THERE, SAGAWA!
HUH?!
SNATCH
CAPTAIN ...!
SLAM
RRRRUUH!
KLAANG

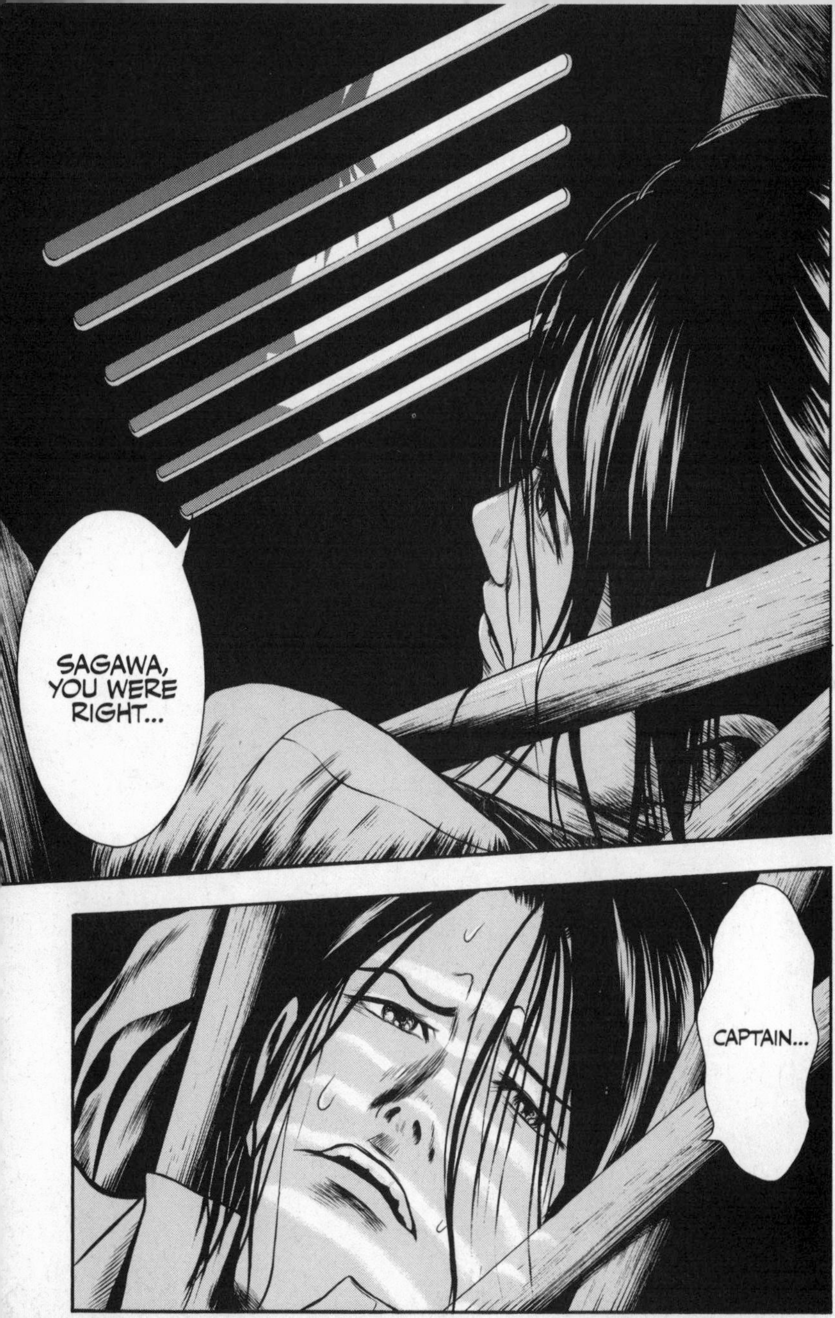
SAGAWA, YOU WERE RIGHT...
CAPTAIN...

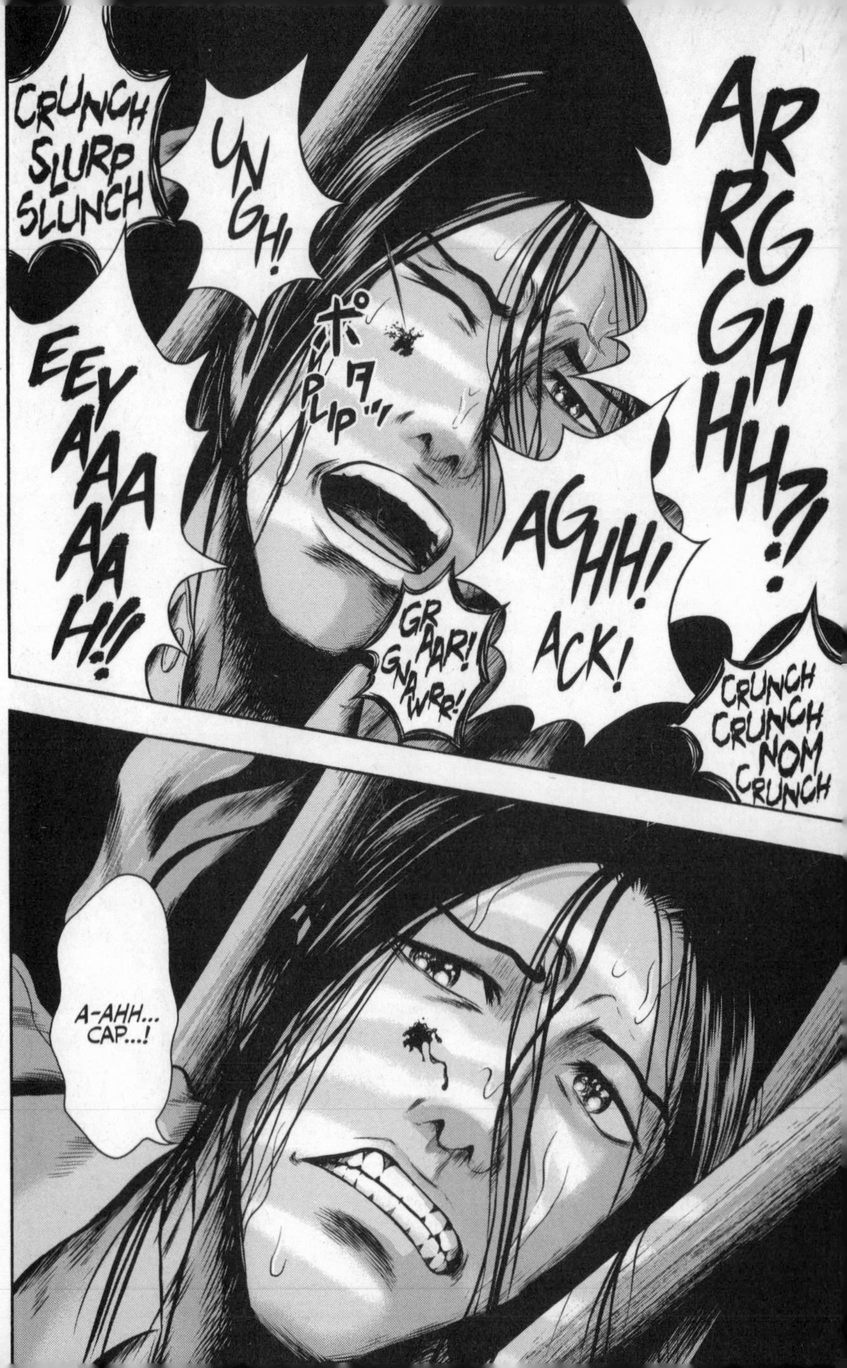
ARRGGHHHH?!
UNGH!
CRUNCH SLURP SLUNCH
ポ
PLIP ッ
EEYAAAAAAH!!
AGHH! ACK!
GRAAR! GNAWRR!
CRUNCH CRUNCH NOM CRUNCH
A-AHH... CAP...!

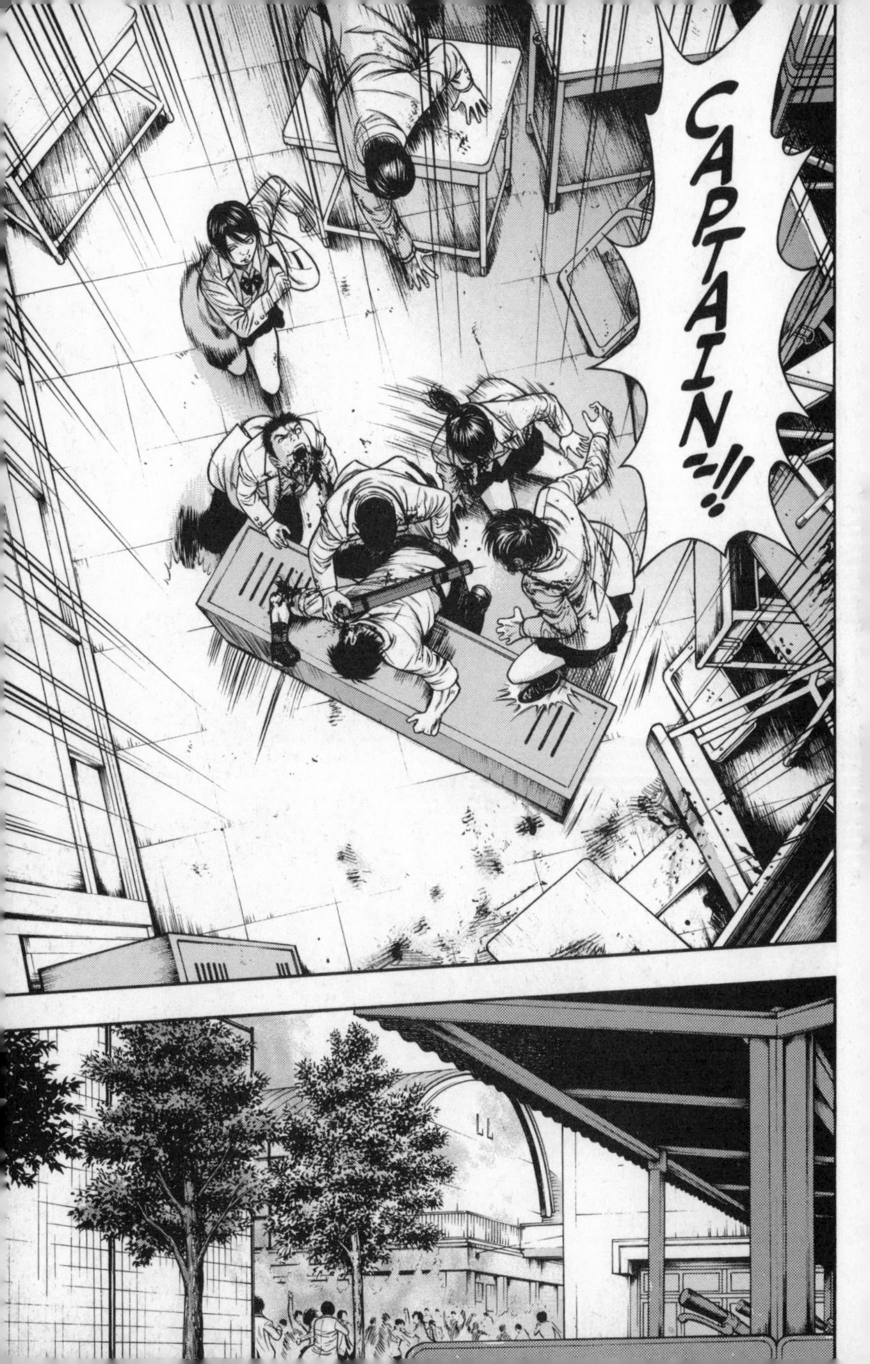
CAPTAIN--!!

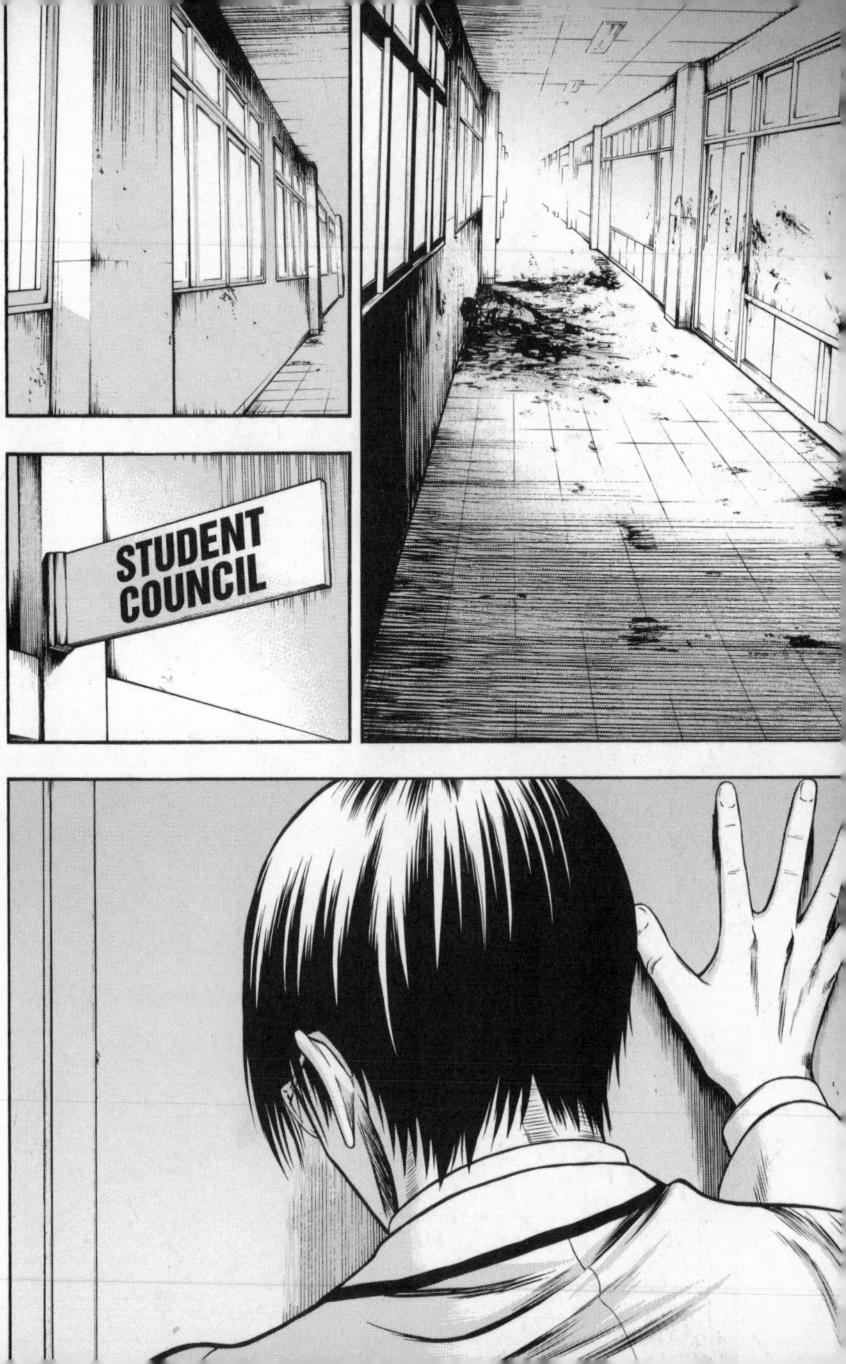
STUDENT COUNCIL

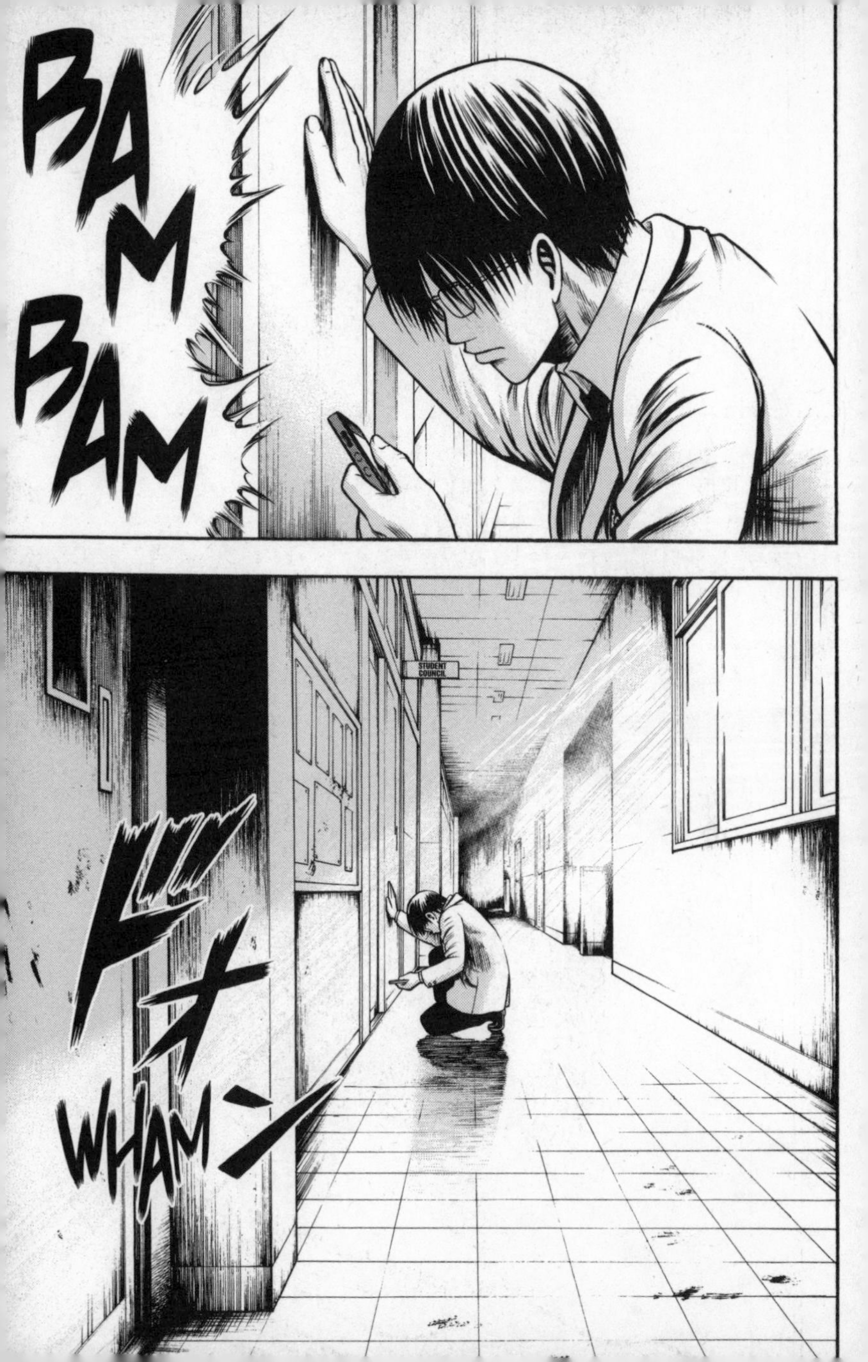
BAM BAM BAM
STUDENT COUNCIL
ドォ
WHAM

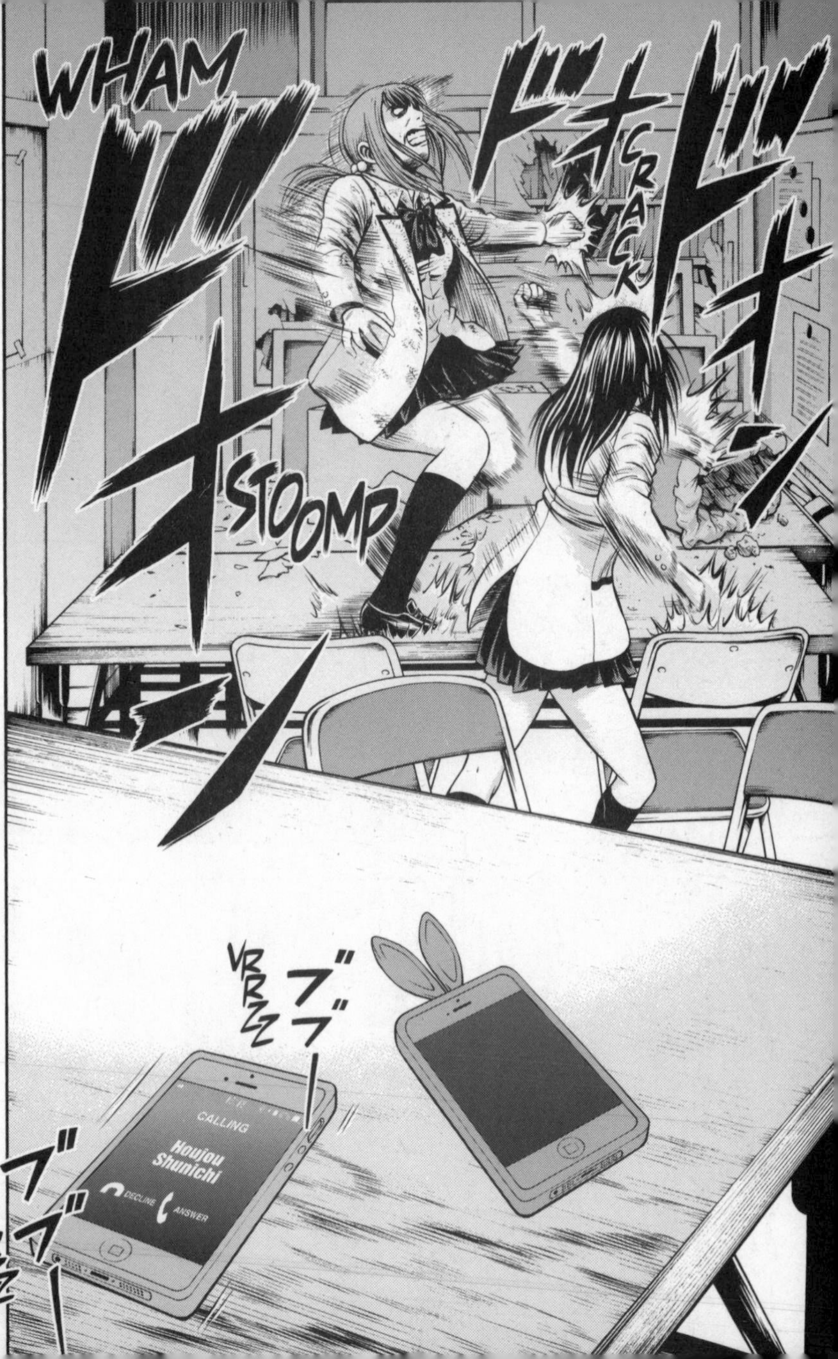
CRACK
WHAM
STOOMP
VRRZZZ
ブブー
CALLING
Houjou Shunichi
DECLINE
ANSWER
ブブー
RRZZZ

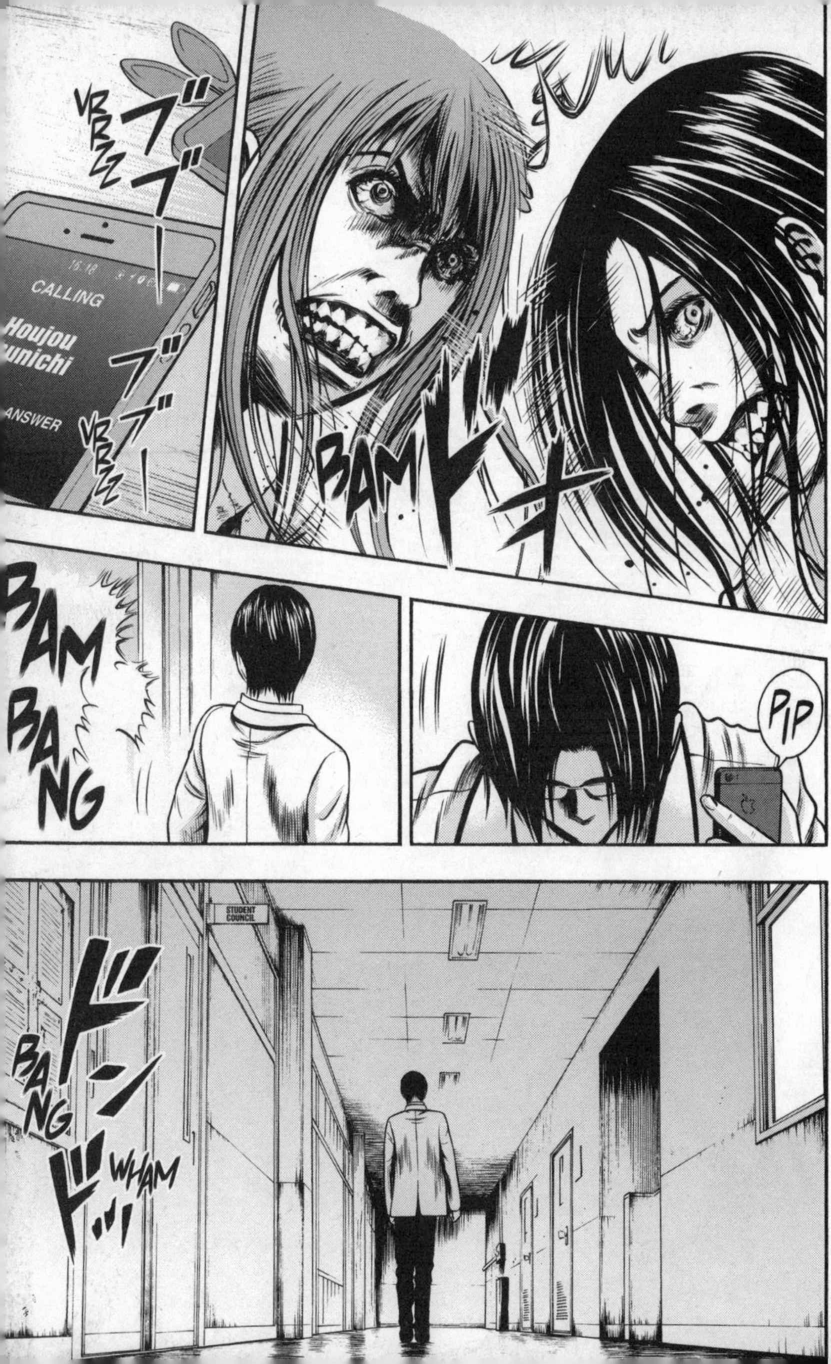
BAM
VRZZZ
CALLING
Houjou
unichi
ANSWER
VRZZZ
PIP
BAM BANG
STUDENT COUNCIL
BANG
WHAM

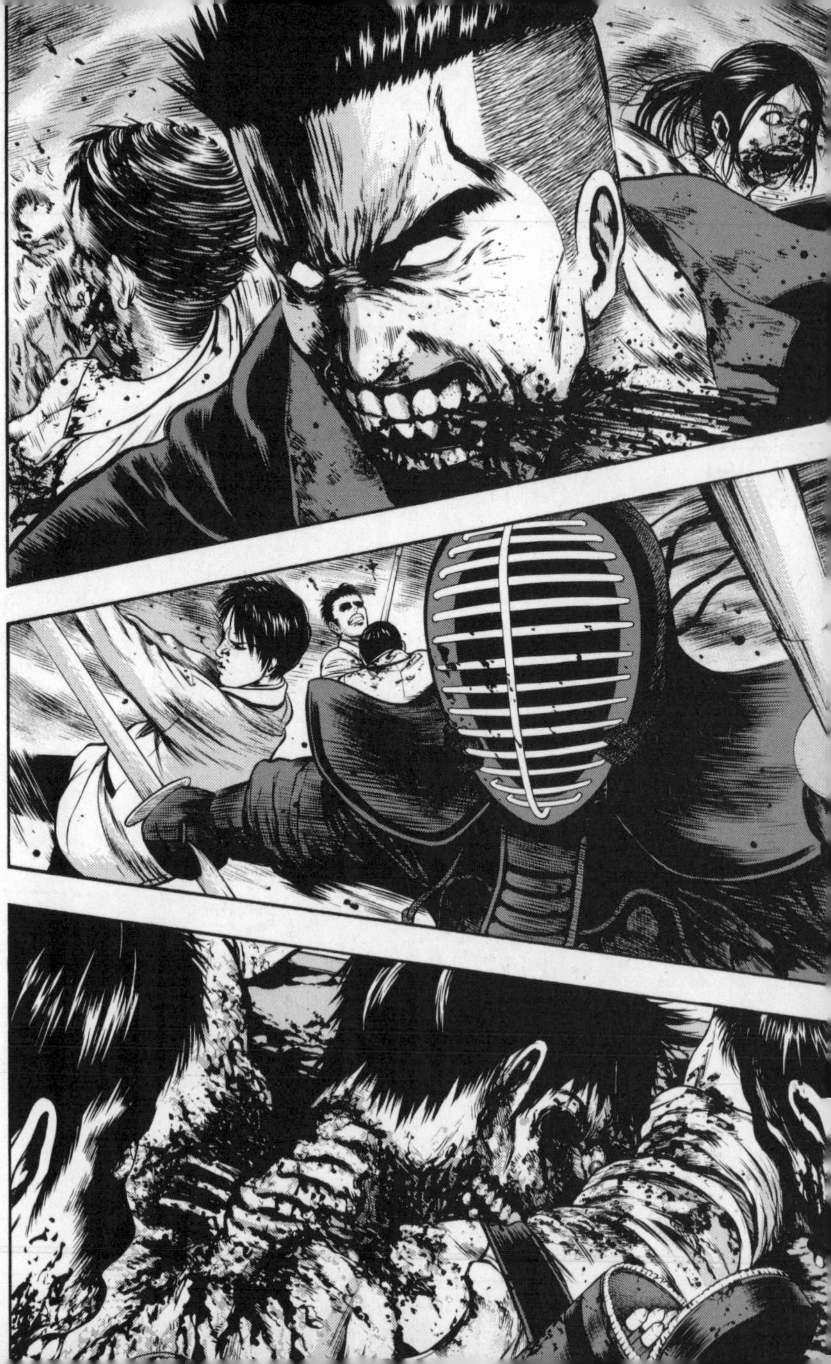

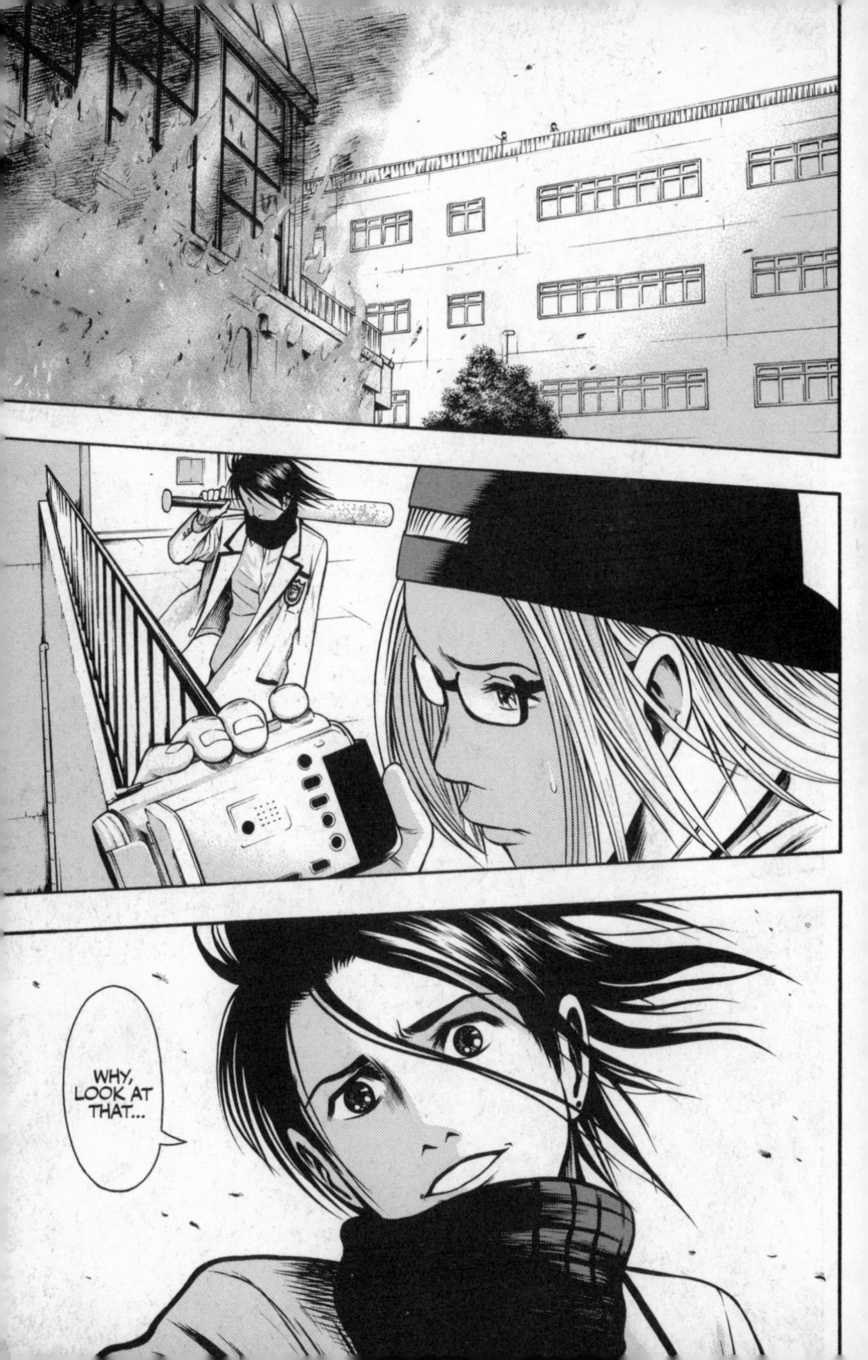
WHY, LOOK AT THAT...

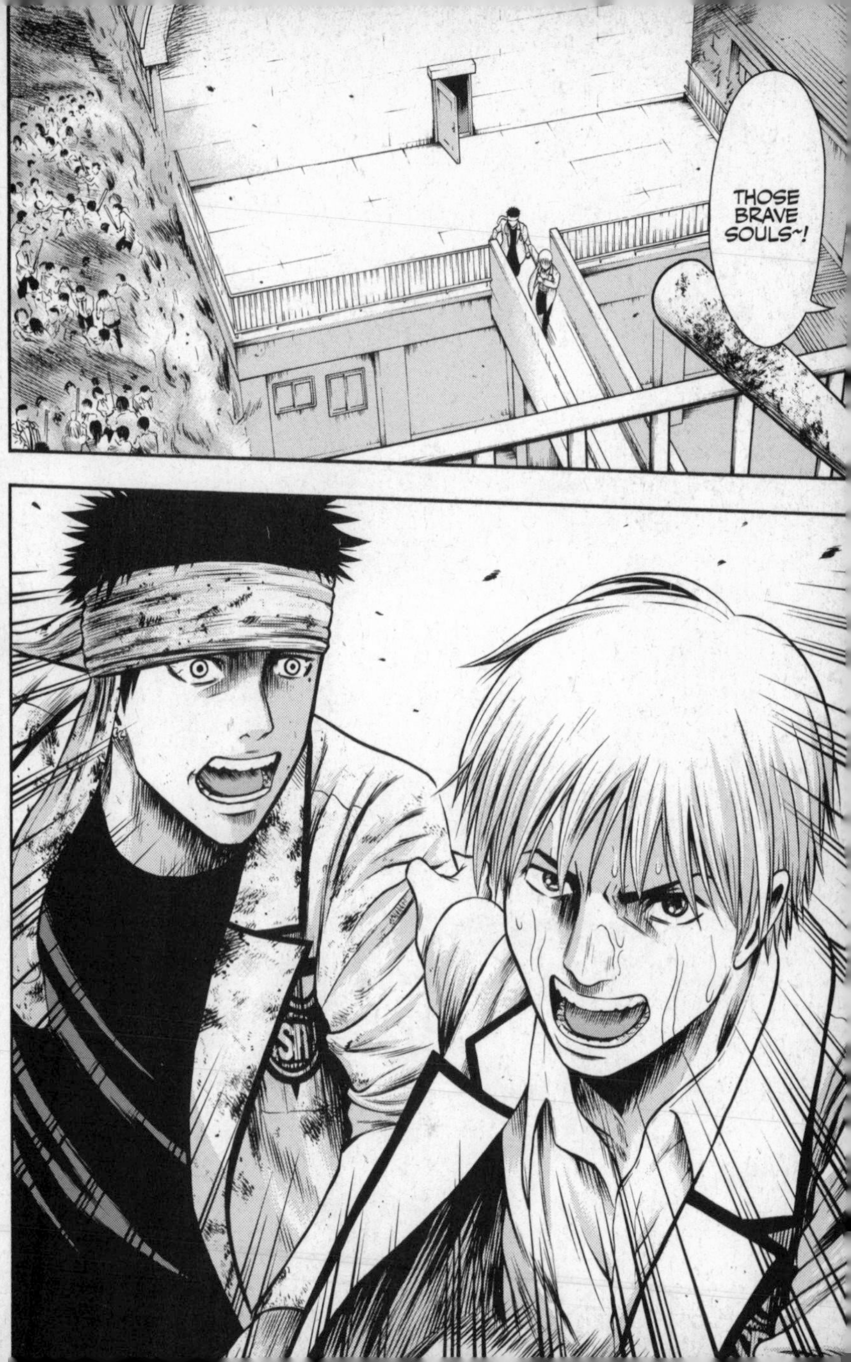
THOSE BRAVE SOULS~!

TO BE CONTINUED...

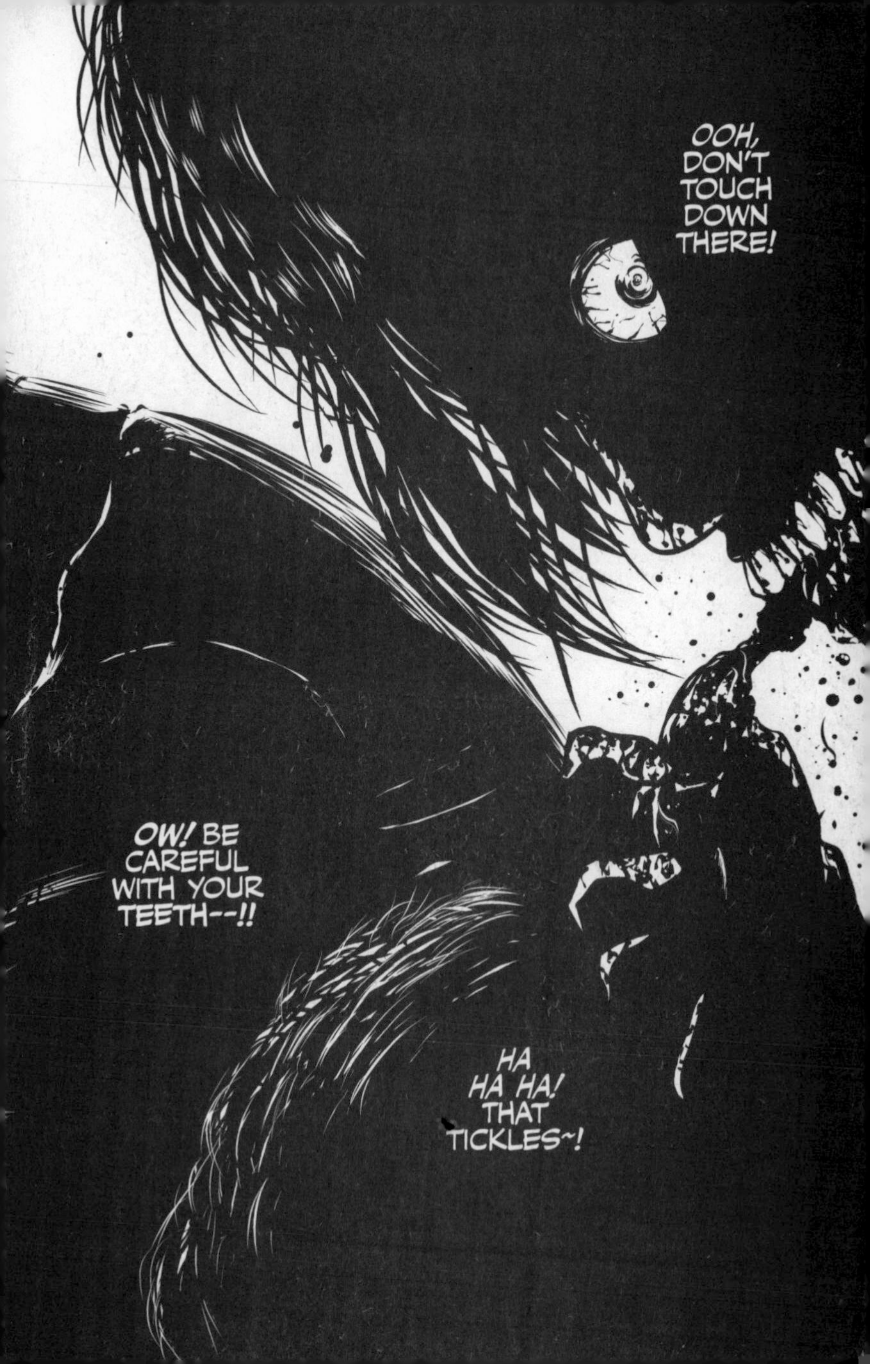
OOH, DON'T TOUCH DOWN THERE!
OW! BE CAREFUL WITH YOUR TEETH--!!
HA HA HA! THAT TICKLES~!

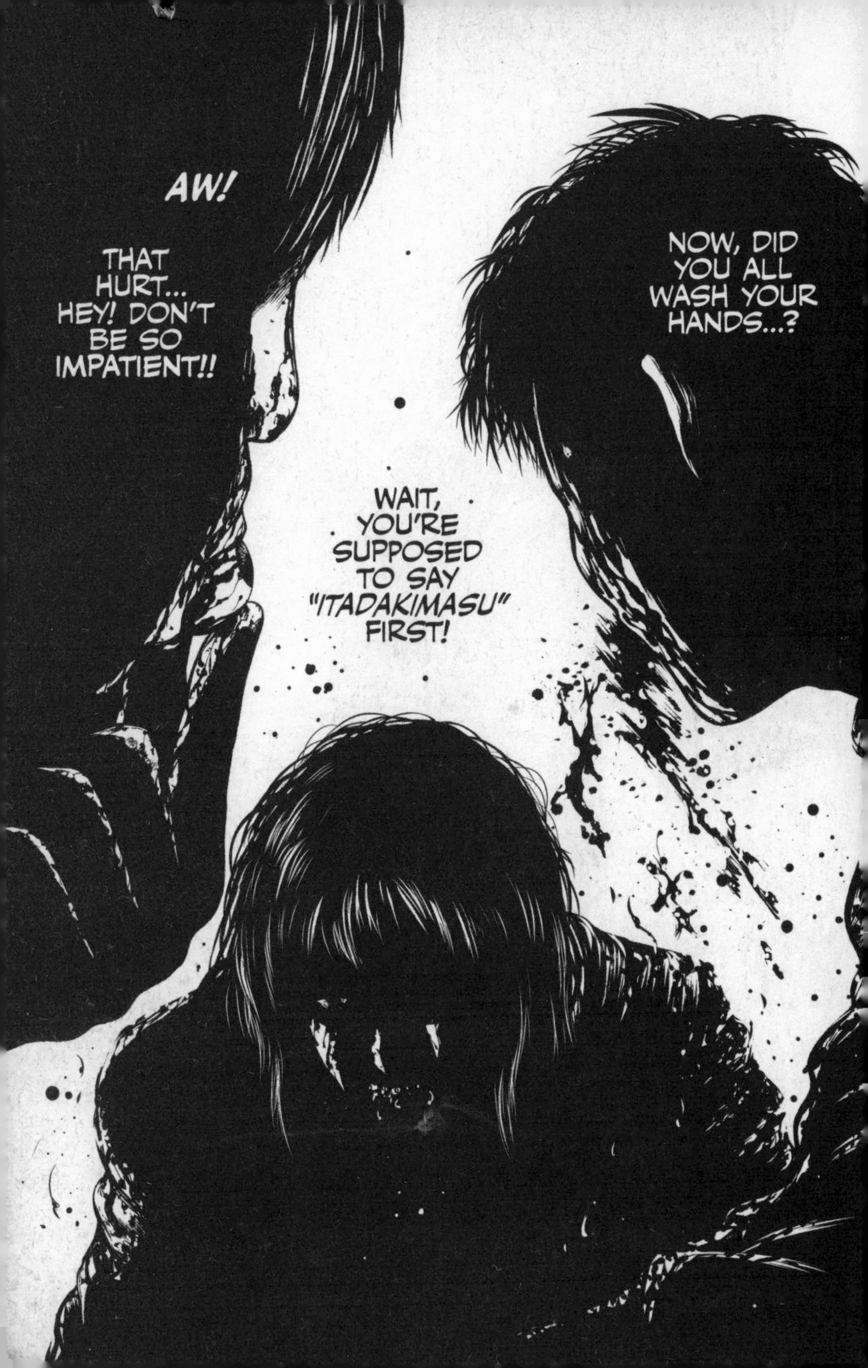
NOW, DID YOU ALL WASH YOUR HANDS...?
AW!
THAT HURT... HEY! DON'T BE SO IMPATIENT!!
WAIT, YOU'RE SUPPOSED TO SAY "ITADAKIMASU" FIRST!

HOUR OF THE ZOMBIE CHARACTER LIST...... 08

HOUJOU SHUNICHI

AGE: 17 years old

CLASS: 3-C

HEIGHT: 171cm WEIGHT: 55kg

BLOOD TYPE: AB

EXTRACURRICULAR ACTIVITIES:
Student Council *(President)*, Shogi
Club *(Vice President)*

HOUR OF THE ZOMBIE CHARACTER LIST...... 09

TAKEDA GOUSHI

AGE: 17 years old

CLASS: 3-C

HEIGHT: 169cm WEIGHT: 61kg

BLOOD TYPE: O

EXTRACURRICULAR ACTIVITIES:
Kyudo Team *(Captain)*

HOUR OF THE ZOMBIE CHARACTER LIST...... 10

SAGAWA SEIICHIROU

AGE: 16 years old

CLASS: 2-D

HEIGHT: 180cm WEIGHT: 59kg

BLOOD TYPE: B

EXTRACURRICULAR ACTIVITIES:
Kyudo Team

HOUR OF THE ZOMBIE CHARACTER LIST...... 11

MISHIMA MASAYUKI

AGE: 17 years old

CLASS: 3-E

HEIGHT: 178cm WEIGHT: 67kg

BLOOD TYPE: A

EXTRACURRICULAR ACTIVITIES:
Kendo Team *(Captain)*

HOUR OF THE
CHARACT

HOUR OF
THE
ZOMBIE